TEACHING READING IN THE CONTENT AREAS
Developing Content Literacy for All Students

Robert B. Cooter, Jr.
Austin Peay State University

E. Sutton Flynt
Pittsburg State University

Merrill,
an imprint of Prentice Hall
Englewood Cliffs, New Jersey   Columbus, Ohio

Library of Congress Cataloging-in-Publication Data

Cooter, Robert B.
  Teaching reading in the content areas : developing content literacy for all students / Robert B. Cooter, Jr., E. Sutton Flynt.
    p.   cm.
  Includes bibliographical references and index.
  ISBN 0-02-324711-8
    1. Content area reading. 2. Reading (Secondary)   I. Flynt, E. Sutton, II. Title.
LB1050.455.C67   1996
428.4'071'2—dc20   95-49734
                                                                                      CIP

Editor: Bradley J. Potthoff
Developmental Editor: Linda Ashe Montgomery
Production Editor: Mary Harlan
Photo Editor: Anne Vega
Design Coordinator: Julia Zonneveld Van Hook
Text Designer: STELLARViSIONs
Cover Designer: Scott Rattray
Cover art: Diana Ong/Superstock
Production Manager: Patricia A. Tonneman
Electronic Text Management: Marilyn Wilson Phelps, Matthew Williams, Karen L. Bretz, Tracey Ward
Illustrations: Jane Lopez

This book was set in Garamond by Prentice Hall/Merrill and was printed and bound by R.R. Donnelley & Sons Company. The cover was printed by Phoenix Color Corp.

© 1996 by Prentice-Hall, Inc.
A Simon & Schuster Company
Englewood Cliffs, New Jersey 07632

Photo credits: All photos copyrighted by individuals or companies listed. Scott Cunningham/Merrill/Prentice Hall: pp. 5, 86, 87, 90, 91, 94, 225, 241, 272. Anne Vega/Merrill/Prentice Hall: pp. 22, 29, 85, 89, 293, 316. Robert Vega/Merrill/Prentice Hall: p. 92. Todd Yarrington/Merrill/Prentice Hall: p. 124.

Printed in the United States of America

10 9 8 7 6 5 4 3 2

ISBN: 0-02-324711-8

Prentice-Hall International (UK) Limited, *London*
Prentice-Hall of Australia Pty. Limited, *Sydney*
Prentice-Hall of Canada, Inc., *Toronto*
Prentice-Hall Hispanoamericana, S. A., *Mexico*
Prentice-Hall of India Private Limited, *New Delhi*
Prentice-Hall of Japan, Inc., *Tokyo*
Simon & Schuster Asia Pte. Ltd., *Singapore*
Editora Prentice-Hall do Brasil, Ltda., *Rio de Janeiro*

For Louise and the late
Louis T. Rizzardi, and for
Charles and Lydia Cooter.

—RBC

For Deb and the kids, and
for my parents, who were
my first and best teachers.

—ESF

Preface

Teaching Reading in the Content Areas: Developing Content Literacy for All Students was written to provide you with scholarly and pragmatic information about teaching in the content areas and to suggest a wide variety of highly successful strategies for incorporating reading, writing, listening, and speaking that can become part of your teaching repertoire. Ideas in this text are drawn from our own teaching experiences in the public schools, as well as our work with teachers, students, and school districts around the country. The writings and teaching practices of many colleagues in the field of education have also informed the writing of this book. Within these pages are methods, techniques, and accompanying examples that not only have the potential to make you a better teacher but can help your students become better learners and thinkers. To that end we show how one can weave innovative teaching methods with proven traditional ideas into a fabric that is understandable, flexible, and most important, highly successful.

The primary audience for this text is pre-service teachers who are seeking middle level or secondary education degrees. However, for those experienced classroom teachers who have not had a content area reading course for some years, this course and text will serve as a valuable resource.

Text Organization and the Content Literacy Model

This book is organized around what we call the *content literacy model*. The model arises from the belief that masterful teaching is based on the practices of reflection and assimilation. We have observed that as teachers reflect, they often change. They assimilate new ideas, techniques, and methods that they believe will increase their teaching effectiveness. This text is therefore structured to maximize opportunities to reflect upon your teaching and assimilate new strategies to create optimum learning environments for students in your content area classes.

We begin the text by introducing you to the content literacy model and what it means in the real world of classroom teaching. In the next four chapters, we focus on fundamental elements of the content area classroom: the students, assessment, learning environment, and comprehension. These chapters construct a platform of knowledge for the remaining chapters, which focus on how to teach literacy skills as you teach content. We have included both the ideal and the pragmatic within each of the chapters in this text. Thus, in some chapters you will encounter teaching suggestions that offer new and exciting literacy oppportunities, while in other places you may find more familiar teaching methods and strategies that have been shown to be effective for content studies. We hope that some ideas will challenge your current beliefs about *what is* and *what can be* in content classrooms.

Special Features

Several unique features are contained in this text. Each chapter begins with a visual diagram of the major content of the chapter and its organization, followed by a series of focus questions to guide your reading. All of these serve as advance organizers to help you assimilate your thoughts about chapter content.

Unique to this text is the rich number of teaching strategies that include methodologies for guiding reading comprehension, teaching content area vocabulary, and integrating literature in content area disciplines. Additionally, an extensive number of metacognitive strategies are provided to illustrate how to guide learners to seek information from expository text and recognize its organizational writing patterns, all with an eye toward helping learners become independent readers and writers. A comprehensive guide to quickly reference these practical teaching strategies can be found at the end of the Contents section. We expect that these strategies will prove to be a valuable resource for you in the classroom.

Each chapter closes with a section on "Students with Learning Problems." These sections suggest ways to assist students experiencing academic difficulties and provide instructional methodologies adapted to meet special needs for exceptional students.

A very special feature has been included as an appendix. Because we believe classroom teachers are in the best position to determine what works and what doesn't work in their classroom, we have developed the Guided Action Research Plan (GARP). The GARP provides you a systematic method for conducting research in your own classroom—a format for trying out ideas described in this text. As more and more school districts search for ways to demonstrate accountability, we encourage teachers to take the initiative to develop, try out, and evaluate methods, techniques, and/or programs. We think the GARP can be the vehicle you need to get started.

Finally, we encourage you to conduct a brief preview of each chapter to get a picture of its focus before reading. We trust that ideas contained in this text will inspire you to reflect on innovative ways to modify and incorporate instructional strategies in your own content area classes. We hope that our book becomes your book and serves as a valued companion as you help students become literate in your content classroom.

ACKNOWLEDGMENTS

We wish to thank all the students, past and present, who have influenced our teaching and our lives. They have been in our thoughts as we have tried to develop a meaningful text. Whether they live in small rural towns in Mississippi or Appalachia or in major cities, we are largely the teachers that we are because of them.

We thank our teachers and mentors who saw in us something that was worth cultivating: Ira Aaron, J. Estill Alexander, Bill Butefish, George McNinch, Reed Mottley, Hazel Simpson, Catherine Gooch, Jeannette Veatch, Bill Fogel, Mrs. Roberts, Mrs. King, and George Mason. Our mothers and fathers, Ellis and Laura Flynt, Bruce and Toni Cooter, were our first and most important teachers.

We express sincere gratitude to Linda Scharp and Jeff Johnston for getting this project going, and to Brad Potthoff (editor and valued friend) for making this book a reality. To Linda Montgomery, our developmental editor, and Mary Harlan, our production editor, thanks for the many ideas and suggestions. We also want to thank all the reviewers who provided their expertise in making this book more readable and complete. They include:

- Lynne Anderson, University of Oregon
- Carolyn Andrews-Beck, Southern Illinois University at Edwardsville
- Gerald J. Calais, McNeese State University
- Joan Elliott, Indiana University of Pennsylvania
- Cindy Gillespie, Ball State University
- Cynthia G. Kruger, University of Massachusetts Dartmouth
- Betty McEady-Gillead, California State University, Sacramento
- Gary A. Negin, California State University
- Ruth DeWill Olle, Northern Illinois University
- Robert J. Rickelman, University of North Carolina–Charlotte
- Diane M. Truscott, Eastern Montana College
- James E. Walker, Clarion University of Pennsylvania
- Liane Holliday Willey, Central Missouri State University

Most important, we wish to thank our families, who encouraged us and persevered through all those trips out of town and long writing sessions. This wouldn't have happened without their support.

Bob Cooter
Sutton Flynt

Brief Contents

Contents

9 Extending Learning Through Literature   265

10 Toward Independent Learning   291

Content Area Teaching Strategies

Did you ever read a text and then try to remember where you saw something you *now* want to use? Let your fingers do the walking in this quickie fingertip guide to teaching strategies that support the development of content area literacy.

Using Literature

Vocabulary Instruction

Writing

Content Area Reading: Developing Literacy in Subject Matter Classrooms

Successful Content Instruction: A Model for the 21st Century

Content Literacy Model

Past Practices/New Directions:
Content Literacy for All Students

The NAEP

Other New Directions

Trends Toward
National Standards

Focus Questions

As you read this chapter, try to discover answers to the following questions:

1 What is the difference between the terms *content area reading* and *content literacy*?

2 What are the basic elements of the content literacy model?

3 Why do successful teachers reflect about their teaching and classrooms?

4 Why do teachers need to know a variety of instructional methods and have access to different teaching materials?

5 How is the student population different from and similar to what you experienced in secondary school?

6 How is the challenge of being a successful content teacher different today than in earlier years?

7 Why is developing content literacy skills more necessary today than ever?

8 What are some of the new directions in content literacy instruction?

9 Do you think moving toward national standards is a good idea? Why or why not?

Content area reading has to do with the strategic application of reading skills within a specific subject domain.

Content literacy is an expanded view of the content teacher's role that includes such literacy language tools as writing processes, listening, oral communications, as well as reading in learning about the subject area.

Each year many of the nation's best and brightest college students choose education as their career. It is a rich and rewarding profession that challenges us to share what we know with young people. Life-long learning is the essence of a literate society, and teaching is the means by which we transmit our knowledge and culture to future generations. Professionals who specialize in teaching a subject domain—such as music, history, mathematics, physical education, the sciences, and so forth—are known as *content area teachers*. The field of **content area reading** has traditionally dealt with teaching students the strategic application of reading skills within a given subject domain. **Content literacy** is an expanded view of the content area teacher's role that begins with applied reading skills as a base but also includes other literacy tools (writing processes, listening, and oral communications) in learning about the subject area. A person who is content literate is able to skillfully learn and apply subject knowledge to accomplish real-world problem solving.

Teachers today frequently receive encouragement from administrators and colleagues to experiment with innovative ideas in their classrooms—to reinvent schooling. For instance, one state commissioner of education recently invited classroom teachers, business leaders, school administrators, and teacher educators to work collaboratively to develop innovative teaching systems and is granting waivers from numerous state-legislated dictates (e.g., out-of-date curricula, state tests) to help create a proper climate for change!

This spirit of innovation and thoughtful change is spreading nationally and aiding in the betterment of schools. John Goodlad (1994), in his book *Educational Renewal: Better Teachers, Better Schools,* writes about teacher attitudes during this time of reinventing schools.

> A spirit of innovation and thoughtful change is sweeping the nation and aiding in the betterment of schools.

> Good teachers are driven in their daily work . . . by a desire to teach satisfyingly, to have all their students excited about learning, to have their daily work square with their conception of what this work should be and do. Yet a strong thread running through everything they do is the expectation that each child or youth will do his or her best and receive unflagging support toward that end. (p. 203)

Many experienced teachers across America have chosen to take advantage of this period of educational experimentation and to create some extremely interesting and effective instructional programs. As researchers of teaching and learning, we have been documenting these practices, experimenting with many of the ideas in our own classrooms, and sharing what we have discovered with other teachers. This process has led to the development of a model useful in explaining to others what successful content teachers do. This model, called the **content literacy model**, serves as the basis for this text and reflects our philosophy about what is needed to develop content literacy for all students.

> The content literacy model explains what is needed to develop content literacy for all students.

SUCCESSFUL CONTENT INSTRUCTION: A MODEL FOR THE 21ST CENTURY

Development of successful content classrooms involves flexibility, knowledge of emerging methods and technologies, and a genuine desire to make learning relevant to the lives of students. We have come to believe that superlative teaching cannot be reduced to a single approach or method. Successful content area classrooms are built by *combining* newer and progressive holistic teaching methods with proven and appropriate instructional practices of the past. Merging the present with the past is accomplished through a process of reflecting, experimenting, evaluating, then assimilating that which works. The content literacy model (see Figure 1.1) depicts how this process may be used to orchestrate dynamic, student-centered classrooms.

> Merging the present with the past to develop innovative programs for the 21st century involves reflecting, experimenting, evaluating, then assimilating that which works.

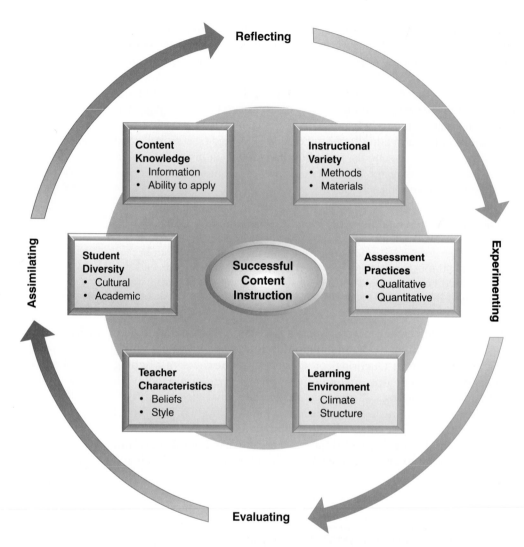

Figure 1.1 Content Literacy Model

The content literacy model features two main elements: reflection and assimilation processes (represented by the outer circle), and basic elements of content classrooms (represented by the boxes within the circle). The content literacy model suggests that the construction of successful content classrooms is an ongoing exploration of the teaching and learning processes. Let's examine the two main elements separately so that you can better understand our perspective.

Reflection and Assimilation Processes in Successful Content Instruction

Skillful teachers are constantly reflecting—about themselves as teachers, their students, and their knowledge of the content field. They are aware of the strengths of their own teaching "personality" or style. This enables them to develop learning experiences that capitalize on their own knowledge, interests, and abilities. For instance, a history teacher with a somewhat dramatic side to her personality may find ways to help students develop content melodramas (Cooter & Chillcoat, 1990) as a way of demonstrating what they have learned in a unit called "Politics of the 1960s." A physics teacher with an interest in applied technologies may help students develop applied projects in electricity for presentation at something she calls "The Invention Convention."

Reflective teachers also consider the special talents and needs of their students. The development of successful content classrooms is predicated on an understanding of the cultural differences among students, the individual needs of students with learning problems, influences that can enhance or detract from learning, and ways of including everyone in the learning arena.

Reflective teachers are well read in the professional literature concerning promising teaching methods as well as new knowledge within their fields of specialization. They seek fresh ideas and information to enhance their classroom instruction. Novel ideas are a source of both fascination and skepticism

Begin to reflect on your own teaching "personality" and ways it might be manifested as you teach your content specialty.

Great teachers are well read in the professional literature of their field as well as in research on teaching and learning.

Successful content teachers use a variety of approaches to enhance students' learning.

to the reflective teacher: *fascination* because new ideas keep their teaching career challenging and interesting; *skepticism* because the education field is constantly barraged with "magic pill" and quick-fix solutions that usually have not been sufficiently proven in real classrooms. Without a regular infusion of new ideas, teaching can become tedious and mundane to the reflective content teacher.

Successful content teachers use the reflection process as a catalyst for experimenting in the classroom. Experimentation is the process by which teachers discover that which works. Masterful teachers are flexible and have a willingness to change, which enables them to experiment with the curriculum fearlessly. Of course, there are the occasional failures, but teacher-experimenters realize that it is through failure that we often learn a great deal. This spirit of risk taking is crucial to building successful content classrooms.

As teachers experiment with various approaches to teaching, they find themselves evaluating results observed in the classroom. Ideas that fail to achieve the desired result are dropped. Likewise, successful content area teachers regularly assimilate that which works into their classrooms. When we say that successful content classrooms are dynamic, it is because successful teachers regularly assimilate new classroom practices and routines after due reflection, experimentation, and evaluation.

Basic Elements of Content Classrooms

The first basic element of successful teaching relates to **content knowledge**. Middle and high school teachers have as their primary function making content knowledge accessible to students. Content knowledge has two main parts: (1) knowledge of the subject matter content and (2) knowing how to use content knowledge. Teachers, therefore, must first become knowledgeable in the field to be taught. This assumes a commitment to life-long scholarship in the subject area so as to remain current in the field. Being a master teacher in the information era, however, does not end with simply knowing a great deal about one's subject; an understanding of the relevance of the specialty field in the world today and how to "put the subject to work" is also essential. This ongoing commitment to scholarship on the teacher's part provides the necessary foundation for a successful classroom.

Instructional variety pertains to the teaching methods and materials that will be selected to help students acquire knowledge in content classrooms. Teaching strategies in content classrooms of the past have chiefly been characterized by lectures and testing; the test–teach–test method. Successful content area teachers today use a variety of methods and approaches (Menlo et al., 1990). Later in this chapter, we examine data from the National Assessment of Educational Progress, which suggest that test–teach–test is still the dominant method in many content classrooms despite the success of more interactive

Experimentation is the process by which teachers discover that which works.

Begin to consider creative ways of making content knowledge accessible to students.

Teaching strategies of the past have relied heavily on the test–teach–test method. What are some problems inherent in this manner of presentation?

student-centered strategies. Throughout this book we examine alternatives to test–teach–test so that readers will be aware of options available to the content teacher. It is also important for content teachers to have knowledge of alternative materials, both print and nonprint, because rarely will a single textbook meet the needs of all students.

Assessment practices are another basic element of successful content classrooms. Assessment practices are an inseparable part of teaching when applied appropriately. Two forms of assessment now commonly used in content classrooms are referred to as *qualitative* and *quantitative*. Qualitative assessments elaborately describe what students know and can do with content knowledge they have acquired. Qualitative assessments use words, rather than the more traditional letter grades or percentage scores, to describe student progress. Teachers interested in using qualitative assessments often make use of such tools as student portfolios (Farr & Tone, 1994) to collect artifacts, or examples, of students' learning.

Assessment is an inseparable part of teaching.

Quantitative assessments, on the other hand, use numbers or letter grades to summarize in simple terms how students are progressing. Grades on homework assignments and scores on periodically administered teacher-made tests constitute traditional forms of quantitative assessment in content classrooms. In Chapter 3 we discuss the basics of content literacy assessment and include other assessment ideas throughout key chapters of this book.

The **learning environment** is a fundamental element of successful content classrooms. There are at least two considerations in quality learning environments: structure and climate. *Structure* pertains to the physical environment of the classroom—furniture placement, learning stations (if desired), learning-enhancement technology (computers, audiovisual equipment), and other physical learning considerations. *Climate* relates to the emotional environment cultivated by the teacher to encourage a spirit of cooperation and collaboration among students. Positive classroom environments are constructed so as to draw students into learning experiences. Reflected in successful content classrooms is the teacher's commitment to making connections between course content and the real world. The learning environment helps teachers to capitalize on student interests as catalysts for motivating them to develop content literacy. As with assessment, we have devoted a full chapter (Chapter 4) to describing the thoughtful construction of content learning environments.

Classroom structure and climate are two important parts of developing a positive learning environment.

Teacher characteristics include the beliefs, pedagogical style, and individual talents embodied by the content educator. Effective teachers carefully assay their own personality, interests, knowledge, talents, and life experiences to determine which aspects of self are useful and appropriate for the content classroom. There should be a match between the teacher's beliefs and instructional practices used. It is always a challenge to discover what works in today's classrooms, and what the teacher brings to the learning situation is central to success. We hope that as you are exposed to strategies and teaching sugges-

Consider some of your own unique abilities and talents that can help you establish a unique and interesting place of learning.

tions presented in this text you will be inspired to adapt and mold them to fit your emerging teaching style.

Student diversity relates to the academic and cultural differences found in content classrooms. Achievement levels, for instance, can range from students who are gifted to those who cannot read and comprehend adopted course materials. A program of **inclusion**, the practice of placing special education students into regular classrooms whenever and wherever possible, adds to the challenge of trying to help all students experience success.

Culturally, the United States has never been so diverse. A recent census suggested that over 15% of our population are from a non-English-speaking background (Kershner, 1993). For teachers, the number of school-age children from non-English-speaking backgrounds will continue to rise significantly (Ramirez, 1985). So, teachers must be prepared for students who are bilingual or speak no English at all. Recognizing and understanding these cultural and learning differences is one of the major challenges of content area teachers. It can also be one of the most rewarding.

Today's students are challenged in ways not previously witnessed by earlier generations in our schools. Academic challenges are all too frequently contrasted against a backdrop of such competing realities as teen pregnancy, threats of violence on the school grounds, and drugs. Even the seemingly mild hazards of youth such as excessive television watching can have long-term negative effects on reading ability. Correspondingly, teachers are often expected to serve as a surrogate parent, social worker, nurse, and psychologist in trying to help students deal with emerging social and emotional problems. That is why simplistic solutions, calls for "back to basics" and a return to the "good ole days" of the past, seem hollow and evasive in light of present realities.

If teachers are to be reflective about their craft and establish successful, dynamic classrooms, then it seems logical to begin the process by considering the present state of affairs in American education and promising new directions in content literacy instruction.

Students today face challenges not previously seen in earlier generations.

PAST PRACTICES/NEW DIRECTIONS: CONTENT LITERACY INSTRUCTION FOR ALL STUDENTS

Richard "Pek" Gunn became quite popular two decades ago as the first poet laureate of Tennessee. We often enjoy sharing his poetry with groups of teachers to make a point as well as entertain. One of our favorites is "June Bug on a String" (Gunn, 1963) in which he describes how children of his youth (on the eve of the 20th century) enjoyed catching a June bug, tying a string around its back, then holding the string while the bug bumbled about in flight. Here is the poem for your consideration:

June Bug on a String[*]

In days way back on Tumbling Creek
     The latter part of spring,
'Twas sport for every boy to have
     A June bug on a string.

The bug would fly like all the rest
     But what impressed me so
Was that the length of string controlled
     Just how far he could go.

Some might have thought he was free
     To go his way but still
I held the string that gauged his flight
     And pulled him in at will.

A man can get entangled too
     No matter when nor where;
And set a boundary upon
     His freedom then and there.

He may fly high and buzz about
     And have a mighty fling
But after all he's governed by
     The one that holds the string!

We think there is a powerful question for teachers embedded within these lines. Are content teachers today more like the June bug or the one holding the string? The answer, of course, depends on the teacher and, perhaps, the school administrators. If teachers choose to conduct classes in a test–teach–test style simply because of tradition, then perhaps they are choosing a June bug's fate— a life of teaching determined by others long ago. But if teachers choose to experiment with fresh alternatives in teaching and learning as part of an ongoing quest for helping students become content literate, then perhaps they are more like the ones holding the string—controlling or orchestrating learning experiences.

> A fundamental question all content teachers must answer is whether they will teach in ways mainly driven by tradition and outside forces or choose to orchestrate creative learning experiences.

The content literacy model presented earlier suggests that great teaching begins with reflection. Before setting off to conquer the world with dazzling new ideas, the wise teacher first considers what is known about past and current practices. One of the more reliable barometers of teaching success is the National Assessment of Educational Progress.

---

[*] *Note.* From *Tumblin' Creek Tales and Other Poems by "Pek" Gunn* by R. M. Gunn, 1963, Nashville, TN: Tumblin' Creek Enterprises. Copyright 1963 by R. M. Gunn.

The National Assessment of Educational Progress: Education's Report Card

Since the early 1970s, the federal government of the United States has monitored the progress of students in our schools through the National Assessment of Educational Progress (NAEP). Specially prepared tests are administered in each of the content areas at the elementary, middle school, and high school levels every 4 years to determine trends in teaching and learning. We reviewed recent government reports (Mullis, Campbell, & Farstrup, 1993; Mullis, Dossey, Foertsch, Jones, & Gentile, 1991) in the areas of reading, writing, science, and mathematics that compare present performances with all previous years since the program's inception. Although NAEP tests are not very exhaustive measures of student abilities, they do represent at least a snapshot of trends in American schools.

The Reading Report Card

The Nation's Report Card in reading presents a rather mixed picture. The NAEP reported that 69% of eighth graders and 75% of 12th graders were estimated to have reached basic level or beyond, indicating only partial mastery of the knowledge and skills needed for proficient work at each grade (Mullis et al., 1993). The National Center for Education Statistics (1992) reported that only one third of eighth graders are able to infer, summarize, or generalize about information they have been assigned to read. The NAEP data (Mullis et al., 1993) report that few high school seniors (2% to 4%) attained the advanced level of reading, implying that the ability to synthesize and learn from specialized reading materials is lacking among most of the school-age population. Although the data suggest that 17-year-olds were reading significantly better in 1990 than they were in 1971, 13-year-olds showed no improvement in reading since 1971 (Mullis et al., 1991, p. 119).

What students do both in and out of school has an impact on reading development. The NAEP reports that students devote considerably more of their leisure time to watching television than they do to reading. This occurs despite considerable evidence from numerous research studies showing that regular reading outside of school is related to higher reading achievement and that watching large amounts of television is negatively associated with reading achievement. Simply stated, students who watch less television and read more tend to be better readers.

Is More Instructional Time Needed in Content Classrooms?

What if we simply spent more time teaching such content area subjects as mathematics and science? Would American students perform better compared to other industrialized nations? Studies reported by the Educational Testing

Service and Kemper Securities (Hokanson, Agasie, & Beebe, 1993) indicate that more instruction is not necessarily better when it comes to amount of instruction! In a six-country comparison, the United States averaged second in the number of hours per week in mathematics instruction but *last* in mathematics achievement. The same was so in science, placing the United States behind such nations as Korea, Taiwan, and Hungary. These data strongly suggest that quality of instruction is at least as important as quantity.

Newer Holistic Teaching Practices Versus Traditional Teaching Methods

The NAEP offers some interesting insights regarding the comparison of newer holistic teaching practices with traditional teaching methods. Concerning the traditional use of skill and drill materials or the "tell and test" method, for instance, 12th graders who reported using workbooks and worksheets less than weekly performed *better* on the NAEP assessment than did students who used these materials more frequently (Mullis et al., 1993). Thus, these "back to basics" materials seemed in some ways to be counterproductive!

> Think of reasons why traditional workbooks and worksheets have been shown to be relatively ineffective in teaching content information.

On the other hand, more holistic instructional strategies, such as those integrating reading and writing and literature-based reading instruction, appear to be generating positive results. For instance, the NAEP reveals that students at grade 12 who reported writing in response to reading almost daily, performed better than 12th graders who said they were asked to integrate reading and writing less often (Mullis et al., 1993, p. 164). Likewise, students with teachers relying heavily on literature-based reading instruction performed at a higher level in overall reading compared to students with teachers reporting little or no emphasis on this type of instruction (p. 140).

> Holistic strategies, those integrating reading and writing and literature in content instruction, appear to be generating positive results.

Additional NAEP data confirm that projects and written responses to what is being read in the content areas increase student knowledge. Unfortunately, these practices occur infrequently. Mathematics instruction, for instance, seems to be struggling to break away from rigid and rote systems of the past that yield lackluster results. Many classrooms continue to be characterized by lecture method, chalkboard computation explanations by instructors, and testing. When students were asked how often they make reports or do projects on mathematics, only 5% said they did so "often" and 23% "sometimes." Most students (90%) stated that they watch their teacher work problems on the board. The NAEP concludes

> Why do you think that many content teachers hold tenaciously to outdated and, many times, ineffective ways of teaching?

> The low degree of participation in reports or projects activities are not consistent with recommendations for reform in school mathematics. . . . [A]bout three-fourths of the 17-year-olds reported never having done these types of activities. (Mullis et al., 1991, p. 88)

The NAEP reporters cite curriculum reformers within the National Council of Teachers of Mathematics who state

The NAEP concluded that more frequent student participation in projects and reports tended to result in higher mathematics proficiency.

If students are going to learn to communicate their understandings and be able to build their own models of mathematical concepts, they need to be able to write reports and carry out constructive tasks that go into completing a project. (National Council of Teachers of Mathematics, 1989)

The NAEP concluded that more frequent student participation in projects and reports tended to result in higher mathematics proficiency.

Trends Toward National Standards

We believe it is likely that the United States will adopt national standards or a "national curriculum" within the next decade.

For over a decade, many politicians, parent groups, and educators have suggested that national standards are needed in each of the content areas to improve learning. This is not a novel concept limited to the United States. England, for example, has had national standards in place for several years and found them to be helpful in most regards, because *how* these standards will be achieved (teaching methods) has been left up to the local school districts and their teachers. We believe that the United States will adopt national standards in the next decade. But even if the United States does not end up adopting national standards, most states will develop state education standards for every subject taught. Indeed, 31 states have been developing state standards since 1991 (Olson, 1995). What seems to be fueling this quest for standards in the United States is a desire for students to demonstrate some level of competence in each major subject area, as a measure of accountability. Theodore Sizer's (1992) Essential Schools model, for instance, has pushed to the forefront the idea of *exhibition,* wherein students are awarded a high school diploma after first successfully demonstrating in some sort of summative way their grasp of the central skills and knowledge of the school's program. The hope is that a concern for quality will shine through, but not in the trappings of test scores (Goodlad, 1994).

Sensing that the discussion regarding national standards is gaining momentum, many of the professional societies associated with the content specialties have generated their own standards. This enables those who know the subjects best to carefully develop standards based on state-of-the-art knowledge in the field. In some cases, the scope and sequence of quite specific information have been delineated. In Table 1.1 we summarize some of these efforts by professional groups.

Other New Directions Addressed in This Book

A key purpose of this book is to help teachers discover innovative ways to promote content literacy in their classrooms.

Teaching Reading in the Content Areas: Developing Content Literacy for All Students has been written to assist content area teachers in discovering innovative ways to promote content literacy in their classrooms. Development of positive learning environments, appropriate uses of writing processes in the content areas, incorporation of quality literature, application of information age technology in the classroom, assisting students with learning needs, authentic assessment of progress, and methods for promoting an interest in content studies are just a few of

Table 1.1 Summary of Professional Standards Committees

Content Area	Professional Organization	Funding for This Initiative	Publication Date of Standards	Grade Level Addressed
Civics	Center for Civic Education	USDOE; Pew Charitable Trust	1994	K–12
Economics	National Council on Economic Education	Three private funds; No USDOE support	Anticipated spring 1996	K–12
Health	Association for the Advancement of Health Education, American School Health Association, others	American Cancer Society, U.S. Centers for Disease Control	1995	4, 8, and 11
History	National Center for History in the Schools (UCLA)	National Endowment for the Humanities, USDOE	U.S./1994 World/1994 K–4/1994	K–4 U.S. History World History
English	National Council of Teachers of English	USDOE, International Reading Association, NCTE	Pending	Not available
Foreign languages	American Council on the Teaching of Foreign Languages, others in specific areas	USDOE, National Endowment for the Humanities	1995	K–12
Science	National Research Council, others	National Science Foundation, USDOE, NASA, National Institute of Health	1995	Not specific
Social studies	National Council for the Social Studies	NCSS	1994	Early grades Middle grades High school
Mathematics	National Council of Teachers of Mathematics	NCTM, AT&T, NSF	1989	K–12
Physical education	National Association for Sport and Physical Education	NASPE	1995	K, 2, 4, 6, 8, 10, 12

the other topics addressed throughout this book. Teaching strategies suggested are frequently ones we have used ourselves with students. This permits us to describe how the strategies are supposed to work and also how they feel to the teacher. We inform you of benefits and pitfalls to consider when attempting suggested strategies for the first time. Our primary goal is to help teachers inspire, set the pace, and lead students through the curriculum using a content literacy perspective.

CHAPTER SUMMARY

This chapter has presented a model for content literacy that will serve as the basis for the remainder of the book. The need for teachers to reflect, experiment, evaluate, and assimilate that which works has been emphasized. We have also addressed some of the past and current trends, including information provided by the NAEP, and examined the national standards movement. Specific trends, issues, and options are discussed in detail throughout the remainder of the book.

Reflection/Application Activities

1. Now that you have read and discussed this chapter, respond to the Content Literacy Survey on page 15. How do your responses and reactions compare with the information in this chapter? Compare your responses with those of a fellow classmate.
2. Contact an experienced middle/secondary teacher, and request an interview. Use the following questions to start your interview. Be prepared to share your findings in class.
   a. How is teaching different now than when you started teaching?
   b. How are students different today than in past years?
   c. If there was one piece of advice you would give to prospective teachers, what would it be?
   d. If there was one thing you could change about your current teaching position, what would it be?
3. Think about one of your favorite teachers from the past. List some of the characteristics that made this teacher one of your favorites. Do the same thing for one of your least favorite teachers. Compare the two.

Recommended Reading

Alvermann, D. E., & Moore, D. W. (1991). Secondary school reading. In P. D. Pearson, R. Barr, M. L. Kamil, & P. Mosenthal (Eds.), *Handbook of reading research* (vol. 2). New York: Longman.

Bean, T. W., & Readence, J. E. (1988). Content area reading: The current state of the art. In J. Flood & D. Lapp (Eds.), *Content area reading and learning: Instructional strategies.* Englewood Cliffs, NJ: Prentice Hall.

Conley, M. W. (1986). Teachers' conceptions, decisions, and changes during initial classroom lessons containing content reading strategies. In J. A. Niles & R. V. Lalik (Eds.), *Solving problems in literacy: Learn-*

ers, teachers, and researchers (pp. 120–126). Thirty-fifth Yearbook of the National Reading Conference. Rochester, NY: National Reading Conference.

Gee, T. C., & Rakow, S. J. (1987). Content reading specialists evaluate teaching practices. *Journal of Reading, 31,* 234–237.

Tierney, R. J., & Pearson, P. D. (1992). Learning to learn from text: A framework for improving classroom practice. In Dishner, E. K., Bean, T. W., Readence, J. E., & Moore, D. W. (Eds.), *Reading in the content areas: Improving classroom instruction.* Dubuque, IA: Kendall-Hunt.

A Content Literacy Survey: Reflecting About What You Believe

We think that it is important for you to begin this course of study by thinking about your beliefs concerning teaching in the content areas. We support the notion that teachers should practice what they believe and that only through reflection and experimentation can teachers begin to examine and modify their beliefs with the goal of improving their classroom teaching. We would like for you to respond openly and honestly to the following survey.

Directions: Read each statement below and decide to what extent you agree or disagree by marking the scale from 1 (strongly agree) to 5 (strongly disagree). Then, using the space provided, comment on why you feel as you do. Think carefully about your responses, and be prepared to share your thoughts with other class members.

1. Teaching students how to learn and study throughout life is more important than how much information they learn in your class.

1	2	3	4	5
Strongly Agree				Strongly Disagree

Comments:

_____

_____

2. Reading and writing should be done on a daily basis in content area classrooms.

1	2	3	4	5
Strongly Agree				Strongly Disagree

Comments:

_____

_____

3. All students in content area classrooms should be required to do the same amount and type of work and be graded accordingly.

1	2	3	4	5
Strongly Agree				Strongly Disagree

Comments:

_____

_____

4. Content area teachers should rely on whole group instruction (lecture, whole class discussions) most of the time.

1	2	3	4	5
Strongly Agree				Strongly Disagree

Comments:

_____

_____

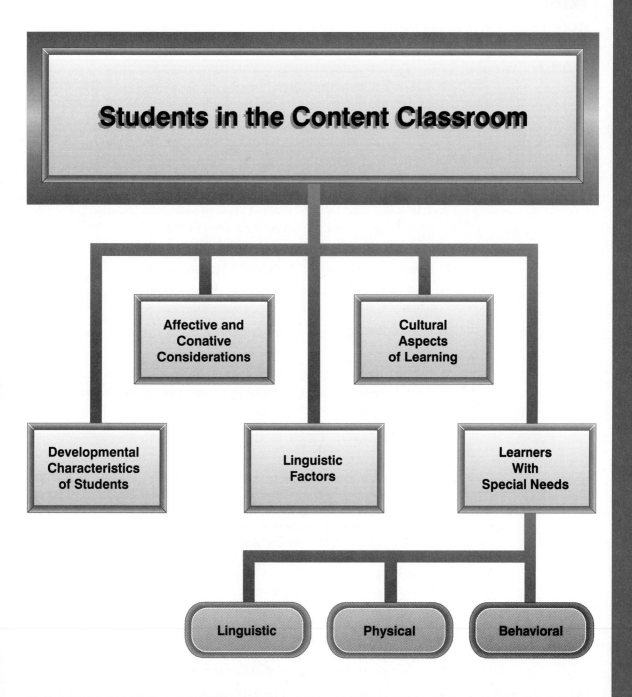

CHAPTER 2

Students in the Content Classroom

- Affective and Conative Considerations
- Cultural Aspects of Learning
- Developmental Characteristics of Students
- Linguistic Factors
- Learners With Special Needs
  - Linguistic
  - Physical
  - Behavioral

Focus Questions

*As you read this chapter, try to discover
answers to the following questions:*

1 What are some general cognitive, physiological, and social changes experienced by adolescents? How do these changes impact adolescents socially and educationally?

2 Define and distinguish between affective and conative factors in learning. How does positive affect make learning easier and more efficient for students?

3 Identify several things you feel teachers in your content area could do to encourage positive attitudes in students.

4 What are the eight motives identified by Mathewson (1985) that seem to trigger the desire to read and learn? Which of these seem particularly relevant to your content specialty?

5 What are some of the linguistic factors that impact content learning?

6 What are the functions of language as described by Halliday (1977)? Is it important to reflect most language functions in content classrooms? Why or why not?

7 How can cultural diversity in the classroom serve as a catalyst for attaining "higher literacy"?

8 What are some of the conditions underlying behavioral problems in students? What are some general classroom ingredients necessary to help these students in the regular classroom?

Reading is like an intricate tapestry of various strands (skills) tightly woven together to form a tool of great power and utility.

Successful content teaching, the type that ignites feelings of excitement during learning experiences, requires an understanding of how students develop as learners. How does reading ability affect learning in the content classroom? While some may think of reading as a simple skill akin to riding a bike (Flesch, 1981), most experienced teachers and educational researchers acknowledge that it is a multifaceted and complicated form of language use. Reading is much like an intricate tapestry of various strands (skills) tightly woven together to form a tool of great power and utility.

One reason some people outside education think of reading as being simple and easy to learn is that they have forgotten how abstract and difficult it can truly be. To reexperience the difficulty of translating written language, try reading the passage in Figure 2.1 called "Diamonds" (Flynt & Cooter, 1995). It is written on a junior high/middle school level but is illustrated here using a dif-

Diamonds

A diamond is one of the most beautiful treasures that nature has ever created. And one of the rarest. It takes thousands of years for nature to transform a chunk of carbon into a rough diamond. Only three important diamond fields have been found in the world, in India, South America, and Africa.

The first diamonds were found in the sand and gravel of stream beds. These types of diamonds are called alluvial diamonds. Later, diamonds were found deep in the earth in rock formations called pipes. These formations resemble extinct volcanoes. The rock in which diamonds are found is called blue ground. Yet even where diamonds are "plentiful" it takes digging and sorting through tons of rock and gravel to find enough diamonds for a one-carat ring.

Gem diamonds' quality is based on weight, purity, color, and cut. The weight of a diamond is measured by the carat. Its purity is determined by the presence or absence of impurities, such as foreign minerals and uncrystallized carbon. The color of diamonds varies but most diamonds are tinged yellow or brown. The cut of a diamond also figures into its value. A fully cut diamond, often called flawless, would have fifty-eight facets. Facets, or sides, cause the brilliance that is produced when a diamond is struck by light.

Figure 2.1 Excerpt From "Diamonds"

Note. From *The Flynt/Cooter Reading Inventory for the Classroom* (2nd ed., p. 163) by E. S. Flynt & R. B. Cooter, 1995, Scottsdale, AZ: Gorsuch Scarisbrick. Copyright 1995 by Gorsuch Scarisbrick. Reprinted by permission.

ferent orthography called *mirror writing.* Because you know something about letters and context it should be easy for you . . . right? Or is it? Allow yourself 3 minutes to read this passage, then be prepared to read it aloud in class or to a friend.

How did it feel to read this passage? Many begin feeling confident and relaxed because they are already successful readers. Then anxiety begins to creep in as the task becomes more difficult than expected. As you continued, did you become more and more tense and sometimes frustrated? If this had been a familiar passage, would it have been easier? This type of experience reminds us how difficult learning to read was when we were children and adolescents.

Once students understand the basic mechanics of reading, are they automatically able to read and understand materials in your content classroom? Not necessarily. As shown in Figure 2.2, other developmental and social factors have a lot to do with whether or not students succeed. These include cognitive and metacognitive, affective and conative, behavioral, linguistic, physical, and experiential factors. Understanding how each relates to content reading and writing development is the focus of this chapter.

Why is reading so much more than a mechanical act?

Figure 2.2 Factors Influencing Students' Content Learning

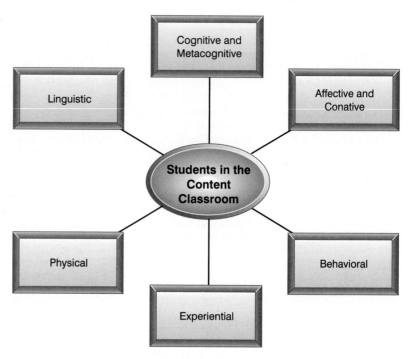

DEVELOPMENTAL ASPECTS OF READING AND WRITING TO LEARN

Know your students and teach them well.

Silvia Ashton-Warner (1963), a celebrated New Zealand educator, once said of her teaching "I reach a hand into the mind of the child . . . and use [what I discover] as the first learning material." The implication is that teachers must know their students—the way their minds work, what motivates them, their physiological/psychological development . . . *everything*! Even though knowing everything about our students may not be possible (or desirable), there are many commonalties about early and late adolescence that we should be aware of, if we are to be successful content teachers.

In this section, we begin by describing in general terms characteristics of middle school and high school students. Next, we discuss the affective factors that influence interest, attitude, and motivation.

Some Developmental Characteristics of Students in Content Classes

In what ways do adolescents change?

Students moving into adolescence experience significant changes in the areas of cognitive, physiological, psychological, and social growth (Alvermann & Phelps, 1994). These changes not only have an effect on students' education but also on their interactions with peers and adults. Teachers, more than ever, must be fully informed and ready to help students at this level with an understanding attitude. Mercer (1992) notes that adolescents

1. Often attain adult stature and appearance
2. Become mobile and function independently of school and home
3. Are influenced by their peer group as they try to establish their identity.
4. Develop abstract and formal thinking
5. Mature sexually
6. Have longer attention spans but little tolerance for boredom
7. Are self-motivating

Studies completed by the National Assessment of Educational Progress (NAEP) and the National Education Longitudinal Study (NELS) (United States Department of Education, 1990) reveal a good bit about students in the middle school and high school years. Students from about 10 to 14 years of age seem to vary a great deal in their ability to read and comprehend classroom materials. Although most can comprehend at the very basic literal level, relatively few comprehend well at the more implicit levels, and most have difficulty with problem-solving tasks. In writing ability, the trend is also not very favorable. Most have difficulty in writing descriptive or comparative essays, as well as responding in writing to what they have read (Tierney, Readence, & Dishner, 1995).

Students in early adolescence, perhaps because of their emotional and biological shifts, tend to be rather egocentric and to shy away from collaborative activities. This can have an effect on their view of the world and their ability to work with peers for problem-solving purposes. As students grow into late adolescence, however, they become better able to view the world from other viewpoints and become more receptive to collaboration. Like their younger counterparts, many students in late adolescence continue to have difficulty with higher order thinking and problem-solving skills (Alvermann & Phelps, 1994), and writing abilities remain underdeveloped in many students. Because reading and writing abilities are developmental, they improve with practice over time. The challenge for teachers seems clear: Discover interesting and motivational ideas for inclusion of reading and writing tasks in the content classroom.

Schema Theory and Metacognition

Schema theory refers to how people store and organize their concepts and ideas about the world. Cognitive psychologists suggest that humans store their prior knowledge in a system of overlapping categories, or *schemata*. Our schemata help us make sense out of events, situations, and things we read by receiving, sorting, classifying, and organizing the information. In general, the degree of prior knowledge (schemata) one has about a topic, event, or idea has a substantial impact on what will be learned. As such, one of the greatest individual differences we observe in content classrooms is the prior knowledge

What are the general strengths and weaknesses of students 10 to 14 years of age?

What you know and have stored in your brain is called your schemata (prior knowledge).

Adolescents explore their ideas and feelings through peer interaction.

students have about topics we expect them to read and write about. To be effective, teachers must assess, activate, and develop the necessary prior knowledge (schema) for topics that we want students to learn about. Without this effort on the part of teachers, many students in the content areas will not be as successful with their assignments.

Prior knowledge of subject matter information is one of the greatest individual differences among your students.

Metacognition simply means knowing about knowing. Specifically, *metacognition* refers to students' knowing about and controlling their thinking/learning processes. This knowing of when, how, and why to engage in specific learning activities is at the essence of being a strategic reader and learner. L. Brown (1991) suggests that competent secondary students often view reading as a meaning-getting process, recognize that strategies for reading depend on the purposes for reading, and monitor their comprehension so that if it is disrupted they use strategies, such as rereading, to preserve meaning. This metacognitive awareness is not shared by all students, and because it is at the heart of becoming an independent learner, teachers must begin to recognize when and how to develop metacognitive behaviors in their students.

Metacognition is knowing when, how, and why to engage in specific learning activities.

We will return to schema theory and metacognition in greater detail in Chapter 5 because of their importance in understanding how students learn. We hope this brief introduction to these topics has made you aware that student differences in prior knowledge and awareness of how to learn are both issues that successful teachers deal with instructionally.

Affective and Conative Considerations in Learning

Affective Dimensions in Learning

Many times we see students in content classrooms experiencing reading problems as a reflection of low interest. Low interest leads to ineffective learning and poor performance when information is needed. Searching for ways to ignite student interest and motivation as well as developing positive attitudes toward learning are part of what is known as the **affective domain**.

Interest and motivation are the basics of the affective domain and essential for learning.

Teachers have observed for many years the powerful influence of affective variables in content classrooms (Alexander & Cobb, 1992). Grover Mathewson (1985), in his seminal essay "Toward a Comprehensive Model of Affect in the Reading Process," has helped teachers better understand which affective factors seem to have an impact on reading and comprehending. Mathewson identified four affective variables that appear to drive the reading process: attitude, motives, feelings, and physical sensation. These variables appear to influence the readers' choice to read in the first place, ability to focus attention, recall information, and comprehend what has been read. Mathewson has also identified through his research some eight motives representing "an amalgam of the higher end of Maslow's need hierarchy: *curiosity, competence,* and *achievement*" (p. 843), which seem to trigger the decision to read and other related behaviors. These eight motives, feelings, or needs students wish to have fulfilled include belonging and love, curiosity, competence, achievement, esteem, self-actualization, desire to know and understand, and aesthetic motivation.

What motives, or needs, are upper level students seeking to have fulfilled?

There is no question that a motivated and interested student will learn more quickly and efficiently than one who is disinterested. Following is a brief case study from our files that illustrates this point.

Brian: The Disinterested Reader

Brian was a 10th-grade student who came in for tutoring assistance in all academic subjects. The idea was to teach him "study skills." His parents said that he was "learning disabled" as a result of reading on a third-grade level, according to standardized test results. It became clear very early during tutoring that he was more *disinterested* than *disabled*. Because of Brian's school passivity, he had simply not read much over the years and, thereby, experienced what we sometimes call **reading atrophy** (the deterioration of reading abilities that is due to lack of regular reading practice).

> Because we feel it is as much a teacher's responsibility to inspire students to *want* to read as it is to teach reading/study skills, we resolved to begin Brian's program by getting him interested in reading . . . anything! Using a standard interest inventory, we discovered that Brian was interested in motorcycles. We used motorcycle magazines (written on an eighth-grade level, incidentally) to help Brian develop basic reading fluency that later translated into content reading success. *Conclusion:* when teachers can accurately assess the affective domain and use the information to make instructional decisions, student learning can be greatly enhanced.

From this example we can see that strong interest in a topic can partially compensate for a student's lack of reading development and be used to increase fluency.

Conative Factors and Reading

How do conative factors differ from affective factors? Why are they important?

John Raven (1992) and Harold Berlak (1992) argue for inclusion of another domain that is quite close to affect called *conative* factors. They state that not only are cognitive and affective aspects of learning falsely treated as mutually exclusive categories, conative aspects of human behavior (i.e., determination, persistence, and will) are also erroneously included under the affective label. Berlak, in summarizing Raven's ground-breaking work in this field, states:

> [A student] can enjoy doing something without being determined to see it through, and he or she can hate doing something, but still be determined to do it . . . [T]aking initiative (which would be categorized as an "affective" outcome in the Bloom Taxonomy) is inseparable from intellectual or cognitive functioning, and from action. (1992, p. 17)

Raven (1992) adds that both affective and conative components are an integral part of what is meant by the ability to cognize.

Which consideration for promoting change in students' determination and willingness do you consider to be of primary importance? Why?

In promoting and changing students' attitudes and willingness to participate, teachers and researchers alike agree on several general considerations (Cooter & Alexander, 1984; Heathington & Alexander, 1984; Rieck, 1977). First, teachers must accept students for who they are, expect them to learn, and interact with them to get to know them. In short, students must feel they belong. Second, teachers should provide the mind-set that it is OK to be wrong, they should encourage participation by using humor and general enthusiasm, and they should be critical only in positive ways. Third, teachers should share reading with their students by reading to them regularly and should make reading rewarding by connecting what they teach to real-world reading assignments. Finally, teachers should encourage students to react to and discuss what they are reading and consider limiting reading assignments based on the reading expertise of their students. All of these ideas are commonsense notions, but to get students to try, simple commonsense ideas are the best place to start.

In summary, when considering the development of students in content classrooms, we should remember that determination and willingness to persevere in the tasks at hand are crucial factors. How we encourage such attitudes is part of the creative artistry of the teaching profession.

LINGUISTIC FACTORS AND CONTENT LEARNING

Vygotsky's (1978) teachings regarding cognitive development strongly indicate that advanced thinking is derived from one's ability to communicate through language (May, 1994). Language is the tool of human expression and assumes four main forms: listening, speaking, reading, and writing. Listening and reading are known as *receptive language* forms because a message is being received from another person when one exercises these skills. Another name for the receptive skills used in reading and listening is *decoding*. The mirror images of receptive language forms are the productive language forms of speaking and writing. Rather than receiving a message, productive language users are sending a message or *encoding* ideas for others to mentally process.

Linguistics is the study of language and how it is used in society. In this field, linguists concern themselves with such aspects of language as *semantics* (word meanings), *syntax* (how words are organized into phrases, sentences and larger units), *phonemes* (sounds in the language), *graphemes* (written symbols that represent phonemes), and *morphemes* (meaning-bearing units or language, such as affixes and free-standing words). **Psycholinguistics**, a field that merges psychology and linguistics (Alexander & Heathington, 1988), focuses on how students use and understand language. A third linguistics-related field is called **sociolinguistics**. These scholars are interested in ways language use relates to societal and human behaviors.

What is the difference in the receptive and expressive language processes? Which of the two is more relied on by students in school?

Linguistics, psycholinguistics, and sociolinguistics are three ways of viewing language, knowledge of language, and how students use language.

FUNCTIONS OF LANGUAGE

Language is used to meet a number of social and functional needs. Halliday (1977) explained that there are at least 10 language uses, which we summarize in the following list (as described by F. Smith, 1977, p. 640):

Which of Halliday's 10 uses of language are most often found in school settings?

1. *Instrumental:* "I want." (Language is used as a means of getting things and satisfying material needs.)
2. *Regulatory:* "Do as I tell you." (Language is used to control the attitudes, behaviors, and feelings of others.)
3. *Interactional:* "Me and you." (Getting along with others, establishing relative status.) Also, "Me against you." (Establishing separateness.)
4. *Personal:* "Here I come." (Expressing individuality, awareness of self, pride.)

5. *Heuristic:* "Tell me why." (Seeking and testing world knowledge.)
6. *Imaginative:* "Let's pretend." (Creating new worlds, making up stories, poems.)
7. *Representational:* "I've got something to tell you." (Communicating information, descriptions, expressing propositions.)
8. *Divertive:* "Enjoy this." (Puns, jokes, riddles.)
9. *Authoritative/contractual:* "How it must be." (Statutes, laws, regulations, and rules.)
10. *Perpetuating:* "How it was." (Records, histories, diaries, notes, scores.)

Once students understand the many uses for language in their own lives, they more easily accept and recognize the purposes and meaning of language found in written language. Success in reading is very much dependent on the quality of the oral and written language students encounter in their studies (Smith, 1988). In light of this fact, experiences with quality texts, extended discussions about their readings, and opportunities to write and respond to what they have read become integral to success in content reading. We have devoted Chapters 8 and 9 to exploring how and when to incorporate these types of experiences into your classroom.

Language, Prior Knowledge, and Vocabulary Building

What two levels of language learning are assumed to have occurred before discussing content in the classroom?

Language is the means by which thoughts are shared between human beings, a point that is especially critical when considering content instruction. When ideas are to be shared and hopefully extended in content area classes, both teacher and students rely heavily on the prior knowledge of class members so that new knowledge bases can be formed. Indeed, the most important variable in learning with texts is a reader's prior knowledge (Vacca & Vacca, 1993, p. 13). There is an assumption that two levels of language learning have already occurred and are contained in students' prior knowledge when new content information is to be presented. First is the assumption that the reader has a relatively extensive *listening vocabulary* associated with the subject. This means that the reader can hear and understand words associated with the field of study (specialized content vocabulary) as well as other common words found in print (nouns, verbs, adjectives, etc.). The second level of learning teachers assume has occurred is a *speaking vocabulary*. This refers to words that not only are understood when heard but also may be used correctly in speech by the reader. When the reader encounters words in print that are understood on these two prerequisite levels, then reading comprehension is possible—and probable. Words that are read and understood comprise the *reading vocabulary*. Teachers who use the writing process successfully with their students help students build a new and sophisticated level of content language known as *writing vocabulary*. The successful content teacher skillfully guides students through the development of each of these four vocabularies when introducing new content. This is how new information is developed into a coherent whole in the minds of students.

CULTURAL ASPECTS OF LEARNING

Diversity in the Content Classroom

Throughout its history, the United States has been a nation of diverse peoples brought together by a common desire for freedom to pursue one's destiny. In recent years, the influx of immigrants from all over the globe has seemingly accelerated such that the so-called majority culture is rapidly becoming a minority. For instance, state officials in Texas announced in 1994 that the combined minority cultures now comprise the majority of residents. Experts (Banks & Banks, 1989; Pine & Hilliard, 1990) predict that by the year 2000 one third of students in public schools will be of African, Hispanic, Asian, or Native American descent. In past decades, classroom diversity was sometimes seen as a negative situation requiring massive dosages of remedial education professionals and federal support dollars. More recently, however, a reassessment of this situation has led many to conclude that diversity may, in fact, be an extremely valuable asset in producing highly literate individuals.

> One third of all students will be of African, Hispanic, Asian, or Native American descent by the year 2000.

Not very many years ago, reading, and content literacy in general, was thought to be text driven. That is, the text one was reading contained all the information, and the reader simply decoded the author's message into language for literal interpretation. But with the work of such scholars as Vygotsky (1978), and to a lesser extent Dewey (1909) and Piaget (1955), came an understanding that meaning is created through an interaction between the text and the reader, not the text alone. This **constructivist** view of literacy suggests that learners are active participants in the creation of their own knowledge, that learning often occurs in social contexts, and that interactions and relationships with others in the learning situation can serve a vital function in the interpretation of what we learn (Hiebert, 1991).

> What is the constructivist view of literacy? What is your view?

This suggests that diversity in the content classroom can help learners to construct understandings of new information from a variety of viewpoints. This is what R. Brown (1991) refers to as *higher literacies*. From this viewpoint it is easy to see that diversity in the classroom can be an asset to classroom instruction rather than a liability (Hiebert, 1991). Skillful teachers exploit this diversity advantage by helping all students develop problem-solving and higher order thinking skills, recognizing language differences as being normal, communicating to all students an expectation of success and acceptance, and capitalizing on students' differing views of the world. Throughout this text, we have interwoven ideas and viewpoints that capitalize on the classroom diversity advantage. Our goal is to help students construct progressively higher level understandings of the world around them and become fully content literate.

> What does the term *higher literacies* suggest about capitalizing on diversity in the classroom?

LEARNERS WITH SPECIAL NEEDS

How will inclusion affect you and your teaching?

Sometimes factors related to language, culture, and physical or mental challenges can lead to difficulty for students in their content learning. Students having major learning needs have tended to be pulled out of content classes to participate in special education programs tailored in some degree to fit their needs. However, a movement gaining renewed strength in American schools in the 1990s calls for greater **inclusion** of students with learning needs in regular classroom settings. The idea is that students' educational needs can best be served when they are placed in classrooms with their peers. Therefore, it is likely that you will be expected to find ways to help students with special needs adapt to the demands of your discipline. Although it is beyond the scope of this text to address each in detail, we summarize some of the more common situations experienced by students and teachers as well as possible adjustments you may wish to consider.

Students With Language Differences

The vocabularies possessed by students (i.e., listening, speaking, reading, writing) reflect the schema structures they have acquired. As an example, consider how a student named Karen who speaks fluently about the field of art history reveals in an indirect way that she has developed extensive knowledge structures in that area. Karen will likely be able to read and understand many books on this topic. Conversely, a student with little language knowledge in art history will likely require much more support from teacher and peers to be able to stay afloat in a class on this topic.

Even more fundamental language factors sometimes cause students to be at risk of failure in content classrooms. A few of these are summarized next. At the end of this chapter, we also list some readings that may be helpful.

ESL Students

What's basic about helping ESL students in the subject matter classroom?

Recently, a teacher came up to us after a presentation and said, "I am an eighth-grade teacher and have been asked to accept reassignment helping students who have just moved into our school district from Mexico, Vietnam, and China. They know very little English . . . yet they are expected to take the same curriculum and state-mandated tests at the end of the year. How can I help them?"

Students who are learning English as a second language **(ESL)** certainly present teachers with significant challenges. These students are (a) trying to learn a new language to cope in basic ways, (b) translating prior knowledge encoded in their native language to the new language, (c) learning how not only to decode English messages in listening and reading experiences but also to encode writing and speaking language forms, and (d) adding new knowledge structures using the new second language. It is an awesome task that

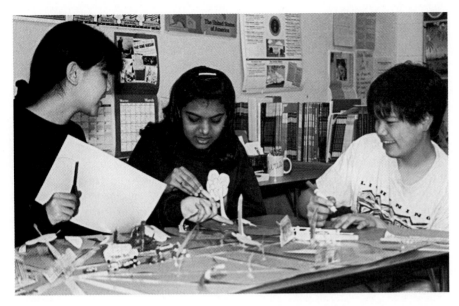

Students from different cultural backgrounds add to the challenges and rewards of content teaching.

requires much study and experimentation on the teacher's part (as well as the student's). Needless to say, students certainly can have difficulty the first few years as they learn English.

The solution seems to be to help students first develop basic listening and speaking vocabularies. This is essential because one cannot read and write what one is unable to first listen to and speak about with understanding. This can be facilitated by immersing the student in English in the classroom, rather than by a gradual phasing in of the language.

Some have argued that it is better to first educate students using their native language, then help them learn English later. Whether to immerse in English first or later has been the subject of hot debate for several decades. Although compelling arguments are on both sides of the debate, we support English immersion first. We feel that if we are to offer students maximum life choices in the United States, then they must learn to communicate in English fluently as early as possible in their education.

Language Registers

Most people use slightly different language patterns, or language registers, in different situations. For instance, most people tend to use informal language when speaking to close friends or family and formal language when they are in a business setting. Similarly, those studying a scientific field tend to acquire a

Can you differentiate between language registers and linguistically different students?

scientific register, or way of speaking. Sometimes students have difficulty making shifts from one register, say street talk, to registers associated with a content field. Modeling by the teacher may not be sufficient, thus role playing and other contrived practice activities may be needed.

Linguistically Different Students

Related to the issue of language registers are linguistically different students. These are students who use a language dialect so different from standard English that it may limit their understanding of school instruction and, consequently, life choices. In the United States, linguistically different speakers are frequently not so much a reflection of a racial or ethnic group as perhaps a geographical region and/or cultural group. Thus, students in urban New York may be just as subject to bias and stereotype as adolescents from southern Appalachia or suburban California. Students should be helped to develop language registers appropriate not only to your content area but also for formal situations requiring standard English forms. At the same time, students must not be made to feel as though they are linguistically deficient, merely different.

Students With Physical or Sensory Challenges

How should you respond if you think a student is experiencing a visual or auditory problem?

An entire constellation of factors related to success in content classrooms is physical in nature. Sometimes students have difficulty in a content classroom, not so much from a lack of prior knowledge or reading ability but as a result of related physical problems. Auditory and visual problems seem to be the most common source of difficulty for students. *Acuity* has to do with a student's physical ability to either see or hear. *Perception* is the ability to understand or process messages received in the brain by the eyes or ears. A number of tests are available to school psychologists for measuring these critical areas. If you suspect that a student may be having learning problems that are due to auditory or visual problems, a referral should be made to the school psychologist or health professionals for testing.

Students Having Behavioral Problems

What conditions often underlie behavior problems?

All too frequently, content classrooms are characterized by student passivity and, as a consequence, a general lack of learning. As students "tune out," they may also become disruptive. As teachers, we not only are interested in maintaining control over the learning environment, we also want to help students begin to learn again! It is important that content teachers first understand conditions that underlie behaviors that cause students to be at risk of failure. Rogus and Wildenhaus (1991) acquaint us with some of the more common determinants:

- Academic underachievement
- Low self-esteem and self-respect (in spite of outward behaviors to the contrary)

■ Inability to communicate intimate thoughts and feelings
■ Limited conflict resolution and problem-solving skills
■ Unrealistic life expectations

Any of these conditions, or a combination thereof, can lead to all sorts of disruptive classroom behaviors and/or reduced student participation. Fortunately, behavior disorder scholars offer suggestions that may be helpful to holistic content teachers.

The first order of business seems to be to establish a cooperative learning climate, as opposed to a more competitive one (Loup et al., 1991; Rogus & Wildenhaus, 1991). This may be accomplished in part by counseling students through disagreements and making it clear from the start that demeaning or sarcastic comments about a peer's work are not permitted. It has also been suggested (Rogus & Wildenhaus, 1991) that students first write about their classroom problems before asking for teacher intervention. This could help them use metacognitive skills to identify what they know and don't know— sometimes helping them solve their own problems. Specific questions that may prove helpful for students to write about include "What is the problem? What did I do? How can I help solve this problem?"

It is also important for behavioral reasons, as well as affective reasons already discussed, that the teacher exude enthusiasm for teaching, learning, and the subject being taught. Enthusiasm is catching, and many behavioral problems can be prevented by the teacher's attitude. Also related to the teacher's behavior is the perception by students that the class is conducted in an impartial way in student interactions.

Obviously, managing student behavior and maintaining classroom discipline can be a complicated matter. A great deal of successful teaching and classroom management comes through experience and a commitment to the enterprise. At the end of the chapter, we also list references that may be of use.

> What can you do to increase the chances of students with behavior problems experiencing success in your classroom?

CHAPTER SUMMARY

Students in content classrooms are at least as different as they are alike. Cognitive development can be affected by past experiences, their interests and attitudes, home environment, and behavior. Linguistic development can also assist students in their content literacy growth or, in some cases, as with students having difficulty learning ESL, language can be a barrier. Content teachers must therefore learn as much as possible about students and growth during adolescence.

Learning appears to be greatly facilitated when students are motivated and interested in the learning tasks and information presented. Studies of the interests, attitudes, and motivations of students are encompassed in what is known as the affective domain. Some theorists further suggest a related conative factor in learning that has to do with persistence and perseverance.

Content classrooms in North America are becoming increasingly diverse in terms of culture and language. We recognize this as an important opportunity for teachers to help students begin to understand multiple viewpoints. Ultimately, if we work together to appreciate our differences, it may indeed be possible to attain higher content literacy levels than ever before.

As content teachers, it is important that we familiarize ourselves with the needs of all students, including those who may have special learning needs. The inclusion movement has alerted teachers to the inherent advantages of special needs students learning in regular classrooms, rather than in pull-out programs. In this chapter, we have highlighted a number of these possibilities including language, physical, and behavioral needs students.

Reflection/Application Activities

1. Develop a tentative plan relative to encouraging positive behavior in your classes. Share this plan with some of your peers or colleagues so that they can help you to anticipate problems and positive solutions in classroom settings.
2. Interview a teacher at a local junior high, middle school, or high school who has a reputation of being a master teacher and popular with students. Find out what this teacher does to encourage positive affect in the classroom and how he or she feels this impacts student behavior. Ask this teacher for recommendations, then share these suggestions with peers or colleagues who have done the same task with other teachers. Construct your own minihandbook on this subject to use in your own classroom.
3. Inquire at your local school district's central office as to the ethnic makeup of the school district. Try to find out what, if any, special initiatives have taken place to train teachers how to better work in diverse classrooms.

Recommended Reading

Brown, A. L. (1980). Metacognition development in reading. In R. J. Spiro, B. C. Bruce, & W. F. Brewer (Eds.), *Theoretical issues in reading comprehension*. Hillsdale, NJ: Lawrence Erlbaum.

Hiebert, E. H. (1991). *Literacy for a diverse society: Perspectives, practices, and policies.* New York: Teachers College Press.

Raven, J. (1992). A model of competence, motivation, and behavior, and a paradigm for assessment. In H. Berlak et al. (Eds.), *Toward a new science of educational testing and assessment.* New York: State University of New York Press.

Rogus, J., & Wildenhaus, C. (1991). Programming for at-risk learners: A preventive approach (The principal's challenge). *NASSP Bulletin, 75*, 1–7.

Smith, F. (1988). *Understanding reading* (4th ed.). Hillsdale, NJ: Lawrence Erlbaum.

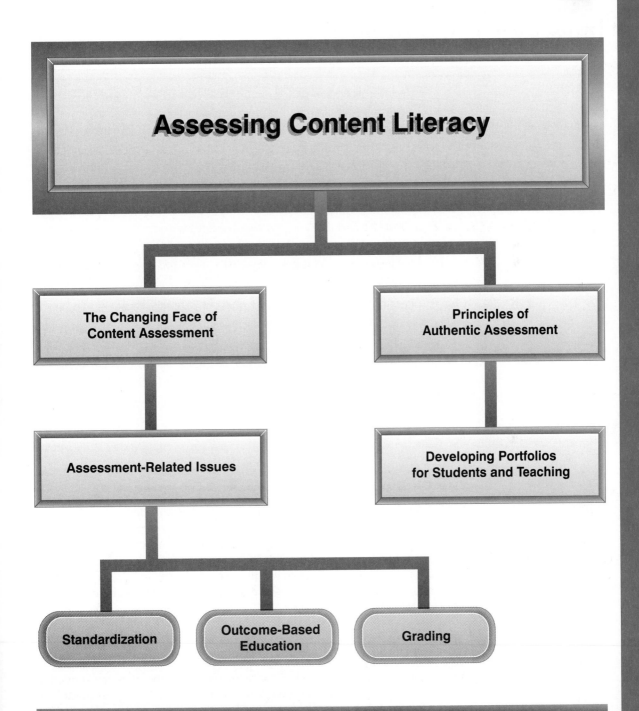

Assessing Content Literacy

The Changing Face of Content Assessment

Principles of Authentic Assessment

Assessment-Related Issues

Developing Portfolios for Students and Teaching

Standardization

Outcome-Based Education

Grading

Focus Questions

As you read this chapter, try to discover answers to the following questions:

1 What is the learning deficit model of learning and teaching? How does it impact teachers and students?

2 What is the authentic model of learning and teaching? How does it impact teachers and students? Summarize the principles of authentic assessment. How does the authentic assessment model fit your content area?

3 What is portfolio assessment? What benefits does portfolio assessment have? What is the difference between classroom portfolios and file portfolios?

4 Describe methods of assessing the affective domain.

5 Why is it important to assess the match between the student and the adopted textbook? Compare the cloze procedure and the content area reading inventory. Which one do you favor and why?

6 How does one determine the considerateness or inconsiderateness of a textbook? Why is using the cross-text comparison procedure recommended to teachers who are adopting a new textbook?

7 What is the central philosophy of outcome-based education (OBE), and can it be applied holistically? Why or why not?

8 How can teachers use authentic assessment strategies to improve the validity of grading and report cards?

The Changing Face of Content Assessment

Assessment helps teachers to document student learning and choose appropriate learning experiences.

Assessing what students know and can do with their knowledge of a subject is at the heart of successful teaching. Assessment serves two related functions: (a) to document student learning, and (b) to help teachers choose learning experiences that best meet the needs of students. In this chapter, we revisit traditional assessment strategies that still have valid uses in the classrooms of today and tomorrow, and we consider newer authentic assessment strategies for documenting student learning.

Changing Views of Content Area Assessment

What is the learning deficit model?

Ways of measuring students' subject area knowledge in the past have tended to be generally simple but also limited. The traditional test–teach–test model has been in existence in one form or another for centuries and continues to be a chief staple in the assessment arsenal for many teachers even today. The main idea is that teachers need to give a paper-and-pencil test to find out what students don't know about the subject to be studied, teach to this deficit, then test again to make sure they have learned the material taught. We refer to this way of viewing learning and teaching as the **learning deficit model**.

The learning deficit model has been a central philosophy governing classroom instruction at all levels for many years. Its central premise is to look for what students don't know, then teach to this need or "deficit." In other words, assessment is the search for what students don't know instead of what they do know. It is somewhat like comparing students' knowledge of a subject or content area to a piece of Swiss cheese: good coverage . . . but full of holes (deficits). Paul Burns (1980) constructed a flowchart explaining this test–teach–test perspective (see Figure 3.1). Called the "diagnostic teaching sequence," this very logical model comprises several basic steps:

Step 1.   Decide *what* in the curriculum is to be taught *(objective)*.

Step 2.   Develop and administer a *pretest* to find out whether students already know the information.

Step 3.   Ask the question "Do the students already know this information (*criterion level reached?*). If the answer is "yes" (they already know this information), either move on to the next objective in the curriculum and repeat the first three steps, or offer the students more advanced information in the subject so they can gain in-depth knowledge. If the answer is "no" (they don't already know this information), then proceed to the next step.

Step 4.   Provide instruction using your preferred methods.

Step 5.   Develop and administer a post-test to find out if acceptable levels of learning occurred. Score the post-test and ask the *criterion level reached?* question again that was described in Step 3. If the answer is "yes," the same choices as described are available. If the answer is "no," then the teacher should reteach the information, perhaps in a different way, and the cycle repeats itself.

As logical as these test–teach–test or learning deficit models are, they do have at least two major drawbacks. First of all, the search for what students *don't* know instead of what they *do* know creates a negative perspective for viewing students. The assumption is that something is wrong or deficient with the student(s), and the teacher's job is to fix the problem. This mentality tends to produce a classroom atmosphere of centering on rewards and punishments with good grades for those having learned the material, and a punishment for those who fail in the form of labels (e.g., *failure, at-risk*). These approaches fail to consider such important factors as students' prior knowledge of a subject, the role of materials provided for learning, the classroom environment, and instructional methods used by the teacher. Teachers who want to establish an

Burns's (1980) "diagnostic teaching sequence" maps the test–teach–test method.

The learning deficit model focuses on what students cannot do, rather than on what they *can* do.

FOUNDATIONS FOR DIAGNOSTIC TEACHING

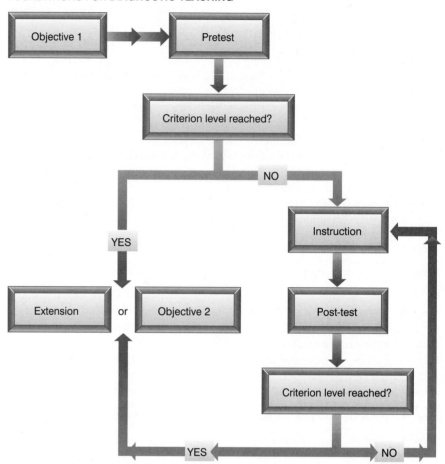

Figure 3.1 Burns's Diagnostic Teaching Sequence

Note. From *Assessment and Correction of Language Arts Difficulties* by P. C. Burns, 1980, Englewood Cliffs, NJ: Merrill/Prentice Hall. Copyright 1980 by Merrill/Prentice Hall. Reprinted by permission.

environment of trust and risk taking on the part of students will most likely find deficit models of assessment and teaching unsatisfactory.

A second problem is that deficit models of assessment and teaching rely heavily on paper-and-pencil tests given on specific test days. If a student is unsettled by such assessment practices, or is simply having a bad day, then he may do poorly on the test when, in fact, he may have an acceptable level of knowledge. These problems have caused many teachers to look further for a more valid assessment model.

Traditional Testing Versus Authentic Assessment: The Growing Debate

Concerns over deficit models of assessment have become rather intense in recent years and have matured into a debate between proponents of traditional testing based on deficit models, and those favoring authentic assessment models (Puckett & Black, 1994). **Traditional testing** typically uses paper-and-pencil formats, sometimes uses commercially produced tests (usually standardized), and focuses on narrowly defined bits of information (e.g., definitions, dates, people's names in a Western civilization course), rather than the application of important concepts and processes. Traditional testing is in some ways like taking a snapshot of an individual student's ability in an isolated area of the content subject.

Describe how *traditional testing* is like a "snapshot" of a student's ability.

Critics of traditional tests generally feel they fail to assess true content knowledge or the ability to apply new learning. In short, taking a paper-and-pencil test is not the same as using the knowledge to solve problems! Goodman (1992), in speaking of language arts assessment, has stated that traditional tests are frequently based on skill hierarchies and lists of information so as to create "an illusion of science." Tierney, Carter, and Desai (1991) add that traditional testing can be both "limited and subversive." They point out that the creative energies of teachers and students are frequently subverted so that students can be prepared to "respond to tests which have very little relationship to literacy as we know it." (p. 4) In a powerful expression of their feelings, two classroom teachers (Nolan & Berry, 1993) summarized the effects of district-mandated testing:

Many teachers feel mandated testing is a classroom intrusion of minimal value. Why?

> [W]e resented how the district's standardized tests intruded on class time, created an atmosphere of anxiety, and failed to reflect the complexity of learning, the quality and presentation of the text, or the conditions of collaboration and discussion that are valued in [the] classroom. (p. 606)

In summary, many educators feel that traditional tests fail to assess many important aspects of learning, ignore individual student needs, and encourage ineffective teacher behaviors.

Authentic assessment, on the other hand, is a concept that implies a much more comprehensive look at students' content knowledge. If traditional testing is similar to a snapshot of students' ability, then authentic assessment is comparable to a color movie. Authentic assessment shifts the focus from merely testing for literal or factual knowledge to surveying a student's ability to internalize and apply information. Authentic assessment activities are drawn from quality classroom activities that carry real-world significance. Thus, authentic assessment is performance assessment (Farr, 1991; Farr & Tone, 1994) at its best and is linked to quality instruction. Learning records gathered while students are involved in realistic content application tasks prove to be far more useful and informative than scores from tests that have little relevance to the needs of students and teachers (Valencia, 1990).

Authentic assessment is like a "color movie" depicting the student's ability.

What are the key purposes that guide authentic assessment activities?

Several key purposes guide authentic assessment (Reutzel & Cooter, 1996; Werner, 1991). First, authentic assessment creates an ongoing record of student achievement in the content area so that growth can be measured over time. Second, authentic assessment helps teachers determine areas of strength and need for planning instruction. Third, authentic assessment can be used to assist teachers in giving grades. Although the notion of grading is not usually considered consistent with a holistic philosophical view, grades can be derived from some forms of authentic assessment to satisfy political realities. Later in the chapter, we offer a system for grading that effectively uses authentic assessment information. Finally, authentic assessment should be used for research. In this instance, we use the term *research* as a descriptor for teachers' career-long search for ways to help students learn about their content area.

Sheila Valencia and David Pearson summed up the assessment debate between testing traditionalists and authentic assessment advocates:

> What we need are not just new and better tests. We need a new framework for thinking about assessment, one in which educators begin by considering types of decisions needed and the level of impact of those decisions. (1987, p. 729)

In the remainder of this chapter, we describe assessment choices for content teachers. These choices help teachers assess all relevant areas of the content domain and facilitate the planning of the best instruction possible.

PRINCIPLES OF AUTHENTIC ASSESSMENT IN CONTENT CLASSROOMS

Teachers often ask us whether one assessment strategy or another is OK to use in their classroom. They are usually classroom veterans of many years who are trying to move toward more holistic models of teaching and assessment. Our response is usually "If the strategy is consistent with the basic principles of classroom assessment and is consistent with your own belief system, then the answer is *yes!*"

So, what are these basic principles of classroom assessment that content teachers should consider? In this section we offer several **principles of content assessment** as a starting point or guide to assist in the selection of assessment strategies. We recommend that you adapt them to fit your own belief system and, if necessary, add others you feel are equally important.

Principle 1: Assessment Activities Should Help Teachers Make Instructional Decisions

A primary purpose of assessment is to inform teaching.

The primary goal of classroom assessment is to help teachers make instructional decisions, or to "inform teaching" (Reutzel & Cooter, 1996). The key factors governing the selection of assessment activities should be the kinds of instructional insights needed and the potential for given activities in yielding that information. Further, assessment activities should reveal rich insights into the effectiveness of certain teaching methods, classroom environmental features, materials selected to enhance learning, grouping strategies, and actual learning of the content.

Principle 2: Assessment Strategies Should Help Teachers Find Out What Students Know and *Can* Do . . . Not What They *Cannot* Do

Assessments should help teachers learn what students know about the subject area *and* their ability to apply the information. Teachers should also be interested in knowing which reading/study strategies the student can use when conducting research in the subject area. When teachers understand what students know or how far their skills have developed in a specific area, appropriate learning activities can be prepared that extend their knowledge. Focusing on what students know instead of what they don't know establishes a positive and safe learning environment in which students feel comfortable trying out new ideas and taking risks with their self-esteem.

Teachers want to know what students can do so that appropriate next steps can be planned.

Principle 3: The Holistic Context for Learning Should Be Considered and Assessed

The term *holistic teaching* implies that teachers consider all factors that have an impact on learning and teaching. Thus, such factors as students' affective responses (interest, attitude, motivation) toward the subject area, classroom environment, parental and cultural attitudes toward schooling, and physiological needs (food, clothing, feelings of safety) should be considered. Surveying holistic factors associated with learning helps teachers make valid judgments about student needs.

Principle 4: Assessment Activities Should Grow Out of Authentic Learning Activities

Good assessment looks like good teaching and vice versa. Authentic assessment strategies usually involve the daily collecting of evidence of student learning as they perform real-world application tasks (Schnitzer, 1993). For example, students in a consumer mathematics course may be asked to find the best deal on an American car selling for under $14,000 as part of a required project. The teacher may ask that they put together a portfolio containing research information they have found on automobiles (consumer reports, cost information, needs assessment for the driver, etc.). Part of the assessment for each student would likely include a qualitative/analytic evaluation of the portfolio contents, an assessment tailored to the task itself, and a learning experience calling for

Think of real-world situations that could be used as a backdrop for assessment activities in your content area.

application of research skills previously learned. Where quality teaching and quality assessments begin and end is often hard to discern, but then, this is as it should be.

Principle 5: Best Assessments of Student Learning Are Longitudinal . . . They Take Place Over Time

The only way to accurately assess what students know and can do is to observe them over time. This is what Goodman (1986) refers to as "kidwatching." Multiple samples of students' work and accomplishments taken from a variety of situations constitute valid evidence of what students can do. Marie Clay, in speaking of reading assessment, helps us understand the purpose and value of multiple observations carried out over time:

> I am looking for movement in appropriate directions. . . . For if I do not watch what [the student] is doing, and if I do not capture what is happening in records of some kind, Johnny, who never gets under my feet and who never comes really into a situation where I can truly see what he is doing, may, in fact, for six months or even a year, practice behaviours that will handicap him in [learning]. (1985, p. 49)

Thus, practicing this principle, although not easy at first, avoids the "quick and dirty" assessment phenomenon created when teachers use only paper-and-pencil tests on designated test days.

Principle 6: Each Assessment Activity Should Have a Specific Objective-Linked Purpose

Assessment all too often becomes a routine exercise with little logic used. For example, giving a test every Friday over readings in the class textbook for the week is a poor rationale for an assessment exercise. Quality assessment grows out of careful observations, discussions, and conferences with students. As teachers discover what students know and can do, natural assessment questions arise about the depth of student understanding of a topic and how well students can use what they have learned. These questions can only be answered through careful and precise, even "surgical" assessment activities that help teachers discover specific answers to specific questions. If a clear and reasonable rationale cannot be determined for conducting a particular assessment activity, then it should not be administered. Development of a clearly delineated curriculum that includes objectives, procedures for learning and teaching, and objective-linked performance assessment is probably the best safeguard against unwarranted assessment activities.

AUTHENTIC ASSESSMENT: DEVELOPING PORTFOLIOS FOR STUDENTS AND TEACHING

As teachers experiencing both the triumphs and tragedies of moving into holistic teaching, we have naturally tried to discover assessment practices that are the most useful. Our "litmus test" questions for assessment strategies, whether holistic or traditional, have to do with their effectiveness, consistency with holistic philosophy, and most especially, how well they work with students presently under our supervision. We have learned that what works on one occasion with students in suburban Knoxville, Tennessee, will not necessarily work nearly as well with students in urban San Antonio, Texas, or for junior high students in Hattiesburg, Mississippi. We offer our suggestions in this section and trust that readers will find them as useful as we have in our own classrooms.

One-size-fits-all assessment programs developed by publishers rarely fit the needs of any classroom well. The Model of Assessment suggests critical factors to consider.

To obtain a comprehensive assessment for content classrooms, it is essential that two major interacting factors be considered: the student and teaching. In Figure 3.2 we present these factors as a **Model of Assessment**. Our Model of Assessment indicates that learning depends on the interaction between student factors, such as background knowledge of the subject and affective variables (interest, attitude, motivation), and how the student reacts to teaching/learning factors (the teacher, text, materials, and learning activities). The Model of Assessment also suggests that learning is also influenced greatly by the context for learning (classroom environment, community factors, home influence, political considerations). The outer band around the model indicates that comprehensive assessment considers, to the extent possible, all of these relevant factors. How teachers do this is the subject of this section.

Figure 3.2 Authentic Assessment Model

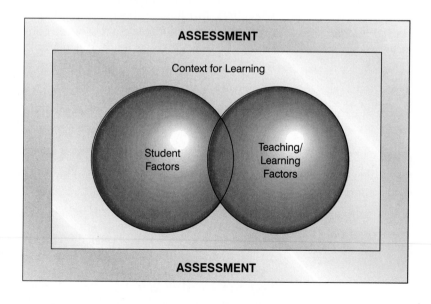

Authentic assessment philosophy calls for self-assessment
as part of learning.

As teachers have moved toward more authentic methods of teaching and learning in recent years, they have searched for compatible assessment approaches. At the heart of authentic assessment philosophy is the notion that both teachers and students should be engaged in ongoing evaluation and self-assessment activities as an integral part of learning. As Sandra Schnitzer so eloquently put it, "From an authentic task—which teaches content and a complex thinking process—flows an authentic assessment of student performance" (1993, p. 32). A popular and extremely effective vehicle for achieving this level of authenticity is the use of portfolio assessment programs (Farr, 1991; Glazer & Brown, 1993; Tierney, Carter, & Desai, 1991; Valencia, McGinley, & Pearson, 1990).

What Is "Portfolio Assessment"?

Portfolio assessment is one
type of authentic assessment.
It is both a philosophy and a
place for gathering learning
artifacts.

Portfolio assessment is both a *philosophy,* or way of viewing assessment, and a *place* for gathering pieces of evidence indicating student growth and development in reading (Valencia, 1990). The philosophy of portfolios is holistic in nature, suggesting that we should consider all factors related to reading when assessing students. The Model of Assessment (see Figure 3.2) described earlier speaks to these factors. Portfolios are consistent with newer curriculum designs (Farr, 1991, p. 2) that emphasize the integration of the language arts (listening, speaking, reading, and writing). They focus on the processes of constructing meaning, use of quality literature and other information aids, problem-solving and application skills, and student collaborations. Therefore, portfolios are a means for dynamic and ongoing assessment (Tierney, 1992).

What examples of student
learning would you want to
include in portfolios in your
content classroom?

Portfolios also represent a place for collecting student work samples that provide windows on the strategies used by students when reading and writing (Farr, 1991; Farr & Tone, 1994; Tierney, 1992). File folders, storage boxes, hanging files, and notebooks are a few of the common portfolio containers used to hold daily samples, or evidence, of student learning. This puts the responsibility and control for content literacy assessment back into the hands of those most affected by it—teachers and students (Valencia, 1990, p. 5) and provides the foundation for teacher–student conferences (Farr, 1991).

We have noticed that effective portfolio programs put into practice the principles of assessment as well as several other important qualities that are worth mentioning.

Portfolios that contain samples
of different language forms can
reveal the depth of student
learning.

First, *both students and teachers make contributions to the portfolio.* Sometimes students completing certain classroom tasks demonstrate that they have achieved new milestones in their knowledge of a subject. These students may be ready to move beyond basic application-oriented projects and create new applications themselves. For instance, Shawn, who is enrolled in an American history course, has just presented a project to the class in the form of a radio news script explaining "The John Brown Incident at Harper's Ferry in 1859." If, in a student–teacher interview following the presentation, Shawn begins to speculate as to John Brown's possible motivations in the rebellion, the teacher may conclude that Shawn is ready to begin thinking and reading about revisionist interpretations of history—differing viewpoints and their pros and cons. The teacher, noticing this learning milestone, will naturally want to add notes taken during the conference and possibly other learning artifacts to the portfolio. Similarly, students may sometimes feel they have achieved something important during the course of a learning task and want to add supporting information and artifacts to their portfolio.

A second characteristic of successful portfolios is that *classroom artifacts are collected that give teachers insights as to specific processes and strategies used by students.* For instance, a general science teacher may want to know how well students can discern cause–effect relationships in the unit on pollution. This actually represents two distinct assessment objectives brought together in an integrated (reading/literacy and science) unit: (a) Do students have adequate knowledge of the reading/study strategy—identifying cause/effect relationships? (b) Do students understand various causes of pollution and their effects on the environment? Asking students to construct a flowchart depicting environmental hazards created by man-made waste described in their text may provide evidence as to how well students can understand the cause–effect relationships presented in the content material, thus assessing both objectives at once *and* offering students quality instruction in the process. The flowchart idea therefore provides one piece of evidence that might be used to inform future teaching and is a constructive teaching strategy.

Finally, *effective portfolios draw on a variety of language forms.* Student portfolios often contain such learning artifacts as writing samples, records of cooperative group meetings and their results, responses to application questions, group project products (radio plays, newspaper accounts, trivia games, content-based melodramas, etc.), records of teacher–student conferences, content-oriented scrap books, student-programmed computer software, and traditional measures including objective and standardized tests (their value is discussed later in the chapter).

Portfolio assessment is helpful not only for assessing student progress in learning but also for evaluating one's teaching. This notion is in keeping with our Model of Assessment (see Figure 3.2) described earlier, namely, that all relevant factors to teaching and learning are included in the assessment program. We take the portfolio assessment philosophy one step further than is usually the case and recommend that teachers use two types of portfolios in their classrooms: *student portfolios* and *teaching portfolios.* Each is described in detail in the following sections.

> Portfolios also help teachers evaluate the effectiveness of their instruction.

Constructing Student Portfolios

Student portfolios are authentic assessment systems for monitoring student learning over time. They usually contain samples of both typical and best efforts. Additions to student portfolios can be made by both teachers and students. Guidelines for the daily workings of student portfolios should be developed collaboratively between teachers and students. This allows students to "buy in" to the portfolio program and understand its parameters. Quality student portfolios become a solid foundation on which useful student–teacher conferences are built.

What is the difference between classroom and file portfolios?

As teachers, we have in some years elected to keep two types of student portfolios: a classroom portfolio and a file portfolio. **Classroom portfolios** are those kept by students at their desk or in a central location. This is the place for storing ongoing projects, work samples the student wishes to place "on the record," and other classroom artifacts that may grow out of cooperative grouping arrangements. **File portfolios** are usually kept by the teacher in a file cabinet (hence its name) and contain classroom artifacts culled from classroom portfolios periodically to keep them from becoming too large and unmanageable. The file portfolio, together with the classroom portfolio, helps create the desired longitudinal record (see assessment principle 5). Even though all student artifacts are eventually placed in the file portfolio, students should continue to have access to their past work. This allows students to evaluate their own progress and set future learning goals (Tierney, 1992). Seeing authentic and tangible evidence of their own growth and development can also be extremely motivational for students (Manzo & Manzo, 1993).

Assessing Affective Factors: Interest, Attitude, and Motivation

Interest, attitude, and motivation are known as affective factors.

Reading teachers and researchers realize that affective factors (interest, attitude, motivation) play key but difficult to measure roles in reading success. For instance, a student who collects and studies spiders around her home environment and finds them interesting will tend to do well on a general science unit called "arachnids." Her informal studies and interests cause her to learn a great deal of vocabulary and to build schemata about this topic. When the student is exposed to reading materials on arachnids, even if it is difficult reading considered to be well above her reading level, the student will almost surely succeed because of her familiarity, interest, willingness to persevere, and positive attitude regarding the subject. Conversely, a student who feels weak in math, even if his ability in the subject is quite adequate, will tend to do poorly on many mathematics assignments—a kind of self-fulfilling prophecy. In both of these cases, if the teacher is aware of these affective factors, then classroom interventions can be planned that can help students succeed to their maximum potential. Following are affective assessment ideas that have proven to be effective.

Interest Inventories

Interest inventories help assess reading attitudes in a given subject area, as well as specific knowledge.

Many authorities suggest administering an **interest inventory** as a beginning point in assessing student attitudes, interests, and self-perceptions (Heathington & Alexander, 1984; Vacca & Vacca, 1993)—also referred to sometimes as an *attitude survey*. An interest inventory usually surveys both general reading attitudes and daily encounters with texts and specific knowledge and practices of the student as they relate to the content subject being taught. The procedure is simple. For most middle and high school students, students simply complete a general interest inventory during the first week of classes and specific surveys several weeks before beginning a new unit of instruction. Students who are learning English as a second language (ESL) may need to complete the surveys with a peer or bilingual teacher. Figure 3.3 is a general interest inventory based on our work (Flynt & Cooter, 1993, 1995), and Figure 3.4 is a specific attitude survey for world history ("The Fall of the USSR").

Self-Rating Checklists and Self-Analyses

Another affective assessment strategy focusing on student self-perceptions is the **self-rating checklist**. As the name implies, students complete a teacher-made checklist tailored to specific reading/study skills that are especially useful in the content area studied. Students indicate whether they feel that they are *strong, good, getting by,* or *not very strong* in the areas specified. Figure 3.5 is a self-rating checklist used in an algebra I class.

What are some of the reading/study skills students rely on in your content area that could be included in a self-rating checklist?

Figure 3.3 General Interest Inventory

INTEREST INVENTORY

Student's Name:_____ Age/Grade: _____

Date: _____ Teacher: _____

Home Life

1. How many people are there in your family?

2. Do you have a room by yourself or do you share a room? (Ask this only if it is apparent that the student has siblings.)

3. Do your parent(s) work? What kind of jobs do they have?

4. Do you have jobs around the house? What are they?

5. What do you usually do after school?

6. Do you have a TV in your room? How much time do you spend watching TV each day? What are your favorite shows?

7. Do you have a "bedtime" during the week? What time do you usually go to bed on a school night?

8. Do you get an allowance? How much?

9. Do you belong to any clubs at school or outside school? What are they?

10. What are some things that you really like to do? Do you collect things, do you have any hobbies, or take lessons outside school?

Figure 3.3 *continued*

School Environment

1. Do you like school? What is your favorite and least favorite class?

2. Do you have a special place to study at home?

3. How much homework do you have on a typical school night? Does anyone help you with your homework? Who?

4. Do you consider yourself a good reader or a not-so-good reader?

   If they respond a "good reader," ask, What has helped you most to become a good reader?

   If they respond a "not-so-good reader," ask, What causes someone to be a "not-so-good reader"?

5. If I gave you the choice of selecting a book about any topic, what would you choose to read about?

6. What is one thing that you can think of that would help you become a better reader? Is there anything else?

7. Do you like to write? What kind of writing assignments do you like best?

8. If you went to a new school, what is one thing that you would want the teachers to know about you as a student?

9. If you were helping someone learn to read, what would be the most important thing you could do to help that person?

10. How will knowing how to read help you in the future?

Figure 3.4 Attitude Survey: USSR

Student Attitude Survey

Class: World History, Block 2   Name _____

"The Fall of the USSR"

Directions: Please respond to the following questions.

1. When did you first learn of the fall of the USSR, and how did you feel about it?

2. What do you think would be some of the problems related to the USSR moving from a socialist society to a more democratic and capitalist society?

3. The Berlin Wall seemed to symbolize to many the problems associated with the old USSR. What did the Wall make you think of and why?

4. If you were the Russian president, what would you do to help the new Russia get through these difficult times?

Figure 3.5 A Sample Self-Rating Checklist: Algebra

"Reading" Algebra

Name _____   Class Period/Block _____

Date _____

Part I

Directions: Rate yourself according to your ability to do the following in past mathematics classes. Please be completely honest in your assessment, as this will help your teacher to plan the kind of instruction that meets your needs.

Your ability to:	*Strong*	*Good*	*Getting by*	*Not very strong*
Read the introduction of a new chapter and understand what the author is saying the first time.				
Translate familiar and new mathematical symbols into spoken language.				
Translate words in story problems into mathematical symbols.				
Write daily learning log entries that describe what I have learned and how to solve problems.				
Explain mathematical processes to another person orally.				
Perform complex addition problems.				
Perform complex subtraction problems.				
Perform complex multiplication problems.				
Perform complex division problems.				
Overall, how do you rate yourself as a student of mathematics?				

Part II

In the space below, please explain what you hope to be able to do as a result of taking this class.

In addition to self-rating checklists, it can likewise be helpful for students to write a **self-analysis** about their academic abilities in a content area. Here students may be asked to complete statements such as the following:

1. What I like most about [topic] is . . .
2. What I like least about [topic] is . . .
3. I feel that I could use some help with . . .
4. People who are successful with this subject tend to . . .
5. My goal(s) for this semester/grading period are . . .

Some students contribute as much or more information by writing free-flowing self-analysis compositions of their own design. Choice in activities and format of assessment tends to yield richer, more descriptive self-analyses, and is a central tenet of holistic teaching.

Research Logs

Research logs list materials used over time by students to complete projects.

An effective and indirect way of finding out the kinds of reading and technical materials students feel comfortable using is the **research log**. Research logs are a simple listing of materials used over time in the content classroom to complete projects. Research logs are kept by students and stored in their portfolios. By periodically reviewing research logs, teachers can usually detect patterns of reading/study behavior. A simple format for research logs is presented in Figure 3.6.

Teacher Observations

Name some of the reading/ study behaviors that could be assessed through teacher observations in your content classroom.

An alternative to paper-and-pencil surveys, like the interest inventories noted earlier, consists of **teacher observations**. Indeed, teacher observations are the most common method used to assess attitudes and behaviors in reading (Alexander & Heathington, 1988) and are a most subtle and nonthreatening technique (Farr et al., 1989). Although some have experimented with various checklists to aid the observation process, many experienced teachers rely on anecdotal or ethnographic records (Manzo & Manzo, 1993) written on a legal pad or index cards, which can be placed in the file portfolio at the end of the day. A number of reading/study behaviors can be assessed through regular teacher observations (Readence et al., 1992; Vacca & Vacca, 1993). A summary of a few of the most prominent behaviors follows:

- Library strategies and habits
- Personal reading habits
- Ability to receive instruction and modify content literacy behaviors
- Class participation
- Interest in recreational reading
- Goal-setting behaviors

Figure 3.6 Research Log Format

Research Log

Name _____

Subject _____ Period _____ Homeroom _____

Date	Assignment/Topic	Materials Selected	Pages/Programs Used	Notes

Assessing Prior Knowledge of Information

As we mentioned earlier in the chapter, authentic assessment and quality teaching activities are often indistinguishable. This point is especially easy to see when attempting to assess prior knowledge of a subject. In the professional literature, many classroom ideas are described for accessing or turning-on schemas in a particular subject area that may be used as authentic assessment strategies as well. In the following list are several strategies for both assessing and accessing prior knowledge that are described in greater detail elsewhere in this book:

Prereading Plan (PReP)

Semantic maps and webs

Analogies

Expectation outlines

Peters' prior knowledge tables

Preview guides

Many activities described in this text are useful in assessing prior knowledge of a subject.

Assessing Student–Text Match

How well students can read and understand required texts and support materials is, of course, an important concern. Even though many supplemental resources can and should be used during the course of a unit of study, there are almost always required readings. Primary strategies include cloze and maze procedures, commercially produced informal reading inventories (IRIs), content area reading inventories (CARIs), and other pretest formats. How to go about using each of these assessment alternatives is discussed in the following pages.

Cloze and Maze Passages

Cloze passages are a most common and effective holistic assessment strategy and have been used in content area classrooms for many years. Derived from the word *closure,* cloze tests cause students to use the schema knowledge of a subject, understanding of basic syntax (word-order relationships), and word and sentence meaning (semantics) knowledge to guess what a missing or familiar word in print might be. Results inform the teacher as to whether the text is likely to be easy reading, instructional level reading (requiring some assistance from the teacher for student success), or too difficult. These results provide one small piece of evidence for teachers regarding individual and class ability to succeed with the textbook. General instructions for the construction of cloze tests using content area texts follow:

1. Select a passage from the adopted textbook of about 300 words in length that you feel is representative of the author's writing style and text difficulty. It is usually best to choose a passage at the beginning of a section or unit so that needed introductory information is included.
2. Type the passage, preferably on a computer. The first sentence should be typed exactly as written in the original text. Beginning with the second sentence, delete one of the first five words, and replace it with a blank, then repeat this procedure every fifth word thereafter. The process is complete when you have 50 blanks in the cloze passage. After the 50th blank, finish typing the sentence in which the last blank occurred. Then, type at least one more sentence intact (no deletions).
3. Have students read the passage all the way through once *without* attempting to fill in any of the blanks, then reread the passage, and fill in the blanks to the best of their ability.

Scoring of cloze passages is simple, using the following percentages. Students who correctly fill in 60% or more of the blanks are considered to be at their independent reading level, at least with the passage selected. Students who get between 40% and 60% of the blanks correct are at their instructional reading level. Those students falling below 40% are considered to be at their frustration reading level. The following example shows a cloze passage constructed using an excerpt from *Reading Inventory for the Classroom.**

Cooking Without Fire: The Microwave Oven*

Microwave cooking is very common today. However, it is_____ recent invention. The microwave_____ one uses today was_____ from the invention of_____ magnetron tube in 1940._____ invention of the magnetron_____ , by Sir John Randall and Dr. H. A. Boot, _____ a very important part_____ the radar defense of _____ during World War II. Neither_____ considered it as a _____ of preparing food after_____ invented it.

It wasn't_____ the late 1940s that_____ Dr. Percy Spencer discovered the magnetron's_____ to heat and cook_____ from the inside out. _____ experimented with many_____ foods and all with_____ same results. The inside_____ hot first. It took _____ years for the company_____ worked for to develop _____ we know today as_____ microwave oven. Not until _____ 1952 could a person_____ a microwave oven, called _____ a Radar Range, for_____ use. These early models were _____ and bulky.

Today, microwave_____ are inexpensive and come_____ a variety of features. _____ features include: defrost, constant _____ cooking, and automatic reheat. _____ cooking, many claim, was_____ first completely new method_____ cooking food since early_____ discovered fire. Why? Because_____ cooking requires no fire or element of fire to cook food. The food is cooked by electromagnetic energy.

* Note: This cloze example is for illustrative purposes and is actually a little shorter than the usual 50 blanks.

Cloze passages are not without their critics. Many people (students included!) feel that cloze passages are extremely stressful and frustrating, because students tend to score less than 60% of the items correct. In a school world where students are accustomed to scoring 70% or more of items correct on most quizzes, expectations for greater success are often dashed. Even when students are told that cloze test performance is supposed to be less than other tests, they find little comfort in this knowledge and often feel discouraged.

---

*Note. From *The Flynt/Cooter Reading Inventory for the Classroom* (2nd ed., p. 162) by E. S. Flynt and R. B. Cooter, 1995, Scottsdale, AZ: Gorsuch Scarisbrick. Copyright 1995 by Gorsuch Scarisbrick. Reprinted by permission.

Another problem is that when content teachers use cloze passages as described, the assessment information tends to reveal more about students' syntax and semantics strategies than their background knowledge of the topic. For these and other reasons, many teachers have opted for a modified version of cloze known as the *maze* procedure.

Maze passages (J. T. Guthrie, Seifert, Burnham, & Caplan, 1974) are a modification of cloze strategies that may be easily adapted to content classroom needs. Maze passages tend to be far less frustrating to students because they have three possible answers to choose from; thus, students will tend to get a larger percentage of the items correct. In our adaptation of maze, we recommend that teachers delete specialized vocabulary of particular importance to the unit. The criteria we suggest as a starting point (you may need to modify the criteria based on student performance in your classes) for the independent reading level is 85% or greater, the frustration reading level range is 50% or below, and the instructional reading level is between 50% and 80%.

The procedure for constructing maze passages is identical to the construction of cloze passages, with the exception that following each blank three choices are offered. One choice is a specialized vocabulary word from the unit which does not make sense in this context. A second choice is usually a foil (incorrect choice) that does not make sense and is an incorrect part of speech: a nonsense choice. A third choice or option is, of course, the correct choice. An example of a maze sentence follows using the content area of sociology discussing the topic of conformity within education systems:

> conformist
> A straight _____ control   is the individual who has learned his place,
> ever
> has accepted it and acts accordingly.

Content Area Reading Inventories

The **content area reading inventory (CARI)** (Farr et al., 1989; Readence et al., 1992; Vacca & Vacca, 1993) is an adaptation of the IRI and is viewed by many as the most useful means for assessing whether students have internalized sufficient reading/study strategies to succeed with content materials. CARIs are usually teacher constructed and administered to whole groups of students. CARIs typically include three major sections (Farr et al., 1989) that assess (a) student knowledge of and ability to take advantage of the usual textbook components (i.e., table of contents, glossary, index) and supplemental research aids (card catalog, reference books, periodicals); (b) student knowledge of important vocabulary and semantic analysis skills such as context clues; and (c) comprehension skills important to understanding text. When students are given the last two sections of the CARI, they are asked to read a selection from the adopted text (usually at least three to four pages) as the basis for the assess-

---

Maze passages are a modification of cloze that we find to be much more functional and nonthreatening.

CARI is an adaptation of the IRI useful in assessing reading/study strategies.

ment. Readence, Bean, and Baldwin (1992) suggest contents for a CARI, which we describe and slightly adapt as follows:

I: Textual reading/study aids
       A. Internal aids
          1. Table of contents
          2. Index
          3. Glossary
          4. Chapter introduction/summaries
          5. Information from pictures
          6. Other aids included in the text
       B. Supplemental research aids
          1. Card catalog
          2. Periodicals
          3. Encyclopedias
          4. Other relevant aids for the content area
II: Vocabulary knowledge
       A. Knowledge and recall of relevant vocabulary
       B. Use of context clues
III: Comprehension skills and strategies
       A. Text-explicit (literal) information
       B. Text-implicit (inferred) information
       C. Knowledge of text structures and related strategies

Guidelines for Developing and Giving a CARI

Although the CARI is considered by many to be a very traditional way of viewing content reading assessment, we feel that with very minor modifications it can be brought in line with authentic assessment principles. Our adaptation of the work of Readence et al. (1992) follows:

Short-term minilessons can be planned from CARI results that help students cope with difficult readings.

Step 1:   Identify a passage from the text or supplemental book(s) to be used of at least three to four pages. It should represent the typical writing style of the author (avoid favorite or least favorite sections as much as possible). Because multiple copies of the text are almost always available, copying will not be necessary.

Step 2:   Construct about 20 to 25 questions related to the text and research/study aids made available. Readence et al. (1992) recommend 8 to 10 questions for part I, 4 to 6 questions for part II, and 7 to 9 questions for part III. The questions may be constructed using either traditional comprehension levels (literal, inferential, evaluative), but we urge the use of questions based on writing patterns used in the sample selection. The questions, whatever the pattern used, should reflect the facts, concepts, and generalizations discovered during the content analysis of the sample selection, as required in Step 1.

Step 3:   Have a briefing session with each group of students. You should explain that the CARI is not used for grading purposes but to help plan instructional activities that will help them succeed. Advise them that no grades will be given but results will be used to decide collective group strengths and needs.

Step 4:   Administer part I first, then parts II and III on a separate day(s). It may well take several sessions to work through the CARI. We recommend devoting only about 20 minutes per day to administering parts of the CARI so that other class needs are not brought to a halt during the assessment phase.

Step 5:   Readence et al. (1992) suggest the following criteria for assessing the CARI:

% Correct	**Text Difficulty**
86% to 100%	Easy reading
64% to 85%	Adequate for instruction
63% or below	Too difficult

While the preceding criteria may be useful for making gross judgments about general reading proficiency, we feel that the identification of specific strengths and needs is the greater product of CARIs. From careful analysis of this assessment, teachers can plan special short-term minilessons that help students cope with difficult readings and internalize important information. Students can be grouped according to need for these short-term minilessons and practice strategies leading to success. In the end, that is what teaching is all about.

Constructing Teaching Portfolios

Teaching portfolios help teachers evaluate their own instructional programs.

Teaching portfolios are authentic assessment programs that help teachers evaluate all aspects of their own teaching and instructional program. They contain such elements as sample lesson plans, long-range instructional goals, teacher belief statements, student progress charts, teaching progress charts, assessments of the learning environment, evaluations of textbooks and other learning materials, and selected professional references that may be used to guide future instruction. It is becoming common practice for teaching portfolios to be used not only as an integral part of a teacher's instructional planning and self-assessment but also as a valid means for teacher assessment by local school officials. For example, teachers in the Carrollton-Farmers Branch Independent School District in Texas have the option of choosing evaluation using the state-designed assessment instrument or assessment via teaching portfolios. Our purpose in this section is to suggest possible teaching portfolio choices that may be useful for content area teachers.

Teacher Belief Statements

The beginning point for effective teaching analysis is identifying what one believes, then considering whether these beliefs are backed up by educational research. This point is crucial to building constructive teaching portfolios.

Evaluating Textbooks

One of the most common recommendations from content reading traditionalists has been the assessment of text readability. **Readability** is an estimate of the difficulty level of books to be used in classrooms based on such factors as average sentence length and complexity of the text. The idea is to screen reading materials using what is called a *readability formula* to determine the difficulty level of the materials (e.g., 5th-, 7th-, 12th-grade level), then compare the level of the materials to the individual reading levels of students. Advocates of readability checks suggest that students with reading development levels below the readability level of the text should receive extra instructional assistance to help them succeed. Two of the more common readability formulas are the Fry Readability Graph (Fry, 1977), and the easier to administer Raygor Formula (Raygor, 1977). Figures 3.7 and 3.8 present each of these formulas and instructions for their use.

> Readability is a simple estimate of a book's difficulty level.

Although virtually every content reading textbook writer recommends readability formulas to content teachers, they do have many drawbacks. First of all, readability formulas and their implied use in classroom assessment are quite time-consuming and tedious to use. Teachers in departmentalized settings often see up to 150 students per day. Attempting to match readability levels of texts to individual students in this setting quickly becomes unmanageable. Second, and perhaps most importantly, readability formulas fail to take into consideration important factors, affect especially, that have a major impact on reading success. A case in point was a 10th-grade student named Michael who came to one of us for tutorial help during the summer break. His teachers indicated that test scores showed that Michael was reading on a third-grade level. However, when we chose materials on an eighth-grade reading level for basic reading instruction purposes that were about motorcycles (a subject Michael said was of keen interest), Michael was able to easily succeed. Obviously, Michael's interest, attitude, vocabulary knowledge, and self-confidence with this topic allowed him to power through texts supposedly *5 years* above his developmental level. The Fry Readability process was unable to account for these important factors.

> What are some of the limitations of readability formulas?

Another problem (alluded to earlier) is that readability formulas tend to make estimates using such elements as sentence length and numbers of syllables in a 100-word excerpt. These formulas ignore other important aspects of writing that contribute to readability, such as the author's writing style and ability to logically sequence information, use of basic writing constructs such as topic sentences, and use of different expository text patterns such as cause–effect, com-

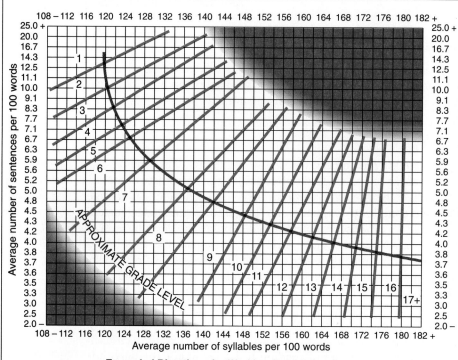

108 – 112 116 120 124 128 132 136 140 144 148 152 156 160 164 168 172 176 180 182 +

Average number of syllables per 100 words

Expanded Directions for Working Readability Graph

1. Randomly select (3) three sample passages and count out exactly 100 words each, beginning with the beginning of a sentence. Do count proper nouns, initializations, and numerals.

2. Count the number of sentences in the 100 words, estimating length of the fraction of the last sentence to the nearest one-tenth.

3. Count the total number of syllables in the 100 word passage. If you don't have a hand counter available, an easy way is to simply put a mark above every syllable over one in each word: then when you get to the end of the passage, count the number of marks and add 100. Small calculators can also be used as counters by pushing numeral 1, then push the + sign for each word or syllable when counting.

4. Enter graph with *average* sentence length and *average* number of syllables: plot dot where the two lines intersect. Area where dot is plotted will give you the approximate grade level.

5. If a great deal of variability is found in syllable count or sentence count, putting more samples into the average is desirable.

6. A word is defined as a group of symbols with a space on either side: thus, *Joe, IRA, 1945,* and *&* are each one word.

7. A syllable is defined as a phonic syllable. Generally, there are as many syllables as vowel sounds. For example, *stopped* is one syllable and *wanted* is two syllables. When counting syllables for numerals and initializations, count one syllable for each symbol. For example, *1945* is four syllables, *IRA* is three syllables, and *&* is one syllable.

Figure 3.7 Fry Readability Graph

Note. From "Fry's Readability Graph: Clarifications, Validity, and Extension to Level 17" by Edward Fry, 1977, *Journal of Reading, 21,* pp. 242–252.

1. Count out three 100-word passages at the beginning, middle, and end of a selection or book. Count proper nouns but not numerals.
2. Count sentences in each passage, estimating to the nearest tenth.
3. Count words with six or more letters.
4. Average the sentence length and word length over three samples, and plot the average on the graph.

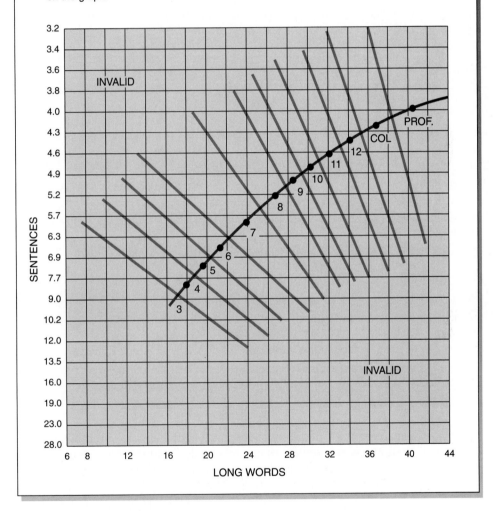

Figure 3.8 Raygor Readability Formula

Note. From "The Raygor Readability Estimate: A Quick and Easy Way to Determine Difficulty" by A. L. Raygor, in *Reading: Theory, Research and Practice, Twenty-Sixth Yearbook of the National Reading Conference* (pp. 259–263) edited by P. D. Pearson, 1977, Clemson, SC: National Reading Conference.

Figure 3.9 Expository Text Evaluation Checklist

Title of Expository Selection: _____

Type of Text: _____

Author(s) and Their Expertise: _____

Publisher/Copyright date: _____

Directions: Evaluate each of the following statements using the following descriptors:

   3 = Excellent

   2 = Adequate

   1 = Poor

 n/a = Not applicable

Overall Features

_____A. The table of contents is logically organized and presents a complete view of the contents of the entire text.

_____B. The index is comprehensive and easily leads to text information.

_____C. The glossary is well developed with adequate definitions, pronunciations, and page numbers as to where the word is found in the text.

_____D. All visuals (tables, graphs, etc.) are uncluttered and aid students' understanding of text information.

_____E. The text provides appropriate models for gender and ethnic groups.

Organization and Writing

_____F. Titles, headings, and subheadings clearly identify the content to be discussed.

_____G. The authors clearly let the reader know the main ideas or concepts in each chapter, and the authors devote most of the chapter to those main ideas.

_____H. Each major heading or subheading lends itself easily to outlining or flowcharting.

_____I. Paragraphs are interrelated explicitly via connectives or repetition of ideas so that important conceptual relationships are clear and do not have to be inferred by the reader.

pare–contrast, and so on. Sentence length is also an unreliable indicator because short, choppy sentences can frequently confuse readers. For these reasons, we recommend readability formulas only as a rough estimate of text readability.

To provide a more comprehensive look at content materials, we support the idea of evaluating adopted textbooks as to their **considerateness** or **inconsiderateness** as suggested by T. H. Anderson and Armbruster (1984). For a text to be considerate, it must be written coherently and be clearly organized (T. H. Anderson & Armbruster, 1986). The **expository text evaluation checklist** shown in Figure 3.9, patterned after the work of Vaughan and Estes (1986) and Readence and others (1992), should prove helpful when evaluating and/or adopting textbooks.

_____J. New concepts are introduced by relating them to previously learned information.

_____K. The vocabulary load is not too dense. The authors only introduce one or two terms in a single paragraph.

_____L. The text uses numerous concrete examples to explain abstract ideas/terms.

_____M. The authors refer back to previously learned concepts when they relate to new concepts being introduced.

_____N. The authors have written the text with the intended audience in mind. They don't assume too much about students' prior knowledge, and they present ideas in a way that is appropriate for the experiences of the intended readers.

_____O. The questions and/or activities presented in the text cause students to think about and apply what they are studying.

Teacher's Edition or Resource Manual

_____P. The teacher's edition provides a variety of methods to develop and/or activate students' prior knowledge.

_____Q. The teacher's edition provides alternative activities/projects, additional readings, and suggestions for accommodating advanced and low-achieving students.

_____R. The teacher's edition provides a listing of accessible professional resources including professional journals, computer software, video tapes, and other supplemental instructional materials.

Determine the text's score by adding up each section's numbers.

Overall Features: 13–15 Excellent; 9–12 Adequate; 0–8 Poor

Organization and Writing: 25–30 Excellent; 15–24 Adequate; 1–14 Poor

Teacher's Edition: 7–9 Excellent; 4–6 Adequate; 1–3 Poor

One final suggestion when evaluating textbooks for adoption: We recommend what we call **the cross-text comparison procedure (CCP).** To conduct a CCP, we recommend the following steps. Using the expository text evaluation checklist, try to narrow the number of books up for adoption to three or four finalists. For each book, photocopy the table of contents, the glossary, the pages that include the discussion of an important common topic and all the "end of chapter" information and activities for the chapter you selected to compare the treatment of the common topic. Using your district's learner outcomes, objectives, scope and sequence, and/or curriculum guide, carefully examine how each text matches up with your curriculum. Additionally, compare carefully which text provides the most meaningful and comprehensive treatment of your topic. This procedure should provide you with insights as to how different publishers in your subject matter area can be. Picking the right text is too important to be left to chance.

Sample Lesson Plans

As part of the teaching portfolio, we recommend that teachers use the following procedure for assessing past lesson plans and teaching as a process for identifying goals for the future.

Step 1:   *Obtain a copy of your belief statements and a lesson plan book from the previous semester.* If you are a new or preservice teacher and do not have a lesson plan book, draw up a class routine/schedule that you feel you will probably use for daily class operations instead.

> Expendable practices are those teaching strategies that you find difficult to justify and that could thus be jettisoned in favor of newer ideas.

Step 2: *Look for patterns of teaching behavior.* Some teachers begin each class with a minilesson of some sort. Others like to start class with a short quiz over the homework assignment. The point is, teachers, like most humans, are creatures of habit and tend to do similar kinds of classroom activities in a predictable pattern. The key question for teachers to ask themselves is this: *Are my teaching practices consistent with what I believe about learning and teaching?* The way to discover the answer to this extremely important question is to carefully compare one's written belief system with past lesson plans and routines. So in this step, we do just that. Look for patterns of behavior in your teaching, and contrast each recurring practice with your written belief statements. Those practices that cannot be justified with what you believe should be considered **expendable practices**.

One method for accomplishing this personal assessment used with success in our own teaching is to first photocopy pages from the plan book that represent typical classroom practices. Next, we take a highlighting pen, and highlight all boxes in the plan book that feature practices that are consistent with our written belief statements. Those boxes not highlighted, namely, the practices we do not really believe in, stand out clearly and become targets for the final step in this procedure. Figure 3.10 is an example of a plan book page with practices highlighted that match our beliefs.

> What are some teaching strategies you would like to try out in your content classroom?

Step 3: *Begin goal setting to replace expendable practices with new ideas that match your beliefs.* Remember that significant changes in classroom practice take time, up to 5 years. Hence, be realistic in goal setting. It is better to set modest goals for each school year that can be obtained easily, then set additional goals as possible. This gives one the sense of accomplishment each year, whereas setting unobtainable goals tends to make one feel unsuccessful when all new goals are not met. Maintaining a sense of enthusiasm and accomplishment is important in long-term curricular change initiatives.

Student and Teaching Progress Charts

One important fact that teachers have come to understand in recent years is that most learning is developmental. That means that human beings add new schemas or understandings of a topic to prior learning. Said another way,

FOR WEEK _____

Grade _____

Subject _Science   11:15–12:00_ _____

MONDAY	Begin insect unit. see science notes —————— p. 45-47 in book Pre-test on vocabulary words
TUESDAY	Discuss metamorphosis do fly-meat experiment in groups also, 2 other types of developments complete wksheets.
WEDNESDAY	Moths and butterflies see unit materials in notes Identify major classes/groups —————— drawing lesson –parts of insects check wksheets
THURSDAY	Kill/pin insects – discuss different types – look up six and write about in science journals —————— Read & do activity on page 48
FRIDAY	filmstrip or video on insects – use anticipation guide drawings of insects —————— finish!! Share insect collection

Figure 3.10 Sample Teacher Plan Book Page

teachers have as a primary mission to add *new* information to what is already *known*.

Curriculum maps chart new learning to take place over the course of a unit.

We have discussed in earlier chapters the need to perform a content analysis on each unit of study and to find ways to link all units of instruction. This process helps ensure that what we teach makes sense and is learned more or less permanently. The content analysis also helps us as teachers to develop a kind of content blueprint consisting of facts, concepts, and generalizations. This can be easily transformed into a kind of **curriculum map** or progress chart for each student and for the class at large. Knowledge maps list important information to be learned over the course of a unit. Individual **student curriculum maps** are generally kept in student portfolios. **Teaching curriculum maps** represent a kind of instructional checklist on which teachers record dates that certain topics were presented and how. Figure 3.11 presents a format for curriculum maps that may be used as a student map. For students, the map acts as a kind of progress chart. The blanks—concerning generalization(s), concepts and facts—are filled in by the students at the beginning of the unit during a whole class discussion. As students work through the unit of study, they fill in blanks, indicating assignments completed. This record becomes part of the students' portfolio. Figure 3.12 presents a similar kind of curriculum map for teachers. As teachers complete basic components of the unit, key elements are logged in as a running record of events in the classroom.

Teaching curriculum maps chart when and how specific topics were presented.

Two advantages of curriculum maps are that they help teachers maintain consistent and sequential instruction and prevent the Swiss cheese effect discussed earlier (holes in learning). Curriculum maps also help teachers provide their administrators with "accountability" data: proof that required information has been presented and assessed.

Assessing the Learning Environment

Chapter 4 is a detailed analysis of how effective classrooms that support learning and teaching are constructed. We also describe processes for analyzing and modifying the learning environment. The reader is urged to review Chapter 4 for activities that can be documented and placed into the teaching portfolio.

Reading Log of Professional References

Many teachers keep reading logs as a tool for noting trends in classroom teaching.

One of the expressions of professionalism in any field is knowing about new and successful trends. Although teachers should not be expected to jump on every new bandwagon in education, because many new ideas have not been adequately tested with students, it is reasonable to expect teachers to remain knowledgeable and current. A conscientious teacher who is well-read in the current professional literature has more choices to consider when attempting to replace the expendable practices mentioned earlier in this chapter.

Figure 3.11 Student Curriculum Map Form

Name: _____			Class: _____		
Unit Title: _____					
Generalization(s) _____					

Content	Reading Log Title/Dates	Type of Text or Materials	Learning Artifact	Group Project?	Other Products
Concept 1					
Fact 1					
Fact 2					
Fact 3					
Fact 4					
Concept 2					
Fact 1					
Fact 2					
Fact 3					
Fact 4					
Concept 3					
Fact 1					
Fact 2					
Fact 3					
Fact 4					
Notes					

At the end of each chapter, we offer recommended readings to help you choose professional writings, especially books, that represent current thinking on various subjects related to the chapter. In addition, we suggest a few professional journals that are of general interest to all teachers and suggest others that pertain to content area reading. In addition, each subject area has

Begin a list of professional journals related to your discipline that can inform your teaching.

Figure 3.12 Teacher Curriculum Map Form

| Name:_____ | | Class:_____ |

Unit Title:_____

Generalization(s)_____

Content	Instruction Dates	Methods Used	Assessment Dates	Results of Instruction	Comments
Concept 1					
Fact 1					
Fact 2					
Fact 3					
Fact 4					
Concept 2					
Fact 1					
Fact 2					
Fact 3					
Fact 4					
Concept 3					
Fact 1					
Fact 2					
Fact 3					
Fact 4					
Notes					

prominent journals that readers may wish to investigate. Here is our own short list:

General Education and Research Journals

Educational Leadership

Intervention

Journal of Educational Research

Review of Educational Research

The Elementary School Journal

The Phi Delta Kappan

Journals Publishing Content Area Reading Articles

Journal of Reading

Journal of Reading Behavior

Reading Horizons

Reading Psychology

Reading Research and Instruction

Reading Research Quarterly

The Reading Teacher

ASSESSMENT-RELATED ISSUES

Few issues in education inspire as much discussion and debate as assessment. The assessment hot potato is a favorite topic of political demagogues (usually proclaiming the virtues of state-mandated testing), parent groups, researchers, teachers, and teacher unions. Of particular interest in the 1990s are issues related to the value of standardized tests, outcome-based assessment, teaching students test-taking or test-wiseness skills, and content area grading in general. In this section we offer a kind of abridged primer on these subjects. More detailed readings are suggested at the conclusion of the chapter.

Standardized or Norm-Referenced Tests and Content Assessment

For various reasons, it is sometimes useful for school districts to obtain information that compares the performance of students locally to other students in the state or nation. Standardized tests fill this need. Generally known in the assessment industry as **norm-referenced tests**, these formal instruments compare individual students to a cross section of students in other areas of the country who were administered the same test. Achievement tests such as the Metropolitan Achievement Tests (MAT), Iowa Tests of Basic Skills (ITBS), and the California Achievement Tests (CAT) are a few examples of norm-referenced tests familiar to many people. Norm-referenced tests are usually formally administered to groups of students, are limited to a set time, survey several content areas (mathematics, science, social studies), and are presented in what is presumed to be an objective format (multiple choice).

Norm-referenced tests compare individual students to others nationally who have taken that same test.

Explain how norm-referenced tests differ in purpose from authentic assessment procedures.

Norm-referenced tests differ significantly from authentic assessment procedures and from portfolio assessment in particular. First and foremost, norm-referenced tests have an entirely different purpose than authentic assessments. Norm-referenced tests are intended to satisfy, almost exclusively, political realities. People want to know how students in their neighborhood schools compare to students across the nation. They feel this is an indicator of whether or not their students (and teachers) are keeping up with real-world demands. Authentic assessment, on the other hand, is intended to inform classroom teaching and provide useful information to teachers for parent and student conferences. A second difference is that norm-referenced tests are designed by test publishers instead of content area teachers. The net result is that norm-referenced tests are not keyed to the local school district's or classroom teacher's curriculum. Instead, they survey broad areas related to content areas with only bits and pieces of the curriculum. Authentic assessments, on the other hand, are carefully tailored to information studied during the course of the year.

Describe some of the ways raw scores can be interpreted.

The information produced by norm-referenced tests is also quite different from authentic assessments. School districts usually administer norm-referenced tests either early or late in the school year, then receive testing reports from test companies a few months later. Data produced are reported both for individual students and for whole schools and districts. **Raw scores**, the number correct on each part of the test or **subtest**, are transformed, or interpreted, in several ways. Grade equivalents, age equivalents, percentiles, and stanine scores are typical forms of reporting student results. It is important for teachers to understand exactly what each form of interpretation means, because many parents, and even other teachers, are somewhat confused as to their actual meaning. Note that in all cases, the norms reported compare the raw score made by a particular student to the average (mean) population of students who took the same test and made the same raw score.

What does a grade equivalent score indicate?

Grade equivalent scores tell us what the average grade level was for students who made the same raw score. For example, let's say that Jean, an eighth-grade student, takes an achievement test and gets a raw score of 35 on the general science subtest. If there were 50 items on the general science subtest, then this raw score means Jean got 35 of 50 correct. Taking our example a step further, let's say that a raw score of 35 translates to a grade equivalent score of 6.1. This grade equivalent score means that Jean made the same raw score as the average student in the first month of sixth grade who was given this test.

The common misunderstanding for many is that the grade equivalent score means a student has developed up to the point indicated by the grade equivalent. Not so. It simply means that on the day a test was given, student X made raw score Y, and the grade equivalent represents the average score made by a certain grade level of student who also took the same test. Does this mean that Jean in our example is 2 years "behind" her peers in development of general science knowledge? Not necessarily. Neither does it mean that a 6th-grade student who scores at the 12.9 grade equivalent in general science level knows what a student in the 9th month of 12th grade would likely know. It is simply a reporting of average scores on a particular test.

Age equivalent scores are exactly the same type of score as grade equivalent scores, except that the score reported reflects the average age of students rather than grade level. In the case of Jean noted in the previous example, the age equivalent score reported might be 11–3 (11 years, 3 months) as opposed to the 6.1 grade equivalent score (6th grade, 1st month).

Percentile scores are a reporting of general standing or ranking of the student compared to other students who have taken the test. A seventh-grade student with a percentile score of 65 has scored as high as or higher than 65% of seventh graders who have taken the same test. The most common misunderstanding of percentile scores is the assumption that the percentile score is a reflection of how many items the student "got right." In our example, some parents will think the percentile score means that student *X* got 65% of the test items correct and that this means he gets a "low grade."

> A percentile score indicates a general ranking of a student compared to other who have taken the test.

Stanine scores divide the total possible range of performance into nine equal parts, with one being the lowest level of performance and nine being the highest level of performance. The word *stanine* comes from the expression "standard nine" and is based on the normal curve.

Two other important terms that relate to assessment issues in standardized testing are *validity* and *reliability*. **Validity** has to do with the question of whether a test actually measures what its makers say it measures. Does a mathematics subtest on the CAT actually measure knowledge of mathematics, or is it really an assessment of other factors (e.g., ability to take multiple-choice tests)? This might be a validity question asked by school district administrators considering the purchase of the CAT. Assessment experts discuss several forms of validity that you may wish to investigate further.

> Validity is perhaps the single most important factor associated with norm-referenced tests.

Reliability has to do with how consistently a test will measure what it is designed to measure. In other words, if I give a 10th grader named Madeline the ITBS this week, then again 3 weeks from now, I should get very similar results. If I do, then the test is reliable. A *reliability coefficient* is a statistical indication of a test's reliability. An overall test reliability coefficient of .90 or better (Cooter, 1990) is considered acceptable for most norm-referenced tests, as is a reliability coefficient of .75 or better for individual subtests. As with validity questions, you will want to investigate further many reliability-related issues. Readings are recommended at the end of this chapter.

> Reliability indicates how consistent a test is from one administrator to another.

Outcome-Based Education

Since the mid-1970s, William Spady and his colleagues have been calling for a system of planning and restructuring of American schools known as **outcome-based education (OBE)**. Closely related to mastery learning models of teaching and learning and behaviorism psychology, it is a philosophy built around

> Outcome-based education has become one of the most politically charged issues of the 1990s.

three basic premises (Spady & Marshall, 1991): (a) All students can learn and succeed, but not necessarily at the same pace or in the same way. (b) Each success breeds more success. (c) Schools control the conditions of success. Spady offered the following explanation of OBE:

> Outcome-Based Education (OBE) means organizing for results: basing what we do instructionally on the outcomes we want to achieve, whether in specific parts of the curriculum or in the schooling process as a whole. Outcome-based practitioners start by determining the knowledge, competencies, and qualities they want students to be able to demonstrate when they finish school and face the challenges and opportunities of the adult world. Then, with these "exit outcomes" clearly in mind, they deliberately design curriculums and instructional systems with the intent that *all* students will ultimately be able to demonstrate them successfully. (1988, p. 5)

Critics sometimes agree that OBE is no different from goal-oriented curriculums of the past.

One of the main problems with most schooling today, OBE proponents would argue, is that instructional programs begin with writing objectives for a curriculum that is already in place (Ellis & Fouts, 1993). For instance, if a geometry course is offered at a given school, the program design begins with writing objectives for the geometry course. OBE supposedly turns this process upside down by beginning with desired *outcomes* (what you would like students to be able to do), then deciding which experiences students will need to gain those abilities. Ellis and Fouts rightly question how this practice differs from beginning with goal statements, as many have done for years (p. 94). Figure 3.13 is a simple flowchart explaining the OBE curriculum design sequence.

Figure 3.13 OBE Curriculum Design Sequence

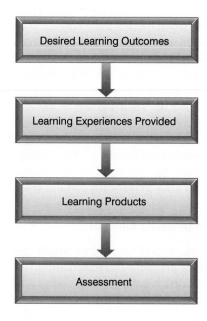

There are both pros and cons relative to OBE, in our opinion. On the positive side, OBE is a philosophy that is quite compatible with holistic teaching perspectives and teaching practices. The idea that all students can succeed, given appropriate time and learning experiences, is at the heart of developmental learning philosophy and constructivist psychology notions. Likewise, not many teachers will argue with the ideas that success breeds success, an idea linked to the affective domain, and that schools control the conditions of success, although this seems to be a somewhat simplistic interpretation that on the surface ignores the role of family and learning environment. Finally, constructing curriculums and assessment practices based on what we want students to be able to do in the real world is another sound idea that is in harmony with holistic teaching principles (but hardly seems like a new revelation to anyone in education). These all are basic education ideas that most can easily support, leading one to conclude that probably the biggest problem with OBE enthusiasts is their tendency to oversell the idea (Ellis & Fouts, 1993).

OBE philosophy can be quite compatible with holistic views, but this is not how it is usually applied.

OBE does, however, have significant problems with implementation. As alluded to earlier, its leading proponents tend to be traditional mastery learning people who almost always suggest these methods for students. Mastery of competencies and success are typically defined by improved scores on standardized tests. Reducing complex abilities and real-world competencies or outcomes to a single test score is the kind of practice that got American education into the mess it has suffered through for several decades! This application of the philosophy, what Spady and Marshall (1991) call traditional OBE, is "an inherently internal, micro, and limiting approach" (p. 69). In our view, this application of OBE does little more than help traditional teachers and administrators justify continuing business as usual.

Mastery learning strategies are the most often seen manifestation of OBE. Unfortunately, this is a very limiting perspective.

The answer to the OBE debate seems clear: Take the philosophy and writings of OBE and apply them using holistic principles rather than retreading traditional mastery learning practices of the past. It is a philosophy with good potential and one that allows a great deal of latitude. As Spady and Marshall (1991) conclude

> OBE takes nothing about schooling today as a given; no existing features are considered untouchable in carrying out a curriculum design. (p. 70)

> [It] takes vision and a willingness to step beyond the givens of curriculum thinking and program design that have left us mired in an Industrial Age model governed by an Agricultural Age calendar. (p. 72)

An example of how holistic/authentic teaching and OBE can be used harmoniously may be helpful at this point in our discussion. The starting point should be, according to OBE advocates, to identify valued outcomes. Let's say that the faculty agree that two of the things people should know are the need for community health standards and the role of citizens in supporting public health officials. Thus, the desired outcome statement might read:

All citizens should understand the need for community health standards and their enforcement.

Once the outcome statement has been written, faculty begin to consider authentic ways of teaching to help students achieve this competency. One solution that would teach to this outcome statement and at the same time illustrate how holistic and OBE philosophies can be merged is through the use of the instructional method called **authentic research** (Schack, 1993). Authentic research involves students working to find solutions to problems of interest using a variety of research skills drawn from two or more disciplines.

Clearly, our outcome statement involves a number of content areas, especially science and social studies, and the authentic research method seems to be a good fit. Stepien and Gallagher (1993) describe a problem of interest to high school students that focuses on unresolved science-related social issues that would fit our outcome statement perfectly. They describe a learning activity wherein students:

> [study] patient files, searching for the cause of pneumonia contracted by 22 residents of a community of 20,000. Taking the roles of public health officials, they will soon discover the chilling fact that the bacterium *L. pneumophila* (Legionnaire's disease) has been found in the lungs of one of the patients. (pp. 26–27)

Real-world problem-solving activities provide a great vehicle for learning and assessment.

After students are placed into authentic research teams, they search for answers to this health dilemma. Over time, this group becomes suspicious of a supermarket misting system used in the produce section. They confer with biologists about possible causal factors and consult with public health authorities about pertinent health standards and legislation. As the students close in on the probable causes of the serious illnesses, one group probes the state statutes concerning the powers that can be exerted by the public health officials to end a potential epidemic. Still other students interview supermarket produce managers to discover why the misting systems are used instead of other alternatives. It is clear that authentic research methods, as one example of holistic teaching, can be used in partnership with OBE curriculum design strategies and can lead to wonderful educational results.

Authentic Assessment and Grading

Many teachers wonder whether grading and authentic assessment are mutually exclusive.

The superintendent of a large urban school district recently appeared on a radio talk show and addressed questions from parents about grading policies. He explained his support for authentic assessment practices, and portfolios in particular. Part of his district's implementation of authentic assessment included a new report card that uses summary paragraphs rather than letter grades to inform parents how their children are doing in school. To the superintendent's astonishment, some parents called in on the radio station's phone lines to complain about the new report cards. When the superintendent asked one of the callers why she was so angry about the new report cards, she responded "How will I know how my child is doing in school if I don't have letter grades to look at each 6 weeks?" The superintendent retorted, "Ma'am, how can you tell how your child is doing *with* a letter grade? What does a letter grade tell you about your child's development in reading, math, or science?" The superintendent then explained about as clearly as one can that letter grades are considerably less informative than most parents think.

Traditional grading systems operate, as do mastery learning systems previously discussed, using a reductionist mentality. It is the belief that complex abilities and knowledge can be reduced to a simple number or letter grade effectively. They cannot—at least, not without sacrificing integrity and validity.

What can teachers committed to authentic assessment do about grading practices in the future? Some have argued that teachers should simply boycott traditional systems and develop their own grading systems—a sort of "Damn the torpedoes!" approach. Others point out that the political realities of bucking the system make grading reform impossible. Our view lies somewhere in the middle. We feel that teachers should work within the system to bring about substantive grading reform and choices for teachers. There is no question in our minds that traditional grading systems do not work well in conjunction with authentic assessment practices. There is also little doubt that permanent change is best achieved systemically. In this section, we offer a transitional approach to grading that can satisfy political realities and provide parents and teachers with a more valid and authentic reporting system. We call it **authentic grading**. Although some will immediately declare the term *authentic grading* an oxymoron, we trust the following description will prove it is not.

Authentic grading is a five-step process:

1. Identify desired outcomes.
2. Identify learning activities that will be used to achieve the outcomes.
3. Determine what kinds of portfolio evidence or learning artifacts can be gathered and used for assessment purposes from the second step.
4. Determine criteria for grading.
5. Decide what other forms of descriptive information can be included in the report card to support grading assessments.

Authentic grading is a natural outgrowth of the curriculum and is drawn from learning activities used in class. Begin authentic grading by reviewing the competencies, abilities, or outcomes described in your curriculum (we assume that the curriculum has been developed up to the point of choosing assessment methods). A listing of these desired outcomes will prove to be useful in authentic grading. Second, identify learning activities that will be used to help students acquire these competencies (outcomes), and write them in under each outcome listed. Third, examine learning activities, and identify those that can yield either qualitative or quantitative evidence of student learning. Fourth, develop a

Authentic grading is an experimental five-step process that satisfies political realities while also meeting the principles set down for quality assessment.

numerical (quantitative) system for grading each student contribution in the portfolio that you deem appropriate for grading. Many times this will involve developing a kind of holistic or analytic scoring system similar to those described earlier in the chapter. Finally, develop a two-part system whereby (a) the grades are included on the report card along with (b) a summary page describing particular areas of development and educational needs demonstrated by the student. This process allows the teacher to satisfy political realities and the perceived need by parents for letter or numerical grades and offers parents the much more valid progress summary. We have developed a short form to help teachers work through the planning stages of authentic grading (Figure 3.14).

Figure 3.14   Authentic Grading Planning Form

Teacher/Group Name _____

School Year/Semester _____

Unit Title _____

Desired Outcomes:

Outcome 1: _____

Learning Activities:

Potential Assessment Opportunities/Methods:

Criteria for Grading:

Descriptive Assessment Procedures:

Outcome 2: _____

Learning Activities:

Potential Assessment Opportunities/Methods:

Criteria for Grading:

Descriptive Assessment Procedures:

We are frequently asked about reports cards and the dilemma between reporting a grade reflective of the student's progress versus reporting a grade reflective of how the student compares to others in the same class. Report cards should reflect both. If teachers use authentic grading, then the three **general report card components** that follow are possible:

1. A letter grade that reflects how well the student has progressed during the grading period (comparing the student to himself)
2. A summary paragraph(s) explaining in some detail what the student has achieved *and* what he still needs to accomplish
3. A letter grade and explanation that reflects how the student compares to others at this level

These three components constitute full reporting of student progress that should fully satisfy and inform parents, students, and school administrators.

CHAPTER SUMMARY

Authentic assessment in the content classroom involves the gathering of learning artifacts that arise as a consequence of learning activities connected to real-world problems. The authentic assessment movement signals a departure from traditional assessment practices based on learning deficit models, behaviorism psychology, and mastery learning pedagogies. The most prominent method for making authentic assessment philosophies part of content classrooms is portfolio assessment.

Portfolio assessment is both a philosophy and a place and is applied in two forms: student portfolios and teaching portfolios. Student portfolios are usually files kept to document students' learning over time. Factors that have an effect on student learning, such as prior knowledge, affective factors, and strategies used to comprehend text, are of interest in constructing student portfolios.

Teaching portfolios help teachers evaluate all aspects of their own teaching and instructional programs. Such aspects of pedagogy as teacher beliefs, textbook selection, lesson planning, and student and teaching progress charts are a few of the factors surveyed in teaching portfolios. Not only do teaching portfolios help teachers direct their instructional programs in productive directions, they may also be used as part of annual teacher/administrator evaluations.

A number of issues directly related to assessment often find themselves in the political arena. One issue that frequently causes sparks to fly is that of standardized testing. Standardized achievement tests continue to be a mainstay of school districts, and their results are often tossed about as evidence of effective (or ineffective) schooling. This happens in spite of the awareness that standardized achievement tests have serious validity problems and are often used to punish groups of students thought to be failures.

Another trend related to authentic assessment is the OBE movement. A close relative of mastery learning, OBE does show considerable promise for content area instruction when used in conjunction with holistic teaching methods and authentic assessment.

Finally, we have recommended that one way of moving beyond traditional grading systems in content instruction is to use authentic grading. Authentic grading encourages teachers to use portfolio assessment methods as described in this chapter, develop reasonable criteria for each authentic assessment activity that can lead to a letter or numerical grade, and use both quantitative and qualitative methods in constructing report cards.

In sum, authentic assessment provides parents, teachers, and students with a vivid picture of how individual learners are progressing in their content knowledge.

Reflection/Application Activities

1. Develop a portfolio assessment scheme—which includes the major components—for a grade level and content unit of your own choosing. (Note: It will be necessary to conduct a content analysis of the unit before attempting to design portfolio alternatives.) You should include grading rubrics if traditional report cards are used in your local school district.

2. Select a passage from a text you would like to use in your content area and construct a maze passage. Then, administer your maze passage to a middle or high school student volunteer in your area. Finally, analyze the results, and note any adjustments that might need to be made instructionally.

3. Visit a content classroom at a nearby school. Ask for permission to interview the teacher regarding the assessment methods used. From this informa-

tion, write a summary about where this teacher seems to be philosophically, which practices you would like to do the same, and authentic assessment practices you would like to try that are different from what was observed.

4. Construct an interest inventory for students based on your content area. It should contain the following components: background information about the student, prior knowledge about the content area, and affect-probing questions relative to both reading/literacy habits and the content area.

5. Arrange through your college instructor or a local school district to tutor for a semester a student having difficulty in your content area. Help the tutee to develop a student portfolio using ideas presented in this chapter.

Recommended Reading

Cooter, R. B. (Ed.). (1990). *The teacher's guide to reading tests.* Scottsdale, AZ: Gorsuch Scarisbrick.

Farr, R., & Tone, B. (1994). *Portfolio and performance assessment.* Fort Worth, TX: Harcourt Brace College Publishers.

Flynt, E. S., & Cooter, R. B. (1995). *The Flynt/Cooter reading inventory for the classroom* (2nd ed). Scottsdale, AZ: Gorsuch Scarisbrick.

Schnitzer, S. (1993). Designing an authentic assessment. *Educational Leadership, 50*(7), 32–35.

Spady, W. (1988). Organizing for results: The basis of authentic restructuring and reform. *Educational Leadership, 46*(2), 4–8.

Stepien, W., & Gallagher, S. (1993). Problem-based learning: As authentic as it gets. *Educational Leadership, 50*(7), 25–28.

Valencia, S., McGinley, W., & Pearson, P. D. (1990). *Assessing reading and writing: Building a more complete picture for middle school assessment.* Technical Report No. 500. Urbana, IL: Center for the Study of Reading. (ERIC Document Reproduction Service No. ED 320 121)

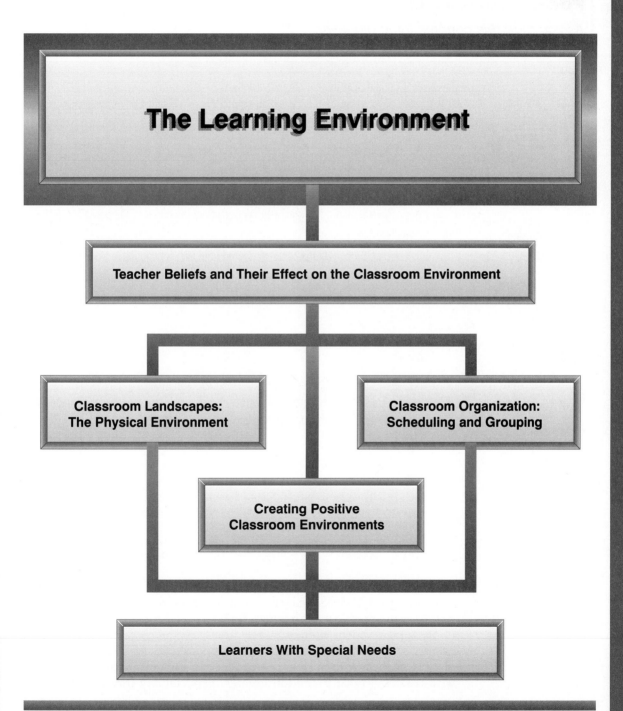

The Learning Environment

Teacher Beliefs and Their Effect on the Classroom Environment

Classroom Landscapes:
The Physical Environment

Classroom Organization:
Scheduling and Grouping

Creating Positive
Classroom Environments

Learners With Special Needs

Focus Questions

As you read this chapter, try to discover answers to the following questions:

1 What constitutes the teaching environment?

2 How should teachers' beliefs about learning and teaching be reflected in the construction of teaching environments?

3 When holistic teachers face a new teaching situation, how do they get started in creating an effective classroom environment?

4 Do learning stations make sense in content classrooms? If so, how are they used?

5 How can walls and other sterile-looking parts of the classroom be used to further instruction?

6 What are some key things to remember in effective scheduling?

7 Are there effective cooperative learning strategies for content classroom use? What about cooperative learning strategies for groups of two? Three? Larger groups?

8 How can teachers create positive learning climates in which students feel comfortable as risk takers?

9 What are some of the behaviors that place students at risk in content classes?

10 How do holistic content area teachers encourage constructive student behaviors, especially for students with learning problems?

> [T]he only way in which adults consciously control the kind of education which [students] get is by controlling the environment in which they act, and hence think and feel. We never educate directly, but indirectly by means of the environment. Whether we permit chance environments to do the work, or whether we design environments for the purpose makes a great difference.
> John Dewey (1916/1966, p. 19)

Begin to consider ways content classrooms can become stimulating learning environments.

Content classrooms can be sterile places with little color and imagination, organized with rows of desks facing the front of the room, and where teachers use lecture as the predominant method. Traditional classroom environments tend to discourage student interaction, rely heavily on the content textbook as the primary curriculum source, and offer few opportunities for creative application of ideas. As the holistic teaching movement has continued to gain in popularity with teachers, not to mention greater respectability through successful research trials, we are now able to apply holistic principles in redesigning content classroom environments.

Research, both past and present, indicates that the interaction between the classroom environment and student characteristics has such a potent impact on learning outcomes that it should not be ignored by those seeking to improve the effectiveness of schools (Fraser, 1986; Lewin, 1935, 1936; MacAulay, 1990). MacAulay (1990) explains that learning outcomes are affected by the interaction between teacher and student characteristics and by the structure and organization of the learning environment.

For example, student performance can be significantly improved by simply altering desk arrangements and can be improved still more when classroom arrangements are matched to teaching style (Rosenfield, Lambert, & Black, 1985). We also know that older students tend to prefer more open classroom styles, or those in which they are allowed to take part in classroom decisions (Arlin, 1976). Other important benefits can also be achieved by altering the learning environment such as the improvement of cross-cultural relations by using cooperative learning strategies (D. W. Johnson et al., 1984; Slavin, 1983).

When speaking of the learning environment, we refer to two important aspects of the classroom ecology: (a) the physical environment, or landscape (Shenkle, 1988; Vacca & Vacca, 1993), and (b) classroom organization factors such as scheduling, grouping arrangements, and other forms of classroom management. These two aspects of the learning environment are the main focus of this chapter. In addition, we also discuss how the physical environment, classroom organization, and teacher attitudes interact to establish the classroom climate (mood of the classroom). The final section of this chapter addresses students with learning problems and how they may be helped to develop constructive classroom behaviors (what are sometimes referred to as discipline policies). We begin with a brief discussion of teacher beliefs and how they relate to constructing effective learning environments.

> It is clear that learning outcomes are affected by the classroom environment (MacAulay, 1990).

> The term *classroom ecology* refers to both the physical arrangement and emotional climate established in learning settings.

TEACHER BELIEFS AND THEIR EFFECT ON THE CLASSROOM ENVIRONMENT

It has been said that one can tell a great deal about what a teacher believes simply by looking at her classroom. Classroom arrangements not only reveal teacher beliefs and attitudes, they also have an effect on learning (Rosenfield et al., 1985). To construct effective content classroom environments, teachers should begin by considering their own beliefs and philosophical stances. For example, when thinking about desk arrangements, a teacher interested in social interaction may want to use a circular arrangement. On the other hand, a traditional arrangement with student desks in rows and the teacher's desk at the front of the room implies a view of the learner as "empty" or passive—a learner who is to be "filled" with knowledge by the teacher (Rosenfield et al.,

> The classroom environment reflects the teacher's beliefs about teaching and learning.

1985). Deliberate planning of the classroom environment can help teachers avoid the pitfall of sending mixed messages about their beliefs and intentions.

We have assembled some belief statements that may be useful in planning classroom environments. They are drawn from holistic philosophy and research on effective classroom environments. These beliefs are suggested as a starting point for self-examination as you begin constructing your own belief systems about content area classroom environments. They are presented in list form, followed by a more detailed explanation.

Think of ways your classroom environment can be used to encourage student choice and independence in learning.

1. The classroom environment should reinforce the notion of student choices.
2. The classroom environment should support the way you teach.
3. The classroom environment should encourage peer collaboration.
4. The classroom environment should encourage risk taking and promote positive self-esteem.
5. The classroom environment should be flexible.
6. The classroom environment should contain the necessary tools for learning.

The classroom environment should reinforce the notion of student choices. One of the great motivators in life is choice. To the extent that teachers can provide students with interesting choices, they are more likely to buy in to the learning process, thus creating a sense of ownership (McWhirter, 1990). The classroom environment sends a silent but powerful message to learners that choice is a regular part of daily operations. Learning stations, self-selected reading and response activities, clustered desk arrangements, sign-up sheets for interest groups, and bulletin boards reflecting student choices are just a few possible demonstrations of this attitude.

The classroom environment should support the way you teach. All teachers have a certain classroom style, or teaching personality. The classroom environment should accommodate both the teacher's style and any goals he may have set for the school year (Novelli, 1990). Perhaps the teacher is considering implementing writing workshops, increasing the role of technology, and/or using small group activities. Whatever goals the teacher may have, the classroom environment should help make it all possible. Beyond these types of decisions, teachers should consider special talents they may possess. For instance, a teacher with an extensive music background may want to use these talents to write special songs or raps for students that teach abstract concepts. Another teacher may enjoy excursions into remote areas to find ways of bringing vicarious experiences into the classroom—like the science teacher who brings in plant samples or photographic slides of geologic phenomena to enhance lecture experiences. Students frequently enjoy getting to know their teachers and their special interests. The types of experiences one brings into

The classroom is a tool that supports teaching.

What are some ways that you could inject some of your personality and interests into the learning experiences?

the classroom reveal a part of oneself to students and help make abstract learning more interesting and concrete.

The classroom environment should encourage peer collaborations. Not everything worth learning comes from the teacher's mouth. Although there may be times when the teacher wishes to disseminate information in group settings using lecture method, or the "sage on the stage" format, there should also be regular times when students work together to solve problems and analyze information. In these latter situations, teachers must know how to act as a "guide on the side" to facilitate student interactions. Creative scheduling along with flexible seating arrangements can help make this a reality.

The classroom environment should encourage risk taking and promote positive self-esteem. Many students make very slow progress in their content learning, which is due to a lack of risk taking. This often happens when students perceive peer and teacher comments about their work to be negative. Students need to be reminded that we all get better at most tasks with practice and that it's OK to be wrong. A supportive classroom environment establishes a kind of safety net for students as they attempt to approximate adult standards of performance. A positive classroom climate begins with the teacher's own attitude toward her students and is learned by other students through the teacher's example. Over time, students' self-esteem grows in a positive direction in this type of classroom environment, and learning will likewise accelerate.

> Teachers need to have a classroom safety net, such that students feel comfortable taking risks.

The classroom environment should be flexible. Although we know that students respond favorably to a classroom environment with clear expectations and a predictable structure (Cordell & Cannon, 1985; MacAulay, 1990), the classroom environment should also be adaptable and easily modified. Flexibility applies to the physical environment as well as in scheduling and daily routines. This point can be illustrated by describing an event that took place in one of our classrooms a few years ago.

One day a fourth grader came to school with an extraordinary cocoon. It was huge, and when students held it, the cocoon vibrated because of the creature's movements inside. For the next hour or so, all usual class routines were suspended while the teacher and class sought answers to such questions as "Is a cocoon a home to a future moth or butterfly?" (Answer: a moth.) "If a moth, then what do we call this metamorphosis stage for a butterfly?" (Answer: chrysalis.) "How does one tell the difference between a moth and butterfly?" (Answer: the antennae are different.) Because the environment was flexible, the teacher and students were able to exploit a naturally occurring event (a teachable moment) and discover answers to these and other questions using different reading/study strategies.

> A flexible classroom environment allows the teacher to exploit naturally occurring events.

The classroom environment should contain the necessary tools for learning. An ideal classroom landscape embodies beliefs about the real world of learning. Such tools as scissors, tape, and extra paper in a writing center, for example, remind student-authors that drafts are temporary and that cutting and pasting is a regular part of the writing process. A research station in a science classroom, for example, investigating the earth's resources can be quite informative. It might house relevant articles on rural ecology and photographs taken at an oil field. This reminds students that multiple sources are needed when conducting research about the science issues of today. Tools in the learning environment serve as silent reminders that learners go through specific and precise processes in solving problems.

CLASSROOM LANDSCAPES: THE PHYSICAL ENVIRONMENT

Reflect on and share with a colleague ways you can breathe life into otherwise sterile classrooms.

Many first-year teachers, as well as experienced teachers facing a new assignment, find themselves placed in unfamiliar surroundings 1 or 2 weeks before the start of school. There is generally not much more in the classroom beyond the requisite number of desks for students and teacher, district-adopted textbooks, and perhaps a few other niceties like an overhead projector and some odds and ends left behind by the previous teacher. It is up to the new teacher to breathe life into an otherwise sterile environment and create a place conducive to learning.

Construction of the learning environment is one of the first and most important creative acts the teacher considers. Newkirk stated, quoting a teacher who compares the classroom setting to a tapestry, "the design of the warp and weft are everchanging . . . with each new experience in the day" (1990, p. 60). Another teacher (Shenkle, 1988) described classroom landscape construction this way:

"I tried to imagine myself as a chief designer . . . to create a whole new learning environment." (Newkirk, 1990, p. 61)

I tried to imagine myself as a chief designer. Ahead of me was the opportunity to create a whole new learning environment. . . . One busy morning, my students and I were having a lively discussion about a class problem. As I stood at the front of the room listening, I suddenly realized that my students were talking to each other's backs. *What kind of communication is this?*, I asked myself. . . . Over the years, I came to see more and more that in defining my classroom's geography . . . I was also defining my values, my teaching style, and my goals for the students. (p. 61)

Routman, in describing holistic classrooms, explains that the

collaborative classroom has a distinctive look and feel that is noticeable when you walk into the room. There are displays of [students'] work and books everywhere. There is space for exploration, learning stations, and a classroom library, and the room is full of attractive, purposeful print. . . . There are open spaces where the class can gather or small groups can meet. There are stations [or] designated areas where students have opportunities for talk, exploration, writing, reading and sharing. In a small room, or secondary classroom, the hallway is sometimes used for conferences and paired collaboration. (1991, p. 423)

This section is devoted to choices for the teacher concerning physical elements of the classroom. Our intent is to focus first on finding necessary furniture and other teaching necessities and then consider ways to arrange things for instruction.

Getting Started: Finding the Bits and Pieces

Perhaps the first and most obvious consideration for constructing the classroom environment has to do with furniture. Early in the school year, furniture and textbooks may be just about the only things in the classroom. In almost all cases, the desks, chairs, and tables are movable—a good thing, because this permits the teacher to reorganize centers of learning according to the demands of a particular activity or unit (Pappas, Kiefer, & Levstik, 1990).

Most teachers begin with a scavenger hunt. They get necessary permissions from the principal and custodian, then begin searching the school's storage places for unclaimed furniture and other things. Items that are especially useful, and may be found in most schools, include the following:

Begin to construct your classroom environment by asking custodial staff to help you scour the campus for needed furniture and learning materials.

Flat-top desks	Movable chalk boards
Comfortable chairs	Movable bulletin boards
File cabinets (2)	Easels (for chart paper)
Tables	Storage containers/cabinets
Bookcases	Overhead projector
Chart paper	Movable projection screen
A-V cart	Small file or recipe boxes

Other items that may be gathered at home or in the community through donations include:

Carpeting	Materials related to the content subject
Aquarium	Old furniture
Pets/cages	Comfortable chairs
Posters	Art supplies (paper, scrap wood, etc.)
Computers	Book-making materials

Developing a Floor Plan: Some Possible Choices

Many teachers find it useful to construct a floor plan of their classroom before placing furniture and other physical elements. Consider what could be used to support and facilitate instruction. Components may include learning stations, storage places, student collaboration areas, walls and windows, desks, group collaboration areas, and private work areas. Each component fulfills a specific purpose and should be included only when it will significantly benefit instruction. Because the classroom should be a dynamic or ever-changing environ-

Construct a floor plan before attempting to assemble your classroom.

Classrooms should be dynamic, ever changing.

ment (according to the needs of the class), these components may come and go during the course of the school year. Remember that simplicity is the key to flexibility in a dynamic classroom. In this section, we offer the reader brief descriptions of potential components, beginning with one of the most effective strategies, learning stations.

Learning Stations

Learning stations are small classroom areas where students can perform an instructional activity without direct guidance from a teacher. A valuable quality of learning stations is that they can be modified to suit your teaching style and needs of the class (Novelli, 1990). Typical learning stations in content classes include writing stations, media stations (listening and viewing), experimentation stations (typically for science and mathematics), computer/technology stations, library/research stations, group collaboration stations, and small group instruction stations. Purposes and descriptions for some of the more common learning stations are summarized next.

Writing stations are essentially publishing areas where final drafts are produced.

Writing Stations.   Writing stations are essentially book-making and publishing stations where students prepare final drafts of reports, student-made books, and other products for sharing with others. Housed in this area are different types of paper (quality stationery, construction paper, newsprint, inexpensive 20-lb. bond, etc.), scissors, tape, laminating supplies, cardboard, tagboard, different color markers, pencils, pens, index cards, stapler, clasps, and so on. Generally, a table and two chairs are all that is required. A typical writing center is pictured in Figure 4.1.

It is important that students have reference tools immediately available in the classroom.

Teachers should search for popular press books to use in classroom investigations that combine accuracy with an interesting writing/reading style.

Library/Research Stations.   Library/research stations are essentially reference materials made available to students from the school library for ongoing units or projects in the classroom. A major benefit of library/research stations is that students can carry on research without having to leave the classroom to do so. All that is required is a little preplanning. For example, if a history class is studying events during the time of the American Civil War, then the teacher might work with the school librarian/media specialist to collect both narrative (fiction) and expository (nonfiction) books related to this period. Or perhaps the science, language arts, and mathematics teachers have joined forces in a middle school using a themed studies approach (Gamberg, Kwak, Hutchings, & Altheim, 1988; Paradis, 1984; Reutzel & Cooter, 1996) called "Touring the Galaxy." The library/research stations found in each classroom would include books specific to the area of specialty but also books of a narrative and expository nature that unite all the disciplines. For example, two excellent expository books related to the "Touring the Galaxy" theme that also involve both mathematics and science are Nigel Calder's (1979) *Einstein's Universe* and Stephen W. Hawking's (1988) best-seller *A Brief History of Time: From The Big Bang to Black Holes.*

Figure 4.1   Writing Center

Another purpose of these library/research stations is getting students excited and reading about the subject. The more students read on a daily basis books in which they are interested, the stronger they become as readers in all disciplines. In other words, time on task in reading pays academic dividends. Content teachers should include not only great books of an expository nature in their library/research stations but also fascinating narrative books that relate to the theme of study. Although some teachers may feel that narrative books have no place in a content classroom, we strongly disagree. Our argument is simply this: If quality popular literature related to the theme of study is chosen, it will often contain factual information that boosts students' understanding of the field of study.

Narrative or fictional materials can serve many valuable learning functions in the content classroom.

Group Collaboration Stations.   We believe that the classroom environment should be a supportive place for students where they feel secure in becoming educational risk takers. In selecting instructional activities, we know that whole class activities alone are not sufficient in creating this type of environment. Lucy Calkins, renowned educator in the writing process movement, remarked "In many middle-school classrooms, small response groups and peer-conferences seem to be safer, more productive settings for giving and receiving responses than the whole-class meetings" (1986, p. 107). Group collaboration stations are one class of small group activities that provide a most constructive setting. Specific types of group collaboration stations include peer conferencing stations, literature-response groups, and various forms of cooperative learning groups, which are discussed more fully later in the chapter.

Students working in small groups often feel much more at ease in giving and receiving responses than they do in whole class discussions (Calkins, 1986).

Library/research stations capitalize on students' intellectual curiosity about topics being studied.

A group collaboration station provides students with a space where they can come together, and it communicates that the teacher values such activities.

An important key to successful group discussions is for the teacher's expectations to be made clear for each assignment.

Reading one's work aloud in front of peers can cause a sense of fear for many. Helping students develop appropriate responses through modeling is crucial.

Group collaboration stations usually comprise a table and chairs where small groups of students can come together. Students generally focus on a project, attempt to reach consensus on an issue, provide suggestions for a student regarding a written manuscript, or engage in problem solving. Although the task at hand tends to dictate what goes on in group collaboration stations, a few general ground rules seem to help things run more smoothly.

First, the teacher needs to help students understand the teacher's expectations in this setting in terms of (a) the assignment itself and (b) group dynamics. Precise directions concerning each assignment, including the relative value of each part of the assignment, will help students better understand how to focus their efforts. Many teachers develop detailed worksheets to help guide students through group assignments. Figure 4.2 is one example of a worksheet developed by a language arts teacher to assist students working in group collaboration stations on literature-response projects.

Group dynamics make up an important aspect of group collaboration stations that should not be left to chance. A seventh-grade teacher once remarked, "You can't just take five 13-year-olds, put them into a center without clear directions, and expect great things to happen!" Calkins, in addressing problems secondary students sometimes have in writing groups, adds

Middle school students often balk at the idea of reading their drafts aloud . . . this behavior is not a reflection of a "bad attitude," but rather of fear. Often the

Small group collaborations develop problem-solving skills in the content area classroom.

fear is well founded. Adolescents can be brutally critical of each other. (1986, p. 107)

Put simply, students who will be working in group collaboration stations need to understand what are acceptable language and behaviors to protect the dignity and self-esteem of others. We recommend as a starting point developing with students an understanding of response models (Calkins & Harwayne, 1987) and group etiquette rules (Reutzel & Cooter, 1996). **Response models** are ways of speaking and behaving in small group situations that are modeled by the teacher, then practiced or performed by students in role-playing activities. For instance, let us suppose that three students in a group collaboration center are reading a draft of another group member's paper dealing with the topic of photosynthesis. In this paper they discover a paragraph that is unclear. Instead of saying something like "This part is *stupid*!" or "What the heck does *this* mean!?" students could be coached to ask clarifying questions of an inoffensive nature. When reviewing student products, Calkins and Harwayne (1987) urge teachers to listen and understand, celebrate with the student what has been legitimately accomplished, then extend and teach. A response model

Figure 4.2 Group Collaboration Guide Sheet

1. Name of Group members _____ _____
                                                    Captain   Recorder

_____ _____ _____
       Reporter   Materials   Checker

2. Name of Group _____

3. Name of Project/ Project Description _____
_____

4. List the things that have to be done, who is doing each thing, and what
   your deadline for each step is going to be.
   A._____
   Who?_____When?_____
   B._____
   Who?_____When?_____
   C._____
   Who?_____When?_____
   D._____
   Who?_____When?_____
   E._____When?_____
   Comments or further things to do_____
   _____
   _____
   _____

5. List the materials you will need and who is to be in charge of each thing.
   _____
   _____
   _____

6. Keep track of who has done their assignments and who has not. Make
   sure to mark the box when you hear positive comments made or when you
   see cooperation between members of your group.

Names	Assign. yes/no	+	+	+	Coop.	Coop.	Notes

Note. Adapted from a group sheet developed by Cheryl Domingues, Alpine, Utah.

that teachers can teach to students that grows out of Calkins and Harwayne's advice follows:

1. Listen to or read what your peers have created.
2. Ask questions about what you don't understand.
3. Compliment your peers about what you like about their product or composition.
4. Help them make it better by making suggestions in a kind way.
5. Don't get angry if they choose not to take your advice—remember, it is up to the author to make that decision.

In addition to offering response models to guide student interactions, it may also be helpful for students to develop, with help from the teacher, **group etiquette rules**. These are student-developed rules for functioning in group collaboration stations. Reutzel and Cooter (1996) offer an example of group etiquette rules that were developed by sixth-grade students in Ohio. They include

Think of some ways you can interact with students about their work that would serve as positive response model behaviors.

1. Remember that the purpose of the group is to learn and help other people learn.
2. Always bring a paper and pencil to the group session.

A small group instruction station exploring how to develop the literacy skill of summarizing.

3. Don't show off in the group.
4. Everyone must take part in the discussion for it to work.
5. Anytime you don't understand what was said, ask the person to explain.
6. When two people don't understand each other, help them out.
7. Don't interrupt people, no matter how good your idea seems to be.
8. Give examples of what you mean, if possible.

More small group learning opportunities are needed in many middle and secondary schools.

Small Group Instruction Stations.   Sometimes teaching is much more effective when taking place in small group settings (four to eight students) than with the entire class. This is especially so when teaching new and abstract literacy, numeracy,science, and computer/technology skills. As with group collaboration stations, all that is really required is a table and chairs large enough to accommodate the group and teacher.

Media Stations (Listening and Viewing).   Media stations are places where students can listen to prerecorded audiotapes matched to expository or narrative books, watch filmstrips on viewers, or view videotapes (such as VHS). As with computer stations, the media center depends on availability of necessary equipment. Because this type of equipment is usually shared in the school, media stations tend to be temporary (3 days to 2 weeks). Likewise, media soft-

Students at a media station reviewing a taped presentation.

A multimedia presentation being prepared in a science class.

ware (films, tapes, books) are usually borrowed from the school library or possibly from a central office collection.

Experimentation Stations.   Effective teachers in the mathematics and the sciences, as with all subjects, seek to link new and often abstract information with concrete experiences. Experimentation stations are one very potent resource toward this goal. Because these stations are defined by the experiment itself, it is really not possible to describe essential elements here, but perhaps a few examples might be helpful (see Tables 4.1 and 4.2).

Linking new and abstract information with what is known is a prime objective of experimentation stations.

Computer/Technology Stations.   Each year, more teachers turn to technology to make education more efficient, interesting, and productive ("Count the Ways Technology Works for Schools," 1990). As most educators are aware, the field of computer technology is one of the most rapidly developing areas. Innovations in computer hardware and software are occurring so swiftly as to make it almost impossible to produce an up-to-date section for a textbook such as this. However, a number of general suggestions for organizing computer/technology stations may be helpful, and these are discussed next.

   Individual classroom computer stations.   Most teachers begin phasing in computer and other technologies on a small scale, primarily for financial reasons. One to three personal computers (PCs) in the classroom, usually Apple

It is important that uses of technology grow out of the needs of the curriculum.

Connecting learning to the real world through an experimental learning station.

Table 4.1   Examples of Science Experimentation Station Activities

Concept and Activity	Materials Needed
Concept: Stems carry water to all parts of a plant. **Activity:** After cutting about 2.5 cm off the bottom of a celery stalk and placing it into colored water, students observe how the water moved up the stalk and into the leaves overnight.	Fresh celery stalks Food coloring (dark blue or red) Water glass and water Science notebooks to record observations
Concept: Effects of streamlining **Activity:** Students bend a long, rectangular piece of tagboard and staple it on one end, creating a teardrop shape. After standing the tagboard on edge with a lighted candle in front of the pointed end (about 4 cm away), students gently blow on the opposite, bowed end of the card to observe how they can blow out the candle.	Candle and stand Long rectangular piece of tagboard Stapler Table Matches
Concept: Composition of soil **Activity:** Students deposit some garden soil in a tall glass cylinder jar (about ⅓ of the cylinder), then fill to within 3 cm of the top with water. After screwing on the top tightly, the jar is shaken. The soil will settle into identifiable layers (gravel, sand, silt, humus).	Garden soil Cylindrical jar with top Water

Table 4.2   Examples of Mathematics Experimentation Station Activities

Concept and Activity	Materials Needed
Concept: Probability and statistics	A partner
Activity: *Fair Game 2.* Take turns rolling the two dice. Player A scores a point if the sum is even. Player B scores a point if the sum is odd. Is the game fair? If not, how could you make the game fair? Explain your reasoning.	A pair of dice
Play the game again, this time figuring the product. Player A scores a point if the product is even. Player B scores a point if the product is odd. Is the game fair? If not, how could you make the game fair? Explain your reasoning.	
Concept: Geometry	Colored tiles
Activity: *The Banquet Table Problem.* A banquet hall has a huge collection of small square tables that fit together to make larger rectangular tables. Arrange tiles to find the different numbers of people that can be seated if 12 small tables are used. Do the same if 24 are used. Record on squared paper.	Squared paper, centimeter or half-inch
Extensions:	
1. *The 100 Table Problem*. If 100 small square tables are arranged into a large rectangular table, find the most and least numbers of people that can be seated.	
2. *Banquet Cost*. If the banquet hall charges by the number of square tables used, what's the least expensive way to seat 16 people? 50 people? 60? 100? Any number?	
Concept: Logic	10 cards, numbered 1 to 10
Activity: *The Card Problem.* Arrange the cards this way: The top card is a 1 and should be placed face up on the table; put the next card on the bottom of the deck; place the third card, which should be a 2, face up on the table; move the next to the bottom of the deck. Continue until all the cards are in order on the table top.	
Concept: Percents	Magazines or newspaper supplements that contain advertisements
Activity: *Comparing Advertisements.* Clip four advertisements that offer discounts for items, and paste them on a sheet of paper. Include one that indicates the percent the customer will save, one that gives the sale price, and two of your choice. Decide which of the advertisements gives the customer the best deal. Record your decision, including an explanation of your reasoning.	
Trade with other groups and decide on the best deal for the advertisements they clipped. Compare your decisions.	

Note. Adapted from *About Teaching Mathematics: A K–8 Resource* by M. Burns, 1992, White Plains, NY: Math Solutions Publications. Copyright 1992 by Math Solutions Publications.

Exploring data bases at a computer station.

Computer, Inc.'s Macintosh series PCs, IBM-PCs, or the compatible clones provide a good place to start. Many educators feel that computer hardware (PC) technology is far more developed than the available software (disks that make the computers work), such that much of the available software amounts to little more than electronic workbooks. Therefore, selection of quality and affordable software can be quite challenging. Most professional journals for educators provide regular articles and reviews of computer software found to be useful and reasonably priced.

Minilabs.   In schools where space is at a premium and the installation of full-size computer labs is not possible, some are opting for **minilabs**. These minilabs often consist of a computer work station or two in each classroom and a small computer classroom/lab with 10 to 15 computers. Minilabs usually provide individualized lessons in reading, mathematics, or other content areas. Parent volunteers, in most cases, can help maintain the materials, but a computer specialist will likely be needed (as with all computer stations) to troubleshoot more serious problems with the equipment. Minilabs can make use of interactive technologies, such as Discourse, or more individualized student programs such as those provided by Jostens Learning Corporation.

Kids' offices.   One Texas school district has joined resources with a utility company, technology vendors, publishers, and a local college to create ultramodern offices for business students ("Count the Ways Technology Works for Schools," 1990, pp. 31–32). The special learning environment includes Macintosh computers linked into a local area network, printers, scanners, a fax machine, copier, modem, and a flat display panel that allows the teacher to

Development of student "offices" is a powerful vehicle for increasing student learning. It is also a great opportunity for business–school partnerships.

project her computer screen to the class using an overhead projector. Students can learn word processing skills, data base management, desktop publishing, and other useful skills. School–business partnerships help to finance the ongoing expenses of this operation. Small-scale duplication of this type of learning center seems possible for most school systems.

Classroom communication network labs.   The Saturn School of Tomorrow in St. Paul, Minnesota, has found an interactive classroom communication network called Discourse to be quite effective in content instruction. Discourse is a computer-driven network designed to transmit learner responses from 8 to 64 individual learning stations back to a central teacher location. Teachers can monitor and record all student responses and deliver feedback as well as measure proficiency levels. Students are prompted to respond to tasks on their own keyboard, and student responses appear simultaneously on the teacher's control unit. Teachers can then provide instant feedback through their own keyboards. This class of technology seems to have great potential for widespread use in the future.

Pen and ink software.   Another emerging technology that seems to hold wonderful potential for content classrooms is commonly referred to as **pen and ink software**. With this technology students use a notebook computer (one not much larger than a common notebook) and a pen-like stylus to literally write notes on the computer screen. The computer's "translation" software leaves an ink-like trail on the screen in an impression of the student's writing. The handwritten notes are later translated into text that can be moved around on the screen just like any other typed letters and words.

Pen and ink software has the potential of making computers more accessible to many, especially for written communications.

The advantages are many. First, students can take notes directly on their notebook computer without disturbing others with the pecking sound of typing. For that matter, this type of software could be most helpful to students who have little or no typing ability. Disadvantages mainly relate to "read errors," that is, computer software misreading what has been written. For example, the student may write (perhaps in a not-so-legible hand) "handsome" and the computer may record "handmade." Cost may also be a prohibiting force, because notebook computers tend to cost between $2,000 and $3,000 per unit, not including the necessary stylus and software. Nevertheless, pen and ink software may be part of the future.

Other Physical Elements Supportive of Holistic Teaching

In addition to various types of learning stations, content teachers will want to consider other possibilities to complement their holistic teaching. Some essential elements include private work areas, a whole group sharing area, student display areas, room decorations, and bulletin boards.

What are some of the benefits students gain in learning to work independently in your content area?

Although there has been much interest in helping students learn to work cooperatively in recent years, there are still times when students should work alone. This does not necessarily mean, though, that teachers must perpetuate the traditional practice of having an individual desk for every student. A brief account of one content teacher's experience is offered to help clarify this point.

Wilder's Revolution

Recently, a workshop was held in a south Texas school district for content teachers interested in making transitions into holistic teaching. The group met once a month with a teacher-facilitator to share information and set classroom implementation goals for the coming month. After discussing ways to reorganize classrooms, a sixth-grade social studies teacher (we'll call her Ms. Wilder) decided to completely redo her classroom.

At the next workshop meeting (1 month later), Ms. Wilder reported that she took the following actions in reorganizing her classroom environment:

- Reduced the number of student desks to 10, which were then clustered in one corner of the room for students who needed a private work area.
- Located three large round tables and necessary chairs to begin forming stations.
- Asked a local carpet dealer to donate a large carpet square for the group sharing sessions in the front of the room.

The result was a new sense of excitement about learning, greater risk taking on the part of students (and the teacher), and a spirit of student collaboration.

> Teachers need to think of bold and untraditional ways to reconstruct the learning environment. In many instances, content classrooms look much as they did decades ago.

What About the Walls?

Many content classrooms seem cold and uninviting, which is due partly to blank walls. Blank walls suggest a lack of ownership or personal investment, as though the message is "No one lives here." Wall space, used appropriately, fosters positive feelings of student and teacher investment. The key concept in decorating walls, aside from making the environment more attractive and inviting, is to immerse students in reading and writing opportunities that reinforce learning. Several ideas are presented next.

Wall Illustrations

One way to improve the look of classroom walls is a decorative paint job. After securing necessary permissions from the school administration, a good place to start is with several colorful illustrations painted on otherwise blank walls. Illustrations can be either abstract or thematic (pictures of objects or people commonly associated with the content subject). Because many of us are not artists, a good way to produce quality illustrations is to first draw or copy the illustration on a sheet of 8½ × 11-inch graph paper (without coloring in the illustration). Next, make an overhead transparency of the design using the necessary equipment found in the school's teacher workroom. With the aid of an overhead projector, it is now possible to project and trace the image on the wall of choice. It is a good idea to use a watercolor marker for tracing so that errors can easily be erased. More permanent acrylic-based paints can be used to finish the project once the image has been traced.

Student-Made Bulletin Boards

Most classrooms have some bulletin board space available. Unfortunately, these useful spaces are typically filled with commercial or other adult-made preformed materials, bordered by the obligatory 2-inch corrugated paper strips. Students pay little attention to this type of display because they reflect little or no student involvement. To reverse this trend, allow student groups to develop all bulletin boards in collaboration with you, the teacher. Specify key elements of the message to be displayed, but leave all creative aspects of the design to the students. Instead of using the 2-inch corrugated paper strips to frame the bulletin board, encourage students to frame their displays with dark-colored paper to emphasize the contrast between background and the information presented (Novelli, 1990). When a new bulletin board goes up, have group members explain and introduce the new concepts. If the bulletin board is to be used in several classes in a departmentalized school, it may be interesting and helpful for students in the design group to be videotaped introducing the bulletin board, which can then be replayed for each class or group.

Bulletin boards and other displays should be conceived by students as a reflection of their learning.

Wall Murals

Another way of immersing students in reading and writing is to have them develop murals depicting important information learned. In the case of history-related or time-sequenced learning, the mural can relate a sequence of events through a progression of pictures moving from left to right. Murals for other courses of study can have a collection or collage look to them. Murals are easily constructed by having students draw or paint designs on long sheets of butcher paper, then displaying finished products on large open wall spaces, or outside the classroom in the hallway.

Murals are a dynamic and interesting way to display student learning and have the added benefit of transforming otherwise sterile classroom environments.

Banners and Barriers

Sometimes teachers like to have private study areas available to individual students or small groups in an otherwise open classroom. Two ways of accomplishing some student privacy is through the use of banners and barriers. Brightly colored banners, with or without thematic designs, can be hung from the ceiling and provide color to the classroom and privacy for students. Hannah (1984) offers some simple suggestions for constructing and hanging banners:

1. Acquire medium-weight fabric in desired colors. Remnants or pieces of sheeting will usually work well.
2. Hems should be sewn or stapled at the top and bottom.
3. Banners can be decorated by painting directly on the fabric (but colors sometimes "bleed" a little) or by cutting out designs from other fabrics and affixing them to the banner by sewing, gluing, or using double-sided iron-on fusible web. Iron-on fusible web is much easier to use than sewing. (It has paper backing on both sides. Remove one backing, iron it onto the fabric, and cut out the desired shape. Remove the second backing, and iron it onto the banner fabric. Fusible web adheres quite well and is available at fabric stores and craft shops.)
4. Wooden dowels or bamboo poles may be slipped through the upper hems, from which fishing line (about 20-lb. test) may be secured for hanging (see Figure 4.3) in the desired areas.

Partitions of various kinds can also be erected for privacy purposes. File cabinets, movable chalk boards, easels, joined pieces of heavy cardboard, and various forms of lightweight particleboard (found at lumberyards) can be used

Figure 4.3 A Banner

for movable partitions. A section or two of garden trellis also provides a sense of privacy at minimal cost.

Putting It All Together: Classroom Landscapes Matched to Teacher Beliefs

Once the teacher has gathered furniture, made decisions regarding stations and wall space, a floor plan should be devised. Think of the classroom environment as a puzzle with only six or eight large pieces or components. It is much easier to construct effective learning environments in this way, rather than trying to thoughtfully place dozens of individual pieces of furniture and other items. Ways of assembling the classroom landscape are as varied as the personalities of those who teach. The point of it all is (a) develop a classroom that supports what you believe, and (b) make sure that the environment is flexible. Figure 4.4 shows an example of a classroom floor plan developed by a content teacher that supports the tenets of holistic teaching described in Chapter 1.

CLASSROOM ORGANIZATION: SCHEDULING AND GROUPING

Once the physical environment design has been developed, the teacher is ready to consider other important elements related to organizing the classroom. Scheduling and grouping are key factors that contribute to teaching success.

> Teachers must try to create a flexible and fluid daily or weekly schedule so as to provide predictability without boredom.

Schedules and Lesson Plans

Traditional lesson plan books and other ways of structuring may be too confining for many content teachers interested in implementing holistic strategies. We have found that it is best to try to create a basic overall pattern or format for scheduling. It should be flexible. Loose-leaf notebooks or other easily modified recording tools should be used. Daily plans should be written in pencil so that changes can be made easily. Routman (1991) states that it may take from 3 to 5 years to finally settle on a scheduling pattern or **scheme** that seems to work just right, so try not to be frustrated if your first ideas are not as functional as you would like.

> Sometimes it takes a few years to settle on a basic overall scheme that satisfies the needs for creativity and function.

Scheduling schemes should contain all aspects of learning and teaching you think are most important. They must also account for nonnegotiable skills required by the state or district for the course of study *(Note: These are usually found in the school district's curriculum guide or are available through the state department of education.)* Begin by identifying major instructional strategies you wish to use, such as writing workshops, individual and group sharing experiences, minilessons, individual or group learning experiences, assessment activities, and center work. Described in this section are two sample schedules for departmentalized content classes that exemplify successful efforts by teachers to integrate holistic principles.

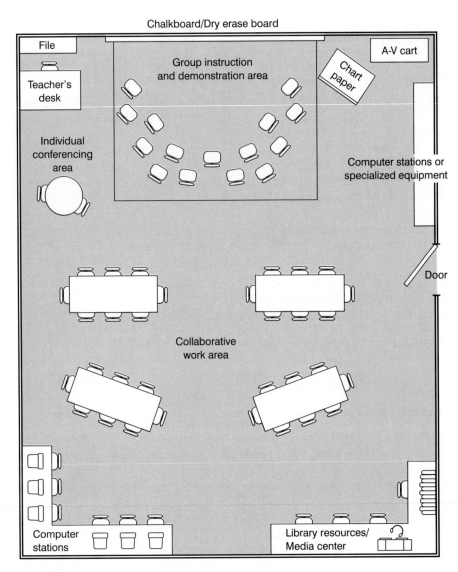

Figure 4.4 Floor Plan

Example: Eighth-Grade General Science Class (55-Minute Period)

The example of an eighth-grade science class in Figure 4.5 reveals that the teacher has at least two goals: (a) establish a regular and predictable routine that facilitates discovery learning and (b) integrate holistic methodologies. It is a rather simple design that includes five basic elements that may or may not be used each day as needs dictate. In other words, this design should be viewed

Figure 4.5 Eighth-Grade General Science Weekly Routine (55-Minute Period)

	M	T	W	Th	F
5–10 minutes	Teacher sharing and mini-lesson	Teacher sharing and mini-lesson	Teacher sharing and mini-lesson	Teacher sharing and mini-lesson	Teacher sharing and mini-lesson
15–20 minutes	Focused group-work session	Individual research	Focused group-work session	Individual research	Focused group-work session
15 minutes	Stations rotation	Stations rotation	Stations rotation	Stations rotation	Stations rotation
5 minutes	Scientific journals	Scientific journals	Scientific journals	Scientific journals	Scientific journals
5 minutes	Student sharing	Student sharing	Student sharing	Student sharing	Student sharing

as *flexible*. Each day begins with teacher sharing and a minilesson. For example, in a unit called "Strange Phenomena in the Universe," the teacher may wish to focus the first week on the topics of black holes and comets. Teacher sharing might include such activities as reading aloud high-interest passages on these two phenomena and conducting demonstrations/experiments for class observations. Teacher sharing activities are usually tied to a related minilesson in which required skills and strategies from the school district curriculum guide are taught. The next part of the routine alternates daily between focused group-work sessions when students work cooperatively to find solutions to problems posed by the teacher and individual research activities that permit students to work independently on more long-term projects. Next, students working in small groups rotate through work stations that help them learn more about the topic under study. These work station activities usually follow a sequence: (a) Conduct an outlined experiment in the center, (b) discuss what was learned in your small groups, then (c) write observations in individual scientific journals. Students also write in their scientific journals a daily summary of usually two or three sentences relative to what they may have learned during the teacher sharing and minilesson phase.

Scientific journals cause students to reflect daily on new information they are acquiring.

The scheme concludes with students sharing projects (one per day, as they conclude projects) that may have been completed and presented to the teacher the day before. Assessment in the scheme is accomplished through individual student portfolios, as discussed in Chapter 3.

Example: 10th-Grade Algebra Class (50-Minute Period)

Discuss with a colleague ways that think–pair–share may be beneficial for some study units in your field.

As Figure 4.6 indicates, this 10th-grade algebra class is organized around a series of cooperative activities to ensure successful participation on the part of all students. On Monday the focus is introducing the topic or theme of the week and making sure that necessary information is shared by the teacher. Next, the students are placed into a think–pair–share grouping so that application of the information can follow the teacher's presentation. This activity allows students to internalize information and discover gaps in their knowledge for teacher clarification (reteaching). Finally, homework/project dyads are formed, groups that stay together for the remainder of the week. Throughout the week, the unit of study progresses to more and more student-directed activities, ranging from dyads on Tuesday to focus trios on Wednesday and paper-chase groups on Thursday. As the week concludes, a unit assessment is conducted that may range from more traditional paper-and-pencil tests conducted in paper chase groups (or independently) to more holistic application problems based on real-world scenarios. Project dyads also have an opportunity to share hands-on projects they have developed both in class and away from school.

Cooperative Learning Groups

Cooperative learning groups help students synthesize information in a collaborative way.

Use of **cooperative learning groups** is a popular teaching strategy that, over time, encourages student independence and growth (Glazer & Brown, 1993). Cooperative learning groups are heterogeneous groups usually ranging in size from two to five students working as a team to accomplish a classroom assignment. These groups are formed for various reasons, such as problem solving in mathematics and science classes or providing extra help for students with learning problems who may be challenged by the reading demands of an adopted textbook. Following are selected techniques that have proven to be effective in content classroom settings.

Cooperative Learning Pairs

Researchers have found dyads to be one of the most effective cooperative learning strategies for students with learning problems.

Paired Reading or Dyads.   Especially effective with students with reading problems, paired reading (Eldredge & Quinn, 1988; K. Wood, 1987) involves two students, usually a special-needs or less proficient reader paired with a stronger peer, silently reading the same text. After reading a small portion, one student acts as a recaller and orally recounts the major points of the passage,

Figure 4.6 Tenth-Grade Algebra Class Routine (50-Minute Period)

	M	T	W	Th	F
5-10 minutes	Topic intro. and project dyads announced	Homework check; group work	Teacher sharing and minilesson	Homework check groups	Weekly assessment and dyads share projects
10-20 minutes	Focused teacher-led instruction	Teacher sharing and minilesson	Problem-solving activity	Teacher sharing and minilesson	
5-10 minutes	Think-Pair-Share	Dyads	Focus trio	Paper chase groups	
5-10 minutes	Homework/ project dyads	Independent projects/ student sharing	Math journals and/or homework dyads	Review and sharing	

while the other student acts as a listener. The listener clarifies any parts that are not fully understood and/or fills in any missing information. Then the process is repeated with the next part of the text with the students swapping roles. If the paired readers find a part of the text that neither student understands, then the teacher can help make the information clear. We find almost universal praise for this technique by teachers who have tried it in their classes. This is also sometimes referred to as *metacomprehension pairs.*

Text-response Pairs. Students read a supplemental text for the topic under investigation in the class, then produce a text-response project that summarizes what they have learned for presentation to the class. For example, projects could take the form of a videotaped "Nightly News" report, radio dramas, game shows (like "Jeopardy"), or dioramas.

Co-authoring/Composing Pairs. The student pairs co-author or compose a book, poem, song, chant, letter, or other writing task that summarizes important information they have learned. The pair works together in all stages of the writing process to compose a product together or to help each other compose separate projects.

Drill Partners.   The use of drill partners is a review activity during which students take turns drilling or testing each other on important facts, vocabulary, formulas, and so forth. Once the drill partners feel they have a good grasp of the information, we suggest that two drill teams get together for a "Drill and Grill" exercise.

Think–Pair–Share.   Lyman (1988) recommends that students sit with a partner during teacher-led minilessons to the class. After the teacher's presentation, the students review the information and try to use it to solve a problem given to the class by the teacher. Once they feel they have an answer to the problem, one of the students shares the pair's response during a class discussion.

Three-or-More Cooperative Learning Groups

Paper Chase Groups.   For paper chase groups, the teacher provides each group (three to four students) with a practice test for review purposes. Students divide the test into segments and distribute it to the paper chase group members. Each student carefully researches full answers for his part of the test, records notes and answers, and makes a photocopy of his notes for each group member. Finally, the group comes together to share what they have learned, discuss each group member's responses, and review the photocopied notes. When the process is complete, all students will have had a detailed discussion of the information and received full notes.

Paper chase groups have been successful even with students pursuing graduate education.

Focus Trios.   For focus trios, groups of three are formed before reading a chapter or portion of text to (a) summarize what they know and (b) develop pre-reading questions for which they would like to have answers. After reading, focus trios get together again to answer their original questions and add to that information other knowledge they have acquired. Students may be assigned to these groups by the teacher, may be randomly assigned, or may form social groups.

A good way to help students working in focus trios, or other similar configurations, is to teach them a strategy known as K-W-L (Ogle, 1986). Students organize their search for information according to *K*, "What do I already *know* about this topic?" *W*, "What do I *want* or need to know?" and *L*, "What did I *learn* from this experience?" To help students put the K-W-L strategy to work, many teachers create a type of worksheet like the one shown in Figure 4.7.

K-W-L is a great strategy, not only with cooperative learning groups, but also as a classroom teaching strategy used by teachers.

Group Reports.   Students conduct joint research on the chosen topic, with each student contributing at least one resource or reference to the project. Reports

Figure 4.7 K-W-L Groupsheet

K: *What do I already **know** about this topic?*

_____

_____

_____

W: *What do I **want** or need to know?*

_____

_____

_____

_____

L: *What did I **learn** from this experience?*

_____

_____

_____

_____

are written and presented jointly with all members having an equal part. The K-W-L groupsheet suggested earlier might be helpful in gathering information for group reports.

Group Retellings.   In a group retelling, each student reads a different book on the same topic of study. Group members then retell the major points made in the book and answer questions. Listeners can also add to each presentation any relevant information they learned in their own readings.

Interest Groups.   Usually applied in thematic units, students are placed into a group based on interest to investigate and report on a specific topic. For example, if a social studies class is learning about Italy, several groups may investigate such subtopics as Italian History: The Ancient Romans, Italian Cuisine, and Italian Art. After indicating their preferences on confidential ballots, students can be placed into interest-driven groups to research specific areas outlined by the teacher.

Pardo and Raphael (1991) offer an "Organizing Thinksheet" (see Figure 4.8), which may be helpful to interest groups. We have adapted it for classroom use and offer the following guidelines:

The Organizing Thinksheet can be quite useful in interest group studies.

1. Group members begin by brainstorming questions or topics they feel should be investigated. For example, a three-member group focusing on the Ancient Greeks might decide that some key areas of interest

(for them) are How the Olympic Games Were Started, Greek Gods, and Ancient Clothing.

2. Once the initial brainstorming has been completed, copies of the Organizing Thinksheet should be distributed (one for each group member). Each student chooses a topic, then group members help each other develop at least three questions related to their special topic. Let's say that one group member, Stacy, selects Ancient Clothing as her special topic. Through group discussion, they decide that three questions for which they would like answers are (a) What kinds of fabrics were used in ancient Greek clothing, and where did these fabrics come from? (b) How did teenagers in ancient Greece dress? and (c) How were summer clothes different from winter clothes?

3. Finally, students conduct research through the school library, interviews, and trips to relevant places (i.e., museums, in this particular

Figure 4.8 Organizing Thinksheet

Question 1: *How did the Olympic games get started?*

Question 2: *Who were some of the Greek gods and what were their special powers?*

Question 3: _____

Note. From "Classroom Organization for Instruction in Content Areas" by L. S. Pardo and T. E. Raphael, 1991, *Journal of Reading, 44*(8), pp. 556–565. Copyright 1991 by the International Reading Association. Reprinted by permission.

case) and complete the Organizing Thinksheet. Information gained through this process is shared and discussed at future group meetings.

Strategy or Concept Clarifiers.   When using strategy or concept clarifiers, as the name implies, students work together in small groups to review and clarify with each other new strategies or concepts introduced in class. It is helpful for teachers to have examples for student groups that may be used for practicing the new strategies or concepts after they have concluded their initial discussion.

Homework Check Groups.   Heterogeneous groups meet each day to review/share homework products, clarify information, and question each other regarding conclusions they have drawn. This has the dual benefit of facilitating deeper understanding and helping students get into the habit of completing assignments.

> Homework check groups are quite effective, but you may need to ask students to consider ways of making sure that all group members pull their own weight and come prepared each session.

Flexible Traveling Groups.   As content teachers add multiple learning stations to their classrooms, they may find it useful to group students into flexible traveling groups (Reutzel & Cooter, 1996) for managing rotation through the stations. Students work together on center activities and assignments as they rotate through. It is recommended that the groups stay together not longer than a month at a time before "shuffling."

CREATING POSITIVE CLASSROOM ENVIRONMENTS

There is an aspect of education that in some ways transcends the importance of books and curricula . . . the **classroom climate**. The way we organize our classrooms affects students' views of themselves as learners and has an impact on their attitudes toward learning and school (Routman, 1991). If the classroom climate or mood is friendly and open, then the learner is far more likely to take risks and participate. If, on the other hand, the classroom climate is closed (Harwood, 1991), such that the teacher uses authoritarian classroom management tactics regularly, then positive learning experiences may be nearly impossible. How does a teacher go about developing a positive classroom climate? Are there essential elements to be included? In this section we offer answers to these questions drawn from our own teaching experiences and the professional literature.

> A positive classroom climate is absolutely essential for optimum learning to occur.

Democratic Classroom Environments

The notion of **democratic classroom environments** has been a topic of discussion and debate for many decades. The publication of the book *Democracy and Education* by John Dewey in 1916 called for such progressive ideals as intellectual freedom for students, as well as free and equitable interaction.

> Respect for others' opinions is the chief cornerstone of building a positive classroom climate.

More recently, Angell (1991) studied democratic learning environments and compared writings in this area by such notable scholars as Dewey (1916/1966); Dreikurs, Grunwald, and Pepper (1971); and L. Kohlberg et al. (1975). There appears to be some agreement among these education scholars as to the development of democratic classroom climate including (a) peer interaction in cooperative activities, (b) free expression, (c) respect for diverse viewpoints, and (d) equal student participation in democratic deliberations and decision making (Angell, 1991, p. 249). Table 4.3 summarizes Angell's findings.

Angell concludes that in a democratic classroom environment "the teacher's primary role is to foster a cooperative spirit and to promote the development of shared values and authentic community life in the classroom" (1991, p. 248).

Democratic classes reflect the ideals on which democratic societies are based, namely, personal rights, responsibilities, and respect for self and others (Holmes, 1991). Students in a democratic classroom environment feel psychologically secure in school. This means feeling respected and being listened to, allowed some privacy, included when appropriate in the decision-making process, treated with fairness, and taught by caring and supportive teachers.

Democratic classrooms exemplify respect for self and others and the assumption of personal responsibility (Angell, 1991).

Table 4.3 Angell's (1991) Comparative Analysis of Democratic Learning Environments

Category: Social Climate

Dewey (1916/1966)	Dreikurs, Grunwald, and Pepper (1971)	L. Kohlberg (1975)
Intellectual freedom Open and equal interaction Numerous connections between the real world and the classroom	Students share responsibility for decision making in the classroom Both teachers and students have a voice in the classroom Students are encouraged to share their thoughts and opinions Differences are respected Collaborative relationships are seen as valuable Role playing is used to develop understandings	Students help govern the classroom community Both teachers and students have rights Group responsibility is encouraged Role playing and discussion are used to develop understandings

Open classroom environments (Harwood, 1991) are one manifestation of the democratic classroom philosophy. The use of the term *open* in this case means that students have an opportunity to participate in structuring the classroom environment and to discuss all sides of controversial topics. *Closed* systems, as mentioned earlier, rely on teacher direction and allow very little student participation in decision making.

Part of what makes adults want to get out of bed in the morning and go to work, or not, is the feeling that work can be stimulating. A great teacher once said "Whoever said that learning has to *seem* hard?" Although many things that must be learned are in fact difficult, a master teacher makes complex tasks seem easy and interesting.

Invigorating classroom designs are classroom arrangements that help teachers create a positive climate. Fulks (1985) states that invigorating classrooms reflect students' real-world interests and sometimes even include music, appropriate television, and movies. Students can pick up and manipulate a wide array of objects. Classrooms and hallways abound with mobiles, posters, art productions, displays, plants, and other connections to the real world. Invigorating classrooms make use of learning stations with movable space dividers, flexible seating arrangements, and portable chalkboards so that the classroom has a changing face throughout the year.

> Invigorating classrooms reflect in an appropriate way student interests and are often filled with stimulating sights and sounds.

Finally, Ann Shenkle (1988) suggests several simple questions and strategies teachers might consider at the start of a new year concerning classroom climate:

Questions for Teachers

- What kind of atmosphere do you want in your classroom?
- What is it that really matters to the students who come to learn here?
- How do you contribute to each student's development?

Strategies for Teachers Interested in Building a Positive Climate

- Hold individual conferences frequently, especially early in the school year. Look for strategies that help each student do his best work, and vary assignments according to each student's ability level.
- On student papers, insert stars on sections that need work, and give up red marks, F's, and zeros. Make all marks in pencil, and carry a pocket full of erasers. Don't grade a task until students have been allowed to make all revisions they wish.
- Provide plenty of time for students to make corrections.
- Let students know you believe in them by offering praise and individual encouragement.
- Show confidence in students by giving them classroom responsibilities at which they can succeed.

> Regular student–teacher conferences build a sense of open communication.

LEARNERS WITH SPECIAL NEEDS

Discussions about student behavior in content classes, a popular topic with both teachers and the general public, have tended to focus on so-called *assertive discipline* strategies. Assertive discipline strategies essentially seek to reward positive on-task behavior and punish negative off-task behavior. These assertive discipline strategies appear to have been a natural outgrowth of educational philosophies based on behaviorism psychology models, such as mastery learning, coupled with authoritarian views of the teacher's role. Although they have been attractive to many people anxious to cause adolescents to adopt adult standards of behavior and performance, assertive discipline strategies have simply not worked very well over time. This has been especially true of attempts to apply highly controlling and manipulative classroom management strategies to special-needs populations. Furthermore, teachers intending to create more holistic and interactive learning environments soon discover the incongruity of limiting student communications through assertive discipline strategies to allow the teacher center stage.

Fortunately, in recent years teacher-researchers have made significant advances in finding ways to improve student participation in content classes, particularly with students with learning problems. In some cases, researchers (Cutler & Stone, 1988; Loup et al., 1991; Tarver, 1986; C. Weaver, 1991) have addressed ways of inspiring positive student behavior with special-needs and behaviorally disordered students in holistic classrooms. We feel that these suggestions have great merit and can be helpful in engaging students, whether they have special learning needs or not.

Behaviors That Place Students at Risk in Content Classroom Settings

Before discussing specific strategies and interventions, it may be useful to briefly describe several conditions that seem to plague students with learning problems.

- *Academic underachievement.* Most students with learning problems have a significant history of low or poor achievement. Over time this creates impressions embedded in the student that she cannot succeed.
- *Lack of self-esteem and self-respect.* As a result of continued academic underachievement, many students suffer lowered self-esteem and loss of self-respect. The unacceptably high dropout rate among American students, particularly among minorities, is one manifestation of lowered self-esteem that severely limits students' life choices.
- *Limited conflict-resolution and problem-solving skills.* When confronted with such classroom-oriented conflicts as disagreements, differences of opinion, and challenges that require problem-solving skills, students with learning problems often flounder. These students often do not understand strategies for dealing with these situations, so they do not know where to begin.

Meadows (1994) suggests a few other factors that seem to confound students' attempts to deal with classroom challenges:

- *Dependent behavior.* Many students with learning problems develop the need for feedback and support from adults, rather than acting independently and accomplishing things on their own. Students who are more self-reliant find it easier to adapt to cooperative group and individual assignments, while the dependent student will require more support and assistance.
- *Perception of educators.* Many students with learning problems view teachers as fountains of information and feel their role is to passively absorb what is presented. Other students see the teacher as a guide who leads and stimulates their active learning. The latter view is essential in a holistic learning environment.

These and other factors must be addressed if a positive learning environment is to be achieved. In the remainder of this section, we present suggestions for teachers that can help overcome counterproductive behaviors of students with learning problems.

Ways Teachers Can Improve Student Participation in Content Classes

Teachers can improve chances for participation and success among students with learning problems by creating an atmosphere conducive for learning and by helping them develop needed strategies. Loup and colleagues (1991), in addressing ways progressive teachers develop a climate ripe for assessment and learning activities, state that the starting place is establishing a classroom climate of courtesy and respect. Warmth and friendliness are demonstrated throughout lessons, and comments to or about students are free of sarcasm, ridicule, and derogatory, demeaning, or humiliating references. Enthusiasm for teaching, learning, and the subject being taught must be communicated to students. The teacher should be perceived as fair and impartial in interactions with students and should provide students with reasons for teacher actions, decisions, or directives as needed.

Weaver (1991) has examined the benefits of holistic principles in meeting the needs of attention-deficit students and found that positive behaviors are encouraged by the sheer flexibility of holistic philosophy. Weaver has described explicit teacher behaviors and attitudes that are most successful. Our purpose in paraphrasing Weaver's findings here is not to display a depressing litany of superhuman traits that few (if any) can attain, but rather to give the reader a sense of the goals to which masterful content teachers aspire.

Holistic teachers tend to be particularly sensitive to the interests, abilities, and needs of their students, both collectively and individually (Weaver, 1991). They emphasize students' strengths, rather than shortcomings, a perspective

> Negative language must be avoided at all costs, especially when working with students with learning problems.

that is consistent with the notion of developmental learning (i.e., we improve at doing things the longer we do them).

Holistic teachers are alert for ways they can alleviate students' difficulties, usually by teaching them learning strategies, and work around their weaknesses. Worksheets, workbooks, and isolated skills work, which are extremely difficult and nonproductive for students with learning problems and most other students, are avoided. However, many opportunities are provided for students to choose learning experiences that are meaningful to them. Students are encouraged to think critically, creatively, and to engage in learning experiences that foster independence of thought and expression.

Holistic teachers allow and encourage a significant degree of mobility in the classroom to help students locate resources, confer with peers, and move from one learning station or area to another. The classroom is organized for collaborative learning activities, such as students working together on projects, sharing what they are reading and writing, and helping each other solve problems. Weaver also notes that holistic teachers tend to communicate frequently with parents, encouraging them to share their understanding of the child, to work together for the child's success, and even to participate actively in facilitating classroom learning experiences.

Finally, Cutler and Stone (1988) suggest intervention strategies that are often found in effective holistic programs for behaviorally disordered students. These include (a) offering consistent reminders of expectations, (b) counseling through disagreements with others, and (c) encouraging students to use language instead of body actions to achieve goals.

> Building learning sessions in ways that take advantage of students' strengths is a crucial strategy for successful content teachers and builds a sense of forward momentum.

CHAPTER SUMMARY

In this chapter we have considered how teacher beliefs about learning and teaching are reflected in the classroom environment. The classroom environment, or landscape, is made up of both physical and organizational factors. Physical features pertain to furniture, classroom work stations, wall spaces, banners, and how the general floor plan is established. Organizational factors pertain to such daily realities as scheduling routines and ways of structuring cooperative groups. The classroom mood, or climate, is another important environmental factor under the influence of the holistic content teacher. Specific ideas were presented that can have an effect on classroom climate. Finally, ideas were presented pertaining to helping learners with special needs to practice constructive behaviors.

Reflection/Application Activities

1. Assume you have been hired by a school district to teach in your subject specialty (choose your preferred grade level). Draw a sketch detailing what you feel would be an ideal classroom landscape (physical environment). Identify elements of your classroom landscape that support the way you would like to teach.

2. After obtaining the necessary permissions, visit either a middle or high school classroom and sketch the environment. If possible, obtain a copy from the teacher of his master schedule or a photocopy of the planbook for a typical week. Finally, observe at least two lessons in this classroom, interview the teacher to clarify what goes on in this classroom, then respond to the following (remember that this is only a limited observation and may not accurately reflect all important aspects of this teacher's environment):

   • What seem to be some of the teacher beliefs represented in this classroom environment?

   • Does the physical environment support the apparent beliefs of this teacher? Explain, using specific instances.

   • How would you describe the classroom climate? What seems to contribute to the climate?

3. Interview four students in content classes at a public or private school: two who excel and two considered to be students with learning problems. Ask them about how the class is run, and ask them to describe typical activities. In your discussions, try to discover to what extent students (a) are able to collaborate or take part in cooperative learning activities, (b) see themselves as successful in this content subject, (c) have the necessary tools for learning, and (d) experience a flexible environment. In a brief paper, contrast your discussions with the students with learning problems with those who excel. What seem to be the major differences in perceptions of the classroom environment?

Recommended Reading

Burns, M. (1992). *About teaching mathematics: A K–8 resource.* White Plains, NY: Math Solutions Publications. (Available from Cuisenaire Company of America, Inc., P.O. Box 5026, White Plains, NY 10602-5026)

Cutler, C., & Stone, E. (1988). A whole language approach: Teaching reading and writing to behaviorally disordered children. In M. Zabel (Ed.), *Behaviorally disordered youth* (vol. 4). Council for Children With Behavioral Disorders. (ERIC Document Reproduction Service No. ED 305 785)

Loup, K., et al. (1991). *The System for Teaching and Learning Assessment Review (STAR): A holistic classroom observation alternative to measures of student perceptions for research on classroom learning environments.* Paper presented at the annual meeting of the American Educational Research Association, Chicago. (ERIC Document Reproduction Service No. ED 335 756)

McWhirter, A. M. (1990). Whole language in the middle school. *The Reading Teacher, 43*(8), 562–565.

Pardo, L. S., & Raphael, T. E. (1991). Classroom organization for instruction in content areas. *Journal of Reading, 44*(8), 556–565.

Tarver, S. (1986). Cognitive behavior modification, direct instruction and holistic approaches to the education of students with learning disabilities. *Journal of Learning Disabilities, 19,* 368–375.

Weaver, C. (1991). *Alternatives in understanding and educating attention-deficit students: A systems-based whole language perspective.* National Council of Teachers of English, Urbana, IL. (ERIC Document Reproduction Service No. ED 337 755)

Wood, K. (1987). Fostering cooperative learning in middle and secondary level classrooms. *Journal of Reading, 31,* 10–18.

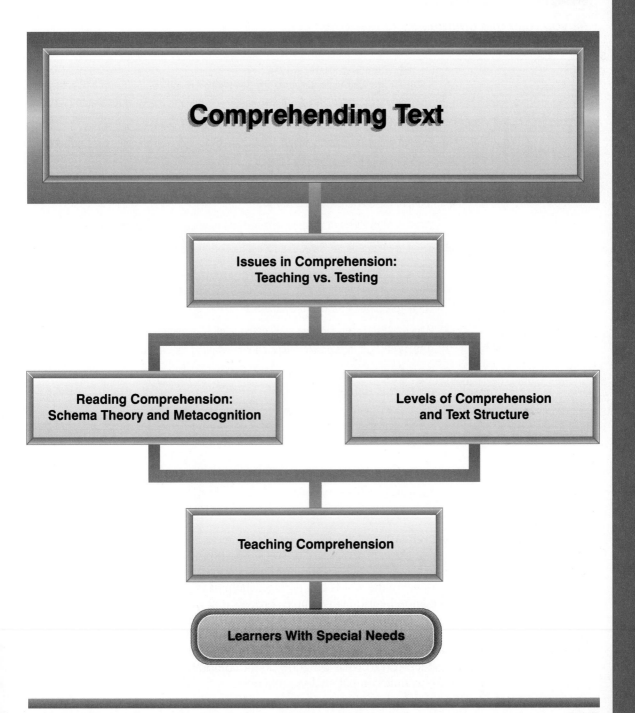

CHAPTER 5

Comprehending Text

Issues in Comprehension:
Teaching vs. Testing

Reading Comprehension:
Schema Theory and Metacognition

Levels of Comprehension
and Text Structure

Teaching Comprehension

Learners With Special Needs

Focus Questions

As you read this chapter, try to discover answers to the following questions:

1 Summarize schema theory and how it explains the kind of mental scaffolding constructed by the brain. What are some instructional implications for teachers that may be drawn from understanding schema theory?

2 Explain the term metacognition. What can teachers do to help students develop useful metacognitive behaviors?

3 What are the instructional implications suggested by the zone of proximal development in the content area classroom?

4 What are the levels of comprehension, and how can one describe them?

5 What are some of the keys to successful comprehension instruction in the content area classroom?

6 How has the constructivist's view of comprehension instruction changed the traditional role of the content area teacher?

7 Why can PReP and KWL be considered student-centered and metacognitive strategies? Which of the two strategies can be adapted for your content area? How?

8 What does the acronym QARs refer to? What is the procedure for teaching students about QARs?

> Reading furnishes our mind only with materials of knowledge; it is thinking that makes what we read ours.
>
> John Locke (quoted in Brussell, 1970)

Before you begin reading, what does the term *reading comprehension* mean to you?

Comprehension of what one reads is the most important aspect of the reading process. As such, it is one of the most heavily researched. Although it was once commonly held that comprehension occurred as a by-product of accurately pronouncing the words in a passage, the past two decades of research suggest that comprehension is a complex process that relies on the interactions among the reader, the text, the teacher, and the educational setting. The ways and means of improving the interaction among these factors are woven throughout this text. For the purposes of this chapter, we use these factors as vehicles to introduce you to what we know about comprehension and how to help students become competent comprehenders.

ISSUES IN CONTENT READING COMPREHENSION

Picture yourself sitting at a desk with an open textbook in your hands. You are reading an assignment for school. Suddenly you stop, look up, and realize that you don't know anything about what you have been reading for the past 10 minutes. What caused this less than rare occurrence? What can be done about it?

We contend that a lot can be done about this scenario. We believe that teachers can equip students with the knowledge, strategies, and perspectives necessary to become strategic comprehenders. In this section, we begin by discussing the issue of teaching versus testing comprehension and then conclude with the issue of whether it is possible to teach someone how to think and comprehend.

Classroom Practice: Teaching Versus Testing

Picture yourself standing in front of a class of students. You've run out of time, so you've decided to make a reading assignment to discuss. You assign the following excerpt (Flynt & Cooter, 1995) to be read, and you are planning to ask the two questions that follow the passage.

> The most significant limitation in an optical communications system is the attenuation of the optical signal as it goes through the fiber. As information in the light is sent down the fiber, the light is attenuated, often called insertion loss, which is due to Rayleigh scattering. Rayleigh scattering refers to the fact that, as a pulse of light is sent down a fiber, part of the pulse gets blocked by microscopic particles, called dopants, in the glass and gets scattered in all directions.
>
> 1. Explain what Rayleigh scattering means.
> 2. What are dopants, and what do they do in fiber-optic cable?

What's the difference between teaching comprehension and testing comprehension?

After the students have completed reading the excerpt, you ask selected students the two questions. One student answers correctly, and the other one doesn't. What has happened in this setting? Basically, you have assessed whether comprehension has occurred. For one student it did, and the other it didn't. What do you do for the unanswered question? You either ask other students until you get the answer you seek, or you provide the answer. The net result being that the answer is heard.

Now consider the same scenario with a twist. First, before students read the passage, you provide background information about optic fiber, its uses, and the fact that it often has to be repaired. You even have a demonstration. Then before the reading begins, you establish specific purposes for reading the selection. Finally, you begin your questioning by having someone summarize what the selection was about and how it related to your purposes for reading.

The difference should be obvious. In the first setting, the teacher only assessed whether comprehension occurred, while in the latter the teacher made specific attempts at increasing the likelihood that students would understand the passage and be able to respond during follow-up discussion. The point should be well taken by practitioners that teaching students how to comprehend is as important as, if not more than, finding out if they did comprehend.

Is It Possible to Teach Someone How to Think and Comprehend?

What are ways teachers can assist students in the comprehension of what they read?

Although the answer to the question "Is it possible to teach someone how to think and comprehend?" depends on who you ask, for us its answer is a qualified yes. As Flood and Lapp (1990) suggested, whether or not comprehension can be taught depends on who you're talking about, what kind of text is being read, for what purpose, and under what conditions. Nevertheless, the past two decades have provided a great deal of insight into how to assist students in the comprehension of text. In a recent synthesis of research about comprehension instruction (Fielding & Pearson, 1994), the four variables most likely to affect a student's comprehension competence included (a) providing significant time periods for actual text reading; (b) teaching specific comprehension strategies; (c) providing opportunities for peer collaboration; and (d) allowing time for students to talk about their responses to reading. These four variables reflect a significant move away from the fragmented subskills approach of the past: Students were taught a myriad of specific skills such as reading for details, reading for following directions, and reading for cause and effect. This shift toward a constructivist view of comprehension supports the idea that the reader, not the text, is the meaning maker. This constructivist view calls for readers to take control of their learning with the teacher supplying support and direction as needed. It embraces the idea of the term **grand conversations** (Eeds & Wells, 1989; Peterson & Eeds, 1990), during which teachers and students are coequals in discussion of passages read rather than on one side or another of an inquisition.

How does the constructivist view differ from the traditional subskills approach?

The remainder of this chapter addresses specific aspects of comprehension and ways of teaching comprehension. This chapter is only an introduction to the topic of comprehension; we will continue to expand on this topic in subsequent chapters. The real issue that this chapter posits is not whether comprehension can be taught but rather, Are you willing to take the instructional measures that are necessary to teach your students how to comprehend?

ASPECTS OF READING COMPREHENSION

Schema Theory

Schemata organize the ever-changing prior knowledge stored in your brain.

Cognition has to do with the ability of the human mind to accumulate, understand, and apply new knowledge. In this century, cognition has been explained by such researchers as Jean Piaget (1955) and Sir Frederick Bartlett (1932) through something known as **schema theory** (Ruddell, 1993). We feel that schema theory is the central construct around which great teaching can be developed. Piaget, whose writings on the subject began to appear in the late 1920s, described schemata, or schemas (both plural for *schema*), as cognitive structures or networks constructed by the brain to organize and add new information to what a person already knows. Schema theory suggests that new learning is built on or added to past experiences by moving from concrete experiences, hands-on experiences encountered in daily living, to the addition of abstract knowledge. A simpler way of saying this is that we progress from the *known* to the *new*. A case in point might illuminate this idea.

Having moved from the sunny South to a northern climate, I awoke one morning to an 8-inch snowfall. My experience (based on the southern inability to deal with snow) told me that today was a day off. I could ease back with some coffee and enjoy, with my children, all the white that was enveloping my home. No one gets out in the snow. To my surprise later that morning, I received a phone call from work and the local school. Both wanted to know what was wrong and why I wasn't at work and why my child was absent from school. Needless to say, I was too embarrassed to admit that I had no idea that people actually drove in snow so deep. At that instant my schema (knowledge base) for snow was changed for all time.

Schema theory offers some explanations about how people acquire new information. First, information is organized in the brain through a kind of systematic framework or scaffolding. When a new piece of information is presented to the brain that fits with what is already known, permanent learning is possible. Second, the brain seeks out and selects information to add to what is already known. This results in greater depth of knowledge, a kind of knowledge evolution or schema expansion. Finally, schema theory suggests that, as these knowledge networks are formed, related concepts become interconnected. Put simply, the more one knows about a topic, the more one will be able to comprehend; and the more one comprehends (reads), the more one learns new information about the topic. Thus, the schemata of your students are among the most important individual differences that must be addressed to enhance their comprehension of text.

As an example of schema theory at work, consider a student named Ross who is taking a basic course in automobile mechanics. The objectives of the course may include such things as how internal combustion engines work, basic maintenance of cars, and other related information. For Ross, his exposure to the world of automobiles is limited to being a passenger in the family car and observing routine tasks performed by most drivers (e.g., cleaning the car, fueling, trips to the service garage). Ross has developed a schema, or knowledge network, for each of these basic experiences. Figure 5.1 graphically portrays some of Ross's car schema. We call a graphic representation of what a student knows a **schema map**.

At this point the teacher of automobile mechanics, Ms. Hildebrand, enters the story. Assume that Ms. Hildebrand learns, through her preteaching class assessment, that her students have a knowledge of automobiles similar to

How do a student's schemata impact on her ability to learn what you teach?

Identify a topic or event that you have a schema of and think about what you would have to do to expand that schema.

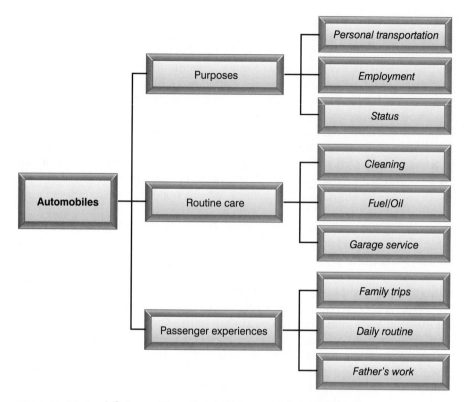

Figure 5.1   A Schema Map: Ross's Schema of Automobiles

Ross's. By contrasting the outline of her curriculum with what students say they know, Ms. Hildebrand establishes teaching goals for the present and the future. Rather than be redundant, she will build her teaching on what students already know. So, for the topic of routine car care, Ms. Hildebrand decides that she will need to add the following to her students' schemata:

- Automobile oil should be changed every 3,000 miles and reasons why this is a good idea
- Information about the thickness or viscosity and when to use different weights of oil
- The value and problems of using oil additives
- How to efficiently change the oil and filter in their own cars

It is through activities that assess students' existing knowledge that teachers can gain a better understanding of what their students need to learn and how best to assist them in learning it.

Metacognition: Knowing What You Know

Remember the example at the beginning of this chapter? You have been reading for a period of time and suddenly realize that you don't remember a thing about what you were just reading. Actively thinking about what you are learning is one example of a self-monitoring behavior known as **metacognition**. Skilled readers develop the ability to monitor their comprehension as they bring meaning to the content material they are reading. For instance, effective readers go back and reread lost sections where their minds have wandered—a metacognitive strategy that enhances comprehension. Similarly, students with good background knowledge (schema) of a subject are aware of writing patterns commonly used in text materials (how the information is being presented) and can use metacognitive strategies to predict and better understand the author's message. Metacognition and associated strategies are the subject of this section.

In what ways do you monitor your comprehension when you read?

Metacognitive Awareness and Its Effect on Learning

Metacognitive strategies help readers to monitor their own learning processes and exercise some control over those processes (Lapp, Flood, & Farnam, 1989; Mason & Au, 1990). In studies of middle school students (Garner & Reis, 1981; Garner, Wagoner, & Smith, 1983), it was determined that students who are good comprehenders were aware of their purposes for reading, could detect failures in their understanding of texts, and could take appropriate action to correct comprehension failures.

Metacognition has several key aspects that seem to be especially relevant when applied to successful reading (Alexander & Heathington, 1988; Flavell, 1981). First is the ability to clearly define learning goals—the student knows what he is looking for. Second is an awareness of the metacognitive abilities one possesses (skills, strategies, resources) to perform a given learning task. Third is the ability to conduct a kind of metacognitive assessment to determine which strategies will be required to do a given task. Fourth is the ability to put all of these together and use self-regulatory mechanisms (cognitive actions, checking, planning, revising, evaluating) to achieve the learning goals. A. L. Brown (1980), who has written extensively on this subject, describes reading skills and behaviors involved in metacognition. Brown's findings subsume those just mentioned and include one or two others:

What are some important aspects of metacognition that apply to successful reading?

1. Clearly understanding one's purposes for reading and knowing the explicit and implicit demands of a given learning task
2. Being able to identify the important parts of a message in a text
3. Monitoring as one reads to make sure comprehension is taking place
4. Engaging in self-questioning to make sure purposes for reading are being met

Which of Brown's (1980) metacognitive skills/behaviors do you think are important enough to teach to students in a content area?

5. Taking corrective action (i.e., rereading) when comprehension is not occurring
6. Recovering from distractions and disruptions and staying on task

Metacognition skills can be taught systematically (Armbruster & Brown, 1984) to help readers become better comprehenders. We feel that it is advantageous for teachers to make students aware of metacognitive strategies because they can assist their students in moving toward a more active role in acquiring new knowledge and developing learning independence.

The Zone of Proximal Development

What is the ZPD?

In conjunction with schema theory and metacognition, both of which are influenced by the interactions of the reader, teacher, text, and educational setting, another notion that has been advanced as a consideration for improving instruction has been the **zone of proximal development (ZPD)**. Originally conceived by Lev Vygotsky (1978), a Russian psychologist, the ZPD is defined as the difference between what a student can do alone versus in collaboration with others. This idea suggests that whenever people learn a new skill or ability they go through predictable developmental stages or degrees of skill. At first they usually require assistance from someone more expert in the skill. Over time, and given appropriate instruction, one progresses from a stage of requiring assistance to a point of independence. As Frank Smith (1988, pp. 196–197) has stated, "what (students) can do with collaboration on one occasion they will be able to do independently on another."

The ZPD is easy to imagine with physical skills. When one learns to play tennis, one usually requires the assistance of a coach who can demonstrate the basics. The student then attempts to approximate the skillful tennis behaviors demonstrated by the coach. Over time the coach is needed less as fundamental skills are learned. Behaviors that require a great deal of attention from a teacher or peer at the beginning of learning (this is the student's ZPD), such as serving the ball and hitting a backhand return, eventually become automatic for the student. When skills are learned and students can do them independently, they have become part of the student's permanent learning or schema structures. At this point newer ZPDs form that can raise learning to higher levels of sophistication or skill. That is how a person like Bjorn Borg progressed from a beginner to a Wimbledon tennis champion.

How does the ZPD apply in your content specialty?

This same pattern of development happens with the process of teaching/learning content subjects. For example, let's say that Mr. Stevens, who is a teacher of economics, is helping one of his students, Melinda, understand how to compute exchange rates for U.S. currency. As a starting point, they focus on British pounds as compared to the dollar. The first several times, Melinda may require some collaborative help computing dollars to pounds, either from Mr. Stevens or another student. But over time and with assistance,

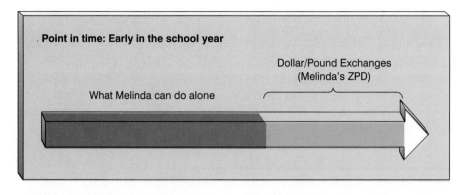

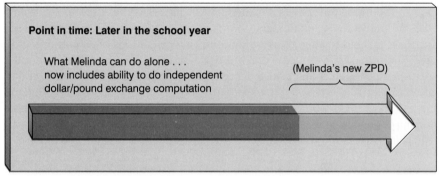

Figure 5.2 Melinda's Development of Pound/Dollar Exchange Computation Ability

Melinda will catch on and soon be able to do the task alone. In Figure 5.2 we illustrate this application of the ZPD.

Note that in Figure 5.2 Melinda eventually adds the ability to compute pound/dollar conversions to her permanent schemata and can do the task independently. Also note that a new ZPD is created. That means that there may be a new ability, say anticipating rising and falling pound/dollar values, that may require assistance at first, but that Melinda will be able to do independently at some later point. This is a reflection of changing and growing schema structures.

The ZPD strongly suggests that the teacher's role changes over time. In the beginning, the teacher must explain and model the skill or task at hand. In modeling, the teacher takes the lead and supports the student as he attempts to use new information. Research (Bandura, 1987) has shown that modeling accomplishes much more than simply showing students what the new skill looks like when used by the teacher. Students often pick up a number of related and useful behaviors (incidental learning) while observing teachers model specific strategies or skills. As teachers' services are needed less and less, students assume more and more responsibility for their own learning. As you have probably figured out, the ZPD is one of the driving forces for promoting more student collaboration in the classroom. Indeed, cooperative learning and reciprocal teaching are outgrowths of the knowledge we now have about schema theory, metacognition, and the ZPD.

In the next section of this chapter, we continue to build a foundation about comprehension by introducing you to the levels of comprehension and the structure of text. We then conclude the chapter by demonstrating some specific applications of teaching students about how to comprehend.

LEVELS OF COMPREHENSION AND TEXT STRUCTURE

Using good questioning techniques is important in the content areas.

One of the most universal of all teaching techniques is the use of questioning. Questioning in the content classroom is often used to guide students toward specific types of learning, to assist students' interpretations of an author's message, and to facilitate student-centered discussions. Although using questioning seems easy enough at first glance, it has become apparent that teachers need to be conscious of the types of questions that best promote desired learning and that students need a heightened awareness of the types of questions, the relationship between questions and their answers, and assistance in determining plausible responses to both teacher-, text-, and student-generated questions.

Student-centered class discussions promote thinking skills.

Levels of Comprehension

A number of taxonomies are available (Barrett, 1972; Pearson & Johnson, 1978) that detail the various skills associated with comprehension. These taxonomies certainly have a place in teacher education courses to study question types; however, most reading professionals favor a simpler and more direct approach to questioning by using what is widely known as the **three levels of comprehension**. As an introduction to these levels of comprehension, read the following passage and answer each question that follows it.

> A diamond is one of the most beautiful treasures that nature ever created, and one of the rarest. It takes thousands of years for nature to transform a chunk of carbon into a rough diamond. Only three important diamond fields have been found in the world—India, South America, and Africa.
>
> Gem diamonds are found deep in the earth's surface. The rock in which diamonds are found is called "blue ground." Yet even where diamonds are plentiful, it takes digging and sorting through tons of rock and gravel to find enough diamonds for a one-carat ring. Gem diamonds' quality is based on weight, purity, color, and cut. The weight of a diamond is measured by the carat. Its purity is determined by the presence or absence of impurities. The color of a diamond varies, but most diamonds are tinged yellow or brown. The cut of a diamond also figures into its value. Facets, or sides, cause the brilliance that is produced when a diamond is struck by light.

1. Where are the most important diamond fields found?
2. What information in the passage supports the idea that diamonds are rare?
3. How do you suppose jewelers distinguish between real and fake diamonds?

What is different about the answers to these three questions?

By examining your responses to each question, we should be able to demonstrate the three levels of comprehension. Certainly, the first question requires you to recall or locate directly stated facts in the passage. We term this level as the **textually explicit level** of comprehension. It is sometimes overused by teachers, and we recommend that this level not be used as a purpose for reading. The second question differs from the first because the reader is required to interpret information. This level we refer to as the **textually implicit level** of comprehension. The reader is required to infer about what was said by the author. Sometimes the inferences are clear, and students converge on the same response. At other times acceptable inferences students may make can be divergent. The point is, Are student responses plausible and based on information in the passage? Finally, the last question requires you to make a judgment based on your prior knowledge coupled with information

Define the three levels of comprehension.

Figure 5.3 Three Levels of Comprehension

Level	Requires Reader To:
Textually explicit or literal	Find or recall directly stated information.
Textually implicit or interpretation	Translate or determine what are the implications of what has been read.
Schema-based or critical reading	Make judgments, problem solve, or apply the information read.

presented in the passage. This level is called the **schema-based level** of comprehension. At this level, the students draw heavily on their prior knowledge. The responses to these questions will vary depending on each student's experiences, perceptions, and values. Figure 5.3 details the three levels of comprehension and what is required of the reader to respond at each level.

Text Structure

Discourse analysis is the analysis and classification of the way an author organizes her writing.

To communicate effectively, writers write in specific ways. Whether the writer is trying to involve the reader emotionally in a scene in a novel or relay a specific set of instructions in a home economics book, she structures her sentences and paragraphs in such a way as to enhance the likelihood that she will be understood. In recent years, the analysis and classification of the way an author presents or organizes her writing, often called **discourse analysis**, have resulted in the identification of specific writing patterns that can be used to help students comprehend text material. Broadly speaking, the five major forms of discourse are explanation, classification, description, narration, and argument. It is recommended that students be alerted or caused to recognize the major form of discourse before detailed reading (Catterson, 1979). To complete our discussion of text structure, we have divided the major forms of discourse into the two broad categories of narrative text (stories) and expository text (textbooks). We address each separately.

Structure of Stories

What is the difference between narrative text and expository text?

Most, if not all, of the stories you have read have been predictable because of the manner in which they were written. This predictable pattern, often referred to as *story elements,* consists of plot, setting, character, theme, and point of view. Because it has been demonstrated that knowledge of these story elements improves students' comprehension of stories (Spiegel & Fitzgerald, 1986; Tompkins & McGee, 1989), it follows that students should receive direct instruction about the elements that make a story a story.

How can you explain plot structure?

Plot refers to the series of events involving conflict that characters encounter across the story. During the introduction to a story, the author presents her characters, setting, and at least one problem. As the story develops, the author introduces conflict to help keep the reader interested. This middle portion of the story is typically filled with challenges to the main characters as they attempt to solve their problem(s). Attempts to solve their problems reach a climax during the latter part of the story. Finally, at the end of the story, often referred to as *resolution,* the reader finds out how the problem(s) of the characters are resolved.

Setting refers to time and location during the story. It can be integral to the story or insignificant, depending on the story line. One should think of the setting as analogous to scenes in movies. *Characters* are the people or animals who the story is about. Characters can be analyzed according to what they say, how they look, and what they do.

Theme refers to the overall message of the story. Generally, the theme of a story speaks to "universal truths" about life or human nature.

Point of view refers to how the author tells his story. Typically, the author chooses one of four viewpoints. *First-person* point of view requires the author to select one character and tell the story from that character's "I" by using the character's feelings, thoughts, and actions. The *omniscient* point of view permits the author to be all knowing and to tell the story in the third person, using words such as *they, he,* or *she.* An author uses the *limited omniscient* point of view when he wants to focus on one character but still wants to be all knowing about other characters. Finally, an author chooses the *objective* point of view when he just wants to reveal what is said and done by characters without explaining the characters' motives or feelings.

What are the main elements that make up most stories?

All of these elements of stories are often known intuitively by students, but we advocate that this knowledge be raised to a conscious level through meaningful writing and reading activities. We address such activities in Chapters 7 and 8.

Expository Paragraph Organization

Just as stories are written with certain elements, content textbooks are also written in specific organizational patterns. For expository writing to be easier to comprehend, excellent writers present their information in an organized manner that allows the readers to recognize what's important and how the important information is being explained. In the field of reading, we have come to recognize over 12 different types of paragraphs used by textbook authors. However, we have chosen to discuss only 10 basic patterns found in textbooks because of their prevalence.

1. *Introductory.* These types of paragraphs appear at the beginning of chapters or major subsections. Often a preview of what is going to be discussed is presented. This paragraph provides the reader with information about what is to come, thus building a mind-set for reading.
2. *Definition.* This is commonly used by authors to define or explain technical terms and concepts. The focus of these paragraphs is usually

Which of these paragraph types are common to your content area's textbooks?

printed in italics or boldface to highlight its importance to the meaning of the topic being read.

3. *Illustrative.*   These paragraphs attempt to use examples, analogies, or illustrations to make a complex idea more understandable.

4. *Main ideas and supporting details.*   These paragraphs have a stated topic sentence or implied main idea, while the remainder of the paragraph supports the topic sentence or implied main idea. This is the most common type of paragraph structure but can still cause students difficulty.

5. *Comparison and contrast.*   These paragraphs focus on describing how ideas, people, or events are alike and different. Often the words *compare* and *contrast* or *similar* and *different* are used in these paragraphs.

6. *Cause and effect.*   These types of paragraphs are organized so that the relationships between events and results are revealed, often implicitly.

7. *Chronological order.*   These paragraphs present information sequentially across time, so that the reader knows what came before and after.

8. *Descriptive.*   These paragraphs attempt to describe an idea, event, or object so that the reader gets a mental picture. Often a single object, event, or idea is identified and described.

9. *Problem and solution.*   These paragraphs often present a problem and then discuss solutions for the remainder of the paragraph.

10. *Summary.*   These paragraphs appear at the end of sections or chapters and often contain the major ideas or concepts discussed in the section or chapter. If well written, these paragraphs contain vital information.

How can knowledge of the various paragraph types be of benefit to students?

Obviously, within a single chapter in a textbook, an author will use an assortment of paragraph types. At this point we want you to recognize that knowing about these types of paragraphs and how they relate to the content area you will be teaching is important. It is important because with this knowledge you can alert students to how information is being presented to facilitate their comprehension, and you can use this information to help generate discussion and questions to be answered.

TEACHING COMPREHENSION IN CONTENT SUBJECTS

Earlier in this chapter, we raised the question of whether it is possible to teach someone how to comprehend. We answered the question with a qualified yes. In this section we introduce you to some specific ways of assisting, motivating, and causing students to comprehend your text more effectively. These initial activities and ideas will form the basis for additional techniques and strategies addressed in later chapters that are designed to help students learn and remember text information.

Before-Reading Strategies

Before being asked to read in their textbooks, students should always be prepared for the reading assignment by providing and/or activating their prior knowledge about the topic. This can take many forms, but typically it involves a teacher–student discussion about or reaction to the topic to be read. Two simple, yet effective, techniques that can be used by the content teacher are PReP (Langer, 1981) and K-W-L (Ogle, 1986). We discuss each of these separately.

PReP (Prereading Plan)

The Prereading Plan (PReP) strategy by Langer (1981) helps determine and activate the prior knowledge of students through three stages. The first stage uses a question to determine any associations students might have with a topic, concept, or term to be studied. These initial associations provide a teacher insights into how much prior knowledge exists in the class and helps students to begin building concept-related associations about the topic. For example, in teaching a lesson about the American Civil War, you might start off by asking your class "What kinds of things do you think of when you hear the words *American Civil War?*" After writing down students' initial associations, the next step is to have students reflect on their initial associations.

During the reflection stage, your goal is to have students discuss and explain why the associations they had about the topic came to mind. "What made you think of . . . ?" This interactive stage develops prior knowledge, builds a common network of ideas about the topic, and allows students to interact in a student-centered discussion.

The last stage of PReP is called *reformulation of knowledge.* Basically, your goal now is to have students recognize and refine what they know about the topic before they begin to study it. For example, students are encouraged to respond to the question "Do you have any new ideas or information about the American Civil War?"

Teachers we know who have tried this simple strategy have suggested that it does help prepare and motivate students for text reading.

Can PReP be adapted for use with printed materials in your content area? How?

K-W-L

The **K-W-L** technique, developed by Ogle (1986), promotes student awareness of what they already *know (K)* about a topic, provides an avenue for students to decide what they *want* to know about a topic *(W)*, and finally, allows students to explicitly determine what they *learned (L)* as they read about the designated topic. Typically, K-W-L begins by the teacher providing a chart on the board or an overhead that identifies the preceding three categories. Then, beginning with the "What do you already know?" column, the teacher ascertains what students think is important and the extent of their prior knowledge.

Which part of a K-W-L session can be the most challenging? Why?

Following the listing of the student-volunteered information in the *K* column, the teacher initiates a discussion about "What do you want to know?" about the topic under discussion. Based on our experiences, this stage is the most difficult to guide. We suggest that the teacher suggest, cajole, and probe in such a way that students suggest things that are conceptually relevant and important. After establishing questions or purposes for reading about the topic, the students read the text selection. An immediate follow-up discussion ensues in which the students reveal what they learned about the topic. This information is written under the *L* column. Some teachers then discuss questions unanswered by the text and assist students in distinguishng relevant information they discovered from irrelevant information. See Figure 5.4 for an example of a student-generated K-W-L chart on the topic of the Oregon trail.

Figure 5.4   Student-Generated K-W-L Chart

What I Know	What I Want to Know	What I Have Learned
•Wagons rode on the trail all of the time	•Did anybody die going on the trail?	1. 1 out of 10 people died on the trail.
•The Oregon Trail crosses through the state of Kansas	•What were some of the reasons for going?	2. People went for a better life and to own land.
•Families mainly traveled together on the Oregon Trail.	•How did the people die?	3. People died of exhaustion or starvation or snake bites.
•They used oxen to pull their wagons down the Oregon Trail.	•If the people ran out of food, what would they eat so they would not starve?	4. So they would not starve they ate shoes and dead people.
	•Did they have clean water to drink and if not, did they die from it?	5. They had to clean insects out of the water as best they could. Sometimes they would get sick because they drank the water.
		6. A lot of people drowned in bodies of water in the desert.
		7. There was a big disease called cholera that killed a lot of people.
		8. A lot of people walked the trail because a wagon did not hold much weight.
		9. The most common animals used on the trail were oxen but some used mules.
		10. Most wagons had 3 yoke of oxen to pull the weight without much water or food.

Developed by Jennifer Hale.

The K-W-L strategy can be adapted in a variety of ways. It can be done with the whole class, small group, or individuals, depending on the capability of the students you teach. One important thing to remember is that students benefit from sharing information. This verbalizing of what they now know about a topic is, according to Pauk (1974), one of the most powerful learning techniques we have.

During- and After-Reading Practices

For the purposes of this chapter, we introduce a couple of strategies that focus on developing metacognitive behaviors among students as they read and respond to what they have read. As recommended by Fielding and Pearson (1994), these strategies begin as teacher directed with the hopes of students' acquiring ownership of them, and they provide opportunities for peer collaboration and sharing. The first strategy has to do with the three levels of comprehension introduced earlier in this chapter and is called Question-Answer Relationships (QARs) (Raphael, 1984, 1986).

Question-Answer Relationships

QARs is a technique that has been demonstrated to enhance students' comprehension and promote independent comprehension processing (Raphael 1984, 1986). QARs' purpose is to teach students directly about the three levels of comprehension described earlier in this chapter. Specifically, students learn about the types of questions and what is required cognitively to respond to each type. Rather than use esoteric terms such as *textually explicit,* QARs use the following concrete, student-oriented labels to describe the relationship between questions and their answers. For the textually explicit level, the label is *Right There.* The textually implicit level is called *Think and Search.* And the schema-based level is referred to as either *Author and You* or *On Your Own.* Figure 5.5 provides an example of each QAR.

What does the acronym QARs stand for?

The recommended procedure for using QARs in the classroom is as follows:

Why is QAR training considered a metacognitive strategy?

1. Using a text selection, the teacher provides questions, answers to the questions, and the appropriate QAR label. Through discussion and explanation, the students are taught what makes a "right there" question and answer and so forth until each type of QAR has been modeled.
2. Next, the teacher provides a text passage that has the questions and answers but not the QARs. The students are encouraged to determine the relationship between the question and the answer and to identify each QAR. This may take more than one session depending on age and proficiency.
3. Once students demonstrate that they have the idea, the teacher then provides a selection with only questions. The students are asked to answer each question and label the QAR.

Figure 5.5   QARs Examples

1. One of the most important technological advances in recent years has been the advent of fiber-optic communications. Whether an on-line computer system or an interactive television network, fiber optics are already a part of most Americans' lives. Because it will continue to replace much of what we use to communicate, it is important for people to understand as much as possible about fiber-optic communications.

   Question: What is one of the most important technological advances made in communications in recent years?

   Answer: Fiber optics

   QARS: Right There

   Explanation: This type of answer is called a Right There type because it is easy to find and the words in the text are similar to the ones in the question.

2. Fiber optic communication is simple: An electrical signal is converted to light which is transmitted through an optical fiber to a distant receiver, where it is converted back into the original electrical signal. The advantages of fiber optic communications over other transmission methods are substantial. A signal can be sent over longer distances without being boosted, and there are no interference problems from nearby electrical fields. Additionally, its capacity is far greater than for copper or coax cable systems, and the fiber itself is much lighter and smaller than copper systems. Notwithstanding these advantages, fiber-optic communications are not problem free.

   Question: What are some of the limitations of traditional ways of transmitting electrical signals?

   Answer: Traditional communications' signals must be boosted over long distances and can't handle as many signals at one time. They also can be affected by electrical sources.

   QARS: Think and Search

4. Finally, students are provided a selection and are asked to design questions whose answers are examples of each QAR. They can exchange papers for application and feedback.

Teachers should consistently reinforce the notion of QARs across the school year. This strategy has been shown to increase students' comprehension of text more than some other questioning strategies (Jenkins & Lawler, 1990).

Reciprocal Teaching

The next strategy we recommend that promotes comprehension of text is termed **reciprocal teaching** (Palincsar & Brown, 1986). Designed to promote independent learning from text, reciprocal teaching capitalizes on the ideas of teacher modeling, student interaction, and collaboration—in short—using the zone of proximal development.

Figure 5.5 continued

Explanation: The answer is suggested but not explicitly stated in the text. Students must infer that the things that give fiber optics an advantage conversely are disadvantages of other forms of communication transmission.

3. The most significant limitation in an optical communications system is the attenuation of the optical signal as it goes through the fiber. As information in the light is sent down the fiber, the light is attenuated, often called insertion loss, which is due to Rayleigh scattering. *Rayleigh scattering* refers to the fact that as a pulse of light is sent down a fiber, part of the pulse gets blocked by microscopic particles, called *dopants*, in the glass and gets scattered in all directions. Some of the light is scattered back in the opposite direction of the pulse and is called the *backscatter*. Since dopants in optical fiber are uniformly distributed throughout the fiber as a result of the way it is made, the Rayleigh scattering effect is like shining a flashlight in a fog at night; the light beam gets diffused, or scattered, by the particles of moisture.

   Question: What would happen to the information in an optic fiber if all of the light was reflected?

   Answer: The communication would not take place because the signal would not reach its destination.

   QARS: Author and You

4. Another type of light loss in optic fiber communications is called *Fresnel Reflection.* Whenever light traveling in a material, such as optic fiber, encounters a different density material, such as air, some of the light is reflected back toward the light source while the rest continues out of the material.

   Question: Describe a common experience that is similar to Fresnel reflection.

   Answer: Shining a flashlight at a window at night.

   QARS: On Your Own

Reciprocal teaching has evolved into many different forms over the years, but the fundamental comprehension processes that are developed include predicting, questioning, summarizing, and clarifying. Other critical ingredients include the teacher modeling all the processes before letting students become "the teacher" and that all reading should use relevant material.

In general, the teacher first has students read a paragraph or two of text. Next, the teacher summarizes the information and asks several questions about what was summarized. If students didn't understand some concept or answered incompletely, the teacher clarifies any misunderstandings. The teacher then asks students to write or volunteer predictions about what will be in the next paragraph or two. When the next segment of text is read, the roles are reversed, and students volunteer to become the teacher.

What is the sequence for conducting a reciprocal teaching session?

As students become more proficient at "being the teacher," the teacher becomes less in control and allows students to reciprocally teach each other. This could mean in a whole class setting or in dyads (pairs). For those of you who try reciprocal teaching, don't expect immediate success. More often than not, the classroom teacher has to model the four processes, explain specifically what she is doing and why, and observe how much assistance students will need to be able to engage in the four processes this strategy employs.

Questions and Questioning

What are the prerequisites for effective questioning?

Besides the strategies discussed in this chapter, your questioning technique can also assist students in more fully comprehending text material. Questions and the subsequent teacher–student interaction are hallmarks of good teaching and very important to any teacher's repertoire. Indeed, through the kinds of questions you ask and the manner in which you ask them, you are providing students with a method for determining what is and isn't important to know and think about in relation to a given topic. There are several prerequisites to the use of questioning in the classroom: (a) Students must feel they can volunteer responses without being ridiculed; (b) the best questions are those that require multiple-word responses (higher levels of thinking); (c) difficult questions require more "wait time" (time to think) before they can be answered; and (d) a variety of students are allowed to respond.

Pick a topic you know well, and think of a focusing, extending, and schema-based question you could pose to students.

As Bloom (1956) suggested, classroom questioning can be clustered in a sequence of focusing, extending, and raising. Within this sequence, all three levels of comprehension, discussed earlier in this chapter, can be used. Generally, when approaching a new reading selection, teachers should begin with focus questions aimed at assessing students' prior knowledge. ("What do you know about the movement West in the United States?" "What does the picture show about the movement West?") Student responses will reveal to a degree what they know about the topic and whether you should ask additional thought-provoking questions to help students extend their thinking about the topic at hand. ("What kinds of things happened to the country as people moved West?" "Why do you suppose the railroad was so important?") These extending questions help students refocus on important topics or information they will be reading about. Finally, you can up the ante by raising students' thinking by asking schema-based questions. ("Why would some people today have a negative view of the Western movement in this country?" "How might our nation's history have been different if Native Americans had not been forced onto reservations?")

LEARNERS WITH SPECIAL NEEDS

What are some reasons students have problems processing text?

Although we recognize that the techniques mentioned earlier in this chapter would be of benefit to students with learning problems, we also suggest a few additional techniques that have been recommended for students experiencing difficulty in processing text information. Before we identify some possible alternatives to try out with students, a few maxims about improving the comprehension of students with learning problems are in order.

1. Often these learners do not see comprehension as the goal of interacting with text (Palincsar & Brown, 1988).
2. These types of learners are not strategic and often do not engage in predicting about text or making decisions about what is important and what isn't (Helfeldt & Henk, 1990).
3. These students do respond to being taught metacognitive strategies (A. L. Brown, Campione, & Day, 1981; Levin & Pressley, 1981).
4. It is important to use materials for instructional purposes that are not too difficult.

With these in mind, the following strategies are offered as additional teaching techniques to add to your repertoire. They, like all strategies in this text, should be used selectively, modified when necessary, and discarded if they do not work with your students or your teaching style.

Reciprocal Questioning

Originally developed by Manzo (1969) as a technique to assist comprehension in a one-on-one setting, reciprocal questioning has come into favor as a means to promote metacognitive behaviors, teach levels of comprehension, and foster students' posing their own questions over what they read. Simply, the strategy proceeds as follows:

What is the role of the teacher during reciprocal questioning?

1. Using a brief but important selection from the textbook, the teacher informs the students that they will read specific portions of the text together. When they finish, they may ask the teacher any questions they want to about what has been read.
2. The teacher and students read the first portion (first sentence or paragraph). The students question the teacher. The teacher is sure to ask for clarification of poorly worded or illogical questions. The teacher also reinforces any "thinking-type" questions asked by the students.
3. Once the students have completed asking their questions, the teacher asks questions about the same paragraph. An option is to have the students read the next segment of text, and the teacher then asks questions first. The teacher models good questioning behavior and periodically asks students to verify their responses and/or predict about the next segment of the text.
4. Once the selection has been completed, then a discussion is held summarizing what was important and the difference between the teacher's

questions and the students' questions. An emphasis is placed on the need for students to pose more thinking questions.

Reciprocal Question–Answer Relationships

How difficult will ReQARs be to teach to students?

A more recent strategy, **Reciprocal Question–Answer Relationships (ReQARs)** (Helfeldt & Henk, 1990) combines the QARs instruction discussed earlier in this chapter with reciprocal questioning. ReQARs use the elements of reciprocal questioning for developing the metacognitive awareness that QARs training provides. Through this type of sequence, you can model your own thinking strategies, students are engaged in discussing a textbook topic, all levels of comprehension are used, and students can talk about their responses. These are the same recommendations mentioned earlier in this chapter as components of successful comprehension instruction. Because you are familiar with both QARs and reciprocal questioning, Figure 5.6 outlines how ReQARs should be implemented over several sessions.

Glossing and Summarizing

What is glossing?

Two possible alternatives for students with learning problems that are included in the regular classroom and have access to support personnel are the techniques of glossing and summarizing. *Glossing* refers to underlining important terms or ideas and writing notations in the margins of texts to explain ideas or to pose questions or reminders to students as they read. Obviously, marking on texts in most high school and middle schools is frowned on, but for special education students, an exception often can be made. Literally speaking, the teacher conducts a walk-through of a chapter, marking and noting via marginal comments what is important to focus on. Another way of providing glosses without marking the text is to provide a photocopy of the glosses page by page, which the student inserts into the text.

How does our explanation of summarizing differ from what your generally think of when you hear the term *summarizing*?

Summarizing of text has proved to improve the comprehension of students with learning problems (Bean & Steenwyk, 1984; Hidi & Anderson, 1986). Although summarizing is not an easy task to learn, our recommendation for using summarizing is to have students read a chapter's summary. Then, the teacher models how to write down the important ideas that will be discussed in the chapter. The students copy what the teacher has written, and then a brief discussion is held concerning what they already know about some of the summary ideas. Eventually, these students should be taught to write their own summaries of ideas.

To assist students experiencing problems comprehending, teachers must be resourceful, patient, explicit in their directions, and flexible. Often this means using a lot of input up front about what is to be read, providing written guides to assist the learner, and working cooperatively with support personnel. In Chapters 6 to 8, we will add additional techniques and strategies that can assist the students experiencing learning problems in your classroom.

Figure 5.6 ReQARs Procedural Outline

Phase of teaching ReQAR	Description	Techniques employed
1. Strategy information	Teacher succinctly explains: WHAT strategy will be learned [self-questioning]. WHY the strategy is important [to increase reading comprehension]. WHEN the strategy will be used [during reading].	
2. ReQUEST	Teacher and student take turns asking one another questions about a segment of text.	Modeling Reciprocal teaching Guided practice Independent practice
3. QAR	Teacher introduces "In the Book" and "In My Head" major categories Teacher differentiates Right There and Putting It Together sources. Teacher differentiates Author and Me and On My Own sources.	Modeling Reciprocal teaching Guided practice Independent practice
4. ReQAR	ReQuest format serves as procedural backdrop for reinforcing QAR strategy: Student asks question. Teacher answers question and identifies QAR category. Teacher asks question. Student answers question and identifies QAR category.	
Gradual release of responsibility	Student asks question and identifies QAR category. Teacher answers question and specifies QAR source. Teacher asks question and identifies QAR category. Student answers question and specifies QAR source. Student asks question and specifies QAR source. Teacher responds, then asks next question. Student answers question and specifies QAR source.	

Note. From "Reciprocal Question–Answer Relationships: An Instructional Technique for At-Risk Readers" by J. P. Helfeldt and W. A. Henk, 1990, *Journal of Reading, 33,* p. 511. Copyright 1990 by the International Reading Association. Reprinted by permission.

CHAPTER SUMMARY

This chapter has introduced the topic of comprehending text. The question "Is it possible to teach someone to think and comprehend?" was answered with a qualified yes. Students can be taught to be competent comprehenders only if teachers know and use those teaching ideas that have proven to be effective with all students. Generally, providing time to read, teaching specific strategies, allowing peer collaboration, and providing opportunities for students to discuss their responses to what they have read will help students develop into competent comprehenders.

Schema theory (from Chapter 2), which explains how the brain stores new information through a network of categories, was revisited because comprehension is greatly facilitated when students' background information is tapped and developed before reading. Metacognitive awareness, knowing about knowing, is an important trait of successful learners. Teachers who provide clear purposes for reading, help students recognize important parts of text, and cause students to engage in self-questioning promote metacognitive awareness.

The three levels of comprehension—textually explicit, textually implicit, and schema-based—were introduced, and the need to ask questions at the higher levels of comprehension to promote thinking was emphasized. The structure of stories and expository text paragraphs was presented as fundamental information students should know because of its impact on one's comprehension of text.

Instructionally, several points in time were identified when comprehension strategies can be used to improve students' comprehension. The before-reading strategies include PReP and K-W-L, both of which build on students' schemata. The during- and after-reading strategies are QARs, reciprocal teaching, and questioning that focuses, extends, and raises students' thinking. Some teaching ideas for students who are experiencing learning problems include the reciprocal questioning procedure, ReQARS, glossing, and summarizing.

Reflection/Application Activities

1. Using a middle school or high school textbook, find an example of each type of paragraph identified in this chapter. Be prepared to share what you find and how your textbook uses these paragraph types to assist the reader.

2. Using what you now know about question–answer relationships, prepare a series of questions, answers, and QARs over a segment of text. Be prepared to explain each one to a peer.

3. Prepare a reciprocal teaching activity using a textbook selection. In small groups, take turns walking the group through how you would model what you eventually want your students to be able to do independently.

4. Interview a middle school or high school teacher and inquire about the following:
   a. How much reading is done by the students in class?
   b. What kinds of things does the teacher do to prepare the students for reading?
   c. Does the teacher refer to the different levels of comprehension?
   d. What kinds of problems do students have with reading the adopted text?
   e. Does the teacher allow students to work together? If so, how?

Recommended Reading

Baumann, J. (Ed.). (1986). *Teaching main idea comprehension.* Newark, DE: International Reading Association.

Brown, A. L. (1980). Metacognition development in reading. In R. J. Spiro, B. C. Bruce, & W. F. Brewer (Eds.), *Theoretical issues in reading comprehension.* Hillsdale, NJ: Lawrence Erlbaum.

Fielding, L. G., & Pearson, P. D. (1994, February). Reading comprehension: What works. *Educational Leadership,* pp. 62–68.

Flood, J., & Lapp, D. (1990, April). Reading comprehension instruction for at-risk students: Research-based practices that can make a difference. *Journal of Reading,* pp. 490–496.

Jones, B., Palincsar, A., Ogle, D., & Carr, E. (Eds.). (1987). *Strategic teaching and learning: Cognitive instruction in the content areas.* Alexandria, VA: Association for Supervision and Curriculum Development.

CHAPTER 6

Vocabulary Development and the Content Area Classroom

Features of Effective
Vocabulary Instruction

Traditional vs. Recommended
Vocabulary Instruction

Learners With Special Needs

Guidelines for Developing
Content Area Vocabulary

Types of Vocabulary

Focus Questions

*As you read this chapter, try to discover
answers to the following questions:*

1 How can words become a barrier to understanding text?

2 What are the guidelines offered to guide vocabulary instruction?

3 What are the cognitive factors involved in knowing a word? What stages must students move through to acquire a conceptual understanding of knowing a word in your content area?

4 Why should vocabulary instruction not be left to chance in your content classroom?

5 Compare and contrast traditional vocabulary instruction with the recommendations in this chapter.

6 Into what three categories do terms in your textbook fall? Which of these categories will require instructional attention?

7 Explain the development and use of graphic organizers. What are the purposes of using them prior to, during, and after reading a text selection?

8 What are some of the most important recommendations about vocabulary instruction and learners with special needs that you think apply to your content area?

The Importance of Developing Content Vocabulary

Effective content teachers systematically teach vocabulary.

Reci, Reci, Reci . . . or *Words, Words, Words!* One of the hallmarks of successful students is their ability to use and understand the vocabulary of subjects they study. Every content area is made up of concepts, and for students, success depends on whether they can acquire, store, and communicate using the vocabulary that represents those concepts. Effective teachers recognize this and do not leave vocabulary instruction to chance. Thus, planned and systematic vocabulary development programs characterize competent content area teaching.

As an example that might help make a point, read the following passage. How well do you understand it? Why?

The tweeter is at the top, and the woofer is approximately in the center of the panel, above the bass port. The woofer uses Quantam's

Quadtric design, with a multiribbed plastic cone and a rubber rim surround to help terminate signals propagating within the diaphragm and
thereby improve midrange detail and dispersion characteristics.

On the rear of the cabinet are separate multiway binding-post terminals for the tweeter and woofer, normally connected by jumper
straps. With straps removed, the system can be biwired or biamplified.
Because the speaker's crossover network is always in the circuit, no
external electronic crossover is needed.

Your comprehension of this passage will, in large part, depend on your knowledge of the vocabulary of consumer electronics. For those who have a limited
awareness or understanding of words like *tweeter* and *multiway binding-post
terminals,* the ability to comprehend the passage is severely limited. These
words can literally be a barrier to understanding, thus making the unknowl-
edgeable reader an outsider. Students are often outsiders because they have
limited schemas about topics and words that make up content subjects,
thereby affecting their ability to read, understand, and communicate about the
subject itself. As Herber noted, "If students hold limited meanings for the
words, they hold limited understandings of the concepts, and hence limited
understanding of the subject" (1978, p. 130). In summary, one of the most
important instructional goals for any content teacher is to take students who
are by and large outsiders in terms of vocabulary and concept knowledge and
make them insiders.

It has become apparent in recent years that content teachers must move
away from merely establishing what Forgan and Mangrum (1989) refer to as
specific knowledge of terms, or a contrived and rote understanding of their
meaning, and move toward assisting students in developing a deeper **conceptual knowledge** of terms. Although no single best approach has been developed for teaching content area vocabulary, evidence in the literature does suggest essential elements of an effective vocabulary development program. A
good summary of this research is found in the work of Simpson and Dwyer
(1991), who have identified five commonsense aspects that tend to enhance
the learning of vocabulary:

1. The use of multiple methods
2. Promoting student involvement
3. The use of contextually based activities
4. Capitalizing on student interests
5. The intensity of instruction

To the extent that teachers can organize instructional activities that embrace
these five characteristics, students will have a greater chance of becoming
insiders in content areas they study. This chapter addresses ways of providing a
coherent vocabulary program that capitalizes on these five characteristics of an

What are the five characteristics of an effective vocabulary
program?

effective vocabulary program. We begin with a few basic guidelines to help guide vocabulary instruction.

TEACHER GUIDELINES FOR DEVELOPING CONTENT AREA VOCABULARY

The following guidelines have proven to be helpful over the years in our own classrooms and in those of our colleagues. They also find support in the work of Simpson and Dwyer (1991) and are offered to assist content area teachers in developing a program of vocabulary instruction.

Keep vocabulary instruction as experienced based or concrete as possible. Direct experience is the best teacher. Whenever possible use real-world objects, displays, actual demonstrations, and other means to connect words to their meanings. Through direct or even indirect experience (it's sometimes difficult to demonstrate concepts like *federalism* in the class), students can be helped to recall what they know about a concept before reading.

Be selective about which terms you emphasize and expect students to retain over time. Because it is often impossible to teach every word a student needs to know, it is imperative that teachers perform a **content analysis** when it comes to selecting terms for which students will be held accountable. The process of selecting key vocabulary has been around for a long time, but some teachers still mistakenly think that students must learn all italicized or bold words in the text (usually for a test); this is not the case. As an alternative, D. W. Moore, Moore, Cunningham, and Cunningham (1986) suggest that teachers list all unknown terms related to a topic, prune the list by selecting words that are important for understanding the topic in general, and then add words that appear repeatedly and are critical to understanding the unit under study. This idea, although decades old, restricts learning activities to words students are actually going to need to know in the future.

Use a variety of strategies to teach vocabulary that will enable students to become more independent. Using a mixture of teacher- and student-centered strategies not only will help students acquire both *definitional* and *contextual* knowledge of important words but also will enhance the probability of increasing student interest and involvement. Strategies that place an emphasis on groups of words and how they are interrelated tend to be the most effective (Nagy & Anderson, 1984).

Provide for both time and exposure to ensure ownership. Often, teachers' pacing of units of study is determined by outside forces other than student needs. In today's content classroom, both time and exposure are variables that require more teacher attention. Time and exposure in this context mean that teachers should allot the necessary time for vocabulary activities for all students to have an opportunity to acquire the necessary knowledge of critical terms before moving on to the next topic in the unit of study. Multiple encoun-

Why is it important to perform content analysis in relation to vocabulary instruction?

What are two apparent benefits of using a variety of techniques for teaching vocabulary?

ters in meaningful settings are necessary for students to actually acquire and store conceptually important ideas represented by words.

Don't ignore the human factors associated with vocabulary instruction. Make sure that strategies are paying off for the students and are not viewed as busy work. Involvement activities with appropriate feedback will communicate the importance you are placing on knowing the language of your field. The tenet to remember is that vocabulary activities should require students to be involved in and elaborate on (apply) what they are learning. This means that students should use all language processes as they study and use the targeted vocabulary.

Be enthusiastic and enjoy the language of what you teach. It is contagious when a teacher demonstrates that she enjoys the language of instruction. This idea means teachers must break the mold of rote drills and present vocabulary using all the communication processes. Such activities as projects, games, humor, analogies, and anecdotes can influence learner attitudes and can stimulate the desire to learn new terminology.

Why is teacher enthusiasm about vocabulary important?

Cognitive Factors Related to Knowing a Word

Estimates suggest that typical high school seniors have a 40,000 word vocabulary (Nagy & Herman, 1984). Hurd (1983) reported that some middle school science texts introduce as many as 2,500 technical and unfamiliar words in a single year. In summarizing this formidable challenge for both students and teachers, Nagy and Herman state, "This astounding rate of vocabulary growth by average children sets a mark against which the contribution of any program of vocabulary instruction must be measured" (1984, p. 6). The task is to somehow relate new vocabulary and unfamiliar concepts to the background of the students being taught. If students succeed in this enterprise, the likelihood of students actually *knowing* the vocabulary and not just memorizing for some routine test will be enhanced.

Why is connecting vocabulary to students' backgrounds and showing how terms are interrelated important in the content areas?

We have defined *schema* as the knowledge one has of a particular event, concept, or experience. As one reads and comprehends text, various schemata for the subject being explained come into play and help complete the communication between the writer and reader. Explicit attention to the vocabulary of a discipline aids in the development of schemata and increases the likelihood of comprehension. But what is *knowing* a word? Stahl (1983, 1985) suggests that a student really knows a word when she has both definitional knowledge and contextual knowledge about the word. **Definitional knowledge** is specific and precise, much like knowing the glossary definition of a term. **Contextual knowledge** is broad, varied, and suggests a complex number of associations about the term. The student has a sophisticated mental model of what the term can mean. To achieve both types of knowledge, the student (often with teacher guidance) usually goes through several stages of learning a term (see Figure 6.1). At the **initial stage**, students become familiar with word meanings as they apply to the topic being studied and begin to recognize **interword**

Contrast definitional and contextual knowledge of what a term means.

relationships. Next students manipulate and compare new words with other related words through a variety of instructional activities. This is what Stahl (1985) calls **comprehension processing**. Finally, students use new terms in independently varied situations through writing, reading, listening, and speaking activities. This process of learning, whether involving new words or other important information, generally moves from teacher-centered activities to student-centered activities (Pearson & Gallagher, 1983). This process builds on the idea that multiple encounters with important terminology are critical to understanding.

Types of Vocabulary

There are basically two types of vocabulary: receptive and expressive.

What causes a student's receptive vocabulary to be larger than his expressive vocabulary?

Receptive vocabulary consists of words that are known when one is reading and listening. **Expressive vocabulary** consists of those words one can use with facility in writing and speaking. In general, one's listening vocabulary tends to remain the largest throughout life, with speaking vocabulary being a close second in size for children. But as most people get older and acquire reading and writing abilities, reading and listening vocabularies tend to converge in size. With some people, the reading vocabulary can actually become larger than the speaking vocabulary because of the influence of context clues embedded in the text. Thus, receptive vocabularies (listening and reading) tend to be the largest for most people, including middle and high school students.

Which category of words do content teachers focus their time and energy teaching? Why?

Vocabularies can be further subdivided into the three categories of general, technical, and special. **General vocabulary** refers to words that are not a part of any particular discipline or subject. Words such as *pervasive, plethora,*

Independent Usage Via
All Language Processes

Instructional Activities
and Multiple Encounters

Exposure and
Background Building

Figure 6.1 Stages of Moving to a Conceptual Understanding of a Word

and *malaise* are considered to be general terms. **Technical vocabulary** refers to words that are specifically related to an academic discipline. Words such as *cosine, federalism, tracheids,* and *dado* are considered to be technical terms. Finally, **special vocabulary** refers to words that, although common, have special meanings in content area textbooks. Words such as *set, bit, bank, love,* and *subject* are considered to be specialized terms used in specific content area settings. Content teachers have to focus their attention on teaching the technical/specialized terminology of their discipline. In addition teachers must be selective about which technical/specialized terms should be emphasized because some high school texts introduce as many as 3,000 unfamiliar terms in a single school year (Holliday, 1991).

STRATEGIES FOR TEACHING VOCABULARY

Teachers who decide to develop a systematic and well-planned vocabulary program should remember several important tips. First, recognize that not all strategies will work with all texts and all students. Teachers must make decisions about which terms are important and which strategies are most appropriate with a particular unit of study. Second, seek allies who are interested in making instruction more meaningful and relevant and are willing sharers of successful techniques and approaches. Finally, remember that vocabulary instruction is only one part, albeit an important element, of a successful content area classroom. The strategies and techniques presented in this section are representative of those that teachers often consider, because they are process oriented, student centered, and capitalize on moving toward a more holistic approach to vocabulary instruction.

Before beginning any chapter or unit of study, the content teacher should conduct a content analysis to determine the major concepts to be emphasized, the important terms or key vocabulary students will be held responsible for, and what product and process outcomes are expected. As part of preparing students to read and learn about any topic, teachers need to address the teaching of important vocabulary, or what we refer to as key vocabulary. The following discussion contrasts traditional with more process-oriented approaches to prereading vocabulary instruction.

Traditional Prereading Vocabulary Instruction

The chief characteristic of traditional practice for preteaching vocabulary is that it is generally limited to emphasizing rote understanding of important words. We have observed in many classrooms that it is common practice for vocabulary instruction to either be nonexistent (the teacher relies on the text and activities at the end of chapter to handle vocabulary instruction) or limited to words taught in isolation with oral definitions. For example, definitions are often writ-

Why is emphasizing just a rote understanding of terms limited in terms of effectiveness?

ten on the chalkboard or overhead projector with hopes that students will copy them down. Much more than simple rote drills are needed, however, if real word knowledge is to occur. For as Nagy pointed out, "Only those methods that go beyond providing partial knowledge, producing in-depth knowledge of the words taught, will reliably increase readers' comprehension of text containing those words" (1988, p. 3). As the following example demonstrates, if all the teacher does with a term is give its definition either orally or written on the board without necessary associations, understanding of the term when first encountering text is at best incomplete and may limit a student's comprehension when reading a section of text about, for example, homeostasis.

Traditional Introduction of Terminology

Sample Lesson Sequence

What are some potential problems with the example of traditional vocabulary instruction?

Step 1:   The teacher introduces the topic *homeostasis* and asks students if they know anything about it.

Step 2:   The teacher writes the terms on the chalkboard.

Step 3:   The teacher either writes the definitions next to each word or has a student find it in the glossary and read the definition out loud.

Step 4:   Next, the teacher conducts a monologue during which most of the information that students need to know about the topic is supplied.

Step 5:   Finally, the teacher assigns students to read the section of the chapter and look up all other italicized words in the glossary and write their definitions or do a set number of questions. These will be collected and graded without feedback.

Homeostasis	The tendency of living things to maintain a constant internal environment
Feedback	The product of an action that influences that action
Negative feedback	An increase or decrease in a system's product to equalize the system
Positive feedback	An increase or decrease in a system that is due to its product

The problems with this type of instruction tend to be as follows: (a) Students are passive in their learning (and often uninterested); (b) it provides a limited view of words, their meanings, and fails to establish relationships among various terms; (3) it emphasizes rote learning and limits the number of encounters with the important terminology; and (4) it fails to capitalize on what we know about the importance of developing prior knowledge of a topic to improve subsequent comprehension.

HOLISTIC VOCABULARY INSTRUCTION: PROCESS-ORIENTED ALTERNATIVES

In process-oriented approaches to vocabulary instruction, teachers apply what is understood about how memory structures are constructed (through schema theory) and translate this understanding into classroom practice. Although many interpretations of this translation of theory into practice are possible, we find that a number of methods meet with great success. In this section, we explore a few of these options.

Using Glossary Definitions

When using definitions provided by the teacher's manual or from the glossary of the textbook, the teacher should remember several things. First, a content analysis should be done to aid in selecting words to be introduced using formal definitions. Remember, you generally cannot teach all the words. Second, the category or class to which the term belongs needs to be identified as part of the procedure because this helps the teacher later describe schema-like connections with what is already known to the reader. For example, irrational numbers belong to a class of numbers called *real numbers.* Finally, any specific characteristics or features of the term should also be noted and described during teaching. For example, irrational numbers are nonterminating and nonrepeating.

What should teachers do when they use glossary definitions?

The teacher should also remember to connect each of the terms, or explain how they go together, using some sort of mapping system (described later in the chapter). For example, the term *bort* belongs to the class of *diamonds* and is characterized by its gray to brown color, industrial use, and poorly crystalized structure. When introducing this term, the teacher connects *bort* to other members of the category of *diamonds* and their specific characteristics (i.e,. carbonado, ballas, and diamond proper) along with the glossary definition, "a low-quality diamond." This teacher-made connection to other members and their contrasting characteristics is critical to fostering learning on the part of students.

An easy but effective method of using definitions with class and feature or attributes of important terms is the **word map**. Originally developed by Schwartz and Raphael (1985), word maps have gained popularity because both teachers and students can develop the maps to foster understanding of key terms. The word map for the term *alkane* in Figure 6.2 illustrates the basic idea.

Can you think of a word from your content area and visualize a word map?

After exposure and the opportunity to compose their own word maps in dyads (groups of two), students should be helped to recognize that they can use word maps to monitor their understanding of what they read. Students should recognize that mentally mapping words as they read is an active method for comprehending text.

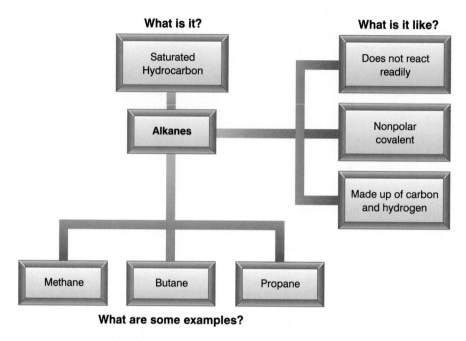

Figure 6.2 Word Map

Using Context to Teach Independent Vocabulary Analysis

Although some researchers (Schatz & Baldwin, 1986) have called into question the practice of using contextual analysis to help students understand infrequently occurring terminology, others (Stahl & Fairbanks, 1986) have concluded that emphasis on context is helpful. Regardless of the debate, we find that the use of context is helpful in determining vocabulary meanings, an opinion seemingly shared by most practicing teachers. We also support teachers teaching contextual analysis techniques to students so that, in combination with other techniques, students can independently figure out unfamiliar vocabulary.

Types of Context Clues

How should context clues be used in content classrooms?

Most textbooks identify the types of context clues encountered in text in the hopes of providing teachers with instructional models. Rather than provide the reader with a list of context clue types, we advocate a more process-oriented approach of emphasizing *how* to use context. This seems to be more beneficial because more recent textbooks do a better job of providing unfamiliar terms in rich contextual settings. Therefore, for the teacher the two main decisions to be made are, (a) Can I effectively use context to preteach the terms I have selected for emphasis? and (b) Do I have sentences contextually rich enough so that students can have a legitimate chance of determining what the word most likely means? An example of a **contextually poor** sentence pertaining to the term *alychiphobia* is

My alychiphobia worries my wife.

A **contextually rich** sentence using the same word, one that might enhance the reader's ability to figure out what alychiphobia means, might be

My alychiphobia is the reason I have worked so hard to be a success and placed more importance on making money and working late than on my home life.

An excellent and entertaining method of introducing terminology through context, as well as demonstrating to students why they should use context whenever possible to figure out unfamiliar words, is a strategy called **contextual redefinition** (J. W. Cunningham, Cunningham, & Arthur, 1981). The steps in this procedure follow:

Step 1:   Select five or six terms that are unfamiliar or probably known by only a few students in the class. Introduce the topic, and display the new terms on the chalkboard or overhead. Ask each student, or pairs of students, to come up with a brief definition for each term. Encourage students to venture a guess at word meanings, reminding them that the goal is to try to come up with logical ideas and not to worry about being right. After the students have had an opportunity to discuss probable definitions (some of which might be funny or totally off base), call for individuals to share their ideas and write them on the chalkboard or overhead projector transparency. Briefly discuss *why* they were unable to do much more than guess. Point out that looking at words in isolation is ineffective unless you already know the word.

Step 2:   Next, tell the students that you have these same words written in sentences and that you want them to read each sentence to see if they want to revise their original guesses. Present each word in contextually rich sentences. During the ensuing discussion, encourage students to explain *why* they think the word means what they now say it means. Record varying responses next to each term as they occur.

Step 3:   Finally, if there are differences, have students either find the word in the text or the glossary and read its definition. Have students copy the finalized sentences in their notebooks/journals.

Now you try it. Without looking at the following sentences, write a simple definition for each of these terms (as best you can):

gynecocracy   ascomycete
sesquipedalian   stipe

What makes a sentence contextually rich?

Be sure to try this activity. Did it work for you?

Now read the following sentences, and see if you need to revise your guesses because of what you can learn through using context.

> If the president were a woman, and the Congress and Supreme Court were made up solely of women, the U.S. government would be a kind of *gynecocracy.*

> No one can understand what he says or writes because he uses such long and unusual words. He is quite the *sesquipedalian.*

> If you don't have any *ascomycetes,* then your bread won't rise.

> That mushroom's *stipe* could barely support its large cap.

Contextual redefinition provides students with opportunities to share their expertise in using context and can be used to promote independent use of context clues. Teachers find it an invigorating means for preteaching terms and showing how the glossary is not the first but the last line of defense in figuring out new words.

Using Morphemic Analysis to Teach Terms

A morpheme is the smallest unit of meaning in the English language.

In the English language, a **morpheme** is the smallest unit of meaning. The two types of morphemes are the free morpheme and the bound morpheme. A **free morpheme** is the freestanding root or base of any word that cannot be further divided and still have meaning. In the word *farmer,* "farm" is the root word or free morpheme. The "-er" portion of the word *farmer* is considered to be a bound morpheme. **Bound morphemes** carry meaning but must be attached to a free morpheme to do so. The most common bound morphemes are prefixes (in-, pre-, mono-), suffixes (-er, -ous, -ology), and inflectional endings (-s, -es, -ing, -ed, -est). **Morphemic analysis** is the act of using knowledge of word parts to deduce meanings. Try to use your knowledge of morphemes to determine the meanings of the following words:

>   claustrophobia   (hint: a fear of enclosed spaces)
>   cardiophobia
>   olfactophobia
>   telephonophobia
>   verbaphobia

Recognize how morphemic analysis and context work together.

Most of you used what is called the **compare and contrast method** of using morphemic analysis. That is, you looked at the unfamiliar word, and using your prior knowledge of other words that look like parts of the unfamiliar word, you figured out what each word probably means. For example, *cardio-* probably reminds you of *cardiac,* which deals with the heart, and *-phobia* means "fear of," therefore, *cardiophobia* must mean a fear of heart disease. To use this technique with students, you must first select words that have morphemes that can be compared to other words students are likely to know and present both the new word and other words that begin or end like the unfamiliar word. Look at the following example:

Because of my extensive vocabulary, my teacher called me a verbivore.

verbi	vore
verbal	carnivore
verbose	herbivore
verbalize	omnivore

The teacher places the sentence on the chalkboard with examples of words that begin and end like the unfamiliar word. Then, through questioning, the teacher leads students to specify the word's meaning by comparing and contrasting the known words to the unfamiliar one, thus concluding: "A verbivore is a person who loves (eats) words."

Another way of using morphemic analysis is to present unfamiliar terms along with explanations of the morphemes that make up the unfamiliar terms to help students deduce meanings. For example, when introducing new terms related to the subtopic of cellular elements of blood, the following procedure might be used as part of an introduction to this segment of text:

Step 1: Identify the terms that need preteaching.

Erythrocytes	Leukocytes
Thrombocytes	Hemoglobin
Monocytes	Oxyhemoglobin

Step 2: Place on the board with these terms a list of appropriate morphemes and their meanings.

leuko = white	thrombo = clot
cyto = cell	hemo = blood
oxy = oxygen	globin = protein
erythro = red	

Step 3: Engage students in a discussion of the topic, and have them determine what each term means *and how the terms are interrelated.* When there is confusion or disagreement, direct students to where the terms are in the text and/or to the glossary for verification.

The combination of context (whether verbal or written) with knowledge of morphemic analysis can be a powerful tool when one must figure out unfamiliar words in texts. However, the combination does not work in every situation. Take, for example, this sentence:

Why doesn't the combination of morphemic analysis and context work in every situation?

You can tell that he is misogynistic.

Obviously, the word *misogynistic* is not in a rich contextual setting or easily morphemically analyzed. You would have to know that *misogynistic* means "having a hatred or distrust of women" to complete the communication intended by the text. However, in much of what we read, the combination of context and morphemic analysis can help the reader figure out the meaning of unfamiliar words. Because morphemic analysis is a potent tactic, students should be taught and encouraged to use it with context as a frequent strategy.

A word of caution. Although we encourage the teaching of how to use context and morphemic analysis, we in no way advocate the overuse of these two techniques or the memorization of lists of morphemes or types of context clues. Teachers who make students memorize common prefixes and suffixes run the risk of having students view the task as an end and not a means to help them become better readers. The story is told of a student who memorized the prefix "trans-" as meaning *across.* Later the same week, the student was reading a science text and was asked what the word *transparent* meant. He replied confidently "a cross mother or father." The point is that all vocabulary instruction in the upper grades should be meaning oriented, connected to text, functional, and capable of being used in the future.

Another strategy that emphasizes the use of prediction and context clues is **possible sentences** (D. W. Moore & Arthur, 1981). In this strategy, the teacher plans an in-class reading assignment using a small segment of text. Before having students read the segment of text, the teacher places four to six unfamiliar or slightly familiar terms that are found in the text segment on the chalkboard. The topic is briefly introduced by the teacher, and then students are asked to compose sentences that use at least two of the terms. The point is to have the students try to predict how the terms will be used by the text author. After students, either individually or in dyads, have composed their sentences, the teacher asks for volunteers to share their sentences. The next step is to have the students read their texts to confirm the accuracy of the predicted sentences. During the follow-up discussion, the teacher has students verify their accuracy or predictions, revise sentences that can be revised, and develop new sentences for words as necessary. It is important to expand the discussion while evaluating the sentences to include why the sentences are inaccurate and how they can be improved based on what has been read. Following is an illustration of the possible sentence strategy.

Possible Sentence Strategy

Sample Lesson Sequence

Step 1: The teacher displays words on the chalkboard or overhead projector and identifies the topic. Say something like "Today, students, we will read the next segment in your text about visual illusions. Who knows what I mean when I say visual illusion? Can anyone think of an example?" Encourage student discussion and perhaps even show some examples of illusions.

What's the major point about vocabulary instruction?

Why can one say that the possible sentences strategy is teacher directed but student centered?

Step 2: Teacher says something like "All of the terms on the board are in the passage you are going to read. I want each of you to predict how your text's author will use these terms in his discussion of visual illusions. I want you to make your predictions by using at least two of the terms in a sentence. You should compose enough sentences so that you have used every word once."

Length distortion	Gateway arch
Hermann's grid	Lateral inhibition
Bull's eye	Illusion

Step 3: "Who would like to share one of your sentences?" The teacher records sentences until all the words have been used. "OK, now I would like you to read the passage in your text about visual illusions. As you read, decide if our predicted sentences are correct or incorrect and, if incorrect, how could they be revised?" (See Figure 6.3 for a copy of this text.)

Figure 6.3 "Visual Illusions" Passage

Visual Illusions

A visual illusion is an unreal or misleading appearance or image, according to *Webster's* dictionary. In other words, visual illusions are caused sometimes from ideas one holds about what one expects to see. In other instances, the illusion is caused by the brain's difficulty in choosing from two or more visual patterns.

If you look at a bull's-eye and move it slowly in circular motions, you should see spokes moving. The spokes, if you see them, aren't really there. This type of visual illusion is called "lateral inhibition."

Another type of visual illusion occurs when a person tries to estimate the height of a vertical object. It is referred to as "length distortion." The famous Gateway Arch in St. Louis is an example of length distortion, because the arch seems much higher than it is wide. In reality the height and width of the arch are identical. Length distortion occurs because our eyes move more easily from side to side than up and down. This greater effort to look up causes the brain to overinterpret the height of vertical objects.

If you look at a series of squares, you should see small gray spots at each intersection. If you look directly at one intersection, the spots should disappear. This illusion is known as "Hermann's Grid." It is often seen in modern high-rise office buildings. Many of these buildings have windows separated by crossing strips of metal or concrete.

The above are only three examples of the many ways that our eyes can deceive us. But they do reinforce the old axiom, "Don't believe everything you see."

Note. From *The Flynt/Cooter Reading Inventory for the Classroom* (2nd ed.) by E. S. Flynt and R. B. Cooter, 1995, Scottsdale, AZ: Gorsuch Scarisbrick. Copyright 1995 by Gorsuch Scarisbrick. Reprinted by permission.

Step 4:   After students have completed their reading, a whole class discussion takes place, and each sentence is evaluated based on the text's information. Final versions are recorded in students' notebooks/journals.

As you can see, possible sentences and variations emphasize vocabulary, use of context, purposeful reading, and all the language processes.

Graphic Displays of Vocabulary

Earlier in the chapter, we mentioned Nagy and Anderson's (1984) finding that content area vocabulary is best taught in interrelated groups. One way teachers might accomplish this is to use the variety of visual techniques available for teaching vocabulary. One technique, the graphic organizer (Barron, 1969), or structured overview, has received much attention in recent years as a viable strategy for both teachers and students.

A **graphic organizer** can be any visual diagram that demonstrates the relationship among interrelated terms, often in a hierarchical fashion. Graphic organizers can range from traditional outlines to tree diagrams to creative visual displays incorporating artwork. As long as the relationships among the terms are readily apparent and logically sequenced, then the organizer is appropriate. The fundamental objective of the classroom teacher is to provide an overview to the unit, chapter, or portion of a chapter before having students read the selection. This overview of the information before reading the text is consistent with the idea of activating or building **schemas** for reading new information.

> Explain what a graphic organizer is.

Graphic organizers require the teacher to examine texts carefully to discern the organization of the information, vocabulary needing emphasis, and the number of major concepts introduced in the passage, as well as to establish purposes for reading about the topic. Graphic organizers are derived from the content analysis. For students, graphic organizers provide a mental map that is useful when they encounter additional information in the text. Graphic organizers also provide assistance in understanding new terminology, an easy way to organize what is read, and a good review tool for study. Graphic organizers can also lead to independent learning if students are taught and encouraged to develop their own organizers—something we strongly advocate.

> Think of a topic and how you would go about constructing a graphic organizer like the one illustrated. What would you do differently?

The most common type of graphic organizer is the **hierarchical tree diagram**. Following is a simple procedure for constructing the tree diagram organizer.

1. Examine the portion of text to decide what information will be emphasized and the major ideas of the chapter or portion of the chapter.
2. After determining the major ideas, make a comprehensive list of all important terminology. This list can be rather lengthy, and for the experienced teacher, this step may be unnecessary.

3. Select only those terms necessary to provide students with an overview of the information. The graphic organizer's purpose is not to replace the need to read the chapter. Neither should the graphic organizer be so complex that the students can't see the proverbial forest for the trees.

4. Arrange in tree diagram form the selected terms so that the relationships among the terms are clear. Sometimes what is clear to the teacher is not necessarily clear to students, so teachers should be careful to view the organizer from a novice point of view.

Following and in Figure 6.4 is an example of a graphic organizer using a portion of a chapter from a 10th-grade biology text dealing with the plant kingdom. First is the list of major ideas and the associated vocabulary terms. Then the teacher must decide how much information to present visually to provide an overview of the topic (Figure 6.4).

Major Ideas/Concepts

■ All plants can be classified as belonging to one of five phyla.

bryophyte	green algae	brown algae
tracheophyte	phylum	red algae

■ Plants in the tracheophyte phylum, the largest in the plant kingdom, are characterized by a vascular system, which is how they receive nutrients and grow.

vascular system	tracheids	pipe-like structures
cytoplasm	phloem	cambium
diffusion	xylem	root hairs
bark	annual rings	tissue

■ The tracheophyte phylum can be subdivided into plants that reproduce by seeds and those that do not reproduce by seeds.

angiosperms	gymnosperms	cotyledons
monocots	dicots	spores
gametes	sporophytes	chromosomes
frond	ferns	corn
apple tree	gametophytes	alternation of generations

As you can see in Figure 6.4, the tree diagram reflects the major ideas about the tracheophyte phylum and how these ideas were organized by the author. The determination of which words should be included on the tree diagram varies from teacher to teacher. In this example, the words included were those that represented the major ideas *(vascular system),* those that were unfamiliar but important to understand *(xylem),* and those that were in students' prior knowledge *(apple tree).*

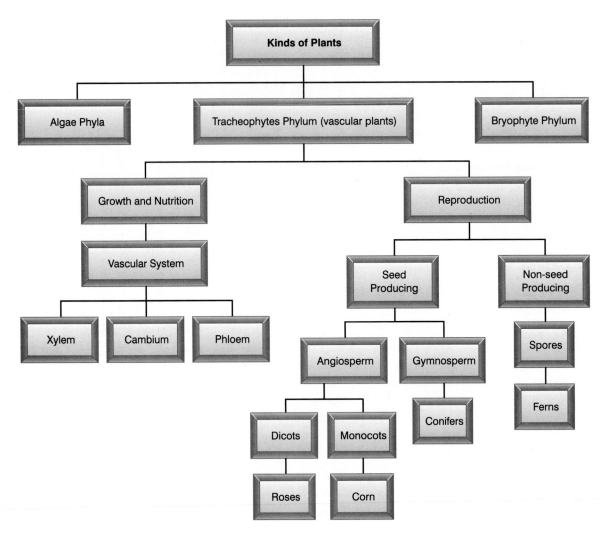

Figure 6.4 Graphic Organizer: Tracheophytes

Figures 6.5 to 6.9 are additional examples of graphic organizers on a variety of topics.

Using Graphic Organizers

Graphic organizers can be used in several ways. The most common is for the teacher to present the organizer on the board or an overhead and reference the prereading discussion to the organizer. We recommend that the students copy basic teacher-made organizers in their notebooks for review and study at a later

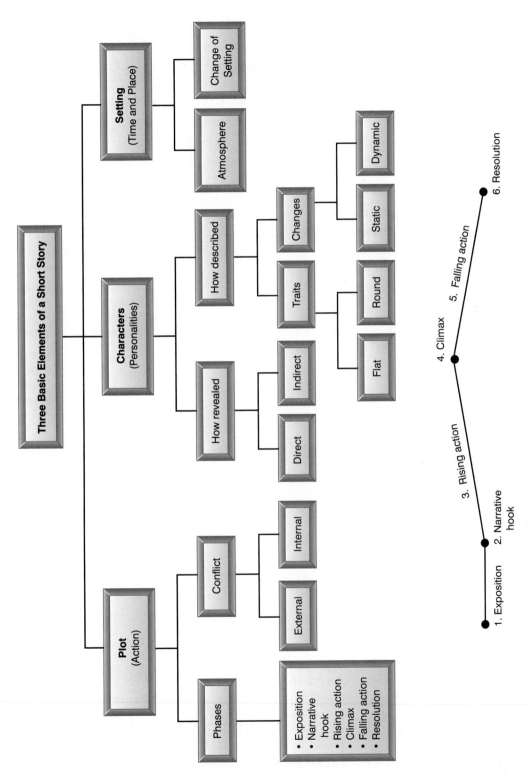

Figure 6.5 Graphic Organizer: Story Elements

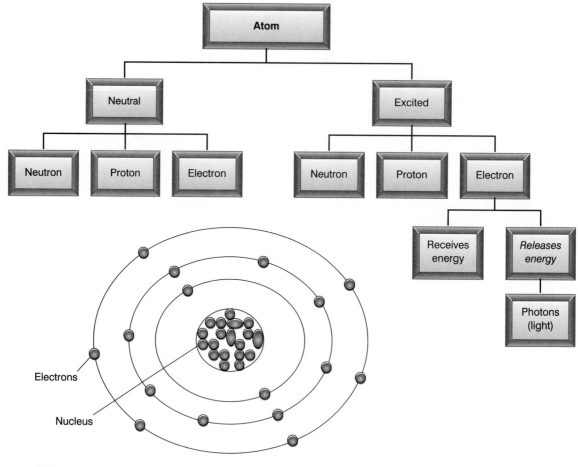

Objectives:

1. Describe the source of light.
2. Tell how the atomic structure relates to light.
3. Compare a neutral atom with an excited atom.
4. List the colors of visible light in an organized way.

Figure 6.6　Graphic Organizer: The Atom

Why are look-back organizers recommended?

date. Another suggestion with the teacher-made organizer is to have students add to the organizer as they read the chapter so that on completion they have a completely organized look at the chapter. These types of organizers are sometimes called **look-back organizers** and have a lot of potential for assisting students in learning how to develop their own organizers. Dinnel and Glover (1986) suggest that learning is maximized the more students become involved in using and developing their own graphic organizers. The example in Figure

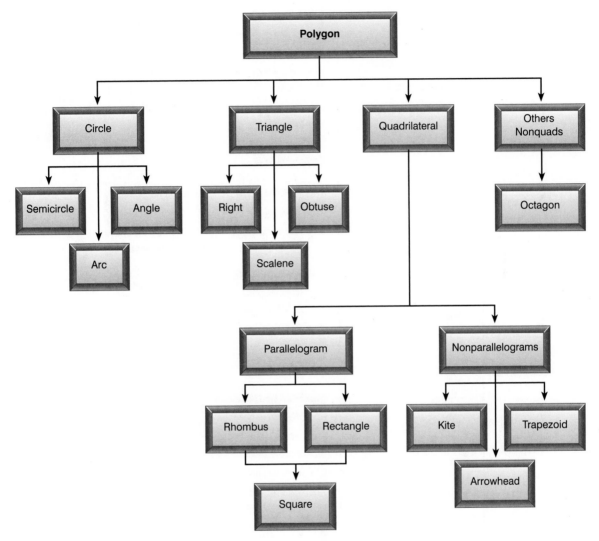

Figure 6.7 Graphic Organizer: Polygons

6.10 is based on a chapter in an eighth-grade earth science text that dealt with the makeup and types of soils in North America. As you can see in Figure 6.10, the teacher uses the top portion of the organizer to introduce and discuss components of soils and to introduce technical terms such as *horizon*. After the initial discussion, which includes a display of soil (direct experience), the teacher assigns in-class reading to complete the organizer by having students determine the location and soil characteristics for each soil region of North America. A follow-up discussion ensues to ensure the accuracy of what students found and to extend the discussion or lead into additional activities or information.

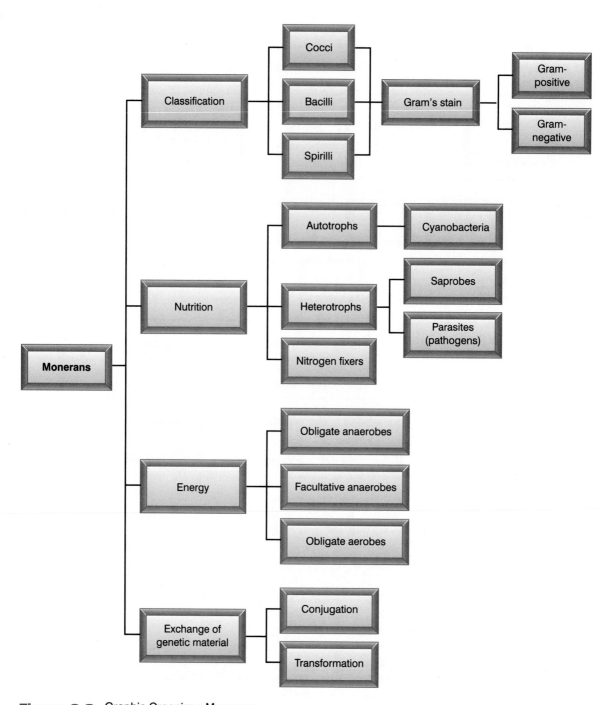

Figure 6.8 Graphic Organizer: Monerans

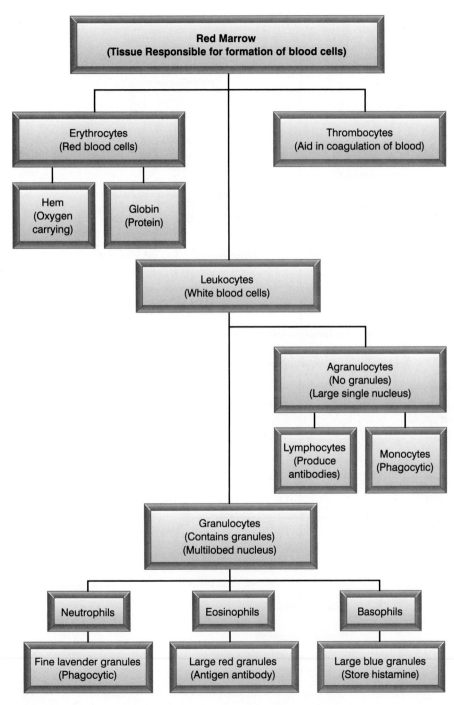

Figure 6.9 Graphic Organizer: Cellular Elements of Blood

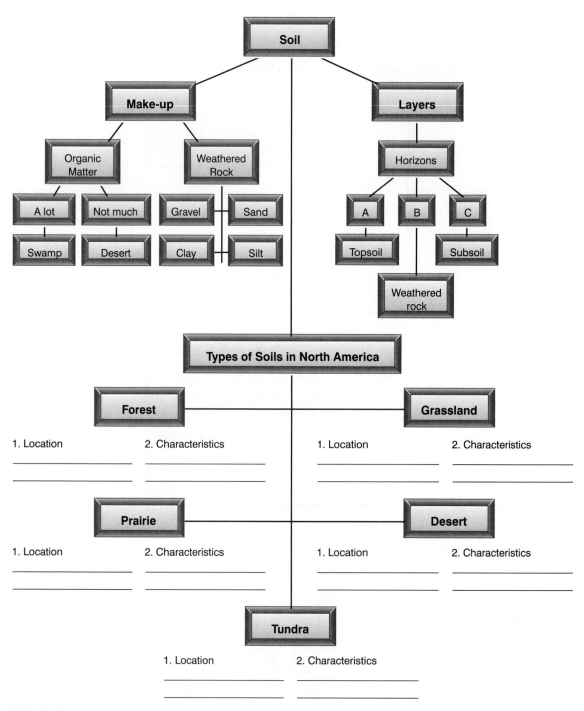

Figure 6.10 Look-Back Organizer: Soil

Using Semantic Feature Analysis

The **semantic feature analysis (SFA word grid)** has considerable research support as to its effectiveness in assisting the acquisition of vocabulary and improving text comprehension (Anders, Bos, & Wilde 1986; Toms-Bronowski, 1983). It is a rather straightforward method of helping students categorize and determine the relationship of interrelated terms. Although often recommended for use as an after-reading activity to reinforce vocabulary, SFA word grids can be used as a method to help prepare students for a reading assignment. The basic steps for using an SFA word grid follow:

Step 1: Based on content analysis of a chapter or unit of study, select a topic or category that is important. For example, we have selected the category *solar system.*

Step 2: On the chalkboard, overhead, or a bulletin board, place the category at the top, and down the left side in column form, list three or four words that name members of the category. In this case, words such as *Mars, Pluto,* and *Neptune* could be listed.

Step 3: In a row across the top of the grid, list several features or attributes shared by some of the words. Characteristics such as *hot, cold, solid, gaseous, outer planet, inner planet* could be listed.

Step 4: Introduce the topic, explain the grid, and engage students in a discussion about which of the listed features apply to the various members of the category. Place a plus (+) if the member has the feature, a minus (–) if it does not share the feature, and a question mark (?) if no one is really sure. This step reflects the extent of prior knowledge that students as a group have about the topic.

Step 5: Next, encourage students to add more members to the grid and additional features. Depending on the topic, you might have to limit the number of additions, while on others you might have to come up with some of the additional features/members.

Step 6: After expanding the grid, individually or in small groups, students use their text and other resources to complete the grid.

Step 7: Once students have completed the grid, a follow-up discussion is suggested, emphasizing likenesses and differences. Students may also be given a writing assignment based on the information in the grid to be included in their journals.

A sample SFA word grid is shown in Figure 6.11.

A variation on the SFA word grid is the **subject area vocabulary reinforcement activity (SAVOR)** (Stieglitz & Stieglitz, 1981). The only difference from the previously mentioned steps is that SAVOR is strictly a postreading

Why is semantic feature analysis considered a categorization activity?

Can you think of a possible writing activity for this word grid?

Planets	Inner planet	Outer planet	Made up of gas	Has more than one moon	Longer revolution than Earth's 365 days	Has rings	Has been visited by a space probe	Stronger gravity than Earth
Venus	+	–	–	–	–	–	+	–
Neptune	–	+	+	+	+	?	+	+
Saturn	–	+	+	+	+	+	+	+
Mercury	+	–	–	–	–	–	+	–

Figure 6.11 Semantic Feature Analysis Word Grid: Solar System, the Planets

activity done for summarization. The grid (except for the category) is completely student generated in cooperative groups.

Using Convergent and Divergent Semantic Mapping (Webbing)

How would you explain the term *semantic map*?

Semantic mapping or **webbing** is another graphic display that capitalizes on teacher–student interaction and groups of interrelated terms and ideas. Semantic mapping assists students in comprehending text by activating their background knowledge, organizing concepts graphically, and discovering the relationships between their prior knowledge and the new concepts. The two types of semantic maps are **convergent maps**, which are typically teacher-made and structured, and **divergent maps**, which are more open ended and student developed.

To use a convergent semantic map, the teacher first selects a key word or phrase about a new topic, places it on the chalkboard or overhead, and identifies three or four categories of subordinate information about the identified concept. These are placed on spokes that radiate from the central word or phrase. Next, students are asked to volunteer any prior knowledge they have about the identified concept and decide which of the categories the information should be placed under. The teacher will need to probe the students for information and suspend judgment about the placement of the information on the map. Finally, students are asked to read their texts and other reference material for the purpose of expanding the map and making any necessary revisions or modifications. Journal entries, class activities, or additional reading and discussion should follow the final version of the map for the identified topic. Figure 6.12 is an example of a convergent semantic map.

To use a divergent semantic map, the teacher first places a word or phrase about a new topic on the chalkboard or overhead and encourages students to brainstorm any words that they associate with the word or phrase displayed in a square or circle. These are recorded in a separate area on the board or trans-

What's the difference between convergent and divergent semantic maps?

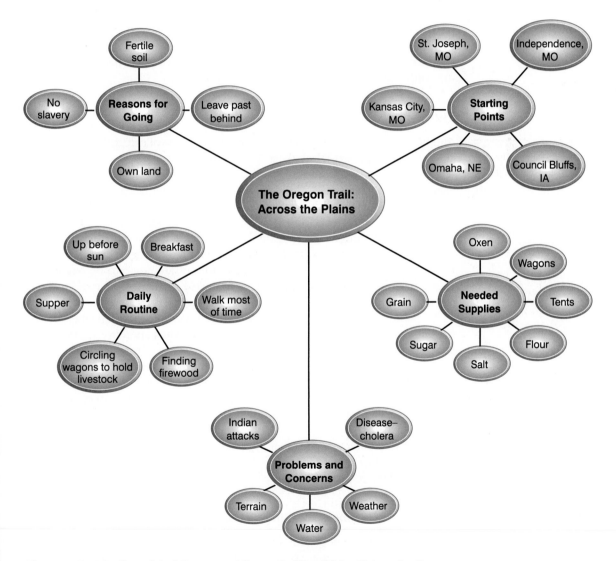

Figure 6.12 Completed Convergent Semantic Map (Major Categories Provided by the Teacher)

parency. Next the students, either as a whole class or in small groups, are asked to identify categories that encompass one or more of the brainstormed words. These category names are placed on the board, and students are encouraged to identify as many words as possible that would fit under each category heading. Finally, after the discussion and arrangement of the organized information on spokes radiating from the map, students are asked to read their text and other sources to find additional information that needs to be added to the map. Figure 6.13 is an example of a divergent semantic map.

The possibilities for mapping or webbing are endless. They do not have to be elaborate as long as they meet the basic criteria of providing insight into students' prior knowledge, helping students organize what they know and what they learned about the topic, and assisting students in other instructional activities with the topic (e.g., writing, reading, and doing).

List-Group-Label

Classifying and categorizing activities, like list-group-label, help students acquire ownership of the terms involved.

Another vocabulary activity that capitalizes on the idea of categorization and classification is **list-group-label** (Taba, 1967). Originally suggested as a social studies technique, list-group-label has possibilities in a variety of other subject matter areas when the focus is on the relationship among the meaning of terms being studied. List-group-label has potential as a prereading technique for activating students' prior knowledge and causing purposeful reading of the adopted text. Likewise, the strategy can be used as a postreading activity to reinforce and expand knowledge of important vocabulary. The teacher begins by writing on the board a topic that students have familiarity with or are going to be reading and learning about beginning that day (e.g., triangles). Students are asked to brainstorm all the words they associate with the topic/category. The teacher records all the words until 20 to 30 terms are on the board. If list-group-label is being used as a prereading technique, the teacher becomes an active participant in generating the list, if students do not brainstorm some of the key vocabulary, by suggesting important terms not mentioned. After the list of terms has been generated, the students form small groups whose purpose is to take the master list of terms and reorganize it into smaller lists that have something in common and give each smaller list a label or title. Each group of students should be allowed to share their results while other groups comment on both completeness of the new list and accuracy of the label. If some terms are left over, students should identify what they are and why there were no other terms that related to the isolated terms. Figure 6.14 is an example of list-group-label for triangles.

Other Ways to Promote Vocabulary Development

Remembering that variety adds spice to life and also the classroom, we offer the following strategies as additional ways to promote interest and acquisition of content vocabulary. These additional strategies should be used selectively by teachers trying to have a planned and systematic vocabulary development program.

Initial Associations by Students:

cold	Eskimos	frozen	polar bears	igloos	oil spills
Alaska	North Pole	Russia	snow geese	blubber	snowy

Categories for Associations and Additional Reading, Expansion, and Discussion:
Climate and Location: cold, snowy, icy, frozen, Alaska, North Pole, Russia
Effects of Man: oil spills, air pollution, endangered species
Organisms (plants and animals): polar bears, seals, snow geese, moss
Eskimos: eat blubber, live in igloos, travel by sled, eat seals

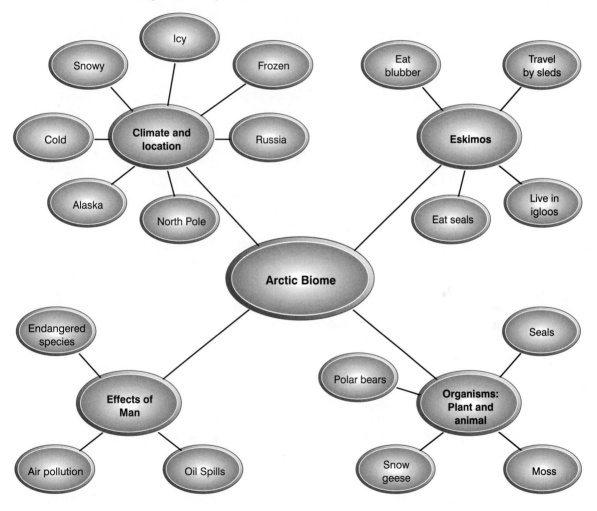

Figure 6.13 Divergent Semantic Map

Figure 6.14 List-Group-Label: Triangles

Triangles			
Master List			
right triangle	acute triangle	angles	base
congruent	isosceles triangle	scalene triangle	b × h
degree	not congruent	equilateral triangle	perimeter
height	side-by-side rule	yield sign	hypotenuse
equiangular	sailboat sails	adjacent angle	house gables
pyramid	tangent ratio	side-angle-side rule	angle-side-angle rule

Examples of Regroupings

Types of triangles: right triangle, scalene triangle, isosceles triangle, equilateral triangle,

Measurement of a triangle's area: base, height, formula b × h.

Everyday things that have triangles: sailboat sails, pyramid, house gables, yield sign

Vocabulary Self-Collection Strategy

Compare VSS and the vocabulary anticipation activity and decide which one would be more appropriate for your content area.

Vocabulary self-collection strategy (VSS) (Haggard, 1982) is a student-centered vocabulary strategy that requires students to decide which terms are important to know. Before, during, or after studying a chapter or unit of study, students (and teacher, too) are asked to select two terms that they think the whole class should learn. They are instructed to be prepared to explain formally or informally what the terms mean, where they found them, and why they chose the two terms. When students enter the class on the appointed day, they write their two terms on the board. After duplications have been eliminated, students explain their terms' meaning and why everyone should learn them. Next, the list of terms is shortened based on an agreed to prior number (no more than 12 for instance), and the owners of the remaining list again discuss the terms. Finally, students are asked to record the terms and their meanings in vocabulary notebooks for that subject matter area.

Vocabulary Anticipation Activity

Vocabulary **anticipation activity** (AA) (Hammond, 1979) is a technique that assesses students' prior knowledge of a topic to be studied, fosters cooperative learning, and provides a stimulus to attend to the meanings of the terms that are unfamiliar to the students. The teacher selects the important words from an upcoming chapter of study, duplicates the list of words, and cuts the lists into sets of word cards. Students are placed into cooperative groups. Each group is asked to place the word cards into groups that have something in common or that reflect how the words may be related in the upcoming chapter. The different groups share their groupings, and then they are asked to read to confirm or find out how the various terms are related. After they read, time should be allowed for each group to reorganize their word cards and to discuss the new information they found out about their terms.

Vocabulary Scavenger Hunt

The vocabulary scavenger hunt (P. Cunningham, Crawley, & Mountain, 1983) is a prereading strategy that capitalizes on competition, creativity, and student-generated meanings of new and familiar terminology. Before the beginning of a unit of study, the teacher makes a scavenger list of important terms that students will be expected to know. Students are placed into scavenger hunt groups, and each group picks a leader and receives a copy of the word list. Each group is to decide how they will accomplish either getting the actual object, a picture that represents the term, a demonstration that explains the word, or any other creative means (actual people could be brought to class). Teams are not allowed to share information. On the day the unit of study is to begin, each group brings their collection of objects, displays, pictures, people, and demonstrations to class. The teacher decides how to award points so that after each team presents their scavenger list findings a winning team surfaces. The winners produce a display for reference.

> Vocabulary scavenger hunts can also include experiments, examples of specific kinds of writing, information about famous people, and so on.

Cubing

Cubing (Cowan & Cowan, 1980) is a postreading activity requiring students to write about important terms. The initial setup is for the teacher to have a large foam cube covered with contact paper. On each side of the cube is written a different direction. The directions need to match the topic under study but could include the following:

1. Describe what it looks like.
2. What else is it alike or different from?
3. What else does it make you think of?
4. What is it made of?
5. How can you use it?
6. Where can you find it?

Obviously, for famous people the directions would have to be changed, likewise for mathematics. Once the cube is rolled and the direction facing the class or group is seen, the students are given a set number of minutes to record an answer. All six sides of the cube can be used or only a few. Once the cubing has ended, students can share their responses with the class or in small groups.

> Cubing could be used as part of a study-response journal (see Chapter 10) or learning log (see Chapter 8).

Figure 6.15 Frayer Model:
Gymnosperms

> *Concept*: Gymnosperms
> *Essential Information or Attributes*:
>   1. Produce naked seeds.
>   2. Do not produce flowers.
>   3. Seeds develop on cones or scales.
>   4. Mainly consist of conifers.
> *Nonessential Information or Attributes*:
>   1. Size of the plant.
>   2. Number of seeds.
>   3. How the plant is used.
>   4. Where the plant grows.
> *Examples*:
>   1. Pine tree
>   2. Spruce tree
>   3. Redwood tree
> *Nonexamples*:
>   1. Corn
>   2. Moss
>   3. Rose

Frayer Model

The **Frayer model** (Frayer, Frederick, & Klausmeir, 1969) is based on the idea that students need to understand concepts in relation to one another. The teacher presents or causes students to determine essential and nonessential information about a concept, find examples and nonexamples of the concept, and recognize coordinate and subordinate relationships of the concept. This classification procedure can be done as a whole group, dyads, or individually. See Figure 6.15 for an example.

LEARNERS WITH SPECIAL NEEDS

Distinguish between work habit demands, knowledge expression demands, and knowledge acquisition demands.

Students with learning problems who are in a regular classroom setting are faced with work habit demands, knowledge acquisition demands, and knowledge expression demands (Schumaker & Deshler, 1984). **Work habit demands** relate to successful homework completion and independent work. **Knowledge acquisition demands** refer to the broad spectrum of classroom activities including listening to lectures, reading complex text, taking notes, and using strategies to understand text. **Knowledge expression demands** are those that require the student to discuss, write, participate, and perform on exams. One of the keys to assisting the student with learning problems in meeting these content area demands is an effective vocabulary program.

Most, if not all, of the teaching ideas presented in this chapter reflect the recommendations of Zigmond, Sansone, Miller, Donahoe, and Kohnke (1986) for teaching adolescents with learning problems. These include the following:

1. Plan activities that cause students to participate actively in new learning. In this chapter, many of the techniques described require active participation and group collaboration. Semantic feature analysis word grids have been found to produce better retention of vocabulary for learning disabled students than the traditional procedure of looking up words in the dictionary and writing a definition (Anders, Bos, & Filip, 1984). Placing students with learning problems in dyads or cooperative groups for vocabulary instruction can also be beneficial because of the mutually supportive climate created and the opportunity for peer assistance.

2. Build background information about new topics before having students read about them. Assist the students in perceiving how text information is organized, and use visuals. Students with learning problems tend to have difficulty organizing information and integrating new information with their prior knowledge (Torgesen & Kail 1985; Wong, 1978). Graphic organizers, if student generated and uncluttered, have proven to be beneficial for students with learning problems. Semantic mapping can also be used as an aid to text organization.

3. Minimize the amount of vocabulary students are held responsible for remembering. Students with learning problems need structure and assurance that efforts will be rewarded. By clearly delineating what is important information to know and remember, teachers can heighten these students' opportunities to increase performance.

Additionally, Alley and Deshler (1979) advocate a **learning strategies approach** for these kinds of students. Students with learning problems should be taught strategies that will help them acquire, store, and express content. The strategies in this and Chapters 7 to 10 emphasize the process (how) over the product (what), because we recognize that knowing how to learn is of paramount importance.

Besides the strategies presented in this chapter, which are appropriate for use with students with learning problems, the following suggestions may be of benefit for increasing the acquisition of new important vocabulary.

■ Students should keep a vocabulary journal/notebook. This notebook should be exclusively for technical and specialized terms. It can include both formal and personal definitions of words and any visuals provided by the teacher or generated by students that are vocabulary oriented.

Summarize the recommendations for teaching vocabulary to students with learning problems.

Which three of the seven suggestions for increasing acquisition of vocabulary do you think are the most important and the ones you will definitely experiment with?

- Students should be made aware of common words that are redefined in the text, for example, the word *set* in a mathematics text. These kinds of words can cause difficulty if not discussed.
- All critical acronyms, abbreviations, and other unique representations of words should be included in the student's notebook along with what they stand for.
- The number of words required of students with learning problems should be carefully considered. Selecting those that relate most directly to major concepts in a unit of study is recommended.
- To learn new words, students should be encouraged or caused to review. Whether using look-back graphic organizers, paraphrased explanations, and/or other vocabulary graphics, review is important for students with learning problems. Support personnel should assist with review.
- Students should benefit from vocabulary study. Students with learning problems need immediate and positive feedback on in-class and out-of-class activities. They also need to have a payoff for study. This means that exams should focus on what has been emphasized, and if the student has been required to study words, then the exam should reflect this requirement.
- The final suggestion, one that runs throughout this text, is to stay in close communication with support personnel for each of the students. Whether it is a special education teacher, paraprofessional, or other resource personnel, your expectations, the students' progress or lack thereof, and the effort put forth should be continually communicated. Likewise, the content teacher should request assistance and instructional recommendations for students who continue to experience problems accomplishing assignments and experiencing success with assessments.

Chapter Summary

Vocabulary development is the foundation for understanding and communicating in any content area. Students' acquiring ownership of important terms in the subject matter areas is not an end but a means to an end, namely, successful learning of content area information and the development of independent learners. The role of the teacher in assuming the responsibility for developing a systematic vocabulary program and the need for students to become active participants in learning how to learn are critical.

The general guidelines for promoting vocabulary acquisition include (a) keeping vocabulary as experienced based as possible, (b) being selective about what words are taught, (c) using a variety of strategies to teach vocabulary, and (d) providing time and exposure to ensure ownership.

Students have receptive and expressive vocabularies, and their receptive (reading and listening) vocabularies are their largest. To increase students' receptive and expressive vocabularies, teachers need to provide students both definitional and contextual knowledge of the word being studied. Teachers who plan to have a systematic program of vocabulary instruction should remember that not all strategies work with all subjects or students and that the real goal is to move from teacher-centered instruction to more process-oriented, student-centered instruction. Word maps, student-generated graphic organizers, and subject area vocabulary reinforcement are representative of student-centered, process-oriented strategies that can promote vocabulary acquisition.

Students with learning problems are faced with work habit demands, knowledge acquisition demands, and knowledge expression demands, and one way to assist them in coping with these demands is a systematic vocabulary program. These students require more structure and explicitness with vocabulary. Uncluttered graphic organizers, fewer terms to remember, and background discussions are general considerations for assisting these students with vocabulary terms. Vocabulary journals, explanations of specialized terminology and critical abbreviations and acronyms, and lots of review are also beneficial for students with learning problems.

Reflection/Application Activities

1. Obtain a copy of a recent content area textbook in your subject specialty. Select one chapter to read, and make a list of all words that are highlighted, italicized, or underlined. From this master list, make a smaller list of words that you think should be pretaught before students should be asked to read this chapter. Finally, prepare a prereading vocabulary activity using the words you selected and one of the strategies introduced in this chapter. You will share your results in small groups.

2. Secure a copy of the teacher's edition of a content area textbook. List the ways the edition suggests for teaching vocabulary. Would you classify the book's approach as traditional or holistic? Why? Does the teacher's edition develop both defini-

tional and contextual knowledge of key words? Explain. Finally, write a letter to the authors of the textbook you selected delineating either why you like how they treated vocabulary instruction or why they need to improve their treatment of vocabulary.

3. Select a topic in a recent content area textbook in your subject specialty. After completing a content analysis of the topic, prepare either a look-back organizer or a convergent semantic map that could be used to assist students in reading about the selected topic.

4. Using your subject specialty, make a list of 10 recommendations that all teachers should read to have a systematic and planned vocabulary program.

Recommended Reading

Cochran, J. A. (1993). *Reading in the content areas for junior high and high school.* Boston: Allyn & Bacon.

Duffy, G. (1990). *Reading in the middle school.* Newark, DE: International Reading Association.

Flippo, R. F., & Caverly, D. C. (1991). *Teaching reading and study strategies at the college level.* Newark, DE: International Reading Association.

Mercer, C. D., & Mercer, A. R. (1993). *Teaching students with learning problems* (4th ed.). Englewood Cliffs, NJ: Merrill/Prentice Hall.

Nagy, W. E. (1988). *Teaching vocabulary to improve reading comprehension.* Newark, DE: International Reading Association.

Pittleman, S. D., Heimlich, J. E., Borglund, R. L., & French, M. P. (1991). *Semantic feature analysis: Classroom applications.* Newark, DE: International Reading Association.

Santa, M. D., & Alvermann, D. E. (1991). *Science learning: Processes and applications.* Newark, DE: International Reading Association.

Sensenbaugh, R. (1992). *Reading and writing across the high school science and math curriculum.* Bloomington, IN: EDINFO Press.

Wallace, G., Cohen, S. B., & Polloway, E. A. (1987). *Language arts: Teaching exceptional students.* Austin, TX: ProEd.

Learning From Expository Text

Complexities of Learning From Expository Text

Preparing Students to Read

Information-Seeking Strategies

Expository Text Structure and Patterns

Responding to Extend Understanding

Learners With Special Needs

Focus Questions

*As you read this chapter, try to discover
answers to the following questions:*

1 Why are textbooks sometimes difficult for students to read?

2 What do successful students do when they read textbooks? What are some things
   teachers can do to promote active reading of texts?

3 What are the common characteristics of the strategies presented as ways of
   preparing students to read your textbook?

4 How do our suggestions for constructing study guides differ from study guides
   you experienced as a middle or high school student?

5 Compare and contrast levels of comprehension guides and selective reading
   guides. Which one would be best for your content area?

6 Why and how do we recommend organizational writing patterns?

7 How would you describe the Guided Reading Procedure?

8 What are the recommendations for helping students with learning problems comprehend text material?

Student–text interaction can be
facilitated by the teacher.

If you ask high school students, "When was the last time you read a good textbook?" the response will probably be one of bemused silence. Yet textbooks
are the most commonly used learning tool in content area classrooms. More
and more content teachers are searching for ways to make textbooks more
interesting and useful in their classes. Furthermore, innovative teachers are
looking beyond traditional textbooks for more exciting learning texts to augment their instruction. Whether textbooks, magazines, computer texts, or consumer materials are to be used, their effectiveness for transmitting knowledge
depends to a great extent on what the classroom teacher does to facilitate the
student–text interaction. In this chapter we focus on ways to help students
improve their comprehension of text materials, using both teacher-directed
and student-driven strategies.

READING TO LEARN FROM EXPOSITORY TEXTS

The old saying "You can't judge a book by its cover" is certainly true in the case of textbooks. Most have gleaming multicolored covers, but once opened they confront the reader with a veritable ocean of words, creating for some students the sense of "enter at your own risk." Supplemental readings can be just as complex and difficult to understand. Students generally have only one person to turn to for assistance, the teacher.

The teacher, or "expert-textpert," is the critical variable for helping students meet the challenges of content text. To assist students, teachers must be equipped with a repertoire of strategies and tactics that can help students develop the skills necessary to succeed with independent reading assignments. Additionally, teachers need to understand factors related to text awareness. **Text awareness** refers to a person's ability to discern how a text is organized and written. Armbruster and Anderson (1984) suggest that texts can be categorized as being either *considerate* or *inconsiderate* to readers based on how well they are written. Teachers who know a variety of instructional strategies and how to assess the internal structure of texts are better able to help students learn from texts. In the following sections, we focus on text awareness, followed by a variety of instructional strategies.

What is text awareness?

Considerate Versus Inconsiderate Text

Expository and narrative texts are the two types of prose most used in content classrooms. They differ both in terms of purpose and internal structure. **Expository texts** are materials written to inform, whereas **narrative texts** tell a story. Most content texts are expository in nature and usually have a hierarchical arrangement of information. The hierarchy is used to organize information around **superordinate ideas** (generalizations), which are explained by **subordinate ideas** (concepts) and further elaborated by **subordinate details** (facts). The content analysis process teachers go through in examining learning materials sets the stage for identifying these superordinate ideas, subordinate ideas, and subordinate details. Whether the text is narrative or expository in design, how well it is organized and written obviously affects the interaction between reader and text.

Note that there are different expository text organization patterns.

Well-Organized Text Facilitates Comprehension

When it comes to text organization, or **internal structure,** textbooks are generally classified as being either considerate or inconsiderate (Armbruster & Anderson, 1984) of the reader. **Considerate text** has logically sequenced ideas, avoids the inclusion of irrelevant information, is written with the back-

Compare considerate and inconsiderate texts.

ground of the intended audience in mind, includes numerous supporting internal aids (visuals, headings), and presents information using specific organizational patterns. **Inconsiderate text** usually lacks these characteristics, which causes it to be more difficult to read and understand. Without repeated exposure and conscious attention to the various organizational patterns in exposition, students can experience problems when asked to read and learn information in expository textbooks.

Global and local coherence can assist comprehension.

When writers create text, they are concerned with making their message as coherent as possible to increase the probability that readers will develop a clear understanding of their message. To improve students' chances of comprehension, texts should have local and global coherence (T. H. Anderson & Armbruster, 1986). **Global coherence**, you recall, has to do with the overall structure of the textbook. A text is globally coherent when readers can view the table of contents and recognize a clear focus, chapters are logically outlined, and information is presented within chapters so that even a newcomer to the topic feels the information will be relatively easy to learn. **Local coherence** is the level at which phrases and sentences are combined to link ideas in a logical way (Mason & Au, 1990). Skillful writers can organize expository text so that global and local coherence come together in a kind of seamless tapestry that boosts comprehension of key ideas.

An early preparatory task for the teacher is to determine the considerateness and coherency of the adopted text. Once this analysis is completed, it becomes easier to find teaching strategies that help students read and understand the content.

Student–Text Interactions: What Successful Students Do

In spite of the fact that adopted textbooks and supplemental readings continue to be the informational mainstay of content classes, many students still do not know how to read and learn from expository texts effectively (Baker, 1991). Unsuccessful students often exhibit dependent behavior, avoid assigned readings, and rely on teacher talk for acquiring needed information for tests. One of the authors recently surveyed his undergraduate content reading classes and found that over 75% admitted that they did not read their textbooks in high school in one or more classes. In follow-up discussions the students added that content teachers frequently restrict their classroom presentations to information in the text, thus making reading outside of class unnecessary. One student added, "Half the time reading assignments were given, and we were never asked to discuss the assignments." Masterful teachers find interesting and creative ways to "honorably seduce" (Cooter & Griffith, 1989) students into reading expository texts. Teachers also realize that successful students develop a number of literacy skills that help them learn and apply expository text information. The teacher's key role then is twofold: Help *all* students (not just the brightest) acquire needed literacy skills relevant to their subject area, and create motivating learning opportunities that draw students into expository texts. So the question we wish to address in this section is, *What do successful middle and high school students do in content classes to learn and apply important information?*

Perhaps the two most common attributes of successful students are familiarity with different types of texts and knowing how to read in strategic ways to obtain important information from them. Teachers can act on this knowledge to promote student learning from expository texts by (a) helping students become active readers, (b) increase student awareness and use of text organization and structure for improved comprehension, and (3) increase student independence by teaching appropriate strategies for learning from text. The ultimate goal, as with education in general, is to help students become independent learners.

What is the teacher's role for promoting student learning from expository text?

Developing Active Readers

Active readers make use of their prior knowledge of a subject and comprehension-monitoring strategies to get the most out of what they read. Teachers can assist students by assessing their background knowledge of upcoming topics, providing needed information about the topic and the text before reading, and encouraging text previews. These **engagement tactics** help students call to mind what they already know and develop an active agenda for what they still need to learn.

One of the distinguishing abilities of highly literate students is knowing what to do when reading comprehension problems occur. Studies have shown that skilled readers monitor their comprehension and deliberately employ techniques that assist comprehension to a far greater degree than do unskilled readers (Baker, 1985; Paris & Myer, 1981; Schommer & Surber, 1986). Self-regulation strategies that involve understanding when and why reading comprehension is not occurring and then taking corrective action are at the heart of what is known as **metacognition** (Baker & Brown, 1984).

Self-regulation refers to strategies readers use to improve comprehension of text.

Some very basic techniques that can be used include predicting upcoming information in text, interspersing questions for discussion of what has been read, postreading reflection on confusing and unclear information identified by the student, and paraphrasing or summarizing activities (Palincsar & Brown, 1984).

Increasing Student Awareness of Expository Text Organization Patterns

We know that students who excel in various content areas—like political science, interior design, geometry, and astronomy—can recognize and adapt to different expository text organization patterns. It would then seem logical that teachers should teach the most common structures to students along with appropriate reading strategies, but not all teachers agree (Manzo & Manzo, 1990; Niles, 1965). In one study (Gee & Rakow, 1987), reading specialists ranked text structure instruction 14th of 23 preferred teaching practices for improving text comprehension. Other investigators, however (Nelson-Herber & Johnston, 1989; Slater & Graves, 1989), claim that the research supports the belief that students who have knowledge of text structures have enhanced comprehension of text. Our view is that making students aware of expository text organization patterns through a combination of reading and writing activities does indeed improve comprehension.

What are the common expository text organization patterns?

In preparing reading assignments, teachers should first identify expository text organization patterns used by the author so that students can be alerted to how the information will be presented. The most common types of expository text organization patterns include comparison–contrast, cause–effect, sequential, simple listing or enumeration, and problem–solution. Associated with these patterns are specific cues that skilled readers use to facilitate their comprehension called **signal words** (Vacca & Vacca, 1993). In Figure 7.1 we offer a

Figure 7.1 Writing Patterns and Associated Signal Words

Pattern	Definition	Associated Signal Words
Comparison & contrast	Information is presented by detailing likenesses and differences among events, concepts, theories, etc.	*however, nevertheless, on the other hand, but, similarly, although, also, either/or*
Cause & effect	The text presents ideas, events in time, or facts that happen as a result of other ideas, events in time, or facts	*if /then, therefore, as a result, so that, because, since, consequently*
Sequential	Information is presented in a chronological sequence, either explicit or implied	*after, when, now, as before, not long,* actual use of dates
Simple listing or enumeration	The text presents information in list form, detailing facts, descriptions, or attributes of what is being discussed	*first, second, next, then, finally, most important*
Problem/solution (similar to cause and effect)	The text presents a problem and solutions to the problem	Same as cause/effect

summary of common expository text organization/writing patterns, a brief definition, and signal words often associated with each pattern.

Although these patterns of writing are often found in combination, generally, a text selection has a predominant pattern that is the key to recognizing and understanding what the author considers to be the most important ideas. Later in this chapter some specific instructional ideas are presented that can help teachers guide students in using these patterns to foster comprehension while they read.

To deepen your understanding of these expository text organization/writing patterns, the examples in Figures 7.2 through 7.6 are presented as practice. Try to determine which pattern is being used by the author to organize and present the information. It is also useful for the reader to try to determine the superordinate idea(s), subordinate idea(s), and any specific details. Finally, classify each selection as to expository text writing pattern used according to the signal words present and their relationship to the superordinate idea(s).

Look for the different writing patterns in Figures 7.2 through 7.6.

Figure 7.2 Organizational Writing Pattern Example

Interaction of Genes and the Environment

In general, no trait is inherited in a simple manner. The picture is almost always complicated by environmental factors. For example, the tendency to become infected with pulmonary tuberculosis is inherited. However, only a small portion of such people actually develop the disease because nutrition, general health, and exposure to infection are more important than genetic tendency to develop the disease. It is uncommon for heredity or environment to be entirely responsible for any particular trait or disease. In most cases, both factors are responsible.

For example, at one extreme there are diseases, such as Down syndrome or muscular dystrophy, that are almost completely genetic in origin. The environment seems to play no direct part in the development of these disorders. At the other extreme, we have infectious diseases that are almost completely the result of environmental factors. Scurvy and tuberculosis are examples of diseases due almost entirely to environmental factors. In between these extremes are such conditions as diabetes mellitus, hypertension, peptic ulcer, and certain cancers. Both environmental and genetic factors are involved in the development of such conditions.

Comparison and contrast.

Note. From *Scott, Foresman: Biology* by I. L. Slesnick, L. Balzer, A. J. McCormack, and D. E. Newton, 1980, Glenview, IL: Scott, Foresman and Company. Copyright 1980 by Scott, Foresman and Company.

Figure 7.3 Organizational Writing Pattern Example

Opening and Closing of Stomates

The amount of gas that can move into or out of a leaf depends on how wide open the stomates are. Opening and closing the stomates involves two things. One is the structure of the cell wall in the guard cells, which surround the stomate. The other is the amount of water in the guard cells. In [the illustration], you can see that the part of the cell wall facing the stomate is thicker than the part of the cell wall opposite the stomate. When the guard cells are filled with water, the water exerts pressure against the cell wall. This causes the thin part of the cell wall to "give," bending the cell wall outward. As the cell wall bends, it pulls the rest of the guard cell with it, opening the stomate.

When the guard cells are not full of water, there is little pressure on the outside walls, and the guard cells do not bend very much. As a result, the inner sides of the guard cells stay together, keeping the stomate closed.

The opening and closing of the stomates are linked to photosynthesis. The guard cells produce glucose from carbon dioxide and water during photosynthesis. Water moves into the guard cells, replacing the water used in photosynthesis. This water exerts pressure against the walls of the guard cells, causing them to open. When the plant is not photosynthesizing, water does not move into the guard cells and the stomates close.

Cause/effect.

Note. From *Biology: A Systems Approach* by E. J. Kormondy and B. E. Essenfeld, 1988, Menlo Park, CA: Addison-Wesley. Copyright 1988 by Addison-Wesley Publishing Co., Inc.

Strategies That Lead to Student Independence

A major goal of content area teachers is to develop students capable of independent learning from a variety of expository text forms. Reading/learning strategies can be internalized and used effectively by students when content teachers follow a three-step process.

First is *awareness* of reading/learning skills. Content teachers need to teach the reading/learning skills that serve their specialty area. For example, skimming and scanning strategies may be useful in such diverse areas as English literature, algebra I, and automobile mechanics. Map reading skills can be useful in world history, geometry, and basics of electronics. The point is to introduce in context various skills related to the unit of study and to provide adequate practice. Second, show students how to cluster individual skills to form a **reading/learning strategy**. For instance, one can combine map reading and scanning skills to locate cities and altitudes in a world atlas. Third, develop creative real-world projects for students that require them to put

One goal is to help students think like historians, mathematicians, etc.

Figure 7.4 Organizational Writing Pattern Example

American Indians

American Indians made significant gains during the mid-twentieth century. Since the 1880s, the federal government had followed a wavering policy toward the Native American people. In 1887, the *Dawes Act* advocated the break-up of tribal systems and the redistribution of reservation lands, traditionally held by the tribe, among individuals. This was supposed to make the Indians landowners in the mode of mainstream American society, but actually made it easier for speculators to grab the Indians' land. Speculators could buy the land more readily from individual owners than from a whole tribe. Not until the Indian Reorganization Act of 1934 was the policy of bringing the American Indians into mainstream society reversed.

In the 1950s, the policy was reversed again. Many young Indians had already moved from the reservations to the cities where opportunities seemed more promising. Native American culture seemed to be dying. In 1953, President Eisenhower further encouraged migration from the reservations into the mainstream of American society.

In the late 1960s, several developments set the course for future Indian sovereignty. In 1968, the *National Congress of American Indians* (NCAI) was founded, and began to push for Indian legal rights. Also in the late 1960s, the *American Indian Movement* (AIM) was founded. More militant than NCAI, the organization protested, sometimes violently, for Indian treaty rights.

In 1970, President Nixon announced a policy of Indian self-determination. Under this plan, Indian people would establish their own tribal systems and customs on the reservations. The federal government would help with housing, vocational training, and economic development.

Sequential.

Note. From *A History of the United States: Our Land, Our Time* by J. R. Conlin, 1985, San Diego, CA: Coronado Publishers. Copyright 1985 by Coronado Publishers.

newly acquired strategies to work. This last step pushes new knowledge to higher levels and causes students to internalize effective strategies. The result is a student who not only knows new concepts but who is beginning to think like a mathematician, historian, health professional, or whichever content area is being taught.

The remainder of this chapter details various strategies teachers may choose to stress to develop independent consumers of expository text. Some are traditional methods that still make sense in light of holistic teaching principles. Others are more recent developments. All have proven to be effective in our own classrooms, as we hope they will prove to be in yours.

Figure 7.5   Organizational Writing Pattern Example

> **The Sunna**
>
> The Sunna were the guiding rules for Islam and were based on the way the prophet Muhammad lived his own life. The most basic of these rules were the Five Pillars of Islam. The ideas behind these five duties came from the Koran, but it was in the Sunna that the leaders of Islam set them down.
>
> The first of these pillars is the profession of faith. To express their acceptance of Islam, Muslims repeat the phrase, "There is no god but Allah, and Muhammad is his prophet."
>
> The second pillar is prayer. Muslims must pray five times a day. Prayers follow special rituals, including washing before praying, bowing, and then kneeling while praying. Muslims must always face Mecca when praying. Every Friday at noon, Muslims assemble for public prayer in a mosque.
>
> The third pillar is giving alms, or showing charity to the poor. Muslims must also contribute to public charities, such as the building of mosques and hospitals.
>
> The fourth pillar is the ritual fast during Ramadan, the ninth month of the Muslim year. Ramadan is a holy time, because in this month Muhammad received his first message from Allah. During Ramadan, Muslims must not eat or drink from the break of dawn until the setting of the sun. Muslims believe that this rigorous fast brings them closer to Allah.
>
> The fifth pillar of Islam is Hajj—the pilgrimage to Mecca. All Muslims who can afford it must make the pilgrimage at least once.
>
> *Enumeration/simple listing.*

Note. From *Houghton Mifflin Social Studies: Across the Centuries* by B. J. Armento, B. N. Gary, C. L. Salter, and K. K. Wixson, 1991, Boston: Houghton Mifflin. Copyright 1991 by Houghton Mifflin Company.

STRATEGIES TO ENHANCE LEARNING FROM EXPOSITORY TEXT

Summarize the beliefs about teachers helping students read to learn.

We hold several beliefs regarding the role of content teachers in helping students read to learn that have helped us select strategies presented in this chapter. They are as follows:

1. Teachers should establish motivation and discussion before assigning reading.
2. Teachers should use structured information-seeking strategies that students can use for obtaining and understanding text material.

Figure 7.6 Organizational Writing Pattern Example

Acid Rain

Acid rain has been recognized as an environmental problem since the 1960s. At that time, the warnings of biologists and environmentalists were largely ignored. Now, however, twenty years later, many people are worried about this unwelcome "rain" that is damaging our environment.

Acid rain starts when sulfur and nitrogen oxide gases are released from automobiles, metal refineries, and from oil and coal burning power plants. The gases interact with sunlight and cloud moisture and are changed into nitric and sulfuric acids. They may be carried hundreds of miles by the winds, then fall to Earth as rain or snow or drift along as fog.

Acid rain has been held responsible for many disturbing events. Crops and forests have been destroyed. Lakes have become so acidic that fish cannot survive. Acid rain corrodes the surfaces of buildings, bridges, and statues and mars paint finishes on cars. When it seeps into the soil, it reacts with some of the clays to release metals that are harmful to living organisms.

Many methods of solving the acid rain problem have been suggested. Scrubbers placed in the chimneys of coal-burning plants wash some of the pollutants from the smoke. Sometimes the coal is washed to remove sulfur before it is burned. Regulations against the burning of high-sulfur coal have been passed. One of the most promising methods appears to be the addition of limestone to coal while it is burning. The calcium in the limestone ties up the sulfur as $CaSO_4$.

Problem/solution.

Note. From *Focus on Physical Science* by C. H. Heimler and J. Price, 1987, Columbus: Merrill.

3. In-class reading of textbooks is necessary for teachers to model what is expected of students.
4. Teachers should encourage students to elaborate about what they read by allowing student discussions to occur on a regular basis.
5. Teachers should place students in situations where they are responsible for their own learning.

Preparing Students to Read

The story is told of a young child from the city visiting his grandparents who lived in the country. As dinner time approached, the boy's grandfather handed him a bucket and asked that he go to the pumphouse and fetch some water. The boy reached the pumphouse and proceeded to work the handle of the water pump. No matter how hard he worked nothing but air came out . . . not one drop of water. After much time and fruitless energy had passed, the grandfather appeared on the scene. Amused by the situation, the grandfather told the boy to take the water gourd hanging on the wall and pour a little water into the top of the pump. As soon as the boy complied, water came gushing forth: The pump had been primed appropriately. This notion of priming the pump also applies to content area instruction.

We believe that the most important part of a content area reading lesson may well be what teachers do to get students ready for new learning. Prereading discussion is far preferable to lecture for motivating students toward the topic at hand. The purpose of prereading discussion is to assess and build prior knowledge about the topic, to allow students to express feelings and attitudes about the topic, and to assist them in recognizing how the author has organized the information and the purpose(s) for reading the text. We offer in the following sections strategies that may be helpful for this part of the lesson.

> Explain the purposes of "priming" students.

Survey Technique

> Why should students survey a chapter before reading it?

A simple technique to prepare and model, the **survey technique** (Aukerman, 1972) is a method for assessing and developing prior knowledge as well as providing students with an overall view of how the chapter or portion of a chapter is organized. The steps follow:

1. Students read only the title of the chapter or chapter subsection and are asked several questions: *What do you think this chapter is going to be about? What do you already know or remember about this topic? What kinds of things do you think we will be discussing about this topic? How does this information relate to what we have just studied?* Any or all of these questions may be appropriate, but the point is for students to activate their schemas related to the topic and predict what will be discussed.

2. Students are then led systematically through the chapter or chapter portion and are asked to examine all visuals, headings, and boldface print. The teacher poses questions about the visuals to ensure they can be interpreted and to stress their importance to the author's message. Students are asked what the purpose of the headings and subheadings are, and if necessary they identify the main topic discussed in that section. Each heading should be changed into a question, providing a purpose for reading each subheading. ("Properties of Emulsions" becomes "What Are the Properties of Emulsions?") Finally, the teacher points out that boldface type is usually a signal of importance from the author. If warranted, the boldface portions can be discussed at this point. By now students have confirmed whether their initial predictions were correct but also begin recognizing the important information and how it is organized.

3. Next, students are asked to read any introductory statements or para-graphs and the chapter summary. A brief discussion is held, with the teacher emphasizing that between the introduction and the summary one should be able to recognize the superordinate ideas discussed in the chapter. At this point the class could generate a chapter-wide superordinate idea.

4. Although this step is not part of the original survey technique, we sug-gest students look at the end-of-chapter questions if they are going to be asked to answer them. Then in small groups students determine as many answers as they can, based on the preview. These can be shared, and discussion can center around which sections of the text would most likely contain information about the remaining questions.

The survey technique lends itself to the building of prior knowledge, help-ing students recognize the organization of information, and developing inde-pendence. It is important that teachers model their thinking when first using this technique. Teachers should also remind students to try this approach inde-pendently with their text and others.

Anticipation Guides

Anticipation guides (Herber, 1978) are used to generate prereading and postreading discussion. These are called **reaction guides** when used *after* students have read. They usually consist of three to six statements about an upcoming topic that students are asked to react to by deciding whether they agree or disagree with each statement and why. Anticipation guides take many forms, but their ultimate goals are to assess students' prereading beliefs and prior knowledge, establish a student-centered discussion, and provide students with a reason for reading and responding to text material. The following guide-lines are offered for constructing anticipation guides:

Identify the purposes of antici-pation guides.

1. Based on your content analysis of an upcoming chapter or unit, deter-mine the major concepts developed by the author.

2. Using the major concepts, develop three to six statements that reflect the ideas discussed by the author. Broad statements, rather than explicit facts are preferred.

3. Display the statements on an overhead projector or handout, and have students react to each statement by deciding whether they agree or disagree with each statement. You should ask for a show of hands of "agreers" and "disagreers" to assist in calling on students to explain their rationale for their position on the statements. Encourage students to elaborate on their reasoning.

4. Have students read the text selection and then return to the state-ments for a reaction to whether they still agree or disagree with the

statements or whether the author supports the statements. During the postreading discussion, students should reference their responses to what they read.

5. An optional step is to reintroduce the anticipation guide *after* a unit of study has been completed so students can observe changes in their opinions based on information learned during the unit of study.

Anticipation guides are easy to construct and very useful as an engagement tactic, because students are asked to respond from their experience base from the outset and because there are no wrong answers—only disagreements of opinion. Figures 7.7 to 7.10 provide examples of different formats that anticipation guides can take.

Engaging students in before-and after-reading discussion is a good way to clarify misconceptions and/or misunderstandings.

Your Own Questions

Your own questions (Vacca & Vacca, 1989) is a simple prediction-verification strategy that causes students to activate their prior knowledge and establish purposes for reading expository text. Our adaptation of the procedure begins with the teacher explaining the process, then asking students to listen carefully as she reads aloud introductory paragraph(s) for a portion of the text. A second reading is usually necessary. Students are then asked to formulate, either individually or in pairs, three to five questions whose answers they predict will be found in the remaining portion of the text selection.

Why is "your own questions" a metacognitive strategy?

Volunteers are asked to share their questions on the chalkboard. Students then read to find the answers to the questions. During follow-up discussion, questions whose answers were obvious are identified and discussed. For questions whose answers were not directly answerable, the teacher encourages students to use inferencing skills to arrive at plausible responses. If students are

Figure 7.7 Anticipation Guide: Immigrants

Directions: Before beginning the unit related to immigrants and immigration, please respond to the following statements. Place a check in the blank next to those you agree with. Be prepared to support your opinion about each statement.

Before **After**

_____ _____ 1. It takes courage to leave everything you know and move to a new country.

_____ _____ 2. Immigrants coming to America found a much better life here than in their home countries.

_____ _____ 3. Unskilled immigrants should be given jobs in preference to American-born citizens.

_____ _____ 4. Living in ethnic communities would help ease the transition to a new country.

_____ _____ 5. Congress should be allowed to limit immigration into the United States.

Figure 7.8 Anticipation Guide: Poor and Homeless

Directions: Before beginning the unit related to the Poor and Homeless, please respond to the following statements by placing an X in the blank next to those statements with which you agree. Be prepared to support your opinion about each statement.

Before	Author	Reaction	
____	____	____	1. Most of the poor in this country could get a job if they tried harder.
____	____	____	2. Poverty is mainly the concern of large metropolitan areas rather than suburbia.
____	____	____	3. The welfare system in this country encourages people to stay impoverished.
____	____	____	4. In most instances, poor people should be required to work for any monetary support they receive from the U.S. Government.
____	____	____	5. The elderly have benefited most from the welfare system in the U.S.
____	____	____	6. More federal problems and monies are needed to solve the problems of homelessness and poverty.

Figure 7.9 Anticipation Guide: Microbiology Unit

Directions: Before we begin the unit on microbiology, read the following ten statements and place a check next to each statement that you think is true. Be ready to explain why you agree or disagree with each statement.

You	Author	
____	____	1. The terms *bacteria*, *germs*, and *microorganisms* may be used interchangeably.
____	____	2. Most bacteria are **pathogenic**, or harmful, to humans.
____	____	3. Bacteria are widely used in industry.
____	____	4. Bacteria actually digest the grass in the stomachs of cattle.
____	____	5. Some bacteria are plant-like and are capable of photosynthesis.
____	____	6. Bacteria are believed to have had a helping hand in the creation of our Earth's atmosphere.
____	____	7. The simple act of rinsing fruits and vegetables before consumption will remove all existing bacteria.
____	____	8. The boiling of foods completely destroys all existing bacterial organisms.
____	____	9. The sole cause of **botulism** is due to the introduction of the microorganism *Clostridium botulinum* into the digestive system.
____	____	10. The main reason that formerly effective antibiotics no longer kill pathogenic bacteria is due to the drastic increase in the cost of these antibiotics. Since the price of medicine continues to skyrocket, pharmaceutical companies continue to add less and less active ingredients to their medications.

Figure 7.10 Anticipation Guide: Federalism

Directions: Before beginning the chapter on Federalism please read and try to answer the following questions. Place your answers in the space on the left marked **before**. After class discussion and reading your assignment place your revised answers in the space on the right of the questions marked **after**.

Before	Questions	After
_____	1. What are delegated powers? Who controls those powers?	_____
_____	2. What is the most flexible part of the Constitution?	_____
_____	3. What phase of federalism are we in today?	_____
_____	4. Concurrent powers give the states and national government powers to do what?	_____
_____	5. Ex post facto laws protect what right?	_____
_____	6. Can a state constitution be overruled by an act of Congress?	_____
_____	7. What determines who has what powers or rights?	_____
_____	8. How can the national government control a state law?	_____
_____	9. Can a criminal escape prosecution by fleeing to another state?	_____
_____	10. Who settles disputes between two or more states?	_____
_____	11. Name two types of grants that the national government can give to states.	_____

unable to arrive at plausible answers for certain questions, then they should be asked to search for other information resources (information from governmental agencies, nonprofit organizations, nonprint media, etc.) for answers.

Prereading Semantic Maps

Convergent and divergent semantic maps are discussed in Chapter 6.

Another useful strategy that can be used to activate students' prior knowledge of a topic and lead to preview of text material is the **prereading semantic map**. The procedure starts with the teacher writing the topic or superordinate concept on the chalkboard or an overhead transparency. Students are then asked to volunteer any information they associate with the identified topic. Experienced-based associations are listed on the chalkboard or overhead transparency. Next, the teacher asks students, individually or in pairs, to examine all headings, subheadings, and visuals in the text selection to gather more information. The new information is added to the chalkboard or overhead list. A prereading semantic map (Figure 7.11) is generated by organizing the information volunteered by the students. Finally, students are asked to read carefully the segment of text to find more relevant information that can be added to the original map. A postreading discussion centers around the various ways of organizing the information including decisions about what is important and not important to remember about the topic.

Directed Reading-Thinking Activity

The **Directed Reading–Thinking Activity (DRTA)** (Stauffer, 1969) is a time-honored strategy that capitalizes on the ideas of prediction and comprehension monitoring. DRTA is cyclic in that students are asked to predict, read, and verify. To begin a DRTA, the teacher places the title or a major heading from a chapter on the chalkboard or overhead transparency. Students are asked to predict, based just on the title, what the chapter will be about and what kind of information they think they will find in the selection. These predictions are written on the chalkboard or overhead transparency. Then, students are asked to examine all headings, subheadings, and visuals. Next, they are asked to verify, if they can, whether the initial associations were accurate and/or to eliminate those that are inaccurate. Also, they may volunteer more predictions about what they will be reading. Finally, students are taken subheading by subheading through the assignment, repeating the predicting, reading, and verifying cycle. To make this strategy successful, the amount of text to be read should be limited to facilitate interaction among students and the teacher's role as facilitator and clarifier.

> DRTA is a prediction, confirmation strategy.

Information-Seeking Strategies

A very important factor in successful reading and learning from any expository text selection is how one mentally approaches the text. Teachers need to make sure that assignments given include more than required page numbers. Providing structure and purpose to reading assignments is an integral stage in helping students move toward independence. Students should be able to answer several questions before they begin an assignment given them: *What am I supposed to read? What is the purpose of reading this assignment? What should I know or be able to do after I read the assignment?* If students can answer these questions, they are likely to be more aware cognitively and likely to meet learning objectives. As an example, please read the following passage and be ready to answer a single question at the end of the passage:

> Why are structured reading assignments beneficial to students?

Initial Student Associations with the Topic

taxes	King George	British Army	Boston Tea Party	Sam Adams
Stamp Act	Tea Tax	George Washington	Ben Franklin	Thomas Jefferson

Additional Associations from Previewing Section of Text

George Grenville   Townshend Acts   Intolerable Acts   Sugar Act
Lord North   *Gaspee*   Boston Massacre   Quartering Act
1st Continental Congress   John Adams   No taxation without representation

Semantic Map categories determined by teacher and students.

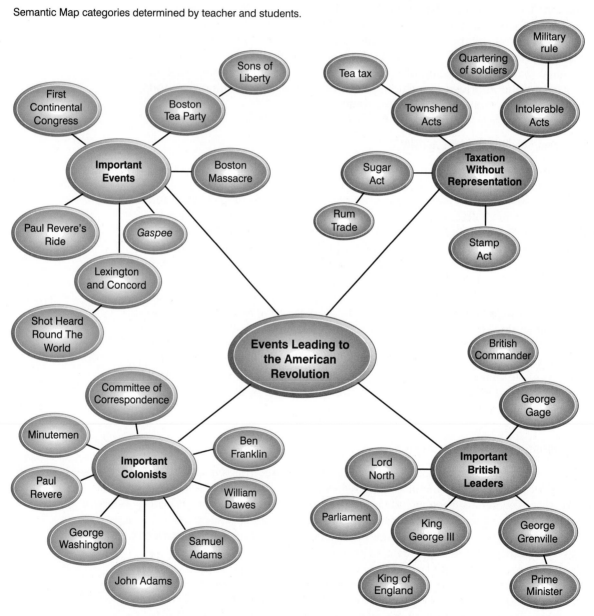

Figure 7.11 Prereading Semantic Map for Events Leading to the American Revolution

A man gets on an empty city bus and rides two blocks where the bus picks up five people. Then the bus goes four more blocks to the next stop and lets off two people and picks up three new riders. Three blocks later the bus stops and lets off four passengers and picks up three new ones. Finally, the bus reaches the last stop. Before the door opens to let everyone off, how many times did the bus stop?

If you assumed that counting people was the relevant task, even though you did read the assignment, you probably did not acquire the information ultimately asked about. The point here is that, if teachers fail to provide students with structure and purpose when giving reading assignments, then students may not obtain the information that was intended. Although strategies previously mentioned in this chapter and included in other chapters may be helpful in this regard, what follows are additional strategies that we believe should be a part of content teachers' structured reading repertoire.

Preview Guides

Preview guides are a series of statements presented to students before having them read a portion of text in class. Students are asked to decide if the statements about the expository text to be read are correct or incorrect. After students indicate yes or no, a brief discussion about student choices takes place, and then they read to verify responses. A follow-up discussion ensues as the teacher encourages students to elaborate beyond their responses. Figures 7.12 and 7.13 are examples of preview guides.

Think of ways preview guides differ from anticipation guides.

Preview guides rehearse prediction and comprehension-monitoring skills and are simpler than study guides because they require students only to recognize information rather than produce it. Hence, preview guides are usually

Figure 7.12 Preview Guide for Light Reception and Sight

Directions: Place a check mark under the **Yes** column if you think the chapter will support the statement. Place a check under the **No** column if you think the text will not support the statement. After you read the selection, review your responses and be prepared to discuss the assignment.

Yes	No	
_____	_____	1. All protists and animals detect and respond to light.
_____	_____	2. Eyespots are the pigment molecules that give your eye color.
_____	_____	3. Most insects, like the honey bee, have sharp vision because of their compound eyes.
_____	_____	4. The human eye can receive light signals up to an angle of 90 degrees.
_____	_____	5. Vertebrate eyes and cameras work according to the same principle.

Figure 7.13   Preview Guide: The Importance of Air

Part I:

Directions: Before you read your class assignment, read each statement in Part I. If you believe that a statement is true, place a check in the **Agree** column. If you believe that a statement is false, place a check in the **Disagree** column. Be ready to explain your choices.

Agree	Disagree	
		1. People can live without air for several hours.
		2. Air is mostly made up of two gases: nitrogen and oxygen.
		3. Water vapor is an important gas in the atmosphere.
		4. Air pressure is not very powerful.
		5. People use air to do work.

Part II:

Directions: Now you will read information related to each of the statements in Part I. If the information supports your choice above, place a check in the **Yes** column in Part II. Then write what the text says in your own words in column **A**, under "Why is my choice correct?" If the information does not support your choice, place a check in the **No** column. Then write what the text says in your own words in column **B**, under "Why is my choice incorrect?"

Yes	No	A Why is my choice correct?	B Why is my choice incorrect?
		1.	1.
		2.	2.
		3.	3.
		4.	4.
		5.	5.

used earlier in the school year as a precursor to study guides. They can take many forms and are easily adaptable for use with most expository materials.

Study Guides

What words do you associate with the term *study guide*?

Let's try a word association task. Quickly list the first five things that come to mind when you hear the term **study guide**. If you are like the majority of our undergraduate students when we do this word association task, words such as *boring, busywork, test, homework,* and *review* come to mind. The reasons for this kind of reaction have to do with how study guides were constructed and used during the past two decades. In the past, study guides tended to comprise a series of questions to be answered independently with little teacher input or student discussion. In spite of their poor reputation among some students, appropriately used study guides significantly improve comprehension of text (Alvermann & Swafford, 1989; Armstrong, Patberg, & Dewitz, 1989). In this section we make a case for increased usage of study guides but in more constructive and interesting ways.

Traditionally, study guides have been used to help students acquire information without much emphasis on necessary processes to acquire that information. Holistically minded teachers now develop study guides that correct this problem by guiding students to discover both the needed information (product) and ways of discovering valuable answers (process). Benefits of using study guides that emphasize product and process include (a) promotion of active reading, (b) facilitation of thinking beyond the explicit level, (c) causing students to spend more time on task, (d) generation of student-centered discussion, and (e) assisting students in acquiring learning skills that build independence.

Before constructing any study guide, teachers should perform a content analysis of the material to be read. Based on the content analysis, the teacher then decides what the students will be held responsible for learning as they read the assignment. Next, the teacher determines what type of study guide might be the most useful for that particular assignment. Finally, the study guide is constructed.

Study guides are classified as interlocking and noninterlocking (Tutolo, 1977). **Interlocking study guides** place all questions and/or statements of the same type together and alert students to this arrangement. Three levels of comprehension—textually explicit (literal), textually implicit (inferential), and schema based (evaluative)—are most often used to differentiate each part of the study guide. **Noninterlocking study guides** send students into text seeking specific types of information but tend to have no prescribed pattern of comprehension activities and questions. As we provide examples of the various types of study guides, keep in mind that it is the teacher who is always in the best position to determine which type of study guide, if any, should be used.

Levels of Comprehension Study Guides.   **Levels of comprehension study guides** (Earle, 1969) can be either interlocking or noninterlocking. They typically make use of questions and/or statements at the literal, inferential, evaluative levels of comprehension, but other comprehension models may be used. Regardless of which version of a levels of comprehension guide you opt to develop, students should be made aware of what level of thinking is required for each question/statement on the guide. Additionally, these study guides should not be used with every selection, and they should not be used as assessment instruments. Rather, they should be viewed as a means for assisting students in developing strategic reading skills and acquiring important information.

We now offer guidelines for constructing levels of comprehension study guides (adapted from Vacca & Vacca, 1989):

1. Determine the implicit information that you expect students to obtain from the assignment. Write questions/statements that address these

Traditional study guides differ from more holistically oriented guides.

How do levels of comprehension guides assist students with process skills?

inferences as simply as possible. You are trying to build into the guide the answer to the question "What is the author trying to say?"

2. Next, analyze the assignment for facts and details that support the preceding implicit information, and write them down in question or statement form. You now have parts I and II of the guide, if it will be an interlocking levels of comprehension guide (Figures 7.14 to 7.16). If you are

Figure 7.14 Interlocking Levels of Comprehension Guide: The Great Depression

I. Literal Level: Check those statements that you feel are taken directly or paraphrased from the text.

____ 1. The effects of World War I were a direct cause of the Great Depression.

____ 2. The California Dream solved all the problems of the Midwest farmers.

____ 3. The Bonus Marchers were unemployed farmers who marched on Washington, D.C.

____ 4. There were early warnings of trouble in the economy before the Great Depression happened.

____ 5. Allied forces had to borrow money to win the war.

____ 6. Factories were a major cause of the stock market crash.

II. Interpretive Level: Several of the statements below may represent what the author means. If you think any of these statements are a reasonable conclusion, check them. Be prepared to support your answer by using part of the text.

____ 1. The farmers of the midwest are to blame for the agriculture failure of the 1930s.

____ 2. Hoovervilles were an economic success.

____ 3. If the farm economy had been stronger, there would not have been a crisis.

____ 4. "Direct Relief" was Hoover's answer to the jobless question.

____ 5. The song "Brother Can You Spare a Dime" reflected the mood of the times.

III. Applied Level: In this section you will be asked to apply what you read. This means that you will be asked to take the information and ideas from what you have read and connect it with what you already know.

____ 1. Installment buying (credit) usually leads to poverty.

____ 2. Government intervention into society (such as Direct Relief) is a good answer to national financial problems.

____ 3. The Hoover plan of putting people to work and reducing taxes was an ideal way to solve the economic problems.

____ 4. Government legislation, such as the Reconstruction Finance Corporation of 1931, will always solve problems in America.

____ 5. Discrimination as a means of cost cutting for factories was a plausible way for factories to lay off workers, thus, "at least some are working," which justified their action.

____ 6. Only the poor or lazy were affected by the Depression because there were jobs if people wanted to work.

constructing a noninterlocking levels of comprehension guide, then the arrangement of these questions is not important (Figure 7.17). If using statements, you may want to include in each of these sections some statements that are not accurate or not directly stated in the text so that students will be required to think with greater discrimination.

3. Determine how the information in the assignment can be used to develop questions/statements at higher levels of thinking. These ques-

Figure 7.15 Interlocking Levels of Comprehension Guide: Lines, Segments, Rays, and Angles

I. Right There: What did the material say?

Directions: Check each statement below that you can find on the pages you just read.

_____ 1. All lines are straight and extend infinitely far in both directions.

_____ 2. Every point on the circumference of a circle is the same distance from the center.

_____ 3. A ray begins at a point called its ENDPOINT and then extends infinitely far in one direction.

_____ 4. An angle is made up of two rays with a common ENDPOINT.

_____ 5. A ray that divides an angle into two congruent angles BISECTS the angle.

_____ 6. An ACUTE ANGLE is an angle greater than 0° and less than 90°.

II. Think and Search: What does the material mean?

Directions: Check each statement you think is true *and* can defend.

_____ 1. Given three points that are *not* collinear, B is *between* A and C.

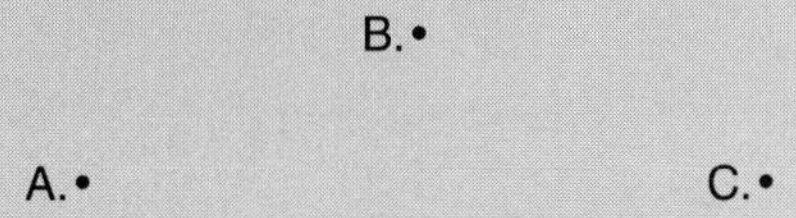

B.•

A.•   C.•

_____ 2. Two angles with the same measure are congruent.

_____ 3. A STRAIGHT ANGLE has a greater measure than an OBTUSE ANGLE.

_____ 4. You can eyeball measures of segments and angles for accuracy.

_____ 5. Geometry's role in everyday life is small and limited.

III. On Your Own: How can you use angles, segments and points?

Directions: Check each item you agree with. Submit with your answers the work you did to show your reasoning.

_____ 1. $\overline{AB} \cap \overline{CD} = \overline{CB}$. This is the diagram for which the statement is true.

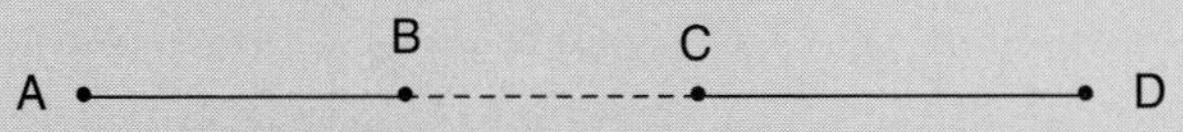

B   C
A •————————•--------•————————• D

_____ 2. The measure of the angle made by the hands of a clock at 4 o'clock would be 120°.

_____ 3. The measure of ∠ ABC = 134°.

Figure 7.16 Interlocking Levels of Comprehension Guide: Composition of Blood

Read pages 310–318 on the composition of blood and answer the following questions. Be prepared to discuss your answers.

I. Answer the following questions. The answers can be found directly in the text.

  1. Name the three most common formed elements in the blood.

  2. What is the process of erythrocyte production called?

  3. Give the common name for the following: erythrocytes, leukocytes, and thrombocytes.

II. Think about the following statements and determine whether you believe them to be correct. Place an X in the blank next to those you believe to be true. Be prepared to defend your answer.

_____ 1. If a person has anemia it would have no effect on the hematocrit.

_____ 2. Leukocytes are the only cellular elements to help in the fight against infection.

_____ 3. People living in the Rocky Mountains would have higher levels of erythropoietin than people living at lower elevations.

_____ 4. The shape of the erythrocyte aids in its function.

III. Applying what you have read, tell which of the cellular blood elements you think would be affected by the following health situations and whether that element would be increased or decreased. (Some health situations will affect more than one cellular blood element.) Be prepared to defend your answer.

Health Situation	**Blood Element**	**Increase or Decrease**
Anemia	_____	_____
Infection	_____	_____
Kidney disease	_____	_____
Severe blood loss	_____	_____

tions/statements should focus on having students solve problems, evaluate what has been read, and/or apply what they read to new situations.

Selective Reading Guides. Selective reading guides differ from levels of comprehension guides in that they tend to be noninterlocking and are designed so that the reader interacts with the guide as he proceeds through the reading assignment. Cunningham and Shablak (1975), calling them the *Selective*

Selective reading guides are comparable to a road map.

Figure 7.17 Noninterlocking Levels of Comprehension Guide: The American Civil War

> **Noninterlocking Levels of Comprehension Guide**
>
> *Directions:* Read pages 350–366 in your text about the Civil War, and respond to the following questions. Notice that the questions have dots next to them. The answers to the questions with one dot can be found directly stated in the reading. The answers to the questions with two dots will require you to interpret or figure out what the author said. These are not directly stated. The three dot questions will require you to make judgments or solve problems based on what you know and what the author said.
>
> •   1. Who was the president of the Confederate States of America?
>
> ••   2. What was the impact of the Dred Scott decision?
>
> •••   3. Why is the Civil War considered a modern war?
>
> •   4. What battle on the Mississippi River was considered a turning point in the war?
>
> •••   5. How does the Civil War continue to affect the U.S. even today?
>
> ••   6. Explain why the South believed in states' rights.
>
> ••   7. How did Lincoln help bring the war to an end?
>
> •••   8. What was the significance of Lincoln having "Dixie" played in the White House after Lee surrendered?
>
> ••   9. Compare and contrast the Southern Soldier and the Northern Soldier at the beginning of the war.
>
> •   10. When and where did the war officially end?

Reading Guide-O-Rama, proposed that selective reading guides accomplish three things:

1. Limit how much of the actual text is read by focusing attention on just those parts necessary to satisfy the objectives of the teacher.
2. Provide information to the student about *how* to read the identified text sections (strategies).
3. Sequence the guide's statements/questions across the reading assignment.

To prepare a selective reading guide, the teacher begins by determining purposes for reading the text selection. It is important to note that if the purpose is to hold students responsible for *all* information in the text selection, then this type of study guide should not be used. However, if the teacher's intent is to hold students responsible for discovering selected information via reading and the remainder through other class activities, then a selective guide may be appropriate. Cunningham and Shablak (1975) recommend that teachers select only those portions of text students must read, then—through the use of statements and questions—lead students through the assignment telling them *what* to read, *how* to read it, and their *choices for responding* to what has been read. Examples and alternate formats for selective reading guides are presented in Figures 7.18 through 7.20.

Selective reading guides are useful to both students and the teacher. For the student, these guides limit the amount of required reading, provide strategies for reading the text material successfully, and offer opportunities for thinking at higher levels of comprehension. For the teacher, these guides let students know of one's desire to have meaningful assignments, provide an opportunity to examine one's own approach to reading text material, and shift some responsibility for learning the text material to the student.

Figure 7.18 Selective Reading Guide: Linear Equations

CHAPTER 8—SECTIONS 8-1, 8-2, and 8-3

The purpose of this assignment is to be able to plot points and draw the graph of a linear equation on a coordinate plane. You are required to read the parts of the sections listed and do the practice activities as directed. (Practice activities are underlined.)

1. Read p. 275, points 1, 2, and 3, and notice the definition of the words in boldface print.

   *Draw a coordinate plane, and label the four words in boldface print on your diagram.

2. Read the first paragraph on p. 276. **This is very important and understanding it is a prerequisite before going on.** Remember, the horizontal number is first, the vertical number is second.

3. On p. 280, the key statement begins on the third line down, with "Any combination . . . " Read this slowly several times. Go over the example at the bottom of the page.

   *Answer the first five Oral Questions on p. 281.

4. On p. 283, read the second paragraph, (it begins, "When x and y . . . . .") and study the diagram.

   *Now see if you can find some solutions to the equation $x + 2y = 8$, and then draw the graph of the equation.

5. Read the red box at the top of p. 284. Notice that the (x,y) solutions to a linear equation will always lie on a straight line.

Figure 7.19 Selective Reading Guide: The Beginning of Civilization in Egypt

The primary objective of this assignment is to enable you to recognize the most important events of the beginning of Egyptian civilization and to realize that Egyptian ideas and culture were unique and very different from our ideas and cultures today.

Directions: Read only those parts of the chapter that are listed in the reading directions. Then respond to the questions as best you can.

Reading Directions	Questions
1. Page 62, paragraph 6.	The form of writing used in Egypt was referred to as what? What, as opposed to the alphabet used now, was used to express ideas?
2. Page 62, paragraphs 2 and 3.	Pyramids in ancient Egypt were built by farmers using their own muscle power. What modern machinery would have helped them make the building of the pyramids easier?
3. Pages 65–66. Look at the questions first, then read the passage on pages 65–66.	Give some examples of why Egypt's soil is referred to as a gift from the Nile. List some other significant gifts of the Nile listed on these pages.
4. Page 67, paragraph 3.	The word *Pharaoh* meant "Great House" in ancient Egyptian. From reading this short passage, what would the word *Pharaoh* refer to today?
5. Page 68, paragraphs 5 and 6. Study the question, and then read page 68, paragraphs 5 and 6.	Describe the burial process for the ancient Egyptians. List some significant practices that were used that we do not engage in today.
6. Pages 72–73, paragraphs 1–3.	Identify the main reason why Egyptians needed a calendar. Specify differences between the Egyptians' use of the calendar and the uses of today.

Expository Text Structure and Organizational Patterns

The major organizational writing patterns used in expository text include time order, simple listing, compare–contrast, cause–effect, and problem–solution. As mentioned earlier in the chapter, helping students understand and use organizational patterns can increase their potential for understanding and remembering text. Therefore, teachers need specific strategies that can be used to help students master these patterns. To this end we recommend three specific approaches for making organizational patterns of text explicit for students. The first is through the use of questions, the second is the use of organizational guides for specific writing patterns, and the third involves the creation of visuals or graphics depicting the organization of ideas presented in the text.

Review with a colleague the main writing patterns in expository text.

There are three approaches suggested for teaching students about organizational writing patterns.

Figure 7.20 Selective Reading Guide: Body Systems

The primary objective of this assignment is to enable you to learn about the human body and its organized systems.

Directions: Read only those parts of the chapter that are listed in the reading directions. Then respond as best you can.

Reading Directions	Questions
1. Page 517, paragraph 1. First read the paragraph, then answer the question.	What are the four basic types of tissues the human body contains? List four characteristics of each. 1. 2. 3. 4.
2. Page 519, paragraphs 1 and 2.	As you read about the skeletal system, focus on its functions. How is the framework of the Statue of Liberty like the framework of your skeleton?
3. Page 522, paragraphs 1 and 2. Read the question first, then read the passage.	List four types of joints and one movement that distinguishes each. 1. 2. 3. 4.
4. Page 524, paragraphs 1 and 2. Study the question, then read the paragraphs.	What is the function of bone marrow? Why do you think it is important for infants and children to have foods that contain calcium and phosphorus?
5. Page 526, paragraphs 1–3.	Read the passage, then give your own example of three things your body does that require voluntary muscles and two things your body does that require involuntary muscles.

Questions and Text Connections

Text-connecting questions assist students in recognizing the way text information is organized.

Muth (1987) has described a method of using questions to cause students to respond to text based on the way it is organized called **text-connecting questions**. This technique has teachers modify their typical diet of questions to include specific questions about *why* the author presented the information using the pattern she did and questions that cause students to *connect* ideas presented across the passage. The chart in Figure 7.21 is adapted from Muth's (1987) suggestions as question prototypes for each expository text pattern.

One should note that the suggested prototype questions may not fit all expository passages perfectly and should be adapted as needed. Also, when beginning to incorporate questions that focus on the organization of text, teachers should begin with brief segments of texts and model answers for the students.

Figure 7.21 Using Text Structure Questions to Understand Relationships Among Ideas

Organizational Patterns	Questions for Patterns
Cause/Effect	Can you tell me the cause(s) of _____? What was the effect of _____? Why did the author use cause and effect for this section? Help me make a chart on the board by placing the causes on the left side of this line and the effects on the right side. Can you think of any cause and effect situations similar to the ones you have just read about?
Comparison/Contrast	Before beginning reading, why do you think this author is going to discuss (topic) by demonstrating likenesses and differences? What was being compared in this section? How were they different? How were they alike? What did they have in common? Now that you have read this section, why did the author use comparing and contrasting to discuss (topic)? Can you think of any other ways (topics) are alike or different?
Sequential	What was the first important idea discussed? When did it occur? Can you remember the sequence of events you just read about? Let's identify the sequence. Why did the author discuss (event or process) using this sequence? Help me make a time line of the events, or help me arrange the steps of (process) in chronological order.
Problem/Solution	What were the problems discussed by the author? Did the author propose any solutions to the problems? What were they? What caused the first problem discussed? How was it solved? (Continue identifying and discussing.) What were some key words or phrases that let you know that you were reading about problems and their solutions? Can you think of any similar problems and how they were solved? How about other solutions than those presented by the author?
Simple Listing	What was the main topic you just read about? What did the author say about (topic)? How did the author present these ideas? Can you make a list (like a grocery list) of the ideas or facts discussed? Why do you think the author just listed information about (topic)? Can you think of any other facts or ideas about (topic)?

Note. Adapted from "Teachers' Connection Questions: Prompting Students to Organize Text Ideas" by K. D. Muth, 1987, *Journal of Reading, 28,* pp. 254–259.

Writing Pattern Guides

Writing pattern guides demonstrate the organization of text information.

Pattern guides help students recognize the pattern of organization that dominates a text selection. Pattern guides explicitly identify the overall pattern and then, via written questions or activities, require students to respond to the material using the pattern of organization. Before providing example pattern guide formats, several suggestions should be kept in mind when developing and using pattern guides. They include the following:

- After identifying the overall writing pattern and before students begin using the writing pattern guide, be prepared to discuss the pattern and how the student can use the pattern to understand the author's message.
- Be prepared to provide assistance to students as they work on the guide by fielding questions and helping students combine necessary information by guiding statements and teacher-posed questions.
- Allow for follow-up discussion that emphasizes what was learned and how the pattern of organization helped to clarify the relationship among the ideas.
- Don't overuse these types of guides.
- Begin with short selections.

Figures 7.22 to 7.26 are examples of pattern guides.

Figure 7.22 Pattern Guide for Cause–Effect Writing Pattern

Teacher presents the series of effects and the students must determine the causes.

Directions: Today in your text you will be reading a selection that discusses the phenomenon called the red tide. The selection presents both the causes and effects of red tide. Below I have identified the effects. You are to read the selection and fill in the cause of each effect.

1. Cause: ______________________________

   Effect: It turns water a reddish color.

2. Cause: ______________________________

   Effect: The movements of people and fish are affected.

3. Cause: ______________________________

   Effect: Scientists have not been able to find a way to stop red tides.

4. Cause: ______________________________

   Effect: Local industry and business suffer during red tides.

Figure 7.23 Pattern Guide for Comparison–Contrast Writing Pattern

Teacher presents the ideas that are being compared and contrasted, and students must read to find out how they are different and alike.

Directions: As you read the section in your text about the armies of the North and South, use the chart below to determine how they were alike and different.

Education

South: _____

North: _____

Adaptable to Outdoor Living

South: _____

North: _____

Political Leadership

South: _____

North: _____

Military Leadership

South: _____

North: _____

Weaponry

South: _____

North: _____

Graphic Aids and Text Organization

Providing visual representations (diagrams, graphic organizers, tables, charts, and other visuals that demonstrate the relationship among ideas in text) of how ideas are organized in text can facilitate learning from expository textbooks (Armbruster, 1991). The term **framing** (Armbruster, 1991) connotes the use of visual graphics to present the organization of content in a text selection. To develop a frame, Armbruster (1991, p. 106) suggests that teachers begin by answering two questions: *What are the important categories of information associated with this topic? How might these categories be subdivided?* Figures 7.27 to 7.31 are various examples of ways graphics can be used to provide students exposure to the patterns of organization.

Visual representations like framing clarify text information.

Figure 7.24 Pattern Guide for Sequential Writing Pattern

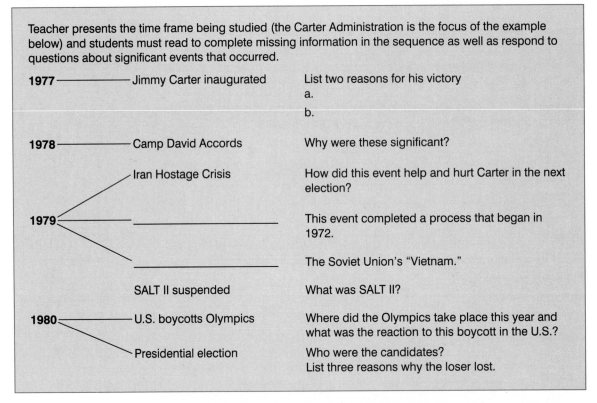

Teacher presents the time frame being studied (the Carter Administration is the focus of the example below) and students must read to complete missing information in the sequence as well as respond to questions about significant events that occurred.

1977 ————————— Jimmy Carter inaugurated   List two reasons for his victory
a.

b.

1978 ————————— Camp David Accords   Why were these significant?

Iran Hostage Crisis   How did this event help and hurt Carter in the next election?

1979 ————— _____   This event completed a process that began in 1972.

_____   The Soviet Union's "Vietnam."

SALT II suspended   What was SALT II?

1980 ————— U.S. boycotts Olympics   Where did the Olympics take place this year and what was the reaction to this boycott in the U.S.?

Presidential election   Who were the candidates?
List three reasons why the loser lost.

Figure 7.25 Pattern Guide for Problem–Solution Writing Pattern

Teacher introduces topic and explains how the author has presented some problems and possible solutions. Then the students are asked to read the section and isolate the problems and possible solutions. The example below is based on the chapter about pollution.

Directions: Many types of pollution are endangering our planet. These major problems are listed below. Next to each one is a root cause. You are to find and list possible solutions to the identified "root problem."

Major Type	Root Problem	Solutions
Air	Auto Exhaust	
Water	Chemicals	
Soil	Pesticides	

Figure 7.26 Pattern Guide for Simple Listing Writing Pattern

Teacher presents discussion topics in this pattern and has students list the examples under each category/topic.

Directions: The section in your textbook lists many facts about **properties of matter**. Some of the properties are extensive and some are intensive. Identify each of the items below as an extensive or intensive property of matter by placing an X in the blank.

Extensive Property	Intensive Property	
_____	_____	1. A 20-gram weight
_____	_____	2. The color of a book
_____	_____	3. The melting point of an object
_____	_____	4. The volume of a container
_____	_____	5. Time
_____	_____	6. Temperature
_____	_____	7. Length of an object

Figure 7.27 Graphic for Comparing and Contrasting Pattern: Halogen Derivatives of Methane

Common Name	IUPAC Name	Formula	Chief Uses
Methyl chloride	chloromethane	CH_3Cl	local anesthetic
Chloroform	trichloromethane	$CHCl_3$	general anesthetic, solvent
Iodoform	tri-iodomethane	CHI_3	antiseptic
Carbon tetrachloride	tetrachloromethane	CCl_4	dry cleaning, fire extinguishers
Freon	dichlorodifluoromethane	CF_2Cl_2	refrigerant

Responding to Expository Text to Extend Understanding

Most of the previously discussed teaching suggestions require interaction between the teacher and the student. However, several other avenues are available for structuring students' response to expository text. They include discussion activities and writing activities that either cause students to monitor, reinforce, or extend their understanding of text material. What follows are some

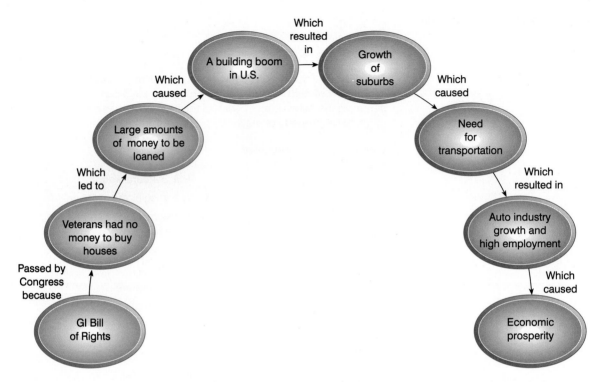

Figure 7.28 Graphic for Cause–Effect Pattern: The GI Bill of Rights

Figure 7.29 Graphic Depicting Time Order Pattern: World War II

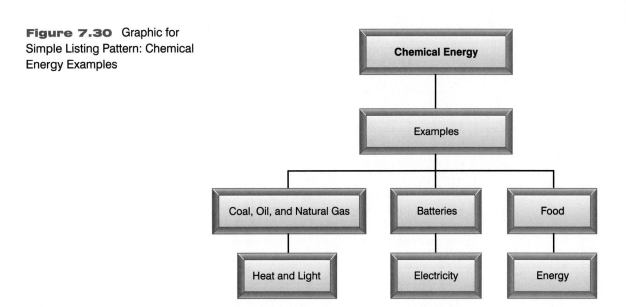

Figure 7.30 Graphic for Simple Listing Pattern: Chemical Energy Examples

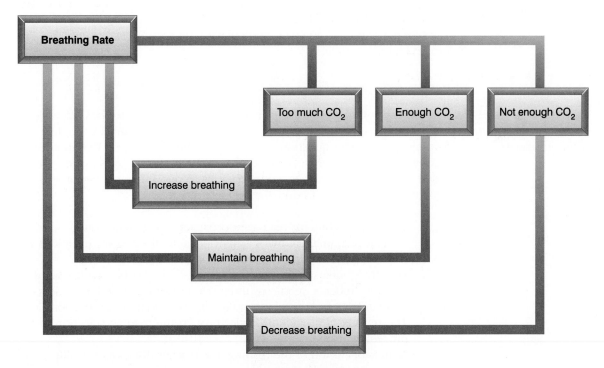

Figure 7.31 Graphic for Problem–Solution Pattern: Breathing Rate

additional ideas that can motivate students and energize the classroom environment.

Discussion Activities

What are the characteristics of a true classroom discussion?

Although most teachers would answer "yes" to the question "Do you conduct class discussions?" Good and Brophy (1991) found very little use of discussion by the teachers in classrooms they observed. They found an apparent lack of sharing-type classroom discussions and an abundance of rote memory responses by students to teachers. According to Alvermann, Dillon, and O'Brien (1987), real classroom discussion should allow for multiple points of view, encourage student-to-student interaction, and cause students to engage in more than one word or short phrase responses. The following strategies embrace these criteria without neglecting the need to focus on all levels of comprehension.

Reaction Guides

Reaction guides can be used after reading a selection to generate considerable discussion. Reaction guides make use of anticipation guides after students have read the expository text selection. Students respond to the original statements on the guide, but the discussion that follows centers around their rationales for continuing to agree or disagree with the previous statements. See Figure 7.32 for an example.

Reciprocal Questioning

ReQuest promotes student-generated questioning.

Student-generated questioning can also be used to invigorate class discussions. One of the most popular methods for causing students to think about text and formulate their own questions is reciprocal questioning, or **ReQuest**. This technique by Manzo (1969; Manzo & Manzo, 1990) has several variations and is based on the idea of teacher modeling of good questioning behavior and student interaction. The procedure for ReQuest is as follows:

1. Teacher and students read a short part of text simultaneously. After the reading is completed, the teacher opens the floor to any questions the students want to ask about the portion of text just read.
2. After the students exhaust their questions to the teacher, the teacher then asks the students questions, using questions that cause the students to make inferences, judgments, and predictions about the information.
3. The teacher and students cycle through the reading selection in the preceding manner.
4. At the conclusion of the reading, the teacher discusses the differences in question type between the students' and his own. Hopefully, this will encourage students to formulate better questions the next time.

Figure 7.32 After-Reading Reaction Guide: End of Unit

Directions: Now that we have concluded our unit dealing with the Poor and Homeless in the U.S., I would like for you to return to some statements used at the beginning of the unit. Please indicate which of the statements below you agree with by placing a check in the appropriate blank. In addition, select one statement to defend in writing, and respond below the statements.

_____   1. Most of the poor in this country could get a job if they tried harder.

_____   2. Poverty is mainly the concern of large metropolitan areas rather than suburbia.

_____   3. The welfare system in this country encourages people to stay impoverished.

_____   4. In most instances, poor people should be required to work for any monetary support they receive from the U.S. government.

_____   5. The elderly have benefited most from the welfare system in the U.S.

_____   6. More federal problems and monies are needed to solve the problems of homelessness and poverty.

Select one of the statements and defend your stance by:

1. Explaining briefly why you agree or disagree.

2. Cite any references (books, films, etc.) that we have used during the unit of study that support your stance.

Modifications to the basic ReQuest procedure can include having longer pieces of text read before the questioning phase; having student-to-student formats (student pairs or small groups can question each other); or incorporating study guide questions and/or statements into the procedure.

Guided Reading Procedure

Another Manzo (1975) strategy that we advocate use of is the **Guided Reading Procedure (GRP)**. The GRP is an example of a strategy that starts off teacher directed but gradually becomes student centered. The procedure requires the teacher to select a well-organized and important section of text that is not very lengthy. Our experience suggests that, for a 50-minute period, time limits of about 10 minutes for high school students and 6 to 8 minutes for middle school students will provide enough time to complete the strategy. Obviously, the maturity of your students and difficulty of the text selection will influence the length of the selection to be read.

The Guided Reading Procedure promotes long-term retention of text information.

The following steps are based on the original recommendations by Manzo (1975) and suggestions by Readence, Bean, and Baldwin (1992):

Step 1:   Assign the text selection to be read, and tell students that they are to read the selection only once but they are to try to remember as much about what they read as they can.

Step 2:   When students finish reading, have them close their books. Then write the topic they read about on the chalkboard, and have the students brainstorm as much information as they can remember from the reading. If students are reluctant, prod them to remember details in the passage.

Step 3:   After writing the things they remembered in random order on the chalkboard, have students return to the passage to find out if they forgot any information and add any new information to the chalkboard.

Step 4:   At this point one of two things can happen. Have the whole group help you organize the random information on the board into an outline, a graphic organizer, or a semantic map. Or, ask students individually or in pairs to take the information and organize it into an outline, graphic organizer, or semantic map. Regardless, encourage students to include only the important and relevant information on the visuals generated.

Step 5:   Administer a short-term memory quiz after students have copied the outline or other visual into their notebooks. The quiz can be objective, short answer, or a combination. Students should score their own tests, and each item should be discussed.

Step 6:   A long-term memory quiz over the same topic should be administered 1 week later to reinforce the importance of retaining text information and to stress the important information in the text selection.

Writing Activities That Extend and Reinforce Expository Text Learning

Writing about what has been read supplements and complements beautifully the kinds of activities presented in this chapter. Santa and Haven (1991) note that writing in the content areas causes active involvement, forces organization, and causes students to demonstrate understanding. To this end we offer the following suggestions that can help students extend and reinforce what they have read about in text material:

Writing about what one reads causes students to demonstrate understanding.

Anticipation/Reaction Guides.   Earlier in the chapter, we discussed the use of anticipation/reaction guides as a means of promoting student-centered discussion. An interesting twist is to have students write their rationales for agreeing or disagreeing with the statements. At the prereading stage, it might take the form of a listing activity. After reading the selection, students return to the original statements and reexamine their beliefs based on newly acquired information. At this point they might be asked to write out their rationales in paragraph form and share them in small groups.

Writing and Patterns of Organization.   Because we have already discussed the point that writers often construct text using writing patterns, then it makes sense to have students write using the same patterns as their textbook authors. Helping students become authors of different text types gives them comprehension insights that transfer to reading. So, to have students experience writing in specific expository patterns, we recommend the following procedure:

What knowledge is necessary for students to write in specific writing patterns?

1. Focus on one writing pattern at a time. Select the writing pattern that is most prevalent in your content area or text selection.
2. Provide exposure and encounters with the identified writing pattern through activities such as those discussed earlier in this chapter. Using an organizational guide for a specific writing pattern (discussed earlier in this chapter) is recommended.
3. Begin the writing activity by modeling what you expect students to do with information from either an earlier chapter or sections recently covered. Your model should include signal words for the identified writing pattern.
4. After you have shown students how you organized your paragraph summary using the signal words, then provide students with an organizational writing pattern (see examples earlier in this chapter) for a section of the chapter currently under study.
5. Based on completed writing pattern guides and the list of signal words associated with that pattern listed on an overhead or chalkboard, students compose summary paragraphs.
6. Follow-up discussion and sharing of paragraphs in small groups should conclude the activity.

Figure 7.33 is an example of an organizational guide for a writing pattern writing activity.

Writing With the Guided Reading Procedure.   The GRP (Manzo, 1975) described earlier offers another avenue for helping students write concise summaries. As you recall, the end result of a GRP could be either an outline, a semantic map, or a graphic organizer. Regardless, each of these graphic aids presents a hierarchical view of the information read, and each is perfect for having students write concise paragraphs that summarize the main points of the authors.

Even strategies like the GRP can be used to promote in-class writing.

The preceding suggestions are just a few of the many possibilities for encouraging students to write to learn. As you will see in Chapter 8, these activities just scratch the surface of integrating writing in the content areas.

Figure 7.33   Organizational Guide for a Writing Pattern Writing Activity

Completed Pattern Guide

Directions: Today in your text you will be reading a selection that discusses the phenomenon called the red tide. The selection presents both the causes and effects of red tide. Below I have identified the effects. You are to read the selection and fill in the causes of each effect.

1. Cause: The right mixture of salt and fresh water enables rapid growth of algae.

   Effect: It turns water a reddish color.

2. Cause: Shellfish infected with the algae and eaten short circuits the nervous system.

   Effect: The movement of people and fish are affected.

3. Cause: The amount of ocean water involved is just too enormous.

   Effect: Scientists have not been able to find a way to stop red tides.

4. Cause: Bans on shellfish, deaths of hundreds of fish, and lack of tourism.

   Effect: Local industry and business suffer during red tides.

Writing Activity

Directions: Using your responses to the pattern guide and the following list of signal words, compose a paragraph that summarizes the main points about red tide.

Signal Words for Cause and Effect: *therefore, as a result, so that, because, since, consequently, if/then.*

Red tide is caused by algae that turn ocean water red. Because it appears infrequently and covers an enormous area, scientists have not found a way to prevent it. As a result, industry and businesses along the gulf have suffered because of decreased tourism and bans on shellfishing. Also, health concerns have been raised because this alga affects the nervous system of humans and fish. Consequently, red tide should be everyone's concern.

LEARNERS WITH SPECIAL NEEDS

Learners with special needs require extra structure for coping with expository texts.

The needs of students with learning problems underscore the necessity for content teachers to include instructional activities that go beyond the typical diet of listening, note taking, and testing. As content teachers, our goal is to help learners with special needs do much more than merely survive secondary school—we want them to become productive citizens knowledgeable of the world in all its diversity. In this section we revisit some ideas previously presented that can be adapted for learners with special needs. We also include additional recommendations for assisting these students with expository reading selections.

Teaching About Text Organization

It is important not to assume anything about how much students with learning problems know about the adopted text. Teachers should make sure that they conduct a text preview at the beginning of the year. During the text preview, the features of the text such as the table of contents, index, glossary, special appendices, and the overall organization of chapters should be explained to students. This can be a whole class activity, or it can be a temporary small group activity for those who need it.

Direct instruction of how to preview chapters may also be of benefit to some students with problems learning. Particularly useful is teaching how to turn headings and subheadings into questions to guide their reading of each section. As a teacher, you may even need to explain that headings and sub-headings are included in textbooks to signal important topics discussed in this section. Textbook visuals can be very important to the student with problems learning. Care and time should be taken to make sure students know how to interpret all visuals within a chapter.

To provide assistance with the hierarchical arrangement of text chapters, Mercer and Mercer (1989) recommend a **direct in-text marking system** for students. The direct in-text marking system is another name for highlighting, but with several new twists. The first idea is that the text is marked before having students use it. All main ideas, key words, and important concepts are highlighted with a light-colored pen. In addition, all unimportant portions of text and terms can be blacked out. Obviously, this is a time-consuming approach, but one that might be warranted in more extreme cases.

Information-Seeking Strategies

For the student with learning problems, preview guides, three-level guides, and selective reading guides can be helpful with expository text reading assignments. Specifically, study guides can be modified to accommodate students in several ways. First, study guides could be done cooperatively. If the ultimate goal is for the students to acquire the information, then what better way for students with problems learning to acquire the information than to be paired up with a more advanced student? Second, three-level guides presented in a question format can include the page number or page and paragraph number where the answers to the questions are to be found. Following are examples from different content areas:

- *American History:* What were three reasons the Southern states decided to secede? (p. 455, para. 1–3)
- *Biology I:* Explain alternation of generation. (p. 233)
- *General Mathematics:* What is the difference between a mixed fraction and a proper fraction? (p. 23, lines 6, 9)

Teachers can also elect to modify assignments. That is, rather than have students respond to 20 items, they might be required to respond to 10. If this

Formal instruction as to how to preview text chapters can be beneficial.

What is meant by a direct in-text marking system?

Summarize ways to modify reading assignments.

tactic is employed, however, a complete follow-up conference is desirable to verify that all important information has been learned.

Consider the procedures you would most likely use in your classroom.

Other techniques that might have merit for assisting students in acquiring text information include the use of **lookback organizers**, **guided notes** (Larazus, 1988), and the **Guided Listening Procedure (GLP)** (Readence et al., 1992). **Guided notes** are teacher-made outlines that are incomplete. The task for the student is to read the relevant portion of text and complete the outline. As a follow-up, the teacher presents a completed outline on the overhead for comparison purposes (Figure 7.34).

The **GLP** is an adaptation of the GRP, which was discussed earlier in the chapter. The main difference is that the text is read aloud by the teacher to the students. Teachers instruct students to listen carefully and remember as much information as they can. A rereading or recording of the text is helpful as a follow-up. Otherwise, the two procedures are identical.

Working With Other Teachers

Collaboration among teachers is important for the learner with special needs.

We encourage content teachers to collaborate among themselves about the kinds of activities that seem to work with students who have problems learning. As part of this recommendation, we urge regular education teachers to seek the advice and assistance of special education teachers and other support personnel who may have suggestions and insights for the regular education setting.

Figure 7.34 Guided Notes: Quadrilaterals

Quadrilaterals: Types and Features

A. Parallelograms

    Opposite sides are _____

    Opposite angles are _____

    1. _____—all sides are equal and all four angles are right angles.

    2. Rectangle—opposite sides are _____ in length.

    3. Rhombus—all sides are:

            angles are:

B. Nonparallelograms

    Only two sides are:

    1. Trapezoid—only one pair of _____ lines

    2. Kite—shaped like this: (draw a small kite)

        _____ pairs of congruent sides

CHAPTER SUMMARY

Certain characteristics of expository texts and strategies can make them easier to read and understand. Teachers should (a) engage student interests before assigning independent reading, (b) teach students how to use information-seeking strategies, (c) provide class time for modeling reading-to-learn processes, (d) encourage students to elaborate about what they read, and (e) try to help students assume more responsibility for their own learning.

The preceding beliefs are reflected by practices and strategies including motivational and preparatory activities, information-seeking strategies, and expository text structure and organizational patterns. Strategies exemplifying each of these topics transform the learner from a state of passivity to activity and gradually move the teacher toward a role of learning facilitator.

Finally, learners with special needs can be accommodated by providing opportunities for them to collaborate with classmates on assignments and assisting them, when needed, with streamlined texts and assignments.

Reflection/Application Activities

1. Select a chapter in a content area textbook in your specialty area or an expository text selection from a well-written popular press publisher. Do the following:
   a. Identify the hierarchical structure of the selection. Write a summary statement representing the superordinate concept or concepts (generalization), identify the subordinate ideas (concepts) that relate to the superordinate concepts, and list the specific details (facts).
   b. Based on this analysis, explain why you think the text you selected is considerate or inconsiderate.
   c. Describe which activities presented in this chapter could help make this selection more accessible to students.

2. Using the same selection, choose a major section and identify the various writing patterns. Photocopy the section, and identify all the signal words by underlining. Then, using the examples in this chapter as a guide, construct an organizational guide for the identified writing pattern.

3. Based on the content analysis of a unit or chapter in a content area textbook, develop an anticipation guide for generating prereading discussion of the key topics.

4. Develop an interlocking levels of comprehension guide for use with an expository text selection of your choice. Use statements rather than questions for this activity.

Recommended Reading

Atwell, N. (1987). *In the middle: Writing, reading, and learning with adolescents.* Portsmouth, NH: Boynton/Cook Publishers.

Cochran, J. A. (1993). *Reading in the content areas for junior high and high school.* Boston: Allyn & Bacon.

Dillon, J. T. (1983). *Teaching and the art of questioning. Fastback No. 94.* Bloomington, IN: Phi Beta Kappa Educational Foundation.

Duffy, G. (1990). *Reading in the middle school.* Newark, DE: International Reading Association.

Mercer, C. D., & Mercer, A. R. (1989). *Teaching students with learning problems.* Englewood Cliffs, NJ: Merrill/Prentice Hall.

Santa, M. D., & Alvermann, D. E. (1991). *Science learning: Processes and applications.* Newark, DE: International Reading Association.

Sensenbaugh, R. (1992). *Reading and writing across the high school science and math curriculum.* Bloomington, IN: EDINFO Press.

Tierney, R. J., Readence, J. E., & Dishner, E. K. (1990). *Reading strategies and practices: A compendium* (3rd ed.). Boston: Allyn & Bacon.

Wood, K. D., Lapp, D., & Flood, J. (1992). *Guiding readers through text: A review of study guides.* Newark, DE: International Reading Association.

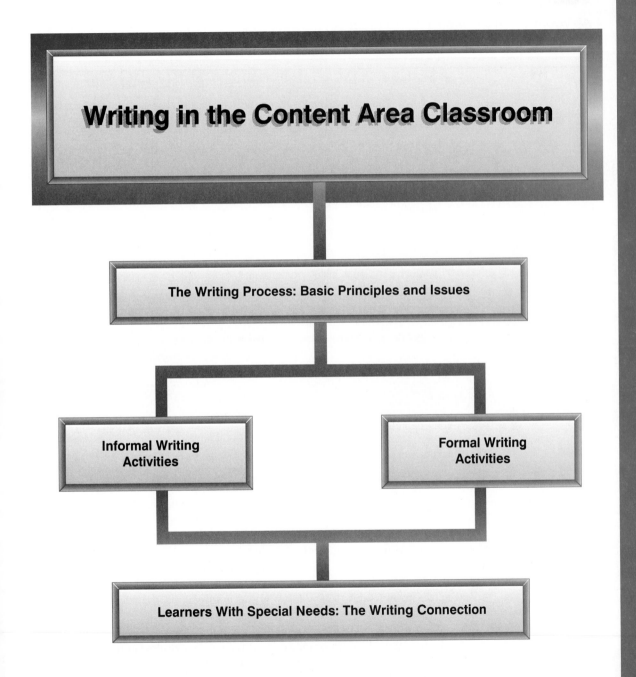

Writing in the Content Area Classroom

The Writing Process: Basic Principles and Issues

Informal Writing Activities

Formal Writing Activities

Learners With Special Needs: The Writing Connection

Focus Questions

As you read this chapter, try to discover answers to the following questions:

1 Why should we include the writing process as an integral part of content learning?

2 How do *product writing* and *process writing* activities and assignments differ?

3 What are some of the different forms of writing? How are they different in terms of purpose?

4 Define and describe the stages of the writing process.

5 What are some of the ways technology can be used to assist in the writing process?

6 What is the role of journal writing in content classes? What are dialogue journals and learning logs?

7 What is an I-Search paper? Name at least three other formal writing activities.

8 What are the differences between quantitative and qualitative writing assessments?

9 Is the inclusion of writing process activities helpful for students with learning problems? Be able to defend your response with examples.

Why Writing in Content Area Classes?

Writing in the content areas is a powerful means for deepening students' understanding in the field of study.

Ancient Romans spoke of a passion known as *cacoethes scribendi,* the compulsion to write. Developing the ability to write coherently is an incredibly valuable language tool for sharpening thinking skills and extending learning. Writing causes us to sort out our beliefs, impressions, insights, and feelings about a subject of interest, then translate our thoughts into text that makes sense to ourselves and others. In this way, writing has the potential to help us "know what we know" (and don't know) about a subject so that deeper study and reflection can occur.

Writing in content classrooms has changed dramatically in recent years. Teachers in past decades often assigned term paper or research paper projects as a way of getting students to review important information and document learning. Students frequently prepared a single draft and turned it in to the teacher, who then graded and returned the paper. This one-draft mentality (Calkins, 1986) did little to deepen students' understanding of the content or to improve their ability to write.

More recently, researcher-practitioners like Donald Graves (1983) and Nancy Atwell (1987) have begun to help content teachers understand new ways of incorporating the writing process so that learning is made more efficient and permanent. Instead of making one-shot last-minute efforts at writing term papers, students are taught how to understand and use the methodical phases of authorship. The result is greater interest in the subject matter and improved communication skills.

We begin this chapter by introducing the basic principles of process writing instruction. Later we take a look at ways of assessing writing projects and some of the problems and issues that sometimes emerge for content teachers as they implement these ideas.

THE WRITING PROCESS: BASIC PRINCIPLES

Process Versus Product

If you ask several adults what they remember about writing assignments during their teen years, chances are they will probably recall unpleasant memories of term papers and red ink. They usually remember being sent off to the library to do research on a topic of seemingly little relevance or interest, perhaps being subjected to the venerable torture known as sentence diagramming, and getting back papers with so much red ink on them that students wondered if the teacher had suffered a terrible wound and nearly bled to death on their project. These are not the kinds of memories that make one think fondly of writing. Small wonder that most citizens write as little as possible to communicate their ideas!

As mentioned earlier, writing in content classrooms has traditionally focused on the product—a paper or research project. In this mode, which we refer to as *product writing*, students essentially spend most of their efforts on gathering and reporting information in a one-shot paper that is awarded a one-time grade based on subjective and objective assessments made by the teacher. Once the paper is graded, the student moves on to something new. Several problems are inherent in product writing. For one thing, this type of exercise does nothing to help students become better writers. What often happens is that many students put off an assignment until it is nearly too late, then go through the motions of hastily gathering information from encyclopedias and constructing a last-minute paper to complete the assignment. Errors in research, composing, and mechanics occur, as one would expect, and are seen by the teacher as points to be deducted from the final grade as a penalty. The student seldom has an opportunity to be coached as a writer, let alone given a chance to revise and try again. It is an up-or-down, thumbs-up/thumbs-down

Traditional writing projects have tended to stifle student interest in writing as a tool for communicating ideas.

Term papers and research papers are examples of product writing assignments.

Writing is an intensely personal process that reveals what we know about a topic.

procedure that puts students in roughly the same position as the early Christians when entertaining the Romans in the coliseum! This feeling of jeopardy and being put at risk is the second problem with product writing. Students need to be encouraged to take academic risks if they are to achieve their potential and compete in the world marketplace. As noted earlier in the book, this also means risking one's self-esteem in the process. Writing is an intensely personal and connected process that reveals what we know about something (and what we don't know) as well as the ability to articulate one's thoughts in print. Teachers must be careful to build students' self-confidence and spirit of risk taking in the classroom. Finally, product writing frequently fails to help students master the content to be learned—a central goal of content instruction. What we desire as teachers is for students to unearth as much information as possible and make new knowledge their own. Half-hearted surveys of encyclopedias and other quick references fail to give students the depth of understanding we hope for and similarly fail to inspire students to want to know more.

> The process writing approach helps students learn to write as professionals and gain penetrating insights into the subject under study.

Realizing that product writing has been unsuccessful in helping many students attain high levels of content literacy, many teachers are now turning to a **process writing approach**. The idea is to help students learn to write in much the same way as professionals. Writers of novels, textbooks, poetry, and other language modes would find it unthinkable to create compositions on a one-shot basis. Instead, writers move through a process of brainstorming ideas, researching the topic thoroughly, organizing information and ideas they wish to present, and sometimes creating several drafts of a composition until they feel the message has been put just right. They seek opinions from colleagues who have read over the material, which often causes authors to yet again rewrite the material.

Process writing, when incorporated in content classes, also helps students become intimately familiar with subjects. In the remainder of this section, we describe the fundamental elements of process writing and how it can be implemented in your classroom.

Topic Selection, Purpose, and Audience

> Student self-selection of a relevant topic is a highly motivating practice in process writing.

Students have traditionally had little to say about topic selection. Instead they have often been assigned a topic they regarded as uninteresting and irrelevant to their lives. But in process writing, students usually choose a topic they can relate to their past experiences. This is not to say that teachers never make writing assignments, for they do. However, in process writing they usually set down guidelines for assignments, then allow students the freedom to interpret the assignment in their own way.

One of the important prewriting considerations for authors is purpose. Is the purpose of the composition to inform or entertain? Persuasion or personal? In Chapter 2 we discussed Halliday's (1977) functions of language. We have found that reviewing these key functions of language with students is a great place to begin in helping students discover purposes for writing.

Finally, students should develop a sense of audience when developing written compositions. Knowing that one's composition will be shared with a group of peers or with parents at the next PTA meeting, printed in the school newspaper, or read by a state senator creates heightened awareness about what is being said. Knowing that there will be a real audience attending to one's composition stimulates a keener sense of awareness to quality of message and attention to detail. Compositions read only by the teacher can stimulate students to higher levels of achievement on occasion, but when used too often this practice will pale in comparison to peer review. Later in this chapter, we discuss the notion of publishing or sharing final versions of compositions, which capitalizes on this sense of audience.

Think of appropriate audiences with whom students could share their finished writing projects.

Forms of Writing

Many forms of writing are used in content classrooms. Each writing form offers unique advantages and should be suggested at different times during the year to help students maintain interest. In this section we discuss a few possibilities we have found interesting and successful.

Last-minute changes to a writing assignment that will be shared with the entire class.

Descriptive Writing

Learning logs, reports, stories, poems, and content-focused melodramas are types of compositions that may use descriptive writing techniques.

Descriptive writing helps students breathe life into subjects by drawing comparisons between familiar events, places, and people in their daily lives. Sometimes dialogue and sensory images are introduced to papers to make them more interesting. Descriptive writing can be used in informal compositions such as learning logs, or in more sophisticated creations such as reports, stories, content-focused melodramas, and even poems. In descriptive writing, authors should include descriptions about specific behaviors of people involved, their names, interesting or pertinent behaviors, the setting in which events occurred, and important dialogue. Descriptive writing is useful in all content area classrooms.

Biographies

Biographies written by students provide insights into real peoples' lives.

Biographies are used to record and describe the lives of important contemporary and historical figures in major fields of study. Not only do biographies chronicle the accomplishments of notable people, they also provide a vehicle for drawing conclusions about life and our own experiences. When the concepts of descriptive writing are employed, rich and interesting compositions result.

Persuasive Writing

Brainstorm a list of persuasive writing forms students could consider in your content area classroom.

Persuasive writing activities help students to see alternative viewpoints, discover techniques for swaying others to their point of view, and develop logical arguments. Frequently, students write about local, state, and national issues in a variety of content-related areas. In a science class, students may prepare arguments for and against state-supported fetus research. Art classes might debate controversies related to projects funded by the National Endowment for the Humanities. Government classes might set up political party teams to persuade classmates as to the correctness of their positions using propaganda techniques. Persuasive writing can be interesting as well as challenging to students because they must build arguments by presenting a position that is corroborated with reasons.

Expository Writing

Expository writing is intended to inform others about a subject. According to Meyer and Freedle (1984) and Armbruster and Anderson (1981), expository writers use five common patterns for presenting information: time order (sequence); cause–effect (showing how something occurs because of another event); problem–solution (presenting a problem along with an answer to the problem); and comparison (examining similarities and differences among things, concepts, events, etc.); and simple listing. Expository writing helps students better understand the relationships and nature of specific facts, concepts, and generalizations about a topic of study.

Narrative Writing

Narrative writing involves the creation of a story to inform and entertain. Although much of narrative writing is fiction, the story may also be used as a vehicle to share truths. Fully developed stories involve common elements: setting, characters, a central conflict to be resolved, attempts to resolve the conflict, resolution, and a theme or moral of the story. These common elements are referred to as a *story grammar.* Narrative writing can employ many of the features of other writing modes including persuasion, description, and exposition. Narrative writers often use this form to present a point-of-view to the readers.

Name the elements of a story grammar.

Journal Writing

Journal writing is a form of writing commonly used to record and analyze information and to carry on written dialogues with others. The types of journals include dialogue journals (usually written discussions between teachers and students, conversational in tone); research journals (used to record information learned during content investigations); double-entry journals (Berthoff, 1981) (students write information learned from text readings on the left-hand side of their paper, then record their response on the right side); learning logs (students record and react to what they are learning in the content class); and simulated journals (Tompkins, 1994) (students write from another person's viewpoint about what is being discussed).

Journal writing has become quite popular in content classes as a means for recording new knowledge.

Stages of the Writing Process

One of the goals of writing process instruction is to teach students to write like professional writers. As students begin to write regularly, their perspective on content learning is transformed. Therefore, an important task for content teachers is helping students learn to "write like the pros" and feel successful doing it.

Professional writers tend to do certain common tasks when creating new compositions and even tend to follow a sort of sequence when performing these tasks. We refer to these groupings of common writing tasks that are presented to students as the **stages of the writing process**. The major stages of the writing process include prewriting, drafting, revising, editing, and sharing/publishing. This is not to say that writing is a lock-step process. Writers often omit some of these tasks entirely, move back and forth repeating certain tasks, and reverse the order in which tasks are performed by other writers. Figure 8.1 illustrates how writers move through each of these stages, sometimes reversing direction, sometimes moving ahead, until they are ready to share what they have produced.

Stages of the writing process are simply descriptions of the major activities of professional writers, not a lock-step method of teaching.

Content teachers find that it often works best to introduce common writing operations to adolescents in a clear, sequential manner. In this section we describe these stages according to prominent scholars in the field (Atwell, 1987; Calkins, 1986; Graves, 1983; Murray, 1985; Temple, Nathan, Temple, & Burris, 1993; Tompkins, 1994) and provide illustrations of how these stages can be applied in selected content classrooms.

Many teachers introduce writing operations using the stages of the writing process and examples drawn from the content area as illustrations.

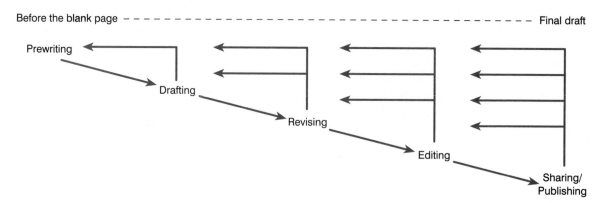

Figure 8.1   Writing Process

Note. Adapted from *Write to Learn* by D. Murray, 1984, New York: Holt, Rinehart & Winston. Copyright 1984 by Holt, Rinehart & Winston.

Prewriting

What are some examples of prewriting activities associated with your content area that you could offer to students?

Prewriting is the constellation of activities one does before actually putting pen to paper. It is what Tompkins (1994) calls the getting-ready-to-write stage. Prewriting is probably the most critical stage because this is when writers discover what they want to say (Temple et al., 1993). The commitment of the writer to the composition depends largely on the topic he selects, so teachers must do all they can to help writers connect with a topic about which they can be excited. Therefore, the first task most writers engage in is choosing a topic, usually through brainstorming.

Teachers should model the topic selection process for students when first introducing process writing.

Donald Graves, in his book *Writing: Teachers and Children at Work* (1983), suggests that teachers model the brainstorming process for students. For instance, a social studies teacher introducing a unit on the Middle East might share with the class a list of several topics she might wish to write about in her soon-to-be-created "book." These topics should be written one at a time and discussed using the overhead projector or chalkboard. It is important that the teacher model topics that she is legitimately interested in so that she can explain why she chose them. In other words, the teacher is demonstrating a way of thinking about writing, not emphasizing the selected topics per se. For the Middle East unit, the teacher might have selected the following topics and offered the reasons described:

Unit Theme: The Middle East

Topic: Middle East Cuisine

Rationale: Cooking is a hobby of mine, and I enjoy sampling different foods from around the world. Therefore, I would love to know more about Middle Eastern culture from the foods they enjoy. I might even want to make a Middle Eastern dish for the class to sample one day.

Topic: Politics of Israel

Rationale: I know that Israel receives a great deal of money from the United States. It would be interesting to learn how this connection was started and why we continue to support Israel. What are our common interests?

Topic: Middle Eastern Schools

Rationale: I think it would be interesting to learn how middle schools and high schools in Middle Eastern countries are like ours . . . or different. How long is their school year? Where do they go for vacations? What subjects do they take in school? This might help us better understand young people there.

Once the teacher has shared her brainstorming list and reasons for choosing topics, students should spend some time separately, and later in groups, coming up with their own ideas. Students should be reminded to consider the purpose of the composition, the form it will take, and the audience that will receive this message (Tompkins, 1994).

> Students need time to work with peers to select appropriate topics.

A critical prewriting activity for authors is organizing their ideas before writing, in other words, developing an outline or map of the ideas to be shared in the composition. Many successful writers construct a very detailed map that includes key information, phrases, references, and supportive details for each major point. Writing from a detailed map helps ideas to be expressed concisely and with clarity. There are many ways to organize ideas before writing including traditional outlines, webs, structured overviews, and pyramid outlines. Figures 8.2 through 8.5 are examples of these different organizational patterns for a topic called "How the United States Touched the Moon."

A major benefit from mapping ideas before writing is that this process helps writers express ideas with clarity and conciseness. Just as important, maps help writers discover not only what they know about a topic but also what they do *not* know and will need to discover through research.

> Mapping is a popular way of outlining and organizing ideas.

Research is the collection of information related to the topic the student has chosen. As mentioned, the student might begin by noting from his map which bits of information are known and can be documented. Next, he should use the map to discover which areas are less known and will require more information. Such skills as using the card catalog in the library, learning about periodicals collections, writing for information from governmental agencies and others, and conducting computer data base searches come into play. As more and more information is discovered, it should be added to the student's prewriting map. Students should be encouraged to overresearch, that is, to seek out more information than they feel is needed to complete the composition, then choose the best material for inclusion in the project.

> Research is the detective work that goes into collecting information related to the topic of study.

Figure 8.2 Traditional Outline

How the United States Touched the Moon

I. Mercury: The Beginning of Manned Space Flight
   A. Suborbital Flight
      1. Alan Shepard, May 5, 1961
   B. First Orbital Mission
      1. John Glenn, February 20, 1962
II. The Gemini Program (Two-Man Capsules)
   A. First flight, March 23, 1965
   B. Enlarged capsule with room for equipment and supplies
   C. Docking system in nose
   D. Enabled first space walks
III. Apollo Program: On to the Moon
   A. Began Moon mission on July 16, 1969
   B. Lunar Module (LM) called "Eagle"
   C. EVA of over 80 hours

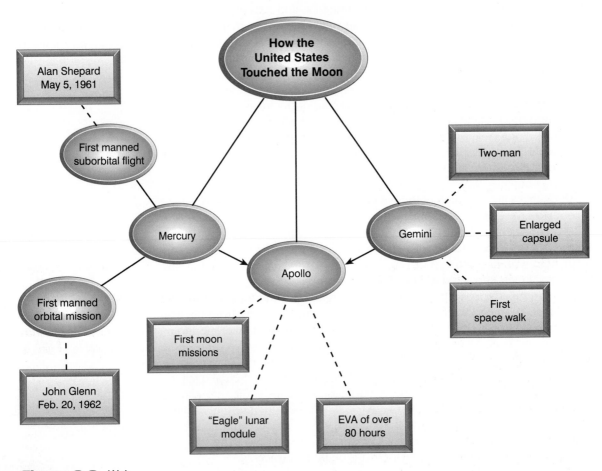

Figure 8.3 Web

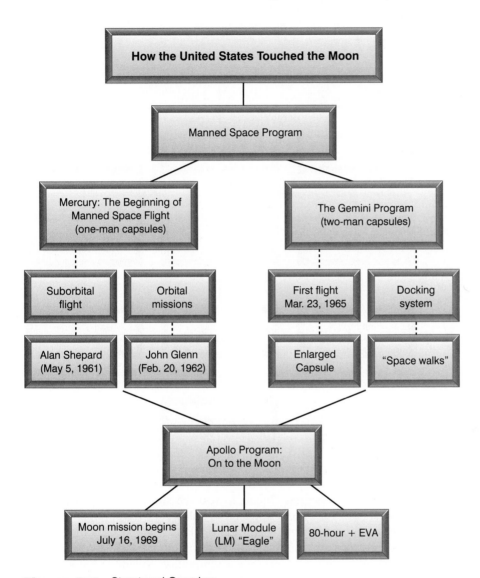

Figure 8.4 Structured Overview

Another prewriting task many authors engage in is the creation of **alternative leads**. Leads are opening lines for a composition intended to grab readers' attention. An executive for a major recording company once remarked, "If you want to produce a hit song, it has to grab the listener within the first 10 seconds." The same is true in written communication. If you don't grab the reader in the first paragraph, he'll lose interest and quit reading. Therefore, suggest to students that they write more than one beginning to their composi-

Alternative leads are opening lines of a composition intended to grab the reader's attention.

Figure 8.5 Pyramid Outline

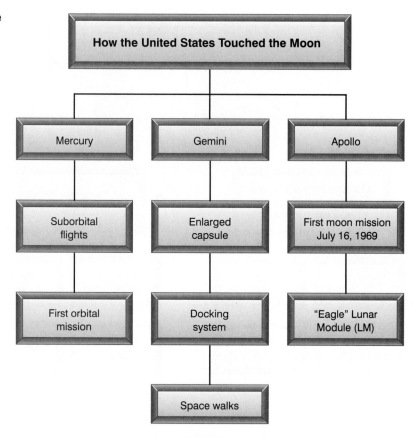

tion, and ask others to read them and offer opinions. These collaborations will yield better compositions.

Finally, teachers often ask, "What do you tell students who can't find a topic to write about?" All writers, especially adolescents, have moments when attempting to conjure ideas to put down in print is difficult. As Thomas Moore said, "inspiration stops and the writer is faced with an intractable empty page" (1992, p. 198). Although it is certainly a temptation to simply tell students something to write about, most writing authorities tell us that this practice does not usually work very well. This is mainly because topics must be of interest to writers for them to devote much creative energy to the project. A topic suggested by the teacher quickly becomes just another required assignment to which they feel little or no connection. One remedy for writers having trouble finding a topic is called **free writing**. In free writing students simply start writing about anything and everything that comes to mind related to the unit of study. For instance, a student having difficulty coming up with a topic in a drama class whose unit is called "methods of creative expression" might free write (or perhaps map or web) for 10 or 15 minutes. The student may then decide from this process that she would like to learn and write about a topic called "Storytelling Through African Tribal Dances."

The purpose of free writing is to help students become aware of topics they may be interested in knowing more about—topics that may be of interest only on a subconscious level until discovered. We also suggest another variation adapted from Calkins (1986), namely, asking students having trouble finding a topic to simply list things associated with the unit of study until they come to an idea they wish to write about.

Drafting

Once students have chosen a topic, mapped or outlined their key points and supportive details, and conducted the necessary research to fill in knowledge gaps, they are ready to move on to the next major activity, called **drafting**. Drafting has to do with the writer's first attempts to get his ideas down on paper. The emphasis at this stage is solely on ideas and content, not mechanical correctness (e.g., spelling, punctuation, etc.); it is a rough draft only. Many writers tell of drafting experiences where the ideas flow so quickly they can hardly get them down. Other times drafting can be a slow and onerous task (Buckley, 1993).

Drafting is a first attempt to get ideas down on paper.

It might be helpful to create with the class and post a series of drafting suggestions for times when drafting is not so easy. Following are a few examples of what might come from such a discussion:

Drafting Suggestions

1. Use your own voice instead of trying to sound like your favorite author.
2. Try to use words that create a picture in the reader's mind. Words should be descriptive and clear.
3. Attempt to use language to create sensory images for important parts of the composition you want to tell.
4. Be succinct. Say what you want to say directly (more is not necessarily better).

Some students have difficulty getting their ideas onto paper because of slow handwriting ability. This can be remedied by letting them dictate their ideas into a cassette tape recorder, then transcribe the composition on paper later. Another option is to let students dictate their draft to another student in a kind of peer tutoring arrangement.

Revising

Revising is the process of reviewing one's draft to find out if the intended message and what is written match. As with drafting, the focus in revising is on the message itself, not the writing mechanics of spelling, grammar, and so

Taking a second look at what has been written is part of what is called revising.

forth, because these aspects are dealt with in the next writing stage. After rereading the rough draft, sometimes the author discovers that the written message is markedly different from what was originally intended. Writers then must decide whether the message presented in the draft is more effective or whether they should reconstruct all or portions of the draft (cutting and pasting) to bring the written message more in line with the original intent.

Peer writing conferences help teach students how to work collaboratively in assisting peers in producing a quality composition.

An important tool for writers engaged in the revising process is the **peer writing conference**. This involves the student-writer conferring with fellow students to try to improve the draft. Tompkins (1994) suggests a routine for this procedure that we have slightly adapted and found to be quite effective with adolescents. We suggest that teachers work through the peer writing conference process carefully with their classes the first time so that students can learn appropriate language to use with peers that is constructive and supportive.

Step 1: *The writer reads aloud.* Students take turns reading their compositions aloud while other members of the group (usually, a group of three or four persons is best) listen respectfully. While listening, each group member should make notes about the strengths of the composition as well as thoughts they may have for improvements. Listening to the composition before reading it, according to Tompkins (1994), keeps the focus on the ideas and content of the piece rather than mechanics like punctuation.

Step 2: *Peer writing conference members offer compliments.* It is always best to begin with positive feedback because students take significant risks with their self-esteem when sharing compositions. Comments made by group members should go further than the nonspecifics commonly heard like "It was really good" or "I liked it a lot." Participants should comment about such writing elements as word selection, opening paragraphs, leads, quality of research demonstrated in the narrative, persuasiveness, and so forth.

Step 3: *The writer questions peer writing conference group members.* One of the signs of growing maturity in writing is realizing that we benefit from constructive suggestions from our peers, but because writing is a personal act, we often find it difficult in the beginning to cross this hurdle and ask for help. To assist young writers in acquiring this habit, Step 3 calls for students to ask their peers for suggestions about parts of the composition they found challenging. Some of the comments may sound similar to the following:

> I had a hard time trying to make Thomas Jefferson seem human. One thing I tried was to tell about his childhood, but I still don't feel like the reader will see him as human. What can I try next?

> My goal is to show how geometry can help you in your adult life. I'm having a hard time figuring out how I can get past just working problems to using them in a real way. Can you guys help me with some ideas?

This part of the conference is initially the most challenging. Once students seek advice more freely and with confidence, however, learning will accelerate through peer interactions.

Step 4: *Peer writing conference group members offer their suggestions.* Many people find it difficult to accept criticism about their writing. Therefore, teachers must help students learn how to offer and accept suggestions during the conference period. Criticisms of the composition, for example, should be stated as questions. This sets a positive tone and allows the author an opportunity to express ideas in his own way. If the author's answer to a group member's question is clearer than stated in the composition, the dialogue helps the group to make constructive suggestions for revisions. Following are a few examples of what we mean:

> At the beginning of your paper, you said that your main point was to discuss how the role of women has changed in America this century. But you spend almost all of your paper talking about their voting rights. Do you think that maybe your introduction should be changed?

> I noticed that you said that some scientists think the Big Bang theory is all wrong, but I don't remember hearing why they say that. Wouldn't it help you make your point better if you told us one or two reasons why those scientists think the way they do?

> It sounded like a lot of your sentences start with "the." Could you check that and think about other ways to start your sentences? I think it would make it more interesting.

Step 5: *Authors make revisions, and the process is repeated.* Students carefully consider comments made by the group and commit to revise their drafts. Suggestions for improving the manuscript are always subject to the writer's judgment, thus, they are not always acted on. Students are often more receptive to making revisions if the first draft was written at the computer using a word processing program, such as MicroSoft Word or one of the many others available for classroom use, because revising rarely means completely rewriting or retyping the composition. Once revisions have been made, the author participates in another peer writing conference, preferably with the same group members, to discuss revisions that have been made. Steps 1 through 4 are repeated and may result in another round of revisions. It is often useful for the teacher to participate in the second round to help with suggestions and brainstorming.

Editing

The most important aspect of writing is the author's message. The impact of that message, however, can be diminished if the composition is marred by poor grammar and incorrect spellings. One of the final stages of writing calls

All writers should attend to the mechanics of writing as a final step in creating quality compositions. This is what we mean by *editing*.

for close inspection of these mechanics of writing, a process called **editing**. In addition to the common problems of grammar and spelling, authors should search for errors in sentence construction, verify the appropriate use of topic sentences, take out awkward language, and look for proper punctuation. Teachers can help students by providing them with opportunities to meet with peers for editing conferences, which are operated in much the same way as the peer writing conferences already mentioned.

Teachers can help students become articulate content subject writers by demonstrating some of the fundamental procedures used by professionals. For example, using **proofreader markings** helps them recall parts of the composition to be corrected during final draft stages. These are notations that an author marks on early drafts to add, delete, or rearrange information. Three of the more common proofreader markings are noted in Figure 8.6.

In most middle and secondary schools, a teacher's time is very precious. Each teacher in a departmentalized school may see upward of 150 students per day. This makes it difficult for teachers to give students the kind of individual attention they would like to offer. Students therefore should be helped to see which of their peers are "classroom experts" in each phase of the writing process and seek their assistance first when they have a question, then present their composition for evaluation by the teacher after it is as complete and ready for sharing as they can make it. When students conference with the teacher, they frequently want to know how close they are to achieving writing goals that have been stressed by the teacher—both in a global and specific sense. We have used a form similar to the one in Figure 8.7 in our experiences with adolescents and found it to be quite functional.

The upper part of the form in Figure 8.7 lets students know in a kind of global or holistic way how their project has progressed to that point by marking the line with an X, indicating how close to perfection you as the teacher feel the composition is according to assessment criteria you have explained to students before beginning the assignment. The bottom portion of the form should include the specific criteria as well as a space for teacher comments and

Prepare a sample composition that may be shared with students and that includes proofreader markings.

The designation and use of "classroom experts" for different stages of the writing process help free up teachers in busy classrooms.

Writing evaluation forms provide students with formative information as they are developing compositions.

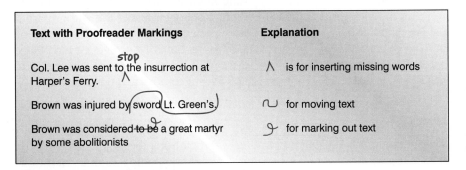

Figure 8.6 Proofreader Markings

Figure 8.7 Writing Evaluation Form

Composition "Feedback"

Student Name _____ Date _____

Title of Composition _____

Overall Assessment of This Draft:

_____

Underdeveloped	Partially Ready	Advanced	Excellent

Areas Needing Further Development

Prewriting/Drafting/Revising

Research on Topic _____

Logical Sequencing _____

Clear Language _____

Appropriate Paragraph Structure _____

Mechanics of Writing

Spelling _____

Grammar _____

Punctuation _____

Capitalization _____

Other Comments:

suggestions. With this information in hand, the student can decide whether she wishes to accept the teacher's assessment or revise and edit the manuscript again using the evaluation form and suggestions made during the student–teacher conference as a guide. We revisit the use of evaluation forms later in this chapter.

Sharing/Publishing

One of the chief motivations for professional writers is publication. It is knowing that one's efforts and labors will be shared with an audience. Knowing that one's work will be made public gives many students purpose and energy to do the necessary and often tedious work of research and drafting. This is what we refer to as the **sharing/publishing** stage of the writing process. Sharing/publishing is a creative enterprise; thus, it may assume many forms. A simple and effective form of sharing/publishing is the **author's corner**. The premise is that after students have completed a composition and been checked out by the

Making one's work public is what we refer to as *sharing/publishing.*

teacher in a writing conference session they sign up for a turn in the author's corner. The author reads the completed composition to the class or a small group, then fields questions about the assignment. Author's corner achieves several worthy goals: Students in the audience are informed by the composition itself, the author has a sense of closure when sharing the composition with a larger audience, and other students are exposed to forms of writing they may not have previously seen in class.

Many other creative forms of expression may be of interest to students. For example, students may want to convert their compositions into classroom resource books on their topic of investigation. Similarly, middle and secondary school students sometimes like to transform their content research reports into simple books to present to elementary classes. The process of simplifying complex content material to an elementary level can actually deepen the student-author's understanding of the topic while enhancing facility with written language.

Begin a list of possible writing projects that could be developed in your content classroom.

Computers, Software, and the Writing Process

Most professional writers produce their compositions with the aid of computers. Name some of the word processing programs that are used by classroom teachers with students.

We have unquestionably entered what has been termed the Information Age. This is an era characterized by rapidly advancing computer technology that nearly surpasses the imaginations of the best science fiction writers. Because of the expense of this technology, not to mention provincial back-to-basics attitudes by many politicians, assimilation of this technology into schools has been slow. However, it is safe to say at this point that the question of infusion of technology into content classrooms is not a matter of "if" but "when."

In preparing to write this book, we wondered about what to recommend to future and practicing content teachers. How can we help you choose technology wisely that can assist in the teaching of content-specific writing long after the purchase has been made? If we suggested particular software programs that seem to be cutting edge or progressive, within 6 months those suggestions may seem hopelessly out of date to the reader compared to the newest innovations. That is the nature of the industry at this point in time. Still, we asked ourselves if there are not at least some valuable generalizations that can be made concerning the marriage of technology and writing process instruction in the content classroom. Happily, there are some constants that we can suggest that will serve you well in searching for and using appropriate computer software and hardware. Here are a few suggestions.

Suggestion 1: Seek Out Technology That Will Help Students Organize, Analyze, and Evaluate New Content Information

Technology should make the critical work of content classes, gaining an understanding and command of the information, easier. A good comparison here is the electronic calculator. For decades, engineers and other scientists relied on the slide rule to assist with complex computations. Although the slide rule worked well, it was no match for the electronic calculator, which made computational tasks faster, more accurate, and simpler.

Learning new information in content classes, as we saw in Chapter 5, is largely a matter of building new schema structures in one's mind. Technology that helps students organize new information and see relationships with what has previously been learned is quite valuable. If the technology then helps students reach higher comprehension levels, such as what Bloom (1956) termed *analysis and evaluation,* then it is indeed worth consideration.

A good example of what we are describing can be found in the Moss Point (Mississippi) School District, where they have adopted what they term The Thinking Networks for Reading and Writing Approach (Cronin, Meadows, & Sinatra, 1990). Although this program was selected for use in all curricular areas, it is primarily targeted for science, social studies, and English classes. This program complements process writing in content classes using highly structured computer programs to help students learn to construct visual maps representing the relationships of major ideas, subordinate ideas, and explicit information. In essence, students begin by completing one of three generic semantic maps portrayed on a computer screen, depending on which map is most appropriate. The format for these maps is shown in Figure 8.8. These maps serve as an organizational guide for ideas consistent with the prewriting stage of the writing process. Many teachers also schedule visits to the library and media center so that staff there can help students collect additional information on assigned topics and teach them word processing techniques. By composing papers at the computer, the process of creating multiple drafts is made easier for students, just as it is for professional writers. The usual stages of the writing process continue until papers are accepted by the teacher.

The important point here is that the teachers and administrators chose technology that complemented their content programs. Too often, technology

Teachers in Moss Point, Mississippi, have discovered an effective program for incorporating writing in content classes.

We must find appropriate uses for technology and avoid being dazzled by the latest "bells and whistles." Otherwise invention becomes the mother of necessity, rather than the opposite.

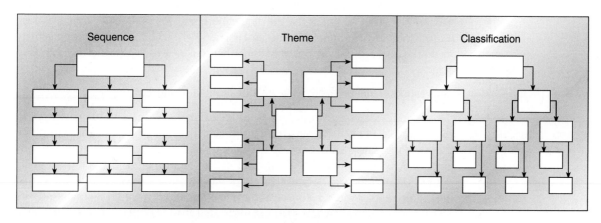

Figure 8.8 Computer-Generated Semantic Writing Map

is selected for style over substance reasons, resulting in the tail wagging the dog phenomenon in education. Know your writing program and what you want, then select technology that improves classroom learning.

Suggestion 2: Provide Students With Easy Access to Microcomputers

Word processors make the revising and editing processes almost painless for young writers.

Many students are not very enthusiastic about the writing process, because each draft at a typewriter requires a tedious rewrite. This problem can be overcome in schools where microcomputers/word processors, like the IBM-PC and Macintosh series, are provided. Such tasks as cutting, pasting, revising, and editing are quick and easy. Second, third, and fourth drafts are as easy to come by as simply pushing the print command, thus saving much time and effort. Word processing programs for classroom computers such as Bank Street Writer can convert existing computers into word processing-like systems. Many schools use conventional word processing programs, such as the best-selling programs by Word Perfect and MicroSoft Word. These programs are probably best suited to high schoolers, although middle school students who have daily access to microcomputers can quickly become proficient users.

Writers simply must have appropriate tools with which to write in the Information Age. Writers, especially neophytes in content classes, need to have access to microcomputers because they make the process so much more enjoyable.

Suggestion 3: Adapt and Insert Technology Into Your Instructional Plans

Computer programs should serve the curriculum, not the other way around.

It is important that technology serve *you* and the students, not the other way around. Great teachers begin by planning learning experiences, the classroom environment, and considering ways of helping students to become independent consumers of information. Technology is only one part of the entire plan and best serves students and teachers when it is integrated sensibly into superior curriculums so as to augment the learning experience. Do not feel locked into using entire software programs (Wepner & Feeley, 1993), when a single writing activity from the package may be the only thing that makes sense with your lesson plans.

Suggestion 4: Make Effective Use of Your Limited Resources

Students can learn quite effectively when working on computers in groups of two.

Making effective use of your limited time and resources is a multifaceted point. For example, school districts have a difficult time keeping up with technology demands because of limited funds. Most classrooms, even in more affluent school districts, will not have sufficient computers for all students to have daily access. Therefore, encourage teamwork with writing software. Not only is this efficient use of limited resources, it is good pedagogy—we know that students learn very effectively when working in dyads (groups of two). This is especially so with students having learning needs.

Learning about new software programs can be quite time-consuming and can keep teachers hopping as they try to help students. There are two ways this problem can be resolved. One way is for teachers to demonstrate new software to the entire class. Be sure to demonstrate the package's commands commonly used in writing: fonts, cutting, pasting, printing, formatting, and so on. Another way to conserve teacher time is to train several students or parent volunteers to be teaching assistants. They can answer the more basic questions and free you up to make house calls on students requiring more specialized help with the content information.

INFORMAL JOURNAL WRITING ACTIVITIES FOR CONTENT AREA CLASSROOMS

Writing in the content classroom can take the form of more relaxed informal experiences that cause students to be reflective about their learning. Journal writing is the most common form of informal writing offering a number of interesting options. With dialogue journals students converse with a classmate or the teacher about what is being learned. Learning logs are another kind of journal wherein students document new information learned in the content class. Simulated journals allow students to assume the role of a historical fig-

Begin a journal of your own that pertains in some way to your field of study.

A student reacting to the day's activities in her response journal.

ure, scientist, or explorer who is discovering the content to be learned for the first time. In this section we elaborate on these journal writing schemes.

Dialogue Journals

Dialogue journals are an ongoing written conversation between a teacher and student or in a student–student format addressing questions and comments about new ideas learned in class. As much as possible, journal entries should be responses and reactions to the ideas presented in class rather than a summary (M. Ruddell, 1993). Dialogue journal entries are usually made once or twice a week, rather than daily, usually in response to questions posed in class by the teacher or in a class conversation. The greatest benefit to dialogue journals is that they give students an opportunity to roll ideas around in their minds and interact with the teacher or peers about their conclusions.

Some content teachers have a problem with dialogue journals. In a departmentalized school, teachers often see too many students per day for individual dialogues to be possible. Ruddell (1993) points out that this problem can be overcome by developing a staggered schedule. For example, the first-period class may engage in dialogue journals for a 3-week period, while all the other classes take part in other less time-consuming activities. In this way, all students are afforded at least *some* contact with the teacher. In self-contained classes, such as in the upper elementary grades where the teacher may have only 25 students daily, dialogue journals can be used for longer periods.

Dialogue journals provide students with occasional feedback on their ideas.

Learning Logs

Learning logs help students record or react to what they are learning in content classes (Fulwiler, 1985; Tompkins, 1994). They also permit students to observe their own thinking (Edwards, 1992) and identify holes in their learning. Learning logs have been recommended for mathematics, science, and social studies but also can be used in other areas. Here are a few ways that learning logs have been recommended for content classrooms.

Learning logs help students record or react to what is being learned.

Learning Logs in Science

Edwards (1992) has found a simple two-part learning log format to be effective with her science classes. Youngsters respond first to a "What I expect to learn" question, then complete a "What I learned" section each day as more insights are gained from teaching–learning experiences. An example of a learning log appears in Figure 8.9.

Another type of learning log in science is the observation notebook, in which students write regular daily entries, usually tracking the progress of an experiment. In some cases this type of learning log will include the question or hypothesis under study, materials and procedures used, data and observations, and a discussion of conclusions drawn by the junior scientist.

Observation notebooks are often used in mathematics and science classes.

Figure 8.9 Learning Log: Science

What I expect to learn (questions I have, what I think I already know, what I am most curious about, etc.)	What I have learned so far (answers to my questions, new information I learned, new questions/ideas I have)
Why are sharks a threat to people? Why do they sometimes eat people? What else do they eat?	They only seem to be a threat when they feel frightened, or mistake a human for a sea animal they like to eat.
Great white sharks are the most dangerous in the Morro Bay area.	I guess I was wrong about sharks in Morro Bay, since they don't live there. I need to go back and reread the newspaper article I found.

Note. Adapted from "Using Dialectical Journals to Teach Thinking Skills" by P. R. Edwards, 1992, *Journal of Reading, 35*(4), 312–316.

Learning Logs in Mathematics

Learning logs in mathematics cause students to translate abstract concepts and computation into language, thus deepening their comprehension and, often, identifying areas requiring further clarification. Learning logs necessarily require students to assimilate and use the vocabulary associated with math and makes them more active participants in their learning. The National Council of Teachers of Mathematics (NCTM) in their Standards for School Mathematics (NCTM, 1989) has included "the ability to communicate mathematics" as one of the five most important needs for students to compete in the 21st century.

Paired or group retellings help students to pool their knowledge and arrive at new understandings of a topic.

We have found at least two learning log approaches to be successful in mathematics. First is to ask students to describe or retell in their own words mathematical processes they have been taught. It can take the form of a narrative with standard paragraph structure or a more step-by-step listing. An effective alternative (Wood, 1992) is to have students engage in paired or group retellings. The advantage here is that students pool their understandings to create the narrative, thereby helping them to clarify misunderstandings in a peer tutoring format. If the group does not collectively grasp the concept, then the teacher is called into the group on a "house call" to clarify as an expert consultant. This makes maximum use of the teacher's time as well. Figure 8.10 shows an example of a math learning log.

Learning Logs in the Social Studies

Many students regard social studies, not to mention *writing* about social studies, to be as exciting as, say, watching paint dry. This is probably due in part to the

Figure 8.10 Learning Log:
10th-Grade Algebra

> Today in Algebra II, we will be learning a method of finding all the zero solutions in a greater than 2 degree polynomial. What I've heard from other students is that the procedure requires the use of all our accumulated knowledge.
>
> After learning the lesson, I found that it was very handy but tedious. The method is very helpful when graphing and solving a problem. The method consists of several steps. The first step is to determine the number of solutions the problem has. You can tell this by looking at the degree of the polynomial. Then you need to use the rational zero test to find possible rational answers. Next you have to interchange the upper and lower bounds rule and synthetic division, using the numbers acquired in the rational zero test. The upper and lower bounds rule tells you how high or low the range of all the possible zeros is. Synthetic division is the actual test used to find the zeros. I'm glad we could use our calculators.

seemingly sterile quality of the enterprise, the lack of a human quality. It may also be that students have difficulty in comprehending time frames and relationships between important events. For these and other reasons, we have sought out some creative options to the typical journal entry type of learning logs.

Minilessons are taught directly to students to help them better understand how powerful, communicative sentences are formed.

Dorothy Grant Hennings (1993) has done a splendid job of summarizing interesting options that we feel can be adapted as learning log entries. In each instance Hennings included a time element to help students see important relationships coupled with summary writing about historic events. In the first example (see Figure 8.11), students construct a time-line entry in the learning log. Writing in this type of learning log entry is limited to one- or two-sentence summaries heavily laden with meaning. Teachers must present minilessons to students, naturally, as to how such concise but powerful sentences are carefully drafted, revised, and revised again to get just the right meaning. Quality and economy of language are the hallmarks of this form of writing. The next type of learning log entry takes the form of a cause–effect map (see Figure 8.12). It is virtually identical to the time-line entry insofar as the writing skills required. The difference is the cause–effect nature of the information recorded. The third type of learning log entry makes use of a generalization (supplied by the teacher at the beginning of the class) and an idea map summarizing evidence that supports or refutes the generalization (see Figure 8.13). Again, precise and brief summaries are used in these entries.

Figure 8.11   Time-Line Learning Log: Early History of Edinburgh, Scotland

Key Events	Dates	Significance
	Before 600 A.D.	
Castle Rock, occupied by Gododdin, a Celtic tribe		A first settlement
	638 A.D.	
Edwin, King of Northumbria, occupies south of Scotland.		Beginning of rulers
	Middle 10th Century	
Kings of Scots expel the Northumbrian rulers; Malcolm Canmore built a hunting lodge on Castle Rock.		Beginning of Scottish rule
Margaret (St. Margaret), Malcolm's Queen, builds chapel on the rock.		Oldest building in Scotland
	14th Century	
Mary, Queen of Scots, becomes the mother of James VI, who unites Scottish and English thrones.		Unification of Britain after a civil war

Each of these modes can put some spice into the social studies class and help students learn more of their world. Teachers must help students know when each style is most appropriate and teach them the skills necessary to develop quality entries.

Figure 8.12 Cause–Effect Map Learning Log: Eighth-Grade Science Lab

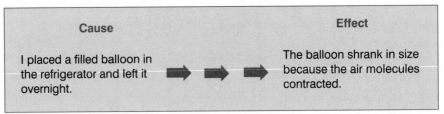

Cause	Effect
I placed a filled balloon in the refrigerator and left it overnight.	The balloon shrank in size because the air molecules contracted.

Simulated Journals

Simulated journals are often used to help students understand the viewpoint of others (Tompkins, 1994).

Gail Tompkins suggests that simulated journals can "help students assume the role of another person and write from that person's viewpoint" (1994, p. 97). Using a kind of "Dear Diary" format, students delve into the content to be learned, find out how this information was discovered, learn something of the people involved, then create a kind of docudrama retelling of the information in memoir style. In math, a student might assume the identity of John Venn

Figure 8.13 Generalization and Idea Map Learning Log: 10th-Grade English

Generalization: Sentence combining is a good way to create more mature sentences.

Evidence to support the generalization

Point 1: Many times I have noticed that short, choppy sentences don't read as well as combined ones.

Point 2: Combining sentences makes the paragraph read smoothly and make better sense to the reader.

Example of choppy sentences: I went to the basketball game. I met my friend Shawna there. It was a great game. The players played hard. Billy scored the last shot. We won.

Example of combined sentences: I went to the basketball game and met my friend Shawna. It was a great game, and the players played hard. Billy scored the final shot and won the game.

and write a simulated journal entry explaining how he developed the now-famous Venn diagram to represent some of George Boole's theories of logical systems. A student of science might choose to create a simulated journal entry based on the work of Candace Pert, a modern scientist whose discovery of the opiate receptor, and other peptide receptors in the brain and the body, led to a better understanding of the chemicals that travel between the mind and the body (Moyers, 1993). In history, a student may decide to author a simulated journal entry based on events in the life of Anne Boleyn during her rather unfortunate marriage to Henry VIII. Whatever the content domain, simulated journal entries are a refreshing alternative to report writing that enhance student learning.

FORMAL WRITING ACTIVITIES FOR CONTENT AREA CLASSROOMS

Many teachers help students use the writing process through formal writing activities proven effective in classroom-based research. These activities are designed to activate students' prior knowledge about a topic to be investigated, provide a kind of scaffolding for future learning, and improve communication skills. In this section are several formal writing activities we have found to be effective and interesting for students. Although we suggest a few illustrative examples, it is important to note that writing takes its own form and style in each of the content areas (Tierney, Readence, & Dishner, 1995).

Formal papers still have a place in content area teaching and learning.

I-Search Paper

The I-Search Paper (Macrorie, 1980, 1988) has students investigate a self-selected topic, conduct field investigations and interviews associated with the topic, then write a report of their research. I-Search Papers help students to capitalize on their natural curiosity about a subject and enjoy the benefits of a hands-on investigative experience. The process for assembling I-Search Papers simply involves choosing a topic, conducting a search for information, and writing the paper. Following is a summary of the procedure.

Selecting a Topic

Self-selection of the topic is an important aspect of the I-Search Paper because this allows student interest to drive the experience. Macrorie (1980, 1988) states that this needs to be an open-ended brainstorming process that allows students a great deal of freedom such that most topics would be acceptable. This open-ended stance works particularly well in language arts classes where composition is the desired end. Our experience, however, suggests that content teachers will probably need to define some boundaries for the I-Search

I-Search Papers (Macrorie, 1988) are a great means for capitalizing on student interest through hands-on investigations.

Paper to be practicable. It does not, for example, serve the requirements of the ninth-grade general science curriculum on "magnetism" for a student to be permitted so much latitude in topic selection that he chooses to write about the history of Rap music. We have found that choice within limits provides a great deal of student satisfaction while also accomplishing curriculum goals.

The Information Search

What are the key steps on an I-Search Paper experience?

A number of useful suggestions have been provided by Macrorie (1980, 1988) to guide the process of gathering information, which we have slightly adapted:

- Students should share their I-Search idea with a group of peers or the class and ask for their thoughts. The group can help each student refine ideas, think of possible sources for further information, and identify possible resource persons who could be interviewed. Ideas should be discussed further with the teacher and approved.
- Next, students should conduct an initial library search for information on the topic. This deepens the student's understanding of the topic with an eye toward interviewing an expert(s) on the topic. Research, as stated earlier in the chapter, is a vital part of prewriting. Information discovered in this initial search should be organized in some sort of outline or web so that knowledge holes can be discovered.
- As information is discovered, students construct a list of local experts on the topic who can further inform them. It is important for the teacher to coach students on appropriate and best ways to contact these individuals and what to say. For some, a telephone interview will be best. Other experts may be willing to have a brief face-to-face interview. Students should come prepared with a list of specific questions and tape-record the interview if at all possible. While interviewing experts, students should be sure to ask where additional information on the topic can be found.
- At this point, students should revisit their first outlines or information webs as part of the prewriting process. Information gaps should be the impetus for further reading and, if necessary, follow-up interviews.

Writing the I-Search Paper

In constructing the paper, students should consider including the following elements:

- Why the topic was selected in the first place
- What the student knew initially about the topic and what the initial library search turned up

- A discussion of the interviews and other field research that took place
- What the student learned, or still needs to learn, about the topic

In presenting the I-Search Paper to the class, students may find that playing back taped excerpts of the expert interview may make the presentation more appealing.

Guided Writing Procedure

C. Smith and Bean (1980) recommend the Guided Writing Procedure (GWP) as a method of simultaneously improving students' content knowledge and writing ability. The GWP begins with students' prior knowledge about a subject, helps them organize their thoughts into an outline, then produce multiple drafts on the topic. Again, we have made some slight adaptations based on more recent research to make this model even more effective.

The Guided Writing Procedure (Smith & Bean, 1980) is a balanced approach to writing that uses explicit instruction as to process and student choice.

Step 1: *Informal discussion of the topic and organization of ideas.* At the beginning of a new unit of study, ask students to brainstorm all information about the topic they can recall. Record all appropriate responses on the board or overhead projector as stated. For instance, in one of our classes, we discussed comets and related phenomena. The initial brainstorming resulted in a listing similar to what follows:

space object	has a tail
appears to be on fire	Halley's Comet
move very fast	some found in our solar system
have their own orbit	

After this has been done, ask students to help you to organize the ideas according to major concepts and supporting details. Students then create a first draft summarizing what they know up to this point. Collect and read the drafts, making comments using a writing checklist or self-adhesive notes. The emphasis at this point should be on the content and organization of ideas, rather than mechanics.

Step 2: *Sharing content and revisions to compositions.* With this common prior knowledge base now firmly in mind, students are ready to receive more information so that knowledge gaps can be filled. Once instruction has proceeded for several days in the preferred mode, ask students to construct a revised draft that includes new information. We find that having students work collaboratively first to construct a revised outline before writing a new draft tends to yield the best results. For instance, a new outline constructed after just several days of instruction may now include some of the following information from which students can construct their own individual drafts:

Comets

I. History
    A. Observed for centuries
    B. Many superstitions about comets came about
    Examples: Influence on Britain in 1066; End-of-the-world episodes
II. Composition of comets
    A. Nucleus made up of ice and dirt
    B. Tail composed of matter and vapor streaking away from the sun
III. Halley's Comet
    A. Sir Edmond Halley (1656–1742)
    B. Regular orbit near the Earth

This process can be repeated several times during the course of instruction so that new information is constantly assimilated and writing improved.

    One of the hazards of the GWP is that it can place teachers in the unenviable position of being the only source of feedback (Tierney et al., 1995). Additionally, the GWP can be quite time-consuming for teachers in secondary grades, who may have six or seven class periods per day. The use of peer writing conferences, as described earlier in the chapter, is a good remedy for these problems. It may also be a good idea to use the GWP with only one or two class periods at any one time to minimize teacher overload.

Peer writing conferences help make the GWP a practicable instructional activity.

Expository Text Pattern Writing

Authors of content texts use several expository text patterns in creating their compositions.

We mentioned earlier in the chapter that Meyer and Freedle (1984) and Armbruster and Anderson (1984) have discovered that expository writers use five common patterns for presenting information: time order (sequence), cause–effect, problem–solution, comparison, and simple listing. Others (Flood, Lapp, & Farnan, 1986; McGee & Richgels, 1985) have found that students can be taught about these patterns to help them better comprehend content texts and concurrently improve their writing communication skills. Each of the patterns can be taught through a series of minilessons (Tompkins, 1994) using a format like the following:

- *Introduce the expository text pattern.* Display on the overhead projector several examples of the pattern to be examined. Pattern guides can be constructed that help students see crucial pattern elements. In Figure 8.14 we offer an example of a pattern guide for a geography class.

Identify several expository text patterns in one of your key content textbooks for discussion with students.

- *Search for other examples of the text pattern in trade books and other text materials.* Once students have been introduced to the pattern, it is helpful for them to work in pairs or individually to try to find examples of the pattern in other books. This is not usually too difficult, because most expository writers use most of the patterns regularly on nearly every page of text. Examples should be shared with the group, and students should explain how the chosen example fits the pattern.

Figure 8.14 Pattern Guide: Comparison for a Geography Class

Three Geographical Regions of Tennessee

Comparison: Geography of Tennessee

After reading pages 287–291 of your text, compare and contrast the three distinct geographical regions of Tennessee.

West Tennessee	*Middle Tennessee*	*East Tennessee*
1. (Hint: Delta region)	1.	1.
2.	2. (Hint: Cumberland River)	2.
3.	3.	3. (Hint: The Smokies)
4.	4.	4.

- *Writing paragraphs that fit the pattern.* The next level of understanding is achieved by having students author their own paragraphs using the pattern being studied. The paragraph should focus on the topic presently under study so that knowledge of the subject matter is deepened. Pattern guides may be used as a prewriting tool along with the usual prewriting research activities described earlier in the chapter. Drafting, revising, editing, and sharing/publishing stages as normally prescribed in process writing usually follow.
- *Repeat the process for each expository text pattern.* During the course of the term, teachers and students can investigate each expository pattern commonly found in the content area. As students become authors of these writing patterns, they become better readers and comprehenders of the subject matter.

Using Frames to Promote Critical Writing

Research has indicated for two decades that middle and high school students have difficulty creating compositions that require critical thinking skills. We feel this is so because students frequently have trouble seeing relationships in abstract content information. Ryder (1994) has suggested the use of graphic organizers called *frames* to help students read and write more critically by identifying relationships in the content. A frame is a kind of matrix that represents knowledge discovered in the content classroom and that helps them to organize information, recognize relationships, and draw conclusions.

Three types of frames may be used in content classes: descriptive, goal, and problem–solution. Descriptive frames are especially helpful in assisting students to see comparison–contrasts, cause–effect relationships, form versus function, or advantages and disadvantages. Goal frames help students understand goals, actions, and outcomes in situations studied. Problem–solution frames, as the

Think of ways you could use the three types of frames in your content instruction.

name implies, help students understand the relationships between an identified problem, actions taken, and the resolution or consequence of that action. In Figure 8.15, an example of each frame type is presented.

Figure 8.15 Frames for Critical Writing

Descriptive Frame of Types of Violence

	Causes	Outcome	Location
Gang violence	Peer pressure, feelings of alienation	Assaults, vandalism, theft, murders	Rural, suburban, and urban settings
Domestic violence	Depression, self-esteem problems, abused in childhood, drug abuse	Broken homes, physical and/or emotional injury	Family settings
Athletics violence	Emphasis on winning, lack of quality leadership, fan expectations	Physical and sometimes emotional injury	Sports arenas

Goal Frame of Ways to Reduce Violence in Society

	Goal	Action	Results
Neighborhood Watch programs	Monitor and eliminate or reduce violence and crime in the community	Awareness of citizens through crime watch programs	Improved crime rate
Gang reconciliation	Eliminate gang-related crime in the community	Bring gang members together through persuasion and negotiations	Reduction in crime rate

Problem-Solution Frame of Causes of Violence

	Problem	Solution
Economic stress	Lack of employment or sufficient employment to provide for most basic needs	Opportunities for improving literacy skills and vocational education
Drugs	Violence committed to acquire drugs and maintain the addiction	Drug awareness programs in schools, access to treatment and counseling programs

To construct a frame, begin by identifying the major concepts or principles and supporting details found in the primary text readings to be used. Next, decide which type of frame (goal, problem–solution, descriptive) best fits the material to be learned. Finally, draw up the frame(s) by creating and labeling the necessary rows and columns.

It will be necessary for the teacher to develop several example minilessons showing students how to complete each type of frame. When doing so, a question requiring critical thinking should be posed, which is answerable using an appropriate frame. Once students grasp how to use frames, which they quickly do, then the stage is set for writing summaries using the information discovered in the frame.

Critical writing experiences using frames begin with the teacher or student group leader restating a question requiring higher level thinking. Discuss in small groups how information noted in the frame(s) might help them in writing their response. They should be sure to also discuss any information in the frame that may *not* be useful in the response, such as irrelevant details. Students should then outline or otherwise organize ideas that are to be included in their response, then construct a first draft. Each student should share her first draft in a peer editing conference, then make revisions according to suggestions received. Final versions can be shared in small groups or by volunteers in whole class sessions.

> Minilessons should be taught to show students how to construct frames.

Extending Learning Through Research Report Writing

Even though research reports have acquired something of a bad name over the years as a result of overuse and poor student preparation, they still can be an important part of content learning. With careful mentoring by the teacher, students can learn to write quality research reports and learn much about the topic.

In truth, following the stages of the writing process described earlier is the most comprehensive way we have found to teach students how to write effectively on most topics. But classroom practice has taught us that several additional areas peculiar to research reports not commonly mentioned as part of the writing process seem to pose challenges for many students.

Formulating research questions is a vital part of the process not always considered. The old newspaper ritual of discovering *who, what, when, where, why,* and *how* is often a good place to start. Webbing out what the student knows often helps him discover what is not known so that further questions can be developed. McKenzie (1979) recommends the use of a data chart to record what is known and sources for obtaining the answers to research questions. In Figure 8.16 we combine the notion of "who, what, when" research questions within a data chart pertaining to an investigation on the history of the automobile.

Another problem students have with research report writing is choosing a topic that is sufficiently narrow in scope. It is often hard for them to judge how

> The stages of the writing process can be used effectively to help students construct superior research reports.

> Formulation of quality research questions is a crucial first step.

Figure 8.16 Data Chart: History of the Automobile

DATA CHART						
Researcher's Name _____ Topic: History of the Automobile						
Information Source	Who	What	When	Where	Why	How
1.						
2.						
3.						
4.						

manageable a topic will be, so a student–teacher conference to confirm the topic is a must.

Finally, many students can work independently on a research paper from the outset, but quite a few otherwise competent students cannot. The answer to this developmental dilemma is collaboration. Some teachers like to begin the year by constructing whole class collaborative reports using the stages of the writing process as major components and as a way to discuss content material in depth. This provides a no-risk environment for students to learn about this type of writing and ask questions. An intermediate stage is *collaborative reports:* Two or three students work as a team to construct a research report on a relevant subject. With this type of groundwork early in the year, most students will be able to construct individual research reports during the second semester using the now familiar procedures.

What are some of the problems students often have in writing research papers?

ISSUES RELATED TO WRITING IN THE CONTENT AREAS

Teachers introducing the writing process to their content classes find that it adds a potent dimension to the learning environment. A general science teacher recently remarked "Once you move into writing as part of teaching [science], you'll never go back to teaching without it . . . it's just too powerful!" Indeed it is, but that is not to say that implementing a writing process component is without some challenges.

Content teachers often ask, "How do I find *time* for a writing process component when each class period is already planned to the maximum?" Still oth-

Assessing writing projects and finding time for writing instruction are two common stumbling blocks for teachers.

ers wonder how they can assess and grade writing products when students can be vastly different in terms of their writing abilities. These two issues can become major stumbling blocks for teachers if not resolved. In this part of the chapter, we offer suggestions based on our own classroom experiences, as well as ideas borrowed from other content teachers currently practicing in classrooms around the country.

Finding the Time: Organizing for Writing Activities

There are no two ways about it—writing in the content areas requires a significant commitment of time. Time is required to teach students about the forms of writing found in the content specialty. It also takes time to react to student compositions, meet with peer editing groups, and teach the minilessons. It should also be noted that effective teachers are writers themselves; teachers must find time to create their own compositions so that they can speak from knowledge and experience (you can't teach what you can't do). Then there is the problem many secondary teachers face: seeing too many students each day to do all they want to do. For us, writing in content classes is not a nice, unnecessary activity; it is essential and nonnegotiable. Some form of process writing should occur in content classes each week, if not daily.

Inclusion of process writing is now viewed as a necessity in building quality content instruction programs.

What is the answer to the time dilemma? For most teachers the solution lies in scheduling. Some of the more complicated assignments and writing activities simply must be staggered in the scheduling. For example, only the first-period class may engage in one of the more complex writing activities, while the other classes perform more routine writing assignments.

Another answer lies in the realization that content teachers need not read and evaluate all writing products themselves. Use of peer editing conferences and other forms of peer coaching, say students paired with upper grade students, can help teachers succeed. Many schools and colleges of education are presently seeking opportunities to create partnerships with schools for field-based teacher education opportunities.

Content teachers should seek out education professors at local colleges and universities for new collaborations. In many instances future teachers are now matched with public school students to assist them with their writing and content learning. Both of the authors of this text are presently engaged in such activities in Texas and Kansas and have found these experiences to be hugely effective and mutually beneficial to content teachers, their students, and future teachers. These efforts are part of a powerful movement in America having as its goal the mutual renewal of schools and colleges of education (Goodlad, 1994).

Universities and public schools are working together to renew and reinvent schooling.

Finding time for writing in content classes is an important part of establishing an effective learning environment. In Chapter 4 we offer some sample schedules that include time set aside for this enterprise. As you plan for instruction, we urge the reader to think of *when* writing will occur, not *if,* then make it happen. The results more than outweigh the complications.

The Correctness Issue: Spelling and Mechanics in Writing

One of the frequent criticisms of process writing seems to be that "these new-fangled methods fail to teach students correct spelling and grammar." Such skills are among the basics referred to in the back-to-basics movement. We agree that these are important skills, and that is why they are addressed in the editing stage of the writing process. So why do many parents and community leaders seem to think that these skills are not taught in process writing?

The fact is that sometimes content teachers who incorporate writing as part of their curriculum fail to address mechanics and spelling. They may feel this is the job of the English teachers or consider correctness of information to be the only really important aspect of a content composition. This is not so. Part of assembling a credible and professional composition is making sure that, when it is completed, it is well written and error free. On the other hand, one of the reasons so many students avoid writing activities is their fear of not doing it correctly. An overemphasis can, in fact, be destructive to the learning environment and cause students to avoid taking risks with their self-esteem as writers. Thus, many teachers avoid teaching the conventions of writing altogether.

How then do teachers help students progress as content writers? How do we keep a proper atmosphere in our classes so that students are helped to write freely and unself-consciously (Calkins, 1994)? How do we do all these things while also helping students to grow in their knowledge of writing conventions? We need to maintain an interest in both the content and mechanics. Prewriting, drafting, and revising activities are geared toward making sure that content is accurate, timely, and presented in an interesting way. Editing is the activity that focuses on the mechanics or conventions of writing. Thus, as we teach students to use the writing process effectively, we ensure that both content and mechanics are properly emphasized.

Assessing Student Writing

In Chapter 3, "Assessing Content Literacy," we go into some detail about such issues as the philosophy and beliefs undergirding modern assessments, how to assess student work, grading, and reporting to parents. After reading this section, you may want to review Chapter 3 for a more comprehensive understanding of assessment and grading issues. Here we briefly describe how one can use authentic assessment like those discussed in Chapter 3 to evaluate student compositions.

Analytic and Holistic Assessments

It is almost tautological to state that the reason we conduct assessments is to find out what students know (and don't know) so that we can offer appropriate instruction in our classes. Said another way, assessment helps us to locate a

---

Spelling and other writing mechanics must be addressed as part of writing in the content areas.

Content and mechanics must both be emphasized in content area writing instruction.

All efficient and effective assessments in writing have an underlying structure.

student's zone of proximal development. An important point to remember is that in *all* teaching–learning activities (not only writing assignments) by which students are to be assessed, assessment criteria should be carefully explained to students before they begin work on an assignment.

Basically two types of assessment are frequently applied to written compositions: qualitative and quantitative. In a **qualitative assessment**, also known as *descriptive assessment,* teachers use words rather than numbers to describe the student's progress as evidenced in the composition itself. In qualitative assessment the teacher usually writes a short paragraph describing how well the student has met predetermined objectives. The advantage of qualitative assessments is that they allow teachers to fully describe what they observe. Thus, qualitative assessments have the potential for being the most valid assessment. The downside of qualitative assessments is that they can be time-consuming. If used exclusively, they can also annoy parents who expect a letter grade rather than a narrative explaining how their child is doing in school. Therefore, parents may need to be educated as to the benefits of qualitative assessment. Following are a few tips to remember when writing qualitative assessments:

> Qualitative assessments use words rather than numbers to describe students' progress.

> Consider some of the disadvantages of qualitative assessment programs and how these problems can be addressed.

1. Begin your analysis by emphasizing several positive aspects of the composition. Students often are hesitant to take risks with their self-esteem, especially in tasks such as these, where they often feel inadequate. Positive feedback is essential in building in students the attitude that helps them think "I am one who writes!"
2. Remember to focus on the objectives of the assignment in your assessment so as to not overanalyze the composition.
3. Instead of using language in your assessment suggesting student "weaknesses," phrase areas to be developed as "suggestions."
4. Be sure to date qualitative assessments and keep a copy in the portfolio (see Chapter 3) for each student. This will help you in determining how much growth students make over the course of each grading period so that you can plan future teaching strategies and content.

As stated, qualitative assessments use words rather than numbers to describe and evaluate students' compositions. **Quantitative assessments** are just the reverse—they use numbers rather than words to describe student achievement. Quantitative assessments are very familiar, because traditional grading is, at least in part, a form of this perspective. However, we do not advocate traditional grading, because it tends to reduce student learning to a single grade based on simple averaging of test scores. Two very effective ways to assess written compositions are vastly superior to traditional grading. When these methods are used in conjunction with qualitative assessment procedures, teachers can inform parents and students in a valid way (see Chapter 3

> Quantitative assessments use numbers or letter grades to describe student achievement.

for a further discussion of this point). The two methods of quantitative assessment are known as holistic scoring and analytic scoring.

Holistic scoring is often performed by awarding students a score of from 1 to 5 on a writing assignment based on how well students achieve predetermined objectives set by the teacher before starting the assignment. A score of 5 indicates a superior level of achievement, whereas a score of 1 is considered a minimal effort. For example, let's assume that a student in a junior-level English class named Lawanda has decided to write a cartoon-like strip summarizing *The Scarlet Letter* by Nathaniel Hawthorne. According to criteria set by the teacher (which, of course, are based on minilessons she has presented to the class), Lawanda must demonstrate the literary elements of suspense and irony, while also observing the mechanical aspects of writing (e.g., appropriate punctuation; grammar, unless affected in the dialogue; and spelling). If in assessing the assignment the teacher decided (a) Lawanda used excellent mechanics in writing her cartoon strip and (b) was able to portray irony and suspense in a way that was substantially better than her peers in the class but (c) not quite as well as seen in the two or three best compositions in this class, then the teacher might decide to award a holistic score of 4 to Lawanda. This score would account for the excellence of the mechanical aspects and the quality with which she was able to portray irony and suspense, while also acknowledging that a few students performed on a still higher level.

Holistic scoring as described here presents one major problem for teachers. In situations like the one just described, where multiple criteria are being used, holistic scoring does not allow the teacher to give different weight to each criterion. Some aspects of a writing assignment may be of more importance to the teacher than others, but this method of assessment does not allow the teacher to differentiate. The 11th-grade English teacher in the example of Lawanda probably considers a student's ability to demonstrate irony and suspense far more challenging and important at this point in her education than the ability to use commas and semicolons correctly! Fortunately, an alternate and more refined quantitative system of assessment is available—analytic scoring.

Analytic scoring is a refinement of holistic scoring that allows teachers to differentiate and place a value on each criterion of an assignment. There are two chief differences: (a) The 1 to 5 score described in holistic scoring is applied to *each* criterion separately, and (b) the score awarded for each criterion is then multiplied by a weighted number to adjust for the relative importance of each criterion. Examine Figure 8.17, which portrays an assessment form developed for the 11th-grade English class described earlier and where the student Lawanda's irony and suspense assignment is evaluated.

The teacher in this instance, Ms. Connor, has developed a form to aid in the assessment process—an idea we strongly endorse. Under the "Specific Criteria for This Assignment" section, Ms. Connor has listed the three main criteria for this assignment: irony, suspense, and mechanics. Note that in each case the criterion is to be assessed using the 1 to 5 system previously described.

Holistic scoring is an efficient strategy for assessing student achievement on predetermined objectives.

Holistic scoring does not permit the teacher to apply different weight to each criterion or objective, whereas analytic scoring does.

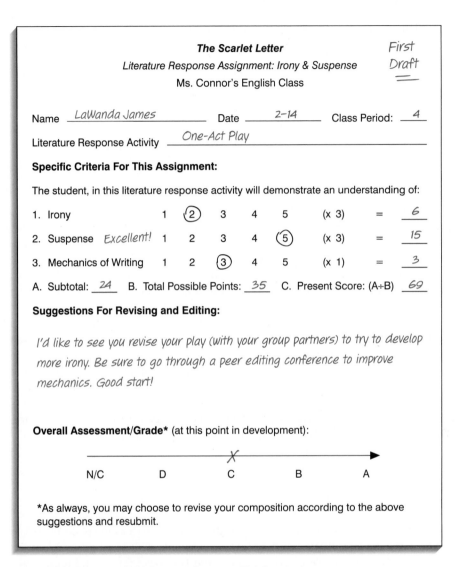

The Scarlet Letter
Literature Response Assignment: Irony & Suspense   *First Draft*
Ms. Connor's English Class

Name __LaWanda James__   Date __2–14__   Class Period: __4__

Literature Response Activity __One-Act Play__

Specific Criteria For This Assignment:

The student, in this literature response activity will demonstrate an understanding of:

1. Irony   1   ②   3   4   5   (x 3)   =   6

2. Suspense *Excellent!* 1   2   3   4   ⑤   (x 3)   =   15

3. Mechanics of Writing   1   2   ③   4   5   (x 1)   =   3

A. Subtotal: __24__   B. Total Possible Points: __35__   C. Present Score: (A÷B) __69__

Suggestions For Revising and Editing:

I'd like to see you revise your play (with your group partners) to try to develop more irony. Be sure to go through a peer editing conference to improve mechanics. Good start!

Overall Assessment/Grade* (at this point in development):

N/C   D   C   B   A

*As always, you may choose to revise your composition according to the above suggestions and resubmit.

Figure 8.17 Analytic Scoring Sample: *The Scarlet Letter*

Next, Ms. Connor will multiply the 1 to 5 score by a weighted figure (1 or 3), which indicates the relative value she places on each component of the writing assignment. Thus, Ms. Connor considers mechanics of writing to be an important aspect of the assignment (as indicated by her assignment of value to it in the assessment), but she considers the demonstration of irony and suspense to be more important than mechanics (hence her assignment of the weighted value of 3 to these factors).

The sections under "Specific Criteria for This Assignment" marked A, B, and C allow Ms. Connor to convert the scores for irony, suspense, and mechanics of writing into an average from 1 to 5. The section marked "A. Subtotal" is simply a totaling of points awarded in 1, 2, and 3. The section marked "B. Total Possible Points" is arrived at by adding up the total possible points in 1, 2, and 3 as follows:

1. Irony: $5 \times 3 = 15$
2. Suspense: $5 \times 3 = 15$
3. Mechanics: $5 \times 1 = 5$

Total Possible Points = 35

The section marked "C. Present Score: $(A \div B)$" is Lawanda's total score divided by the total possible points. The final section simply converts Lawanda's score on this assignment into a letter grade (if required). Please note that the student is allowed to revise and edit the composition to arrive at an improved assessment of the assignment. Students should be encouraged to do so, because it is in revising and editing that writers seem to learn a great deal and extend their communication skills.

Finally, it is necessary to say a word or two about grading. Many authorities do not like to link processes like reading and writing with grading, because they are developmental skills (i.e., we all progress at different rates over time). Although we wholeheartedly agree with this sentiment, the reality is that most teachers are still required to award grades. In Chapter 3 we provide a comprehensive discussion of this issue and offer a three-way system for grading that is fair to the student and satisfies political realities. Please read this section carefully before attempting to award grades for writing assignments.

> See Chapter 3 for a discussion of grading alternatives.

LEARNERS WITH SPECIAL NEEDS: THE WRITING CONNECTION

> Writing process instruction is quite beneficial for learners with special needs.

It may well occur to you that many of the writing process ideas described in this chapter would be just as beneficial to students with learning problems as they are for other students. This assumption is correct for several reasons. In teaching special needs students about the process of writing, say, applied to the creation of research papers, we are basically breaking the task down into manageable components and adding more structure to the process (Graham, MacArthur, Schwartz, & Page-Voth, 1992). Thus, the enumeration of several special strategies for students with learning problems is unnecessary and might well create the illusion that an entirely different curriculum is required. However, we offer a description of one study that capitalized on the use of process writing and teacher modeling to help students with learning disabilities become more successful in writing essays. We do so as an illustration of the power of writing.

The PLANS Strategy

A group of students with learning problems recently found success in composing essays and stories using a strategy referred to as the *PLANS* (*p*ick goals, *l*ist ways to meet goals, make *n*otes, *s*equence notes) (Graham et al., 1992). Before describing this method, it is important to note several abilities that were developed before PLANS was introduced. For example, all students received instruction on microcomputer operations and typing. This resulted in their ability to perform basic word processing tasks, such as editing, revising, printing, and other functions critical to process writing. Students were also instructed on the components of quality essays and stories. This is an important step because other studies (see, e.g., Vallecorsa, 1990) have shown that many students with learning problems have a poorly developed sense of story and essay form compared to other students. As a net result, these students with learning needs were made knowledgeable about the writing process and how to create compositions on the microcomputer.

Teachers next introduced the PLANS strategy using a chart, describing why and how each step of the strategy was used in planning compositions. These teachers modeled PLANS by writing an essay and thinking out loud as they went through the process. They also showed students how to set up planning sheets to aid in the structuring of compositions. These documents addressed problem definition, planning, and self-evaluation tips. Teachers and students discussed the importance of what we say to ourselves while we work (metacognition) and thought of examples. Then they proceeded to experiment with the strategy. It reportedly took six to eight 40-minute training sessions to enable students to master the process.

There are three steps to this method we call PLANS (Graham et al., 1992, p. 325):

> **Step 1:** Do PLANS (*p*ick goals, *l*ist ways to meet goals, *a*nd make *n*otes, *s*equence notes).
>
> **Step 2:** Write and say more.
>
> **Step 3:** Test goals.

In step 1, students go through prewriting using the PLANS ideas noted in parentheses. It is important that teachers make clear project goals and ways to meet these goals with students. Goals should be discussed, enumerated on chart paper or the chalkboard, and left up so that students can refer to them throughout the writing process. Listing different ways goals can be met and discussing each option with the class help students have a clearer understanding of expectations and with far less ambiguity. The different options also provide students with some choice in the matter, a necessary precursor to motivation. Making notes on the subject of the essay and organizing these notes are usual steps in the writing process, so methods described earlier in the chapter are appropriate here. The second step of the strategy, write and say more, is what we normally call the draft-

The PLANS strategy offers an effective strategy for many special needs learners.

Think of examples you could use from your content area to develop a PLANS chart.

ing stage. The third stage, testing goals, is an evaluation stage that can be accomplished through a student–teacher conference, a peer editing conference, or both.

Is PLANS markedly different from the suggestions made earlier in the chapter? Not really, but it does represent an effective composite strategy that we strongly endorse. The winning combination for student success seems to be providing necessary background instruction related to process writing and appropriate uses of technology, clearly describing learning objectives, and providing necessary structure in the early stages.

CHAPTER SUMMARY

Incorporating writing process instruction into content classes can provide quantum leaps in learning. Replacing the one-shot essay papers of the past, which seemed to do little for the cause of content learning, process writing causes students to experience their content studies as authors in search of answers and information. Using different forms of writing, such as descriptive, persuasive, narrative, expository, and journal entries, helps to keep students motivated as they peruse content information. Use of the writing process is beneficial for all students, especially for those with learning problems, because these methods help students break learning tasks into manageable bits and provide a simple structure for project completion.

Teachers concerned about how to schedule writing activities can do so in a variety of ways. The use of peer writing conferences encourages students to work collaboratively in refining compositions and frees the teacher to work individually with adolescents who may need special assistance. Staggered scheduling also helps teachers use more time-intensive writing activities at different times during the school year and make them manageable. A range of assessment options provides both qualitative and quantitative evaluations of student work.

Process writing initiatives can be maximized in the classroom through appropriate uses of technology and teacher modeling. Teachers should encourage school district leaders to provide students with daily access to microcomputers, instruction in keyboard skills, and carefully selected software programs that make drafting, editing, and revising activities simpler for learners. In this way, youngsters are transformed from passivity to active authors and content researchers.

Reflection/Application Activities

1. The best way to learn about the writing process is through experience. As a first step, choose an area of focus from your own content area specialty about which you feel you need to develop greater expertise. Develop an essay using one of the forms of writing described in this chapter using each stage of the writing process. Be sure to document each step by keeping a personal portfolio of the experience. Present your best draft to a group of fellow students, and solicit their advice for further

revisions and improvements. After you have completed the composition, share (publish) it with the same peer group.

2. Develop a mock daily schedule on topics related to your subject area, assuming that you teach in a six-period departmentalized school setting. Decide how you will factor in process writing on a regular basis and which forms of writing will be appropriate. Once this schedule has been drafted, visit with a teacher in your content specialty at a nearby school who includes process writing in the curriculum, and share your tentative schedule. Ask for advice on refining the schedule so that it takes into account real-world realities. (Note: Your college instructor should be able to assist you in locating an appropriate teacher, if you need suggestions.)

3. Visit with a college or public school media specialist regarding software programs available for assisting in the writing process. If you are not already familiar with basic word processing programs and how to use them, inquire into courses that are geared toward practicing teachers. Begin a file of possible computer programs that you may wish to try out in your content classroom in the future.

4. Develop an outline of a presentation to parents as to why you feel process writing should be included in middle school and high school content classes. Be sure to include classroom-based examples to make your points. This may necessitate an interview with a practicing teacher who regularly incorporates the writing process. Preparation of a talk of this kind will assist you in future parent–teacher conferences.

Recommended Reading

Atwell, N. (1987). *In the middle: Writing, reading, and learning with adolescents.* Portsmouth, NH: Heinemann.

Gomez, M. L., & Smith, R. J. (1991). Building interactive reading and writing curricula with diverse learners. *The Clearing House, 64,* 147–151.

Macrorie, K. (1988). *The I-Search Paper.* Portsmouth, NH: Heinemann.

Ryder, R. J. (1994). Using frames to promote critical writing. *Journal of Reading, 38*(3), 210–218.

Tompkins, G. E. (1994). *Teaching writing: Balancing process and product* (2nd ed.). Englewood Cliffs, NJ: Merrill/Prentice Hall.

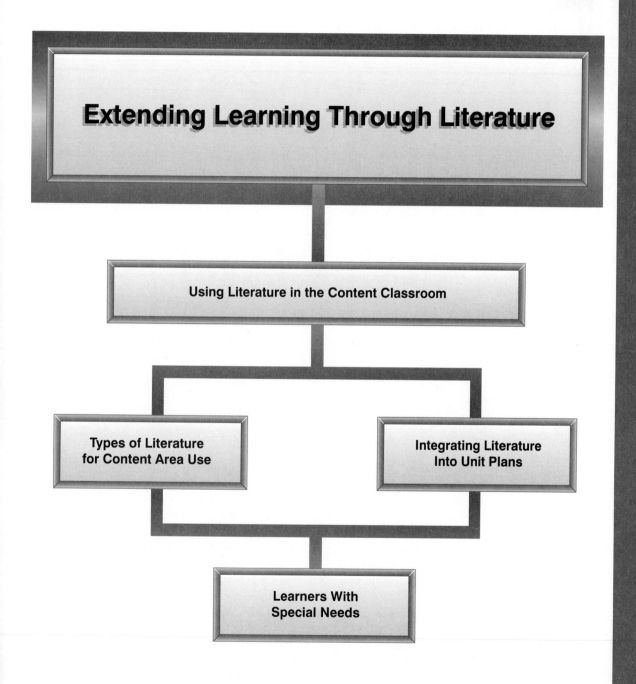

Extending Learning Through Literature

Using Literature in the Content Classroom

Types of Literature
for Content Area Use

Integrating Literature
Into Unit Plans

Learners With
Special Needs

Focus Questions

*As you read this chapter, try to discover
answers to the following questions:*

1 What is the role of literature in the content areas?

2 What three things can literature do for the content classroom?

3 Why is salesmanship important in today's content area classroom?

4 Identify the major types of literature appropriate for the content classroom. Summarize how teachers can select the best books of each type of literature discussed.

5 How does a content teacher go about preparing a unit of study that incorporates adolescent literature?

6 What are some good sources for determining trade books that are available in the content area in which you teach?

7 What are the goals of themed literature units in the content areas?

8 What purposes do book talks and other activities associated with themed literature units serve?

9 Why is it important for content teachers to read widely in their field of expertise?

Integrating adolescent literature with content instruction helps sell what you are teaching.

Recently, a retired high school math teacher advised us that three essential ingredients make for successful content area teaching: knowledge, dramatics, and salesmanship. Everyone recognizes that knowledge of what one teaches is important, but the other two ingredients often do not receive the attention they warrant. *Dramatics* refers to the need to have a high energy level in class such that through voice, body language, and enthusiasm one captures student attention and interest. *Salesmanship* suggests that teachers must "market" what they teach so that students become avid consumers of the topics and ideas presented. In this chapter we advocate the integration of adolescent literature as a means of marketing what you teach and as a way to help students connect the ideas of various content areas with the real world. A simple case in point might give you an idea of what we mean by marketing what is taught.

A biology teacher we know during a unit on monerans decided to address the issue of viruses and their impact on society both historically and futuristically. One day the teacher brought to class the popular book *The Hot Zone* by Michael Preston (1994). Excerpts from the book, which is based on a true story of the outbreak of a deadly virus in Africa, were read aloud to the class across several days. The teacher was careful to read just enough of the book to pique student interest. These read-alouds also provided a great introduction for each day's discussion about viruses. Almost overnight the book became a "best-seller" in this class composed of 9th, 10th, and 11th graders. In fact, a waiting list was created because so many students wanted the rest of the story. Because of the demand, the biology teacher recommended several other books, such as the *Andromeda Strain* by Michael Crichton (1972) and articles in such periodicals as *Scientific American* that involved the topic of viruses and how they are spread. This is what we mean by salesmanship!

In this chapter we explore ways of using adolescent literature to enhance your teaching and improve student learning and motivation. We begin by addressing the role and benefits of integrating literature into every content area.

Using Literature in the Content Classroom

In the early 1990s, there was an explosion of what we call "mega-bookstores." These stores not only are huge but even have areas where customers can sit, sample books, and drink espresso. On the surface it seems as if everyone is reading all types of books on a regular basis. However, some research reports suggest that only a small percentage of Americans read widely. Some report that 40% of adults who can read choose not to, and that less than 1% of children spend leisure time reading (R. C. Anderson, Heibert, & Wilkinson, 1985; Honig, 1988). In 1990, the National Assessment of Educational Progress Report (NAEP) concluded that about 50% of secondary students read 10 or fewer pages each day for schoolwork across all subject matter areas (Langer, Applebee, Mullis, & Foertsch, 1990). On the other hand, Moffit and Wartella (1992) report that 78% of their sample of high school students claim to read books as a leisure time activity. So what is one to think? Do our students read? If not, why not? An ancillary question is, Do teachers read, and if not, why not? Regardless of which statistic is correct, we all agree that in this technological age reading is still a most meaningful way to study, analyze, and reflect about topics of interest. For the content teacher, reading and encouraging students to read are keys to being successful and promoting content literacy for all.

How much time do you spend reading for pleasure?

The Role of Literature in Content Area Instruction

As students move to higher grade levels, they often experience **single-text teaching.** Many teachers, novice and experienced, adopt a single textbook and use it exclusively as the vehicle of instruction. Unfortunately, this approach does not recognize the diversity of needs in the classroom or the need to interest and

Single-text teaching has many limitations.

motivate students to know. We are convinced that library books or **trade books** should be used to complement and supplement any core text. As Crook and Lehman noted, "The integration of both fiction and nonfiction helps [students] experience two ways of knowing literature" (1991, p. 35). Through this knowing of literature, students can continue to refine their reading skills and acquire information and insight related to topics they are studying. In short, students will experience your subject matter in a way that is both motivating and rewarding.

Trade books can be the spice for your classroom.

If you think of your classroom as a "gumbo" rather than as a chicken broth you might get a better picture of what we mean. The basic ingredient in gumbo, a popular New Orleans entrée, is a flour and water mixture called a *roux* (pronounced "roo"). It's just not gumbo without a roux. However, what makes gumbo come to life are all the spices, shrimp, sausage, crab, and okra. Such is the content classroom. Certainly, the textbook is equivalent to the roux, but by itself you don't have the kind of classroom that everyone will enjoy, so to the adopted text, masterful teachers add many different instructional components and techniques. The use of fiction and nonfiction trade books, we believe, can be the spice so many teachers are looking for to help them get students interested and motivated.

If developing lifelong learners and readers is a goal of education, and we think it is, then the reading experiences teachers provide may help determine if students become avid readers and effective thinkers. Additionally, because adolescence is the age of discovery and definition of self (R. Kohlberg & Gilligan, 1972), what better way to promote discovery than through books that students can relate to and be influenced by. As Bruner states, "the foundations of any subject may be taught to anybody at any age in some form" (quoted in Egan, 1992, p. 50). The key is to engage each individual's mind, and books can do that for the student and teacher.

Advantages of Using Literature in the Content Areas

Teacher's editions of textbooks can be a limiting factor in the content area classroom.

For most content teachers, the adopted textbook is viewed as advantageous because of the wealth and organization of information. Also, texts are viewed positively because of the accompanying teacher's edition, which provides suggestions on how to teach and use the information contained in the textbook. Unfortunately, these benefits are also viewed as liabilities by increasing numbers of teachers. The very fact that a vast amount of information is presented in conjunction with the typical organization of most content area textbooks often makes the text too difficult for many students. The problems associated with many of the teacher's editions are twofold. First, the quality of teacher editions varies quite a bit in terms of teaching suggestions and connections between what is being studied and the real world. Second, overreliance on the teacher's edition, particularly if it is a poorly developed one, can limit a teacher's methods and ideas for promoting interest in the topics presented.

What are newer teacher editions providing that can assist the content teacher?

On a positive note, informal evaluations of recently copyrighted teacher editions by undergraduates and graduate students in our classes indicate that even the most traditional publishers are providing supplemental reading lists and projects related to both fiction and nonfiction for adolescents. Coupling this trend with the fact that many texts are too difficult for many students, it is clear why more and more teachers are turning to adolescent literature—it is instructionally beneficial! Several advantages of incorporating quality literature and other reading materials in your content area follow.

Improved Motivation

In the best-selling satirical novel *Forrest Gump* (Groom, 1986), Forrest summarizes one of his school memories by saying,

> She give me *Tom Sawyer* an two other books I can't remember, an I took them home an read em all, but then she give me a test where I don't do so hot. But I sure did enjoy them books. (p. 11)

One factor many upper level teachers face is the lack of interest and willingness of students to learn and interact with the topics that are being taught. We believe, as many do, that the use of literature can improve levels of motivation and interest in your content classroom. N. M. Johnson and Ebert (1992) reported that incorporating literature as a part of social studies units resulted in higher motivation and increased knowledge.

Trade books can increase interest and participation.

Using trade books, which come in a range of reading levels, as a part of a unit of study will greatly enhance the teacher's ability to capture student interest and provide opportunities for them to participate in class discussions and sharing groups. For instance, informational trade books such as *1001 Things Everyone Should Know About Science* (Panati, 1994) are often more up-to-date than adopted science texts. Remember, the copyright date of a textbook does not reflect the several years of prepublication work and production delays that can cause many books to be nearly out-of-date on arrival. Finding information that is new and perhaps even challenges statements in the adopted text sends the powerful message to students that to read is to know. Historical fiction and science fiction, for example, can appeal to the interest of the reader while introducing myriad facts and terms that connect directly to what is in the adopted text. *Jurassic Park* (Crichton, 1990), which is about DNA cloning, and *Fallen Angels* (Myers, 1988), a story about the Vietnam War, are two good examples of books that can put the student in touch with classroom topics in unique and motivating ways.

Depth of Learning

The use of fact and fiction trade books can improve students' understanding of terms related to specific content areas. Their use can also cause students to use higher order thinking skills by presenting various views or perspectives related to units of study. To a unit in social studies about the Western expansion in the

Trade books can promote higher order thinking skills.

United States, trade books such as *Native American Testimony: An Anthology of Indian and White Relations, First Encounter to Dispossession* (Nabokov, 1972), *The Adventures of the Negro Cowboys* (Durham & Jones, 1969), *The Way West* (Guthrie, 1979), *The Chisholm Trail* (Gard, 1969), *Borderlands* (Carter, 1990), and *The United States in the Indian Wars* (Lawson, 1988) can provide students with an in-depth look at a variety of events and individuals from perspectives no single textbook can offer. In an art class, books about adolescents and art abound. Trade books such as *Treasure Keepers* (Mills, 1973), *In Summer Light* (O'Neal, 1986), *The Monument* (Paulsen, 1991), and *Great Moments in Architecture* (Macaulay, 1978) not only can promote reading and artistic endeavor but can assist students in acquiring a real-world view of why art is important and what it takes to be an artist.

Because of the appeal generated by the way trade books are written, students often encounter many facts and ideas incidentally while they are immersed in a good story line (Speigel, 1987). Additionally, some writers (Butzow & Butzow, 1989) suggest that in many of today's integrated approaches to content area teaching the use of age-appropriate literature is essential. Literature helps students encounter facts and concepts in a form that is motivating and understandable.

Incidental learning can occur while reading interesting material.

Increased Student Involvement

Think of the last time you were really interested in finding out about something. If it was how to repair furniture, you probably sought out informational texts that explained how to do the repairs effectively. If it was women's role during World War II, you probably read both fiction and nonfiction books that detailed events on the home front. The point is that because you wanted to know, you read. Remembering the earlier discussion about the lack of substantial amounts of time spent reading by upper level students, it follows that adolescent literature can be the catalyst for increasing the time allotted by students for reading and involvement in what you are trying to teach. Literature can literally break the nonreading–lecture–test curriculum cycle.

Opportunities for deeply involving students in the topics they are studying using adolescent literature are many. Whether through book talks, read-alouds, or **reader-response activities** (all of which are discussed in subsequent sections of this chapter), when students are asked to present, discuss, or write based on entertaining and informative selections they have read, their involvement and investment naturally rise. As Chatton noted, "Literature used across the curriculum extends and enriches the life of the classroom and the attitudes, knowledge, and understandings of the students who work there" (1989, p. 69). Literature can also be used to raise issues and questions about topics being studied as well as to provide sources for students to use to find solutions or answers. In short, literature can provide students with a view of topics across curriculum areas that cannot be provided by single textbooks or group lecture alone.

Consider the advantages of integrating literature across the curriculum.

Arthea Reed (1994) suggested several reasons why literature is important for upper level students. Following are those advantages applicable to content teaching:

Which of these reasons are the most important to you as a teacher?

1. Reading books of interest increases the potential of improving students' reading skills.
2. Reading fiction and nonfiction trade books increases students' higher level thinking skills.
3. Students recognize the various reasons for reading and can be encouraged to spend more time reading.
4. Students can develop an appreciation for different forms of literature and varying viewpoints about the same topic.
5. Teachers who use literature in conjunction with an adopted text will not be locked into a nonreading or lecture-only approach to what they teach.
6. Through the use of literature, classrooms become a place for sharing and reacting to what students have been reading.
7. The variety of literature available for use in any one subject matter area provides students with a window for exploring and experiencing their world, times past, and other cultures.

In the remainder of this chapter, we present a discussion of the types of literature that may be used in your classroom, as well as useful sources for locating the titles you need. Later, we present ways of incorporating literature into content units of study that will help students use the literature they read in meaningful and productive ways.

TYPES OF LITERATURE FOR CONTENT AREA USE

Over the years, we have discovered that three specific types of literature can be extremely helpful in content classrooms: informative literature, fiction, and poetry. They increase depth of student learning and improve student interest and motivation in the field of study. In this section we describe each form and offer examples for clarification.

Informational Literature

Book publishers have come to realize in recent years that there is considerable interest in using informational literature in public and private schools. Where curriculum budgets in the past were almost exclusively spent on state-adopted content textbooks, teachers now insist that monies be reserved for the purchase of quality literature of all types and formats. Content teachers know that informational literature brings a depth to the curriculum not possible when

Informational literature is a logical starting point for most content teachers interested in expanding beyond a single textbook.

A teacher selecting library books to be integrated in an upcoming unit of study.

using content textbooks alone. Written by experts on specific topics in the field of study, informational books often inspire and stimulate students.

It is helpful to keep several points in mind when selecting informational literature: What should teachers look for as they choose informational books? What are the different types of informational literature available? Does informational literature serve different functions? These issues are addressed in the next section.

What to Look for in Informational Literature

A trip to the local bookstore will quickly convince you that literally hundreds of new informational books flood the market each year in all content areas. They are often quite appealing in terms of graphics and photography and seem to call out to readers from the display racks. But how can content teachers discern quality in the almost limitless numbers of informational literature available? Drawn from the advice of children's and adolescent literature authorities (Huck, Helper, & Hickman, 1993; Norton, 1995) and tempered by our own teaching experiences, selection criteria for choosing informational books follow.

Why is a curriculum match important?

Curriculum Match. Informational books selected should share a common thread of information with the curriculum presented in the classroom. This is important for schema building or creating mental scaffolding for the acquisition and accommodation of new information. The primary reason for selecting informational literature, however, should be to enrich and extend learning.

Therefore, informational literature should go well beyond that which is presented in the regular textbook and unearth new perspectives for the reader. *Lives of a Cell: Notes of a Biology Watcher* (Thomas, 1978) is an excellent example of such a text that is often used in science classes.

Accuracy of Information.   Choosing informational literature in the Information Age can sometimes be a little tricky. New knowledge is constantly coming on line, thus causing some books to quickly become inaccurate. This is especially true in the sciences, where yesterday's theories are sometimes discovered to be inaccurate. Content teachers therefore must be lifelong scholars (i.e., students) of their discipline. Selecting current informational literature written by qualified authorities in the field is probably the best way to ensure accuracy of content. *The Last Rain Forest: A World Conservation Atlas* (Collins, 1990) is an example of such a book. In fields where new understandings occur frequently, it makes sense to invest in relatively inexpensive print and nonprint media that can be updated or replaced every year or two.

Think of ways you can make sure information you teach is current.

Graphics That Clarify.   Graphics, such as photos, maps, charts, figures, and so forth, should help make abstractions as concrete as possible for the learner. Books such as *The Formula Book* (Stark, 1979) exemplify this trait in informational literature. Check whether graphics use captions with clear labels and descriptions, check whether the format is enticing to the reader, and decide if the media used are appropriate for the intended purpose.

Graphics are an important consideration when selecting informational trade books.

Style and Organization.   The author's style of writing has everything to do with whether or not students will stay with the informational literature source. Rich, colorful descriptive language is a desired attribute, along with logical organization. Good style and organization promote reader interest and cause students to persevere. Glasser's (1979) *The Body Is the Hero* is a good example of a reader-friendly writing style.

Fiction

Fiction is imaginative writing that portrays events that could or could not actually happen to people living in the past, present, or future. This type of writing enables readers to vicariously experience events and see the world from another perspective. In fiction, the division between what is real and not real becomes blurred so that students can catch a glimpse of what could be. Much of the fiction appropriate to content classrooms helps students feel like actual participants or insiders in the field of study itself. For instance, a book about African-American and other minorities struggling for equal educational rights in Boston during a time of insidious oppression in the 1970s can awaken a sense of awareness and frustration in the reader. Reading about the search for faster, more efficient means of working through complex mathematics computations

Reading fiction can offer fresh new perspectives on topics under study.

and the subsequent invention of the electronic calculator similarly fosters in students an appreciation of the tools of a discipline. This is the power of quality fiction in content classrooms.

Two types of fiction are often used in content classrooms: **realistic fiction** and **historical fiction**. Even though both forms used in content classrooms should conform to essentially the same standards, it may be useful for teachers to at least be aware of their differences. Realistic fiction may be set in the past, present, or future, but it frequently deals with social issues. Topics like racial and ethnic diversity, sexuality, peer acceptance, relationships, and discovering one's self are commonly dealt with in realistic fiction. These stories help students develop vicarious insights into real-world situations and give readers a sense that they are not the first to face certain choices and dilemmas. Because of their content, such books can be helpful in classes like biology, psychology, sociology, and special classes established to help students prepare for adult choices.

Historical fiction, by definition, is set in the past and helps students better understand the needs of people from another time. Some forms forge a story around actual events and people of the past, while others describe fictional lives of characters with little or no reference to recorded history (Huck et al., 1993). Historical fiction is useful in virtually every content area because one can travel back through time to learn about great innovators in each field of study. For historical fiction to be useful in content classes, selections must do a good job of portraying factual information abundantly and accurately while still holding the reader's attention. The only way to make sure these two conditions are met is to carefully review each book. In the next section we suggest some criteria for reviewing both types of fiction.

> Distinguish between realistic fiction and historical fiction.

What to Look for in Fiction

Fiction is perhaps the most popular form of literature today. Stories set in the past provide a tantalizing backdrop for many romance and mystery novels, just as futuristic stories permeate much of science fiction. Here are a few guidelines that can help you decide which books to include in your classroom library.

> Why is accurate information so important when using fiction to supplement the adopted text?

Inclusion of Accurate Information. Make sure that the content-related information is consistent and accurate with what is known in the field. This is what makes the story believable and informative. For example, Michael Crichton's (1987) book *Sphere* provides a great deal of information about deep-sea life that could be quite interesting and informative to some students in a biology class investigating marine species. Events described in historical fiction should be consistent with what actually happened, and science fiction should project plausible scenarios in light of current knowledge. Sometimes past and present knowledge can be successfully merged through a genre known as alternative history. Accurate information makes a story believable and invests it with potential instructional value.

Honest Presentation of Information.   Many writers find it tempting to discuss "hot button" issues (e.g., racism, sex equity issues, AIDS, etc.) in sensational and biased ways that sometimes ignore the realities of the times or people involved. Search for books that honestly reflect the sentiments, knowledge, and other important factors that provide valuable insights for the reader. The goal is to put students into the shoes of those about whom they are reading. Avoidance of stereotypes also goes a long way toward portraying information honestly. Dizenzo's (1977) *Why Me? The Story of Jenny,* about a girl's reaction to being raped, typifies an honest portrayal of a social issue.

Convincing Dialogue.   Language can be a powerful tool for writers as they attempt to re-create the past or create a believable mood in contemporary settings. For instance, having characters use modern-day slang in a medieval story can cause readers to reject the book no matter how good the story line and how interesting the content facts may be. Dialogue should be as carefully researched as any other factual tidbits by the author. Lasky's (1986) *Beyond the Divide,* the story of a 14-year-old's participation in going West for the gold rush, is a good example of convincing dialogue. This is not to say that old English, for example, should be used in a medieval story, for that would be unreadable; rather, dialogue should blend into and complement the story.

> Both honest portrayal of hot-button topics and convincing dialogue can increase the likelihood of students reading trade books.

Insight for Content-Oriented Problems and Needs.   Keep in mind the primary function of selecting fiction for the content classes you teach: to augment readings from the textbook and to help students better understand how this information can help them solve real-world problems. Some fiction has so little factual information as to be useless in content learning and should be rejected. Fiction with characters who use factual information for problem-solving related to the field is the best possible literature. A good example of this trait is J. Anderson's (1987) *1787.* It is worth mentioning, however, that some books and other media (e.g., films) weak in content information may, in the end, serve the development of positive affect toward the field. What we mean is that a great story about a person loosely associated with a field of study may, in fact, create enormous interest in that field. One need only recall the great popularity of the *Indiana Jones* movies and the resulting interest they created for many students in the field of archeology.

> What is the primary function of selecting fiction for use in your classroom?

Poetry and Content Instruction

The value of poetry in the content classroom is its ability to help bring depth to the learning experience. Poetry is the distillation of experience that captures the essence of an object, feeling, or thought (Huck et al., 1993, p. 452). When added to the content learned from textbooks and other instructional media, poetry has the ability to help students gain sympathetic appreciation for the sum and substance of the new material.

> Of what benefit is the integration of poetry into the content classroom?

Many content teachers hope to instill in their students a greater appreciation and respect for the field of study. These teachers want students to see what they see and develop some of the passion for their field that caused them to become content specialists in the first place. Poetry can help teachers accomplish this affective goal by helping students participate in the field on a sensory level and thereby improve student interest, develop positive attitudes about the field, and motivate them toward further studies.

The search for just the right poem, as with all other forms of literature for content classes, is a lengthy process. We have found that it is a continual search that becomes part of life in and out of school. Teachers discover great poems for their classrooms when they least expect them: on vacations, during trips to the shopping mall, or while visiting friends who happen to mention a poem in casual conversation. Most content teachers become habitual collectors of information anyway; it is just a matter of including the notion of poetry in one's subconscious menu of classroom possibilities. This kind of teaching schema addition is first initiated by choosing one or two units of study and actively searching for poetry and other literature forms to supplement the learning experience; doubtless, a novel experience (pun intended) for many teachers of such subjects as chemistry, business math, biology, and other areas not typically considered language arts in orientation.

Content teachers may find several forms of poetry interesting. Narrative poems describe events or tell a tale. Lyrical poems are usually descriptive or personal and are song-like in their cadence. Limericks are five-line poems featuring first and second lines that rhyme, third and fourth lines agreeing, and a fifth line that has some sort of humorous statement or surprise. Raps or chants are a relatively recent form of poetry that many students respond to because of their frequent use in popular music. Free verse is a kind of poetry that does not rhyme but does feature rhythm and cadence. Haiku is an ancient poetry form from Japan. Having only 17 syllables in each poem, the first and third lines have five syllables, and the second line has seven. Haiku causes students to use their wordsmith skills and to carefully consider specialized content vocabulary at the microlevel.

Having students create their own poetry to retell what they have learned has been a strategy used for years in many elementary and middle school classrooms but basically unexploited in high school content classes. This is a practice with which we have had success and strongly recommend.

What to Look for in Poetry

Because of its ability to evoke emotion in readers, poetry must be selected carefully to obtain the desired effect. Following are some points we consider when choosing poetry for content classes:

Age/Interest Appropriateness.   Stick to poetry written for adults. Using poems written for elementary audiences generally puts middle and high school stu-

---

Collecting appropriate poetry can be a challenge.

Which types of poetry do you recognize?

Summarize the recommendations for choosing poetry.

dents off. This is often true of authors like Shel Silverstein and Jack Prelutsky, who mainly write for young children.

Modern Versus Old Favorites.   When possible, it is wonderful to have a combination of classic or old favorite poems that may be familiar to the students, as well as works from contemporary or modern writers.

Appropriate Illustrations.   Related to age/interest appropriateness, illustrations should complement the poem and not cause students to feel it is written for children. More importantly, illustrations should be accurate and consistent with the factual information presented.

Support Materials.   It is helpful if books of poetry on a specific topic or theme include support materials to aid the reader in locating information. A good introduction to each poem is especially helpful. Commentaries may or may not be helpful, depending on whether they are aimed at the artistry of the poem (most often the case) or the content (what we actually need most in content class situations). Indexes and glossaries are especially helpful but rarely included in books of poetry.

Sources for Locating Literature

Because it is impossible to keep up with all the quality literature coming available each year, teachers must identify resources that can identify specific literature by topic. We have found a number of books and data bases to be quite helpful in locating an initial pool of possibilities. Once the pool is established, we simply review each book to find the ones best suited to our purposes. Here is a list of sources for locating literature we have found helpful:

Abrahamson, R. F., & Carter, B. (Eds.). (1988). *Books for you: a booklist for senior high students.* Urbana, IL: National Council of Teachers of English.

Benedict, S. (1991). *Beyond words: Picture books for older readers and writers.* Portsmouth, NH: Heinemann.

Dreyer, S. (1977–1989). *The bookfinder: A guide to children's literature about the needs and problems of youth ages 2–15* (4 vols.). Circle Pine, MN: American Guidance Service.

Gillespie, J. T., & Naden, C. J. (Eds.). (1990). *Best books for children: Preschool through grade 6* (4th ed.). New York: Bowker.

Harris, V. J. (Ed.). (1993). *Teaching multicultural literature in grades K–8.* Norwood, MA: Christopher Gordon.

Huck, C. S., Hepler, S., & Hickman, J. (1993). *Children's literature in the elementary school* (5th ed.). Orlando: Harcourt Brace Jovanovich.

Kennedy, D. M., Spangler, S. S., & Vanderwerf, M. A. (1990). *Science and technology in fact and fiction: A guide to children's books.* New Providence, NJ: Bowker.

Lima, C. W., & Lima, J. A. (Eds.). (1989). *A to zoo: Subject access to children's picture books.* (3rd ed.). New Providence, NJ: Bowker.

If you need a book on a specific topic, one of these sources will have it.

Moir, H., Cain, M., & Prosak-Beres, L. (Eds.). (1990). *Collected perspectives: Choosing and using books for the classroom.* Norwood, MA: Christopher-Gordon.

Norton, D. E. (1995). *Through the eyes of a child: An introduction to children's literature* (4th ed.) Englewood Cliffs, NJ: Merrill/Prentice Hall.

Pilla, M. L. (1990). *The best: high/low books for reluctant readers.* Littleton, CO: Libraries Unlimited.

Ryder, R. (1989). *Easy reading: Book series and periodicals for less able readers.* Newark, DE: International Reading Association.

Sinclair, P. (1992). *E for environment: An annotated bibliography of children's books with environmental themes.* New Providence, NJ: Bowker.

Subject guide to children's books in print (annual). New Providence, NJ: Bowker.

VanMeter, V. (1990). *American history for children and young adults: An annotated bibliographic index.* Englewood, CO: Libraries Unlimited.

Webb, C. A. (Ed.). (1993). *Your reading: A booklist for junior high and middle school students* (8th ed.). Urbana, IL: National Council of Teachers of English.

INTEGRATING LITERATURE INTO UNIT PLANS

Literature as a Component of Unit Planning

Carefully study Figure 9.1.

It is important to have a kind of structure or unit scaffolding in mind that can accommodate the use of literature in the content classroom. The organizational structure for unit planning suggested by Wepner and Feeley (1993) mirrors our own beliefs and can serve as a splendid vehicle for integrating literature. Figure 9.1 portrays our slightly modified version of Wepner and Feeley's "steps for organizing content-based materials" and serves as the outline for this section.

Phase I: Gathering Learning Resources and Ideas

Step 1: *Select content area topics and subtopics.* This is the first step in all lesson planning, as was previously discussed in Chapter 3. Facts, concepts, and generalizations to be developed in the unit are identified.

Step 2: *Identify materials and learning resources.* Once the teacher has carefully reviewed the adopted textbook and the school district's curriculum guide (Step 1), a determination is made as to whether the textbook is an appropriate resource for inclusion as a regular reading resource in the unit. Because of the concept density and stilted language found in many content textbooks, they often serve the teacher best as a reference tool or information base to which quality readings may be linked.

In steps 1 and 2, decisions are made about which books and other materials will be included as part of the unit of study.

Next, a survey of possible literature, or trade books, is conducted. A decision is made as to which forms of literature will be included and how many. Some selections may be read aloud (Atwell, 1987) by teachers as part of formal lectures and presentations. Other selections will be introduced to students through book talks that cause students to want to read the complete work for themselves. Book talks are discussed later in this chapter. Books for these purposes, as well as other

Phase I: Gathering Learning Resources and Ideas

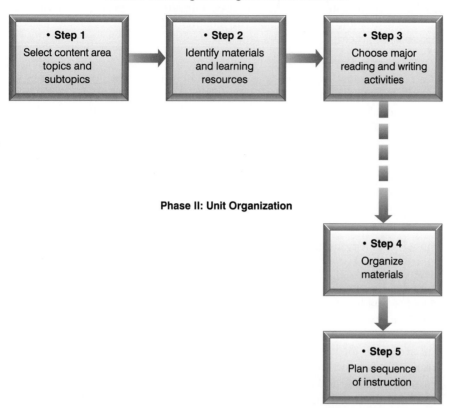

Figure 9.1 Steps for Organizing Content-Based Materials
Note. Adapted from *Moving Forward With Literature: Basals, Books, and Beyond* by S. B. Wepner and J. T. Feeley, 1993, Englewood Cliffs, NJ: Merrill/Prentice Hall. Copyright 1993 by Merrill/Prentice Hall.

content-related literary selections, are made available to students in a library center where they may be checked out. Teachers should work in collaboration with the school librarian in preparing these unit-oriented classroom libraries. Some teachers having classes at several different locations in the building move their unit libraries around on library carts checked out from the school media center.

Other print and nonprint materials should also be identified at this early planning stage. Period news articles, videotapes, photographic slides, computer software, filmstrips, artifacts, and other materials add color to the learning experience and inspire interest.

Step 3: *Choose major reading and writing activities.* Two major kinds of reading and writing activities are to be selected: those done by students, and those done by the content teacher. Student reading and writing activities might

Think of the kinds of activities that might be appropriate for step 3.

include reading and **learning logs,** research projects, literature-response group activities, and writing projects. Literature-response activities are described in some detail later in this chapter. Writing project ideas are discussed in Chapter 8.

Book talks can tease students into wanting to read specific books.

Reading and writing activities involving the teacher vary greatly according to unit requirements and student needs. Common teacher-initiated activities include read-alouds, book talks, and modeling activities. **Read-alouds** are just as the name implies: The teacher reads aloud all or portions of literature chosen to enhance the learning experience. **Book talks** are activities designed to share just enough of a book to cause students to want to read the entire selection on their own. **Modeling** has to do with showing students how to do something. In this instance, we refer to showing students how one can read certain kinds of content resources efficiently (content textbooks, journal articles, technical papers, etc.) or how to write in a specific style common to the field of study.

Phase II: Unit Organization

Organizing the materials is important.

Step 4: *Organize materials.* Decide when literature will be used during the course of the unit and for what purpose. Some literature may be used to help students build new schemas and vocabulary related to the subject. Informational literature and realistic and historical fiction can sometimes help in realizing these goals. Other literature may be selected to help build understanding and sympathy for key people related to the topic. Poetry and some forms of alternative fiction can be helpful in establishing these affective connections between the topic and learner.

Some purposes may be accomplished using the textbook alone, whereas other purposes are best achieved using a combination of textbook and literature selections or literature selections only.

Step 5: *Plan the sequence of instruction.* The final step involves actual scheduling of daily activities. A unit could be sequenced in many ways. The content analysis in Step 1, which decides the facts, concepts, and generalizations to be studied, often suggests a logic for the sequence of instruction. A more inventive and interesting way of sequencing units is the approach called *themed literature units.* We examine this organizational alternative in the next section.

Themed Literature Units

Describe the overall organization of themed literature units.

Themed literature units (Cooter & Griffith, 1989; Reutzel & Cooter, 1992, 1996) organize reading and writing activities around a central theme or topic. In our adaptation of themed literature units for content classes, students begin by choosing a book from a list of teacher-selected options. In content classes, multiple (three or four) copies of each book are usually available with about 8 to 10 different titles. After students have read their book, literature-response groups are formed to develop a project that demonstrates their growing knowledge of the topic. Completed projects are presented to the class, thus serving the dual function of deepening the learning experience for group members and classmates, while also providing a convenient forum for student assessment. Following are some of the major activities and time lines for themed literature units for content classrooms.

Week 1: Introducing the Theme or Topic

Many teachers begin themed literature units with introductory activities that activate students' prior knowledge and motivate students to want to know more about the topic to be studied. A collage bulletin board depicting aspects of the new topic, interviewing a visiting expert, and various group participation activities are common introductory ideas.

Brainstorm some ways to introduce and begin a themed literature unit.

Other theme introduction activities may involve drama. Role playing, readers' theater, and even an occasional video production can be used for theme introduction (Reutzel & Cooter, 1996). Once a mental mind-set has been created for the theme, the teacher is ready to introduce the books.

Book Talks. An important and stimulating part of the themed literature unit, for both teacher and students, is book talks (Fader, 1976). The purpose is to lure students into the books and interest them deeply so they will want to read. Cooter and Griffith (1989) refer to this activity as an "honorable seduction," a bonding of sorts between students and the topic under study. When the book talk is well executed, all students want to read several of the books mentioned. A little frustration may even result as each student tries to narrow his choices to the one book he most wants to read.

The book talk activity is very easy to do. First, find a most enticing section in each of the books to be used. We recommend that the book talk last about 5 to 10 minutes and be drawn from the first third of the book. Second, enthusiastically tell the class about each book, perhaps adding some background information about the topic or author, then read a "spicy" part of the book to the class. The more drama and excitement you put into the book talk, the easier it will be to get the class "hooked" on each book. Third, conclude the reading without giving away the best parts of the book. If done correctly, the suspense of not knowing what happens should create an almost overpowering urge to read the book. After each book has been introduced, the students are ready to make their selection.

Book talks are opportunities to "sell" great books to students.

Student Self-Selection. An important element for the success of any learning program is for students to feel that they have choices. In themed literature units students are allowed to choose the book they will read. Because only a few copies, or only one copy, of each book are available, students should be asked to write down their top three choices on a slip of paper and turn it in to

Self-selection is a crucial motivational tool.

the teacher. The teacher can then sort the ballots and assign books according to preference.

Sustained Silent Reading. Once the book assignments have been announced, students are ready to begin reading. We recommend that the unit begin in earnest by allowing students time to read their books in an uninterrupted fashion, or **sustained silent reading (SSR)**. SSR serves three primary functions in this situation. First, students are given time to read, an activity that improves reading ability and deepens their knowledge of the topic. Second, students are allowed to become interested in their books, creating a strong motivation to continue reading. A third purpose is to allow students who may have selected a book that is too difficult time to change their minds and trade in their selection for one of the remaining titles. Usually, a 24-hour grace period is allowed for exchanges. The equivalent of two or three class periods on consecutive days is a good start for SSR.

Week 2: Forming Literature-Response Groups

Literature-response groups essentially process and apply what has been read.

During the second week students begin working in their **literature-response groups (LRGs)**. Students are grouped based on mutual interest, namely, which book they chose. For example, all students who chose to read the novel *Beyond the Divide* (K. Lasky, 1986) as part of the Westward Movement theme become the "Beyond the Divide" group. Students reading the informational book *The Oregon Trail* (Fisher, 1990) become the "Oregon Trail" group, and so on. This type of grouping capitalizes on students' intrinsic interests and motivations and enables them to work cooperatively in discovering new information.

A primary goal of the LRG is to develop a project that demonstrates their comprehension of the chosen book and growing knowledge of the factual information. All project ideas are subject to approval by the teacher because some refinement of project ideas may be required. Following are some LRG project ideas recommended by Reutzel and Cooter (1996) that may be useful in content classrooms.

Contrast student dramas and radio plays.

Student Dramas. Reenactment of major events in a book is a particularly popular LRG activity. Student dramas facilitate content mastery and provide a marvelous forum for practicing oral presentation abilities. Only minimal props and costumes are needed. Students begin by choosing a favorite part of the book to retell, then develop a script based on a combination of actual dialogue in the book and narration. Usually, the narration is delivered by a reader or narrator, who explains such story elements as setting, problem, and other pertinent information. Typically, the drama is presented as a one-act play.

Martinez (1993) points out that modeling can be especially helpful in encouraging students to choose this option for literature response. Inviting a drama teacher or amateur actor to explain to students some of the rudiments of performance is a great way to stimulate interest.

Radio Play.   A radio play uses the same process as a student drama, except that it is performed a bit differently. Students first write a one-act play based on their book as described in the preceding section. Next, sound effect materials are gathered and practiced (e.g., recorded train sound effects, door opening/closing, the sounds of wind or other forces in nature). After thorough rehearsal of the script with sound effects, the radio play is taped on a cassette recorder and played over the school's public address system into the classroom. Recordings of old radio shows, such as *The Shadow,* help students better understand the radio play concept.

Evening Newscast.   Students enjoy acting out book summaries in the form of a nightly newscast. Each student prepares a news story script using the writing process previously described in Chapter 8 that retells an important event or piece of information in the book. After LRG members have refined their scripts, they rehearse as news readers until the performance is ready for presentation to the class. The evening newscast can either be acted out before the class or recorded using a video camera, then replayed to the class on television.

Evening newscast integrates all language processes.

Meeting of Minds.   Steve Allen hosted a television program called "Meeting of Minds" in 1977 to 1978 in which famous people of the past were played by actors. They enacted high-level discussions about issues of their time and problems they were trying to solve.

   Peggy Lathlaen (1993) has adapted Meeting of Minds in her classroom and found it especially useful with biographies. Students begin by carefully reading the biography they have selected pertaining to a famous person from the past so that they can later become this person for the class. This usually involves careful reading of more than one book; construction of a time line for this person's life (which is compared to a general time line recording significant inventions and world events at the time for perspective); research into costumes of the era; construction of comparison–contrast frames comparing their person to others being researched in the LRG; and searching books like Bartlett's *Familiar Quotations* for memorable quotes made by the individual. Famous historical figures portrayed in Lathlaen's classroom include Thomas Jefferson, Queen Elizabeth I, Barbara Jordan, and George Bush.

Think of ways you can adapt this idea to your specific content area.

Discussion Webs.   **Discussion webs** are a kind of graphic aid for teaching students to look at both sides of an issue before making final judgments (Alvermann, 1991). They may be useful with novels and other narrative selections, but we feel they can be particularly useful with nonfiction materials. Adapted from the work of social studies teacher James Duthie (1986), discussion webs basically comprise five steps. The first step is much like traditional reading activities in that a discussion is held to activate background knowledge, to discuss new or challenging vocabulary, and to provide a purpose for reading. Students then read, or begin reading, the selection. The second step is to state the

Carefully study Figure 9.2, then summarize it to a peer.

central question to be considered and introduce the discussion web. Students complete the *yes* and *no* columns individually, usually recording key thoughts as opposed to complete sentences. The third step is for students to be paired for the purpose of comparing responses and begin working toward consensus. Later, the groups of two are paired to construct groups of four for the purpose of further consensus building. In the fourth step, a group spokesperson reports to the whole class the reasons that best reflect the consensus of the group. Usually, a 3-minute period is allotted for reporting. The final step suggested is that students individually write a follow-up position paper about their judgment on the matter. In Figure 9.2 we present a discussion web for a history class completed by students researching whether they would choose to move West with the early North American settlers.

Home-Made Filmstrip. Home-made filmstrips are an interesting way for students to retell the sequence of a story (Figure 9.3). Pictures are made with captions that retell important parts of the book. The pictures are then taped together in sequence and viewed with the aid of an opaque projector (if available). This activity is in some ways similar in purpose to the creation of big books or predictable books described earlier.

Consider rules of etiquette to be discussed before forming LRGs.

Finally, it should be mentioned that students do not always work in groups naturally and harmoniously. It typically takes some training and practice. Sometimes role playing can help students understand the kinds of appropriate behavior expected from LRGs (Reutzel & Cooter, 1996). One group of middle school

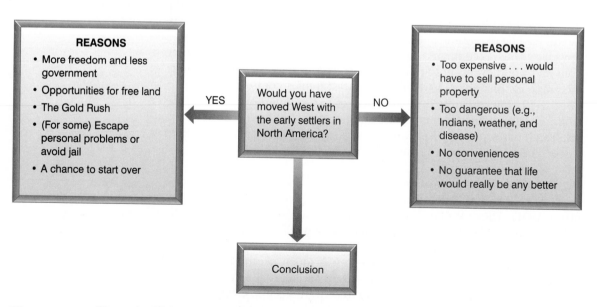

Figure 9.2 Discussion Web: Westward Movement in North America

Frame 1   Frame 2   Frame 3   Frame 4

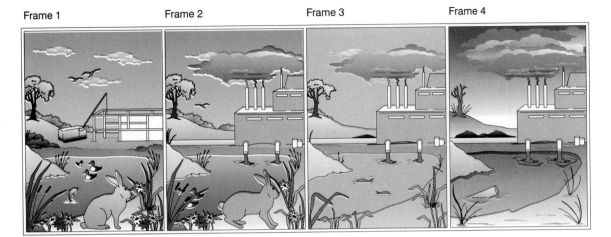

Figure 9.3   Home-Made Filmstrip: Ecology
This is a general example that might be appropriate for such books as Michael Brown's (1981) *Laying Waste: The Poisoning of America by Toxic Chemicals.*

teachers in Kenton, Ohio, came up with a wonderful idea for teaching what they termed "group etiquette." One day after school, teachers at each grade level met to dramatize both positive and negative group behavior. They dressed in the popular clothing styles of young adolescents in their classes, then role played negative group behavior then positive group behavior. These performances were recorded on videotape and shown to their classes during the introduction phase of their themed literature units. Students enjoyed viewing the production and were able to identify some critical "do's and don'ts" for their LRGs.

Weeks 3 and 4: LRG Projects, Teacher-Directed Sessions, and Minilessons

Work continues on LRG projects in weeks 3 and 4, but time is also reserved by the teacher for minilessons and other teacher-directed sessions. In weeks 3 and 4 of the unit, students should be allowed approximately one half of the time for working on LRG projects. LRGs who feel they require more time to work on their projects should do so out of class as homework.

Week 5: Project Presentations and Closure Activities

The final week of themed literature units is reserved for students to present their projects to the class, which serves two important functions. First, this is an opportunity for LRGs to share with peers the fruits of their labors. Second, students in the class are introduced or reintroduced to important content information and books they did not read, a process that often serves to stimulate further interest and outside reading.

What are the culminating activities that bring the theme literature unit to a close?

Themes should be concluded with some sort of closure activity. Closure activities bring about a sense that the work is now complete and the class is ready to move on to something new. Closure activities, like introductory activities, sometimes include a guest speaker, a field trip, or viewing a film related to the theme.

LEARNERS WITH SPECIAL NEEDS

Book Talks, Books on Tape, and Picture Books

Interest in topics can promote reading development.

Over the years we have noticed that many students with learning problems respond quite favorably to the infusion of quality literature into content curriculums. In fact, a most successful tutoring tactic for improving the reading habits and fluency of students with reading problems is to assign high-interest magazines and best-selling books as homework. Why is this tactic so successful? Because the students are interested in the topic and simply *want* to read. When students with learning problems, all students for that matter, have a strong interest in a topic, they will spend the necessary energy to read and welcome needed assistance from the teacher as necessary.

Book talks, as described earlier, are an excellent teaching strategy for getting learners with reading problems hooked on books. Teachers who do book talks regularly find that they are able to include many titles and topics of special interest to learners with special needs. The goal is to create a compelling interest in all learners so that books will be received as a reward.

Books on tape can allow students with problems learning to participate in classroom discussions.

Books on tape are another valuable resource for students with learning needs. The number and types of books on tape continue to grow by leaps and bounds. Many popular novels for adults and adolescents as well as informational books are now available on tape at new and used bookstores and in public libraries. Some high school libraries are also beginning to stock some books on tape. For marginal readers, books on tape serve as an excellent means for them to participate in discussion groups and literature assignments. We recommend that content teachers begin advocating specific titles for purchase by their school librarian/media specialist and make them available to students with learning problems as part of themed literature units.

Picture books sometimes can be used with older students.

Picture books, although traditionally thought of as belonging to the world of primary-age children, have been promoted as having a legitimate role for upper level classrooms (Brozo & Simpson, 1995; Gilles et al., 1988). Their use may be appropriate, depending on the type of picture books selected and how students use them. By type of picture book, we mean that any picture book recommended should have a direct connection to what is being studied and should be age- and interest-level appropriate. Picture books should also provide students with insights into the time, place, topic, or emotions of an era being studied. For instance, *The Wall* (Bunting, 1990), about the Vietnam Memorial; *Hiroshima* (Hersey, 1975), about Japanese life before and after the atomic bomb fell; and *Shaker Lane* (Provensen & Provensen, 1987), about the changing American society, are all good examples of the type of picture books that should be used in content classes.

Several kinds of literature-response activities may be used with picture books, including in-class sharing by students and as a stimulus for a writing/illustrating activity. One example of a writing activity is to have students develop their own picture book illustrating topics or concepts that are currently being studied.

We believe that for students experiencing reading problems, an important solution is to move away from the exclusive use of lecturing and the adopted text toward inclusion of quality supplemental literature. The right book in the hands of the right student is the key to enriched learning and academic success.

CHAPTER SUMMARY

The use of literature in content area classrooms has great potential and valuable functions. The advantages of using literature to supplement and complement teaching include increased motivation and interest, improved depth of understanding, and heightened student involvement in classroom discussion and activities.

The types of literature suitable for content classrooms include informational literature, fiction, and poetry. Teachers should be aware of criteria for the selection of each form of literature as well as how to construct a themed literature unit using quality literature.

Students with learning problems can be helped through the use of content-oriented literature. We are convinced that if teachers in all content fields share, encourage, and use literature as part of unit planning, students will enjoy greater learning benefits.

Reflection/Application Activities

1. Secure a copy of a recently copyrighted teacher edition of a textbook in your content area specialty. Examine all suggestions for outside reading and projects. What evidence is there that the authors are interested in students' reading beyond the text? Are any fiction or nonfiction trade books suggested to go along with various units? If so, make a list by unit topic.

2. Go to a local high school or middle school librarian/media specialist and conduct an interview. Find out how the library is used by content area teachers and which of the various resource books mentioned earlier in this chapter are available in the library. Ask the librarian if teachers regularly conduct themed literature units in content areas other than English. Create and ask three other questions of your own that relate to the content of this chapter. Be prepared to present your findings.

3. Select one unit topic that you might someday teach. Using public, university, high school, and middle school libraries, identify all the books available that could be used to supplement and comple-

ment this topic. From your list identify five books that you think sound like they would definitely be a good fit with the unit topic. Read them and be prepared to do a book talk on your favorite book.

4. Using the five books from Activity 3, develop three activities that students could do to share, discuss, or demonstrate what they have been reading in small group settings. Describe each activity in detail.

5. Arrange to meet with a peer that will be teaching in the same content area. Develop a themed literature unit, using the unit topic from Assignment 3. Your plans should include a web of the unit, list of books chosen, possible reading strategies to be taught in teacher-directed sessions, and a list of literature-response activities or projects that students could do individually or in small groups.

Recommended Reading

Examples of Literature for the Content Classroom

Historical and Alternative History

Turtledove, H. (1992). *The guns of the South.* New York: Ballantine Books.

Science Fiction

Crichton, M. (1987). *Sphere.* New York: Ballantine.

Biographies and Autobiographies

Art

Peet, B. (1989). *Bill Peet: An autobiography.* Boston: Houghton Mifflin.

Business

Iacocca, L. (1984). *Iacocca: An autobiography.* New York: Bantam.

Civics/Government

Freedman, R. (1990). *Franklin Delano Roosevelt.* New York: Clarion.

History: Women's Roles

Williams, S. R. (1976). *Demeter's daughters: The women who founded America 1587–1787.* New York: Atheneum.

History: Geography

Levinson, N. S. (1990). *Christopher Columbus: Voyager to the unknown.* New York: Lodestar (Penguin).

Mathematics

Billings, C. (1989). *Grace Hopper: Navy admiral and computer pioneer.* Hillsdale, NJ: Enslow.

Science

Yeager, C., & Janos, L. (1985). *Yeager.* New York: Bantam.

Journals and Documents (Historical)

Freedman, R. (1980). *Immigrant kids.* New York: Dutton.

Murphy, J. (1990). *The boys' war: Confederate and Union soldiers talk about the Civil War.* New York: Clarion.

Myers, W. D. (1991). *Now is your time! The African-American struggle for freedom.* New York: HarperCollins.

Experiment and Activity Sources

Biology

Seuling, B. (1986). *You can't sneeze with your eyes open and other freaky facts about the human body.* New York: Ballantine.

Nutrition

Burns, M. (1978). *Good for me! All about food in 32 bites.* Boston: Little, Brown.

Science

Math, I. (1988). *Wires and watts: Understanding and using electricity.* New York: Scribner's.

"How to . . . " Books

Art

Reid, B. (1989). *Playing with Plasticine.* New York: Morrow.

Home Ecology/Historical
Walker, B. (1979). *The Little House cookbook.* New York: Harper & Row.

Language Arts
Bauer, M. D. (1992). *What's your story: A young person's guide to writing fiction.* New York: Clarion.

Photo Essays

Astronomy
Simon, S. (1985). *Jupiter.* New York: William Morrow.

Biology
Goodall, J. (1989). *The Jane Goodall chimpanzee family book.* Saxonville, MA: Picture Book Studio.

Ecological Studies
Ancona, G. (1990). *Riverkeeper.* New York: Macmillan.

Geology
Lauber, P. (1986). *Volcano: The eruption and healing of Mount St. Helens.* New York: Bradbury.

History
Freedman, R. (1987). *Lincoln: A photobiography.* New York: Clarion Books.

Language Arts
Charlip, R., & Miller, M. B. (1980). *Handtalk: An ABC of finger spelling and sign language.* New York: Four Winds (Macmillan).

Topical Surveys

American History
Grun, B. (1975). *The timetables of history: A horizontal linkage of people and events.* New York: Simon & Schuster.

Government
Boller, P. (1984). *Presidential campaigns.* New York: Oxford University Press.

Language Arts
Varasdi, J. A. (1989). *Myth information.* New York: Ballantine.

Mathematics
Paulos, J. (1991). *Beyond numeracy.* New York: Knopf.

Science
Meyer, J. (1967). *Great accidents in science that changed the world.* New York: Arco.

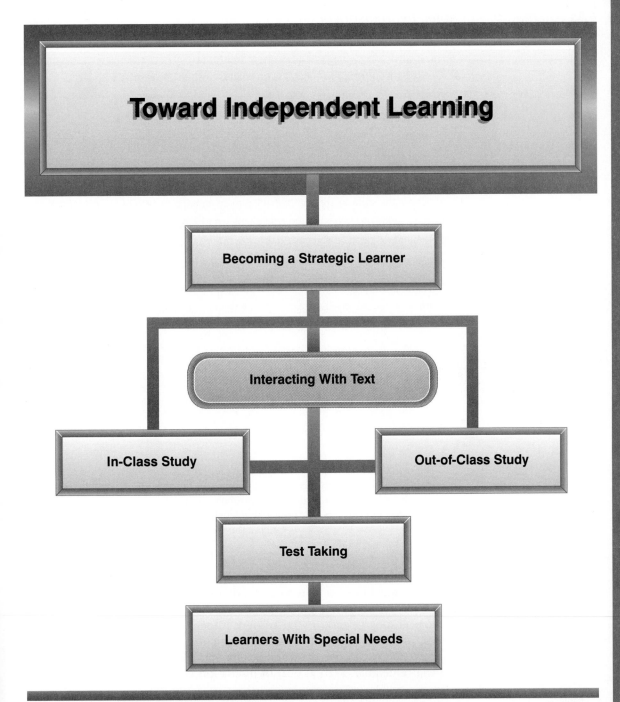

CHAPTER 10

Toward Independent Learning

Becoming a Strategic Learner

Interacting With Text

In-Class Study

Out-of-Class Study

Test Taking

Learners With Special Needs

Focus Questions

*As you read this chapter, try to discover
answers to the following questions:*

1 What are some of the major characteristics of strategic learners?

2 What is the role of the teacher as students are encouraged to improve their studying both in class and out of class?

3 What do successful teachers do to improve the note-taking skill of students in their classrooms?

4 What role does writing play in a student's becoming an independent learner?

5 Why is the study-response journal the most appropriate type of journal for out-of-class studying? What are the characteristics of this type of journal?

6 What are some ways you can help students prepare for exams?

7 How should studying in the middle school differ from high school?

8 Learners with special needs require additional support for studying out of class. What are the recommendations for assisting these students?

The major asset a high school graduate can have is the ability to learn and adapt. You never reach obsolescence if you are trainable and adaptable. High school teachers have a "primary responsibility" to teach basic intellectual skills before teaching any specific body of knowledge.

Panel of the National Academy of Science (1984)

The title of this chapter reflects our view that content teachers should have as a primary goal teaching students how to learn and not just what to learn. However, our experience leads us to conclude that many content classrooms continue to reflect traditional practices (teacher-dominated instruction with a rote memory emphasis and limited student interaction) rather than embracing holistic practices (student-centered instruction with a conceptual learning emphasis and expanding opportunities for students to interact). In Chapter 5, you will remember, a great deal of discussion centered around helping stu-

Students developing independent research skills in social studies.

dents comprehend text. In this chapter the focus shifts to the idea of learning by oneself, without assistance. To this end, this chapter begins with a discussion about what it means to be a strategic learner in the content areas, and it concludes by examining specific techniques teachers and students can use to create an environment that integrates how to study and learn in and out of the content classroom.

BECOMING A STRATEGIC LEARNER

For many content teachers, learning is associated with the "power task" of acquiring specific information and being able to remember it and regurgitate it on tests. Rarely does it occur to these teacher that teaching students how to acquire and use the specific information of their content area is part and parcel of their job responsibility (Durkin, 1978–1979). This traditional view of teaching is caused by lack of knowledge (how can someone know something if they don't know); the assumption that students already know how to learn (Gall, Gall, Jacobsen, & Bullock, 1990); or a reluctance to assume more responsibility on top of current demands (Gee & Rakow, 1987). For many other teachers, however, learning is associated with the development of the whole student— one who can and will see learning as a natural activity that can open doors to the future. This holistic view reflects a sincere desire, on the part of the teacher, to impart the knowledge and develop the skills that are characteristic of strategic learners. This desire is coupled with the realization that many students need encouragement and opportunities to learn how to learn.

Reflect about the teachers you had in middle/high school and how you would characterize the most and the least effective.

What are strategic learners?

- *Strategic learners engage the text before beginning to study.* Before reading text information, the strategic reader often attempts to obtain an overview of the topic to be read by previewing the text selection. During this preview the student attempts to ascertain what concepts are being discussed, what he already knows about the topic, how difficult or easy the reading will be, the purpose(s) for reading, and a focused attempt to become interested in the topic. This preview enables the reader to actively attend to the author's message and decide how he must read the text selection effectively.

- *Strategic learners interact with text as they read.* Perhaps one trait that separates the strategic reader from those who are not strategic is how he reads text for understanding and remembering. We have all experienced reading, let's say, our educational psychology textbook, when three pages into the chapter we realize that we don't have a clue about what we have just read. This doesn't typically happen to the strategic reader, because of the tactics he uses to understand and remember text information. The strategic reader, when study-reading, attempts to translate text ideas into his own words, tunes into the unfamiliar vocabulary, tries to determine the main ideas that exist across paragraph boundaries, notes transition words that signal changes in the author's line of thinking, rereads complex sections, and forms mental pictures of what is being read. All of these habits tend to cause the strategic reader to remain focused and attentive to the author's message.

- *Strategic learners do more than just read the assignment.* Following a flexible reading of a text selection, the strategic reader conducts a **self-assessment** of what he has learned and understood. Decisions are made about what is important to remember, how the information can be organized, whether anything still needs clarification, and what he needs to do to remember the information across time. This kind of reader frequently reviews material depending on the classroom assessment schedule.

- *Strategic learners know how to listen and record information effectively.* Listening and taking notes, high-use study skills in the upper grades (Gall et al., 1990), are typically learned through trial and error. Strategic learners tend to acquire insightful listening strategies and skill in recording organized lecture or discussion information, whereas below-average and average students do not experience as much success via the trial and error of learning to take notes (Caverly & Orlando, 1991). Strategic learners tend to take responsibility for learning from lectures or group discussions, they recognize verbal cues that indicate important information, and they organize their notes systematically.

What do you do when you study?

- *Strategic learners know how to study.* Strategic learners, when preparing for exams or other assessments, tend to focus their attention on relevant information; organize text and lecture information via outlines, graphics, or summarization activities (they write); develop strategies for memorizing lists and details that they know they will be held responsible for on exams; and are self-disciplined so that they review and rehearse the information across time. They predict what kinds of questions will be on exams, and they have strategies for taking exams that often provide superior results.

SPECIFIC APPLICATIONS FOR DEVELOPING INDEPENDENT LEARNERS

The idea of content teachers employing strategies and techniques to help develop students' skill in becoming independent learners is not a new idea. However, the idea that teachers provide instruction not only in the techniques but also in how and when the particular technique should be employed is relatively new. Fundamental to this idea is the gradual release of responsibility model of instruction (Pearson, 1985). This model, as you recall from Chapter 2, suggests that the initial onus for study skill instruction lies with the content teacher and not some special course. Common sense suggests that the place students should learn how to read and study biology, math, and/or power and energy is in that subject's classroom (Herber & Herber, 1993). It follows then, that only after demonstrating how to select and use a strategy or technique, and causing students to practice the strategy, should the teacher expect students to become capable of applying the strategy independently. This pattern of modeling, practice, and application is extremely important in the area of studying because study habits take time to develop and they have transferability from course to course. Studying is used by students at two distinct times: in class and out of class. In the following sections are some instructional strategies that can empower students to become strategic learners.

The gradual release of responsibility begins with you.

In-Class Studying

As students begin in-class assignments, one thing they need to do is to evaluate the material and mentally make a decision about what strategy they will need to employ to successfully complete their study goals, whether a teacher-generated or student-generated study goal. Such instructional activities as metacognitive questioning, listening and note taking, study diagrams, and learning logs are some of the many strategies that can be used for in-class study activities. These types of activities break the mold of traditional content instruction because the teacher assumes the role of expert reader by modeling the strategy with adopted course material. Additionally, as teachers such as yourself begin to provide more opportunities for students to experience success and learn how to become strategic learners, levels of participation and motivation in your classrooms will increase.

Define in-class studying.

Metacognitive Questioning

As discussed in Chapter 2, knowing about knowing, or metacognition, is an important part of being successful in the content classroom. Teaching students

Can you think of how you have used metacognitive questioning?

about what kinds of questions to ask of themselves as they interact with text is one avenue for promoting efficient study of content textbooks. In conjunction with the development of this type of self-questioning, students should also be taught how to preview text information because it will help with the formulation of answers to metacognitive questions. In Chapter 6 the survey technique (Aukermann, 1972) is identified as a structured method for conducting previews of text selections. The survey technique includes (a) predicting what the text selection is to be about and discussing how much students know about the topic, (b) analyzing subheadings and visuals to confirm predictions and build prior knowledge, (c) reading introduction paragraphs and the chapter summary, and (d) recognizing why the text is being read and actively seeking answers to questions formulated during the preview. By previewing text, using the survey technique or an adaptation of it, strategic learners often ask questions similar to those found in Figure 10.1 as they proceed.

Teacher-led instruction on how to pose metacognitive questioning can take many forms. The following scenario, using two class sessions, exemplifies one way the integration of metacognitive questioning with content instruction can be modeled by the teacher and applied by the students:

Causing students to use metacognitive questioning begins with the teacher.

Figure 10.1 Metacognitive Questioning Can Aid Studying

Before careful reading

What are the major topics being discussed?
What do I already know about these topics?
What has the teacher emphasized about reading this topic?
What do I really need to know when I get through reading?
Why am I really reading about these topics?
Which highlighted words are ones I don't know?

During reading

Does this heading give me a clue about what is important?
What major idea is being discussed in this section of the reading?
How would I paraphrase each section?
What examples are being used to support the author's ideas (studies, visuals, etc.)?
Do I understand the answers to questions posed by the teacher?

After reading

Did I accomplish my study goal?
Are there any parts that are still unclear?
What details or specific bits of information do I need to memorize?
What do I need to write down now because I know it is important information to remember?

Day 1:   Begin by having students divide into dyads. Identify the main topic of the selection, and have each dyad list some things they already know about the topic. As they observe you, conduct a preview of the first portion of the chapter under study, being sure to explain why you examine each visual, heading, and term that is highlighted. Point out the kinds of questions you are considering as you do the preview (see Figure 10.1 and select those or others that are applicable). Once completed, discuss what you found out about the topic, and have the dyads note any new information about the topic that was not part of their original predictions. The preview having been discussed, begin the process of reading the chapter by modeling how you would read the chapter based on your preview. Indicate which questions you will pose to yourself as you read using the chapter's headings and/or questions similar to those in Figure 10.1. Assign the reading, and have immediate follow-up to discuss answers to the questions posed and to elaborate about the section just read. Conclude the session by pointing out the benefits of previewing and thinking about what you need to ask yourself to improve your understanding of what is being read.

Day 2:   Briefly review the previous day's activity. Then have each dyad conduct their own preview of the next portion of the chapter, being sure to exchange ideas about the visuals, terms, summary, and any questions at the end of the chapter. Follow the preview with each dyad listing what they know about the topic(s) and sharing their ideas with the class. Then have each dyad generate a series of questions that they think will be important to find answers to in this portion of the chapter. As each dyad shares their questions, discussion should center around why the questions are important, how they can be clarified, and whether other dyads have similar questions. Each dyad reads the selection and discusses which questions were answered. A whole group discussion about what is the most important information to remember from the assignment should follow. Finally, the dyads or whole group can decide how best to record the important information in their course notebooks (e.g., outline, semantic map, or simple listing of ideas).

> How does day 2 reflect the teacher releasing responsibility?

Obviously, with some groups of students, small segments of text should be used at the outset. Regardless of how much text is used, this type of in-class activity should be used across subject matter areas (with modifications for specific types of text) to encourage it as a habit and hopefully promote its transfer to out-of-class studying.

Listening and Note Taking

Listening and taking notes on important information shared in class are the most widely used study skills of students from junior high through college (Gall et al., 1990). Unfortunately, there seems to be a paucity of direct instruction of how stu-

> When and how did you learn to listen and take notes?

dents should record class information. For 5 years, we have been informally surveying our undergraduate and graduate content reading courses about whether they were ever required to take notes in high school and, if so, whether they were taught how to do it. The results every semester suggest that almost all students remember taking notes during their high school years, but less than 10% remember a teacher actually teaching them how to do it. Those that had been taught how to take notes typically received instruction by one teacher in one content area (most often in either English or science), and no one recalls a cross-subject matter emphasis. You can probably relate to these findings, because for most of you, learning to listen and take notes was a trial and error process. Common sense suggests that if listening and note taking are widely used, then how to do them should not be left to chance. Therefore, the following is a summary of what we know about note taking and how to integrate it within the context of a student-centered classroom. Two caveats before we begin our discussion follow: (a) Teaching students how to take notes should include causing them to use their notes. (b) There should be a payoff for the student who listens and records notes (assessment should reflect lecture content).

_____

What would be a payoff for a
student in your class?

_____

What are some things that
make a lecture effective?

Teacher Responsibilities for Promoting Note Taking.   For students to become efficient note takers, teachers need to model **appropriate lecture behaviors** that promote successful note taking and provide students insight into how to listen and record information. The following guidelines are offered as teaching tactics that assist students in recording meaningful notes.

1. Provide students with the purpose of the lecture (Fleming & Leet, 1989). The purpose of the lecture should be visually presented, on chalkboard or overhead, so that students' active attention will be focused on what is important to record. So, if a lecture's purpose is to compare and contrast platforms of the various political parties during the election of 1860 or to describe the preparation, reactions, and uses of halogens and noble gases, the students should know this information at the outset.

2. Emphasize important points by presenting them on the chalkboard or overhead projector (T. H. Anderson & Armbruster, 1991). Alert students to key points by explicitly stating that they are important. Tell students to copy important information from the chalkboard or overhead.

3. Tell students when information is being presented that is nonessential or unimportant for recording. If information is being presented that students are not going to be held responsible for or that is just an aside, teachers should literally inform students of that fact.

4. Pace the lecture so that students have time to record the information. When covering complex information, encourage thinking about the topic by pausing, restating, and using appropriate examples or analogies (T. H. Anderson & Armbruster, 1991). Teach students how to use appropriate abbreviations such as "geo" for *geological,* "evol." for *evo-*

lution, "B of R" for *Bill of Rights,* and others that they may need before you lecture (Gall et al. 1990).

5. Check out students' note-taking proficiency. Early in the school year, examine students' notes to determine their completeness and to identify those students who need more assistance and structure. For some classes or students, providing **listening outlines** (Figure 10.2) that must be filled in may be a necessary first step in teaching students how to record notes.

6. Construct tests that reflect important information emphasized during note-taking sessions. Nothing will encourage good note taking more than the knowledge by students that their notes will help their performance grade-wise.

7. Cause students to rehearse their notes. This can be done by having open notes tests, having pop quizzes that allow students to first review their notes and then respond to questions, and having students develop discussion or test items using their notes.

> Rehearsal, or practice, is the most commonly used study technique.

Recommendations for Recording Notes. Many different systems are available for teaching students how to record notes as they listen, ranging from the Cornell System (Pauk, 1988) to the REST system (Morgan, Meeks, Schollaert, & Paul, 1986). The common threads of these various systems are exemplified by recommendations about how notes should initially be recorded, the need for subsequent reorganization and expansion of the notes, and a strong recommendation for frequent review. Before discussing each of these components, we first suggest a couple general guidelines. First, students should be asked to use a single notebook for note taking in your class. This will help them keep the notes organized, and it will be easier for you to examine the notes. Second, if note taking is important to you, then some type of credit or grade should be given to students who do a good job of recording and organizing their notes. Finally, adapt the amount of lecturing and style of lecturing to your students. If you have an advanced class versus a low-achieving one, more sophisticated lecturing might be warranted. On the other hand, if your class is inexperienced with note taking and listening, you might want to begin slowly and use a lot of visuals or maybe even a listening outline to assist them in recording important information.

> When you take notes in college, how do you do it?

Two of the most popular note-taking systems are the Cornell System (Pauk, 1988) and A Notetaking System for Learning (Palmatier, 1973). Both of these systems share several features that we recommend for training students how to listen and record lecture information. Figure 10.3 is an example of how notes should look once students have progressed through the following sequence:

1. Students should divide their notebook paper into two columns. The left column should be about 2 or 3 inches wide or one third of the width. The remaining two thirds of the page is used for recording the notes as students listen.

> Do you do any of these recommendations?

Figure 10.2 Listening Outline: The First Americans

Purpose of the Lecture: To recognize who were the First Americans and what kinds of civilizations they established and how they lived.

I. First Americans arrive on the continent.
  A. Landbridge to North America
    1.
    2. Indians began to spread out across North America.
II. North American Indians
  A. Climate, land forms, and forests contributed to diversity.
  B. Indian Culture of North America differed in many ways.
    1.
    2.
    3.
III. Advanced Cultures of the South
  A. South America, Central America, and Mexico
    1. Most advanced Indian cultures
    2.
  B. Incas
    1. Location
      a.
      b.
    2. Accomplishments
      a.
      b. Master road builders
      c.
      d. mita—
    3. Government
      a.
      b.
  C. Mayas
    1. Located on Yucatan Peninsula
    2. Accomplishments
      a. Writing system
        i.
        ii.
      b.
      c.
    3. Government
      a.
      b.
  D. Toltecs and Aztecs
    1. Location
      a.
      b.
    2. Accomplishments
      a. Agriculture
        i.
        ii.
      b.
      c.
    3. Government
      a.
      b.

Figure 10.3   Split-Page Note Taking: Forms of Energy Lecture

What is energy?	I. Energy = ability to do work
f × d =	A. Work = force × distance
Macroscopic	II. Macroscopic particles—large objects
Mechanical energy	A. Possess mechanical energy
Types and examples	1. Potential energy (stored energy)— wound up spring in watch
	2. Kinetic energy (energy of motion)— hit baseball
Submicroscopic	III. Submicroscopic particles—can't be seen by
Nonmechanical	microscope
Types and examples	A. Possess nonmechanical energy
	1. Chemical energy (gasoline)
	2. Electrical energy
	3. Electromagnetic
	4. Sound energy
	5. Magnetic energy
	6. Heat energy
Classify nonmechanical	B. Nonmechanical energy is really kinetic and
as kinetic and potential	potential energy
Joule	IV. Measuring energy
	A. James P. Joule
	1. Joule
	2. Heat produced

2. Students should record information in a modified outline form on the right side of the page. During the recording of the notes, students should use indentations for subtopics and minor ideas using letters and numbers. They should be encouraged to use abbreviations to minimize how much time is spent recording information. Notations identifying heavily emphasized points should be made by using asterisks or stars.

3. Students should organize and expand their notes as soon as possible. Considerate teachers provide in-class time for this part early in the school year. At this time the students, if necessary, literally rewrite their notes on paper divided as described in steps 1 and 2. The purpose is for the students to write all abbreviations, expand phrases, and make sure that the information is sequentially organized. This is obviously a form of practice.

4. Students fill in the left margin for aid in study and review. As they reread their notes, students identify topics, key terms, and questions

that might assist them in remembering the lecture information recorded on the right side of the paper.

5. Students use their notes for study and review. Students can now cover up the right-hand side of the paper and use the memory triggers they have recorded on the left side for review. As they move down the left side of the page, students use the headings, key terms, and questions as a means of assessing whether they can remember and paraphrase what they have recorded.

Which of our recommendations do you see as workable in your subject matter area?

Remembering our suggestion regarding modeling, practice, and application, teachers who want to encourage the development of note-taking skills by students should begin with explicit models of what notes ought to look like. This can easily be done by conducting a lecture during which you place on the chalkboard, overhead, or a chart an example of what the students' notes should look like. Students can compare theirs to yours, and via the ensuing discussion, you can explain the system discussed previously. Using your model, encourage students to help you fill in the left margin. Remember, whether the system you adopt is the same or different from ours, it will take time and practice for students to become proficient. So, start slow, use brief lectures, and make sure students are rewarded.

Study Diagrams

Do you use visuals or graphics when you study?

Although semantic mapping has been discussed earlier in this text (see Chapter 6), organizing text information into diagrams that reflect the relationships among ideas has shown to be effective in helping students remember the information (Caverly & Orlando, 1991). **Study diagrams** can take the form of semantic maps, graphic organizers, or simple outlines, as long as the information being organized is accurately reflected. Obviously, before students can be encouraged to organize text into organized diagrams, teachers should model the process using adopted materials students will be expected to read and study. Although there is no one way a study map is supposed to look, we do recommend some general guidelines that need to be communicated to the students.

- The main topic should be clearly identified via boxing or circling and placement at the top or middle of the page.
- All major ideas and/or subtopics should be clearly identified via boxing, circling, or size.
- All details should be evaluated for inclusion on the map, and lines should be used to connect them to appropriate ideas or topics.

How can study diagrams be used in your subject matter area?

As you can see in Figures 10.4 and 10.5, maps may take different forms, the main point being that relationships are clearly delineated and the maps lend themselves to review and study. Because these types of study aids can take many forms and require time for students to become proficient in developing,

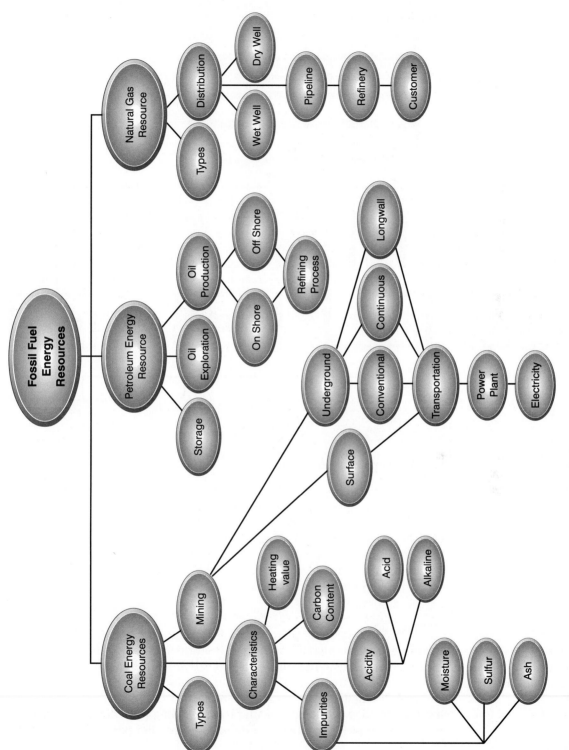

Figure 10.4 Group Study Diagram: Fossil Fuel Energy Resources

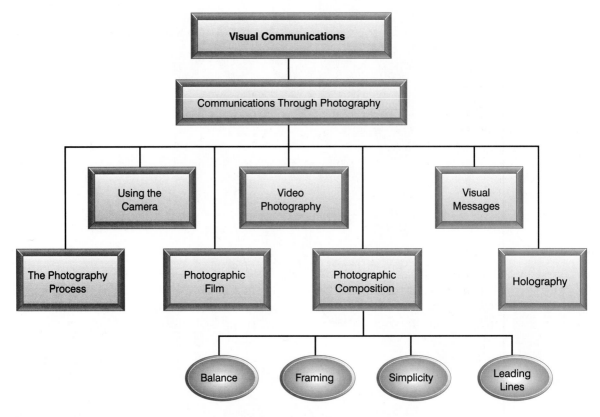

Figure 10.5 Group Study Diagram: Visual Communications

we suggest teachers use in-class collaborative activities to assist their development and use. Teachers can form small collaborative groups whose assigned task is to create the best study diagram over a specific text assignment or lecture. Each group can present their version, and a discussion can include critiquing each group's visual and deciding which ones are the best representation of the important information in the selection.

Learning Logs

Learning logs are journals used to record or react to topics being studied in class (Fulwiler, 1985). These types of journals are informal and often are cluttered and messy. The types of entries into learning logs can include but are not limited to listing important vocabulary; reactions to lecture or text reading; listing steps in an experiment or math problem-solving procedure; word associations with a topic; comparing two events or ideas; and personal responses to

Learning logs are reactions or records of what is being studied.

such questions as, What did I learn today, what do I still need to know, or what is it I don't understand? These running entries are designed to promote thinking about the topics being studied and to allow students time for reflection in class.

Out-of-Class Studying

Completing out-of-class assignments and preparing for upcoming exams are two facts of life students face on an ever-increasing basis as they progress through our public schools. Because both of these activities begin and end in the classroom, it follows that teachers have responsibility for assisting students with out-of-class studying. Notwithstanding that the ideas about in-class studying are supposed to have transfer value to out-of-class studying, we have additional recommendations and strategies to teachers regarding out-of-class studying.

Did you ever fail to turn in assignments? If so, why?

Daily Assignments

In general, teachers typically have two concerns when it comes to making daily assignments: (a) Will the students copy it down, and (b) will they do the assignment? The first concern is easily remedied by requiring students to obtain and use **assignment notepads**. Additionally, teachers should write out assignments for all to see rather than just verbalize it. Having it in written form makes it take on more prominence, and students will perceive it as more meaningful. Students, on recording the assignment, should be able to answer the questions (a) What is the assignment, (b) why am I being asked to do the assignment, and (c) what should I know or be able to do when I complete the assignment? This last point is very important because it helps avoid giving busywork and provides students with a real study goal. So, whether the assignment is to attend a city commission meeting because issues related to the local landfill will be discussed and acted on or to complete the reading of Chapter 10 about the French Revolution, students need to be able to answer the previously mentioned questions.

How do you keep up with assignments and responsibilities during the week?

The second concern requires a different tactic. Teachers should advise students that studying and completing homework assignments at the same time each day works better than randomly deciding day by day. This idea should be communicated to parents early in the school year via a newsletter or some other form of communication. Setting strict time limits is not the purpose of this recommendation, rather the development of a habit of studying on a regular and organized basis is the intent, because research has shown it improves academic achievement (Risko, Alvarez, Fairbanks, 1991). Students should also be instructed to establish a set of priorities for assignments that must be completed over several days. By rank ordering from the most important or most pressing study goal to the least important, students can better schedule their time and efforts.

How much homework do you think is reasonable for high school students on a nightly basis?

Reading, Responding, and Study

Throughout this text, we have advocated providing students the support and structure necessary to promote interest, motivation, and literacy development in your subject matter area. We realize, however, that there will be times when students must assume the responsibility for reading, writing, and studying printed material of your subject matter area. We again recommend some specific ideas that you can use to assist students in coping independently with the demands of learning on their own.

Were you ever taught a systematic study strategy?

SQ3R.   All effective reading/study strategies are metacognitive in nature because they cause readers to establish purposes for study, determine whether they have been successful in satisfying their purposes, and adjust their tactics if they haven't been successful in achieving their purpose for studying. They require the students to actively attend to text information; respond to text in some way (taking notes, underlining, answering questions); spend more time on task; and review the material for long-term retention. If one examines a reading/study "how-to" book, one often finds a plethora of reading/study strategies that are touted as either effective or tailor-made for specific subject matter areas. They are usually presented by an acronym that reflects the various steps of the strategy. The most time-honored of all these reading/study strategies is SQ3R. Originally developed by Francis Robinson (1946) as a technique to help soldiers study manuals during World War II (Stahl & Henk, 1986), SQ3R has been used widely in public schools as a way of providing students with a specific, albeit intense, method for independent study. SQ3R has spawned many other similar reading/study strategies; however, because most of the other reading/study strategies reflect much of what SQ3R recommends, we will confine this discussion to SQ3R. First, in Figure 10.6, we present the steps of SQ3R and then discuss its relative usefulness in content reading and study.

Having viewed Figure 10.6, how practical do you think SQ3R is?

As you can see, SQ3R and its many clones require a great deal of effort on the part of the student and the teacher. Estimates suggest that a minimum of 10 hours of teacher-lead instruction are required for low-achieving students to use SQ3R effectively (Orlando, 1986). In addition, the effect of SQ3R on student achievement is questionable (Caverly & Orlando, 1991). So, where does this leave teachers who want to assist students in becoming independent learners? We think it leaves the teacher in a decision-making position. Specifically, those components of SQ3R that can best serve the student with a particular assignment should be modeled and practiced in class first. Then, when an out-of-class assignment warrants the use of SQ3R or some of its steps, the assignment should include directions to the students that will require them to use SQ3R. Figure 10.7 provides an example of how such an adaptation can be made.

Paraphrasing and summarizing are critical to successful studying.

Response Journals and Study.   Responding to what one reads can take many forms. In the content areas, having students respond to instruction and/or reading can take the form of learning logs (Norton, 1993), **study skills jour-**

Figure 10.6 The SQ3R Study Strategy

The acronym SQ3R represents the sequence survey, question, read, recite, and review.

Survey   The purpose of this step is for students to preview the chapter closely to get a general idea about what the chapter will be about and to build prior knowledge before reading the chapter.
1. Read the introduction and summary to the chapter.
2. Examine all visuals.
3. Read all the headings and subheadings in the chapter.
4. In a notebook make a list, with definitions of all boldface or high-lighted terms.

Question   This step will cause students to establish purposes for reading the material as well as to think about what they are reading.
1. Read the questions at the end of the chapter and/or any teacher-assigned questions.
2. Make up questions from the headings and subheadings using the six indicators of information (who, what, when, where, why, and how). Write these questions down.

Read   This step requires students to actively read, searching for specific information determined by the previous two steps.
1. Read one heading or subheading at a time.
2. Try to answer the questions you have posed for each section. If you can't, reread the section now.

Recite   This step requires students to actually write the answers to the posed questions.
1. After reading a heading or subheading, without looking back at the text, try to write an answer to the question(s) posed for that heading or subheading.
2. After writing your answer(s), look back at the text and expand your answers, if warranted, by including key words, examples, and more complete information.
3. Proceed through the assignment, repeating this procedure.

Review   The purpose of this step is for students to practice the information for improved memory, to clarify relationships among topics, and to prepare for tests.
1. Without looking at the answers, read all the questions posed and either mentally or in writing try to answer them.
2. Check the answers with the notes already recorded for accuracy. If there is a discrepancy, those questions should be noted for additional review.

Figure 10.7 SQ3R Adaptation for a Specific Study Assignment: Food Processing

Directions: We will begin discussing Chapter 8, Food Processing, tomorrow. To prepare for our discussion and in-class activities, you will need to be familiar with the information in the initial section of Chapter 8, pp. 238–242. Please complete the following activities using your textbook.

1. Survey this section of Chapter 8.
   a. What is the main topic of this subsection?
      The main topic is how food is acquired and processed.
   b. Make a list of all italicized terms by topic.
      Acquisition of Food
         ingestion   taking food in
         food cavity   part of consumer's body
         digestive tract   where the food is acted on by the body
         food vacuole   an amoeba's food cavity
      Food Processing
         mechanical digestion   breaking down of large chunks of food
         chemical digestion   use of enzymes to break down food molecules
         intracellular digestion   chemical digestion within a single cell
         extracellular digestion   chemical digestion within a digestive tract
         absorption   means by which digested food is distributed
            throughout the organism's body
         egestion   process of ridding the body of waste and unused food

2. Question
   a. Using the words for review for this section, rewrite each question in your own words.
      1. What are the ways consumers use food?
      2. What is the difference between chemical and mechanical digestion?
      3. What are some examples of chemical and mechanical digestion?
      4. Why is egestion necessary?

3. Read
   a. Read those parts of this section that will give you an answer to your questions.
   b. Write out your answers to each question using two or three sentences.
      1. After obtaining food, consumers break the food down into nutrients so that they can be delivered to the body by absorption. After the body stores or uses the nutrients, the leftovers and waste are gotten rid of.
      2. Mechanical digestion is when you chew, grind, or tear up incoming food. Chemical digestion is when the body uses chemicals it produces to reduce the food to nutrients.
      3. Chemical examples are amylase, which produces the nutrient maltose, and protease, which produces amino acids. Both of these are enzymes. Mechanical examples are the gizzard of a chicken and tongue and teeth.
      4. Egestion is necessary because an organism never uses up all of what it swallows. There's always going to be waste that has to be gotten rid of or the organism will get sick or at least feel bad.

nals (Brozo & Simpson, 1995), **dialogue journals** (Gambrell, 1985), or **study journals** (Manzo & Manzo, 1990). All of these are attempts to have students integrate writing as a way of learning and study, with the added benefit of personal reactions to what is being studied. The most appropriate of these for out-of-class studying is what we will call the **study-response journal**. The study-response journal is a hybrid of the study skills journal (Brozo & Simpson, 1995) and the study journal (Manzo & Manzo, 1990). This type of journal requires that the teacher train students how to paraphrase and summarize text information, neither of which is an easy task. Additionally, this type of journal requires the student to personally react to what has been read and written about. The setup for the journal is to divide notebook paper in half. The left half is used for paraphrasing and summarizing, and the right half is used for personal reactions to what is being studied. See Figure 10.8 for an excerpt from a study-response journal.

Paraphrasing refers to taking the author's message and putting it into one's own language. It parallels the idea of unaided recall. Students can be taught how to do this by first reading a short segment of text, with the teacher demonstrating how he would paraphrase the segment. Then, in cooperative groups, students could be assigned a segment of text to read and paraphrase,

Contrast paraphrasing and summarizing.

Figure 10.8 Study-Response Journal Excerpt: Tundra

Text Paraphrase/Summary	Personal Reaction/Response
The tundra is one of six main biomes on Earth. It is extremely cold, dry, and barren. It is found in Northern Canada and Russia. The ground is always frozen, and the top layer is called the *permafrost.*	This is my least favorite biome. I think living there would be terrible. The fact that the permafrost is always present means no gardening.
The plant life is sparse. The few trees that exist are tiny. Mostly fungi, grasses, and tiny wildflowers grow during the short growing season.	I couldn't stand not having trees and bushes. It sounds like a cold desert.
The tundra biome is home to a variety of water and land animals. Polar bears, arctic foxes, and seals are a few of the main animals. Humans don't venture into the tundra except for hunting and oil exploration. The oil exploration has caused the tundra to become polluted.	I think the hunting would be great. I don't understand how so many different animals live there since it's so cold and there's not much to eat. The pollution of this and all other biomes needs to be prevented when possible.

in writing, the main points. Each group can share their paraphrases and judge which is the most accurate and why. With practice activities like this, students' proficiency at paraphrasing should result in better study-response journals.

Summarizing refers to identifying and organizing important information into a concise series of notes, sentences, and/or paragraphs. To develop summarization skills, teachers should consider the recommendations of Taylor (1986) for teaching students how to develop a hierarchical summary. Students should be taught how to perform the following:

- Conduct a preview of a short segment of text.
- Develop a cursory outline using Roman numerals for main headings, capital letters for subheadings, and Arabic numerals for any details.
- Read the segment of text, and complete the outline by adding additional information.
- Using the outline as a guide, write a summary using one's own words.
- Above the summary try to write the major idea for the whole segment of text.
- Below the summary list any critical details that are not addressed in the summary.

What value can study-response journals have in your classroom?

As with paraphrasing, students should learn how to summarize in class before they are asked to summarize out of class. The same kind of scenario as mentioned about paraphrasing should be used to provide students practice in summarizing. One additional suggestion is to provide student groups with two summaries, one a complete summary and the other an incomplete one, and let them evaluate both by discussing which is better and by identifying the flaws in the incomplete one.

Finally, as study-response journal entries are made, students are asked to respond and react on a personal basis to what they have read and written. Typically, these responses should center around ideas that students recognize as important, ideas that are confusing, ideas about how this information relates to what has been previously studied or discussed in class, and ideas about what is being learned.

BECOMING A PROFICIENT TEST TAKER

As students progress through the grades, testing becomes more and more prevalent and important to overall class performance. Because tests are only a one-time demonstration by students that learning has taken place, we support the use of the portfolio approach to assessment (see Chapter 3) in the content areas. However, we would be remiss if we did not share with you ideas that you can use to help students improve their test performance. We begin by discussing how to improve test performance generally and conclude with techniques for specific kinds of exams.

Improving Test Performance

A cartoon we remember shows two students discussing their results of a test. One student comments that he made an A, and the other asks how. The first student says, "I studied for the test, and I guess the ploy paid off." We recognize that preparing for upcoming exams is the responsibility of the student; however, caring teachers often provide insights and recommendations for taking their exams. These teachers recognize that providing students with guidelines about how to prepare for examinations and what to do during the examination session can influence students' performance (Wark & Flippo, 1991). General knowledge that teachers should communicate to students for taking any type of examination includes the following:

Name three things that could improve your test performance.

- *Amount of time for completing the exam.* Students should know in advance whether the time allotted for an exam is limited or not.
- *Format and purpose.* Students need to know the structure of the exam in advance because it impacts how they should study for the exam. So, if the exam will be essay, students should know how many questions, the weight of each, and which topics will be covered on the exam.
- *Conduct exam preview.* Regardless of exam type, students should be encouraged to look over the entire exam before launching into the exam. This preview can help students use their time more effectively, decide which part of the exam they should tackle first (always the most familiar), and reduce anxiety.
- *Pace yourself.* Students need to recognize that all exams are timed and that to improve their scores they need time to attempt all items. Additionally, if some items carry more weight, then those items should receive more attention.
- *Read carefully.* Students need to read carefully all directions and items. There is no excuse for mistakes that were made because directions were not followed appropriately or test items were misread. They should pay particularly close attention to key terms in each question that specify what is being asked of them.
- *Reconsider answers.* Contrary to popular belief, higher scores result from changing answers than from sticking with one's first choice (Wark & Flippo, 1991). Students should be encouraged, time permitting, to return to difficult items and reconsider their answers in light of logic and information gained from the rest of the test.

Summarize the general recommendations for taking exams.

Intellectual Preparation

Besides knowing the exam's format in advance, students should consider a number of things to prepare for an upcoming exam. First, students need to plan to review for the test across time rather than trying to cram everything in at the

As a student, how do you review for an upcoming exam?

Predict two questions that will
be on the exam for this chapter.

last minute. To encourage this type of reviewing, teachers can establish **in-class review groups** that can meet for short periods to discuss the upcoming exam's information. The one caution about using review groups is that at least one member of each group should be a strategic student who is well versed in the topic under study. Second, students should predict the questions that are likely to be on the exam. Combining information from lectures, readings, and possibly old exams, students can become proficient at predicting exam content. Third, students should develop skeletal outlines of course content that can be used as a memory aid when taking the exam. This type of outline should contain only major terms and key ideas and should be rehearsed until memorized. Fourth and finally, students should use the night before the exam to conduct a final review. During this final review, students should try to commit to memory those specific details and facts that they can assume will be on the exam.

Emotional and Physical Preparation

Exam taking can be a physical and emotional strain on students. Ranging from all-night study sessions to test anxiety, internal and external factors can reduce a student's performance on exams. A bit of common sense can help mediate the effect of these types of factors. Teachers can help students with test anxiety by teaching effective ways to study and prepare for their exams and by providing instruction in how to approach taking their exams (Wark & Flippo, 1991). Physically, students should be well rested and well fed. All-night study sessions can reach the law of diminishing returns if students are not careful. Some experts (Flemming & Leet, 1989) recommend that when students find it necessary to cram for an exam the sessions should not last for more than 2 hours at a time without a significant break away from the material. Test performance can be affected by lack of mental alertness because of hunger or lack of sleep.

Do you have test anxiety?
What can be done to help students relax and concentrate?

Emotionally, students should remember two words: relax and concentrate. Teachers should point out that the pretest banter among students often can be counterproductive and heighten anxiety. The solution, of course, is for students to concentrate on points they want to remember, avoid distracting conversations, and record those points on the test as soon as the exam is passed out by the teacher. One final note is the idea of thinking positively about the exam. Most study skills handbooks suggest that students who have prepared for the exam should expect to do well on the exam.

Taking Objective Exams

Although we do not support the overuse of objective testing, we do recognize that objective testing will continue to be a predominant method of assessing students' knowledge of specific subject matter information. Besides the previous discussion about how to prepare for tests, we advocate that teachers spend a little instructional time (before the test and when test papers are handed back) discussing with students effective ways of taking objective tests. Figure 10.9 contains

Figure 10.9 Recommendations for Taking Objective Exams

1. Read all items very carefully, anticipate the answer, and then look for it. Be sure to consider all alternatives before responding.
2. Never leave a question unanswered.
3. Skip any items you are unsure of, and come back to those later. Pacing is important.
4. For multiple-choice items, if you don't know the answer, try to eliminate some of the choices, then make an informed guess. Remember to relate all the alternatives to the question or stem in making your guess.
5. Looking at the four choices on a multiple choice item, note whether there are two answers that are opposite, an answer that has a broader application than the rest, or whether some answers are not correct grammatical extensions of the stem. These clues can help you make an informed guess on items when you don't recognize the answer.
5. For true or false items, words such as *always, never, without exception,* and *only* often signal false statements, while words such as *generally, usually,* and *most of the time* often signal true statements. These kinds of signals are called *specific determiners* and are useful mainly on poorly constructed tests.
6. When you encounter a matching section that has an equal number of statements and possible answers, try using the process of elimination.
7. Be aware that some items later in the exam may provide you with information about earlier items. Use this information to change your answers when warranted.

our recommendations of what teachers should share with students about taking objective tests. The time spent discussing this type of information not only can benefit student performance but also can help reduce test anxiety.

Taking Essay Exams

Unlike objective tests, which are recognition exams, essay exams require students not only to recall information but to discuss it in a coherent fashion in writing. In preparing for essay exams, experts (Flemming & Leet, 1989; Simpson, 1986) suggest, students should be encouraged to begin their preparation by doing three things:

Should you combine objective and essay exams?

1. Predict what the essays will be about using class notes, textbook, and input from the teacher.
2. Develop skeletal outlines or other diagrams to concisely represent what they need to know about the topics being assessed (these can be done in class as collaborative activities).

3. Commit the outlines and diagrams to memory so that they can be used as reference points when responding to test items. Other suggestions about essay exam preparation include the idea that students should actually write out predicted essay questions before the exam and conduct a self-evaluation for completeness (Simpson, 1986; Simpson, Hayes, Stahl, Connor, & Weaver, 1988). This latter suggestion would be a very good in-class review exercise done in collaborative groups.

Students should also be taught how to respond once the exam is passed out. Our recommendations are as follows:

Develop a "top 10" list for studying and taking exams.

1. *Don't look at the test immediately.* Rather, write down the skeletal outlines or diagrams that you have memorized for ready reference.
2. *Carefully read the directions and exam questions.*
3. *Respond to the easiest question first.* This tactic will cause students to relax, establish confidence, and give them a running start at the exam.
4. *Before beginning to write, think and organize.* Students should analyze what the question requires. If the question wants them to describe, list, compare, or discuss, then their answer should reflect the intent of the question.
5. *Reference responses to prepared outlines or diagrams.* Students should begin their responses with an introductory paragraph that includes a restatement of the question, proceed to the body of their response that includes the specific details necessary to support their answers, and finally end their response with a concluding or summary paragraph.
6. *Reread all responses.* Rereading is done to determine if anything was left out and to correct mechanical errors that went unnoticed while writing.

This discussion about improving exam performance has centered on the more traditional type of exams found in content area classrooms. As you will remember from Chapter 3, on assessment, we do not view assessment in the narrow vein of paper-and-pencil exams. We hope you recognize that the authentic assessment strategies already discussed are as valid and more meaningful than one-time assessments of students' knowledge via paper-and-pencil exams. We encourage you to experiment with the many alternatives to paper-and-pencil exams in hopes of promoting real assessments of student progress in your classroom.

LEARNERS WITH SPECIAL NEEDS

Organizational skills are a critical variable for being a successful student.

Students experiencing problems learning at the postelementary level are typically described as disorganized, limited in reading and writing skills, poor test takers, and poor listeners (Mercer & Mercer, 1993). For these types of students, direct instruction about how to study and instructional modifications to assist them in studying should be provided by the regular classroom teacher in consultation with the special education teacher. Even though much of what has been discussed in this chapter has applicability to these types of students, we suggest some additional techniques that have merit for helping students with learning problems become better at studying. These additional ideas also can be used with nonlabeled students.

In-Class Studying

One area that can be directly addressed by the classroom teacher concerns structured listening activities. Besides listening outlines (see Figure 10.2), other structured listening activities that can be used to assist these students include the Guided Lecture Procedure (Kelly & Holmes, 1979), the Directed Listening Procedure (P. M. Cunningham & Cunningham, 1976), and the Guided Listening/Note-Taking Activity (Mercer & Mercer, 1993).

If students can't read your text, then structured listening is one way to communicate important information.

Guided Lecture Procedure

The **Guided Lecture Procedure (GLP)** capitalizes on focused listening, integration of all communication skills, and collaborative learning under teacher direction.

1. The teacher lists the objectives for a class lecture on the chalkboard or overhead and has each student write them in their notebooks. Students are then asked to listen without taking any notes.
2. The teacher conducts a tightly organized lecture that lasts no more than half the class period. The lecture should include the typical kinds of visuals and chalkboard writing associated with a good lecture.

Learners with special needs have short attention spans.

3. On completion of the lecture, students are asked to write down as much as they can recall from the lecture that relates to the original objectives.
4. Students then form collaborative groups to discuss, revise, and organize the lecture information. This type of interaction and support is crucial for students with learning problems and will probably result in their receiving more information than they volunteer.

Consider the makeup of collaborative groups carefully.

5. Finally, a whole group teacher-lead discussion should follow to clarify confusion and to make sure that the students' notes are as complete as possible. Early in the school year, it is advised that the teacher provide a model of what information should be in their notes and how their notes should be organized.

This technique is a bit unorthodox, and many students may resent at the outset not being able to record notes as they listen. However, if the teacher

A teacher exploring students'
responses to the Guided Lecture
Procedure.

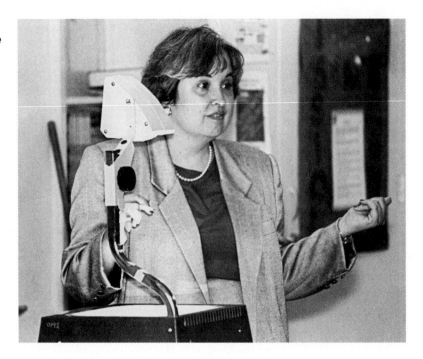

explains ahead of time the purpose of the procedure and the fact that students will end up with complete notes, this type of complaint should not be a problem. Added benefits of this procedure for the student with problems learning are the interaction with her peers and the use of writing, reading, talking, and listening to learn content information.

Directed Listening Activity

Think about how you could use the DLA in your subject matter area.

The **Directed Listening Activity (DLA)** begins with the teacher preparing the students for listening to him read or lecture on important information that students will be held accountable for knowing. Initially, the prelistening discussion centers around activating the background of students by asking what they know about the topic and discussing some of the key terms that they will hear. Before reading or lecturing, the teacher establishes specific purposes for students' listening. On completing the reading or lecture, the teacher asks students to volunteer what they learned from the reading or lecture. Discussion of what they heard allows the teacher to fill in gaps and misinformation and may result in the teacher rereading portions of text or going back over parts of the lecture. Finally, in dyads or small groups, students help each other record the information into their learning logs or study journals.

Guided Listening/Note-Taking Activity

Although the **Guided Listening/Note-Taking Activity** is intended as a technique that support personnel can use to assist students in developing note-taking skills, it certainly could be used in the regular classroom setting with small groups or as a paired learning activity. If it is used as a paired learning activity, it is imperative to match students with learning problems with a competent student. The steps of the procedure as intended for use by support personnel follow:

1. Using an 8- to 10-minute recording of a lecture over content material, the student and her teacher record notes.
2. After listening and recording of notes are completed, the teacher shares his notes with the student for comparison purposes and for explaining note-taking strategies. The teacher may replay the tape again to point out signals used in the lecture that alert the listener to important information (voice cues such as transition phrases, repetition of information, and overall organization cues).
3. Next, the student relistens to the tape and records a new set of notes. The new set is compared again with the teacher's model notes, and corrections are made.
4. Subsequent opportunities are provided with other short tapes made by regular classroom teachers. A number of practice trials may be necessary before the student can develop skill and completeness.
5. Finally, the student is asked to record notes from live lectures in the regular classroom. A set of model notes should be provided by the classroom teacher to assist the student in comparing her notes and correcting them.

This strategy is ideal for building a bridge between support personnel and regular faculty because both are involved in cooperatively trying to help students with learning problems in a **shared responsibility** atmosphere.

If special needs students are to be held responsible for the same amount of information as regular students, then teachers should encourage the use of cassette players by students with problems learning. Taping of class lectures provides these students an opportunity to relisten, study, and remember what you have emphasized in class.

Out-of-Class Studying

Again, many of the ideas already discussed in this chapter can be adapted to assist students with learning problems. Ideas already discussed that are recommended for use with these types of students include previewing of text, study diagrams, and modified versions of SQ3R (Meese, 1992). In addition to these, other recommendations for out-of-class study include time management, study cards, and text marking.

Margin notes:

What other ways can support personnel be used?

Shared responsibility means that all students belong to all teachers.

Time Management

The student with learning problems often needs instruction in time management. Making schedules, establishing priorities, and estimating how long study assignments will take are all a part of time management. Students with learning problems need to visually see their schedule of after-school time. These students should record how they spend their after-school time for a week. Based on that information, time allotments for schoolwork should be negotiated. A record of time spent listening to lecture information, doing homework, and studying for exams should be kept by these students.

Another area of time management these students need help with is establishing priorities for assignments and projects. Students with problems learning should keep a calendar of assignments and their due dates. Also, they should try to predict how much time will be required by assignments. This can be easily done by having them list assignments that are due during a week's time, prioritize them, and estimate how much time each one will require. If students are consistently mistaken about how much time will be needed to complete assignments, they should adjust their estimates for future assignments.

Study Cards

Study cards are a way of conducting a review of information a student needs to remember. Simply, key terms and questions are placed on one side of the card, while the terms' definitions and the questions' answers are placed on the other side. These study cards can be done in class, with support personnel, or at home based on completed work. The purpose is obviously for the student to be able to explain what each term means and answer each question completely without looking at the back of the card.

Text Marking

Although public school students are told not to mark in their texts, many special educators secure copies of textbooks for their students with the intent of highlighting the important information. S.O.S. (Schumaker, Deshler, Alley, & Warmer, 1983), which stands for *survey, obtain details,* and *study,* is a **text-marking strategy** that incorporates listening and writing. Support personnel highlight a chapter by marking only main ideas, important words, key facts, and important lists. Then a paraprofessional makes a recording of the chapter as it has been marked. Students are provided a partial outline as a listening guide and record the information on the outline as they listen to the recording. After listening the students can examine the marked text and compare their notes to what is highlighted. The structure of S.O.S. causes students to be active listeners and also allows them to study with assurances of success.

Test Taking

For many students with learning problems, course examinations pose quite a challenge, first, because they have to study differently from students who can read and write adequately and, second, because the exam requires them to be able to read and write. Therefore, we recommend that all regular education teachers consider alternative testing for students whose performance is hampered by the literacy demands of the exam. We believe that mainstreamed students should be held responsible for the same information as the rest of the class, but their demonstration of their knowledge is what should be varied. (We are, of course, referring to mildly handicapped students.) For objective exams, students with learning problems should certainly receive test-taking instruction similar to recommendations made earlier in this chapter, but they should also have the test items read to them if reading them by themselves penalizes their performance. Special education personnel will be very receptive to this idea and will record their responses and let the regular education teacher score the exam. Essay tests for these students should be recorded if their writing skills have been identified as delimiting. Again, the test and student can be sent to special education personnel who will read each question and have the student record his response. Later the responses can be transcribed by support personnel for evaluation by the regular education teacher. Neither of these ideas is novel, but they do warrant more attention by regular education faculty for all students.

What students know, not how they demonstrate what they know, is the point.

Chapter Summary

Content teachers need to assume an active role in promoting effective study habits in their classrooms. Because independent learning is an important goal of content area instruction, teachers must be willing to model study strategies and techniques before expecting students to be able to apply them.

Listening and note taking are among the most frequently used in-class study techniques. The split-page approach to recording lecture information should be coupled with explicit input from teachers as to what is and is not important to record. Note taking becomes meaningful only if teachers demonstrate how to take notes, provide opportunities for students to expand their notes, and cause students to practice their notes. Students can also be taught to use visual diagrams to organize and study important text information. This idea of graphically organizing text cannot be underestimated in terms of benefits to both regular and special education students. Learning logs (see also Chapter 8, "Writing in the Content Areas") are useful, because responding in writing to class learning activities is an excellent way to keep students involved and for you to gain insights into what is and isn't being understood.

Out-of-class studying can be enhanced by specific methods for encouraging students to practice content information. Although we do not heartily support the use of SQ3R because of its time requirements and reluctance among students to use it, we do support teaching students how to preview texts, pose their own questions, and respond in writing to what they are studying. We recommend modifying SQ3R to satisfy specific study goals teachers might have for students. Study journals are also recommended because they require both summarization of important information and personal reaction to what is being read and studied.

Test taking is an area of instruction that needs more attention. Students can be taught general test-taking strategies for objective and essay tests. However, pencil-and-paper tests need to be supplemented with more authentic assessments. Students need opportunities to demonstrate learning in a variety of ways, and as Chapter 3 points out, pencil-and-paper assessment is only one of many ways to get a view of student learning.

Finally, some alternative techniques can be used to accommodate students who have problems learning. Structured listening techniques, time management ideas, and alternative testing recommendations can be used with students with learning problems as well as with regular education students who would benefit from them.

Studying is not an easy task. Studying is even harder when students do not receive instruction in how and when to do it. We propose a much more active role for the content teacher in demonstrating how to study. We hope you will reflect on your past habits of study and recognize that you too would have benefitted if a teacher had taken the time to provide some assistance.

Reflection/Application Activities

1. First, evaluate the method you use for recording lecture notes in your current university classes. Then, using the recommendations in this chapter, try to adopt the split-page approach for at least one of your courses that is lecture intensive. Continue recording notes for the remainder of the current semester, using the split-page approach (don't forget the practice recommendation). At final exam time, compare the split-page notes with your other method. Which one is clearer? More organized? Which of the two note-taking techniques helped you more in preparing for your final exams?

2. Use this chapter to experiment with the concept of the study journal. Divide your notebook paper in half, and as you read the chapter, summarize important text information on the left side and write personal reactions to what you read on the right-hand side. Be prepared to discuss the effects of this approach to reading and studying.

3. Write three essay questions that you think could and should be asked by your instructor about the information in this chapter. Compare them with your classmates questions. Your instructor should also be prepared to share his with the class.

4. If your university or college has a developmental reading program for unprepared students, try to either review material being used to teach these students how to study or request an interview with one of the instructors. During the interview, ask questions about what the characteristics of the students in the program are and what specific study techniques are taught to these students. How do this chapter's recommendations compare?

Recommended Reading

Flemming, L. E., & Leet, J. (1989). *Becoming a successful student.* Glenview, IL: Scott, Foresman.

Flippo, R. F., & Caverly, D. C. (1991). *Teaching reading and study strategies at the college level.* Newark, DE: International Reading Association.

Gall, M. D., Gall, J. P., Jacobsen, D. R., & Bullock, T. L. (1990). *Tools for learning: A guide to teaching study skills.* Alexandria, VA: Association for Supervision and Curriculum Development.

Pauk, W. (1988). *How to study in college* (3rd ed.). Boston: Houghton Mifflin.

Tompkins, G. E. (1990). *Teaching writing: Balancing process and product* (pp. 317–369). Englewood Cliffs, NJ: Merrill/Prentice Hall.

GUIDED ACTION RESEARCH PLAN

Successful content area teachers are those who reflect—about themselves as teachers, their students as learners, and their classroom environment. To this end, skillful content teachers are those who make their classrooms varied in terms of environment, teaching activities, and assessment practices. They do not, however, shape their classrooms and teaching haphazardly; rather they engage in a practitioner's form of research often referred to as **action research**. In this context, action research is defined as things teachers do (experiment with) to improve the quality of their teaching and subsequently the success of their students. Action research is most often based on the following:

- Self-analysis and reflections from observations made of student behavior and responses in the classroom.
- Inservice workshops that introduce new ideas and strategies.
- Collaborations with other staff members about commonly shared concerns and discussions about how to deal with them.
- Reviews of current professional literature through university course work and/or personal reading.

Professional Growth and Action Research

The advent of teachers becoming involved in action research is a direct outgrowth of efforts to rethink education and to improve learning conditions for all students by promoting professional growth and development. Gove and Kennedy-Calloway (1992) suggest three themes of professional growth that are influenced by teachers becoming action researchers. The first is the idea that teaching is a problem-solving profession and to be successful one must recognize problems and determine how to solve them. The second theme suggests that teachers should not view themselves as islands in a large ocean. They have colleagues and resources that can aid them in the problem-solving process. One goal of staff development in every school district should be to develop collegiality and promote a sense of shared problem solving. The final theme has to do with teachers recognizing that they can be systematic data collectors and make educationally sound decisions about changing instruction based on data they collect and analyze. Action research causes teachers to fine tune their teaching and influences their attitudes toward their students and teaching situation. As Gove and Kennedy-Calloway noted,

They change from "Johnny has a problem. His home life is dysfunctional" to "I know I can find ways to work with Johnny." They change from continuing to use the same teaching patterns to "Oh, I wasn't aware of that! What can I try which might be effective?" (1992, p. 533)

Action Research Models

Several models can be used by classroom teachers to implement action research. The first, and probably the most common, is the **individual teacher model**. Although self-explanatory, this model refers to the actions of a single teacher who decides to experiment with a new idea, strategy, or method. Often, teachers engaged in individual action research use a single section of students for experimentation. That is, they conduct a unit of study in their more familiar or traditional way, and then in a subsequent unit of study, they infuse the new idea, activity, and/or method to see if it makes a difference either attitudinally (students are more motivated) or academically (students perform better on assignments and/or assessments). Sometimes these teachers elect to compare the traditional and the new between two different class sections. One section receives the traditional unit of instruction, while the other receives the infused unit of instruction.

Another model that is gaining popularity is the **dyadic partnership** model. This type of action research can take more than one form. The partnership can be between two teachers teaching the same subject matter, two teachers who have the same students but don't teach the same subject matter, and/or a teacher and a university professor or other professional who work together to implement and evaluate the new idea being tried.

Finally, the **collaborative group model** is beginning to be used in many schools as a number of teachers from various content areas are placed on teams that have common planning periods and the same students. These types of action research teams often focus on how to integrate literacy skills and coordinate units of study across subject matter areas. Sometimes university professors or other professionals are involved when some specialized knowledge or training is necessary.

Developing a Guided Action Research Plan

To conduct action research, one must either observe effects of the learning environment that may hinder student motivation and achievement or determine an area of instruction that needs improving. Through this awareness and analysis comes the desire to try something new. Once an area of concern or dissatisfaction has been identified, the next step is deciding what to do. Most action researchers do two things at this stage of the sequence. First, they talk to other teachers and/or professionals about their concern, soliciting input and advice about what to do and/or where to go for additional information. Second, they seek information from sources as varied as a university course, an educational regional service center, a few good books, or an in-district specialist. The next phase is to conduct the research by developing an action plan.

The three goals of an action plan are to decide: (1) what questions are trying to be answered, (2) what needs to be done instructionally to conduct the "experiment," and (3) how success/failure will be determined. The questions should be simple and direct. The instructional procedures may include only one strategy or new idea, or several. The form of evaluation for determining success can include single or multiple measures.

Of these three goals, it is the evaluation of the implementation of a new or adapted instructional strategy that provides realistic information about its value. The most often used forms of evaluation include teacher observations and reflections recorded in teacher-response journals, student reactions solicited verbally and in writing (learning logs or student response journals are commonly used), questionnaires used to measure student attitudes and reactions, student work samples, and teacher-made tests. One or all of these types of data can be part of the evaluation of a newly infused idea, strategy, or method. Finally, based on teachers' observations and student reactions and performance, a decision is made as to whether the new idea or method should be assimilated as is, modified for reevaluation, or dismissed. See Figure A.1 for an example of a **Guided Action Research Plan (GARP)**. Figure A.2, a blank GARP form, is provided for duplication and personal use. As professionals, you are encouraged to do your best, and action research is one avenue to achieving that goal.

Figure A.1 Guided Action Research Plan (GARP)

Area of Concern: My students don't seem to be able to retain important text information in an organized fashion. How can I help them organize text information to improve their retention and help them write essay items more effectively?

Information Needed: I need to find out about some techniques or strategies for increasing my students' ability to organize and retain important text information that can also help them formulate organized responses to essay items.

Sources That Can Help: Mrs. Leap, Dept. Chair of Science, fellow science teachers, assistant superintendent for instruction, Dr. Lee at the university, and textbooks from the school's professional library.

Action Plan: Based on input and information, to experiment with graphic organizers.

    Questions: 1. Will my students' retention be increased if I begin using graphic organizers and teach them how to develop their own graphic organizers to organize text information? [See Chapter 6 for examples.]
        2. Will my students be able to respond in a more organized manner on essay items if I incorporate graphic organizers as part of my teaching repertoire?

Instructional Procedures:
1. Use graphic organizers to introduce the first two chapters of the next three-chapter unit.
2. Have students expand each graphic organizer I have prepared. Make them look-back organizers. Assign short writing assignments based on the look-back organizers.
3. Have small groups of students work together on the last chapter of the unit to develop their own graphic organizers of what they think are the important ideas in the chapter. Have each group share its organizer, and use the discussion to help each group finalize its graphic organizer. Have each group decide on a writing assignment based on its reading and graphic organizer. Let each student select one of the writing assignments, and have groups evaluate the completeness and accuracy of each member's response.

Determining Success:
1. Keep a personal log of how students are reacting and performing as well as my perceptions about the effectiveness and worthiness of graphic organizers in terms of time commitment and results of assessment.
2. Collect student and group work samples. Provide feedback.
3. Ask students to share their reaction to whether graphic organizers are beneficial and whether we should continue using them on a regular basis. Ask all students to keep a response journal as we go through the unit of study.
4. Include essay questions on the end-of-unit exam and student-generated writing assignments. Evaluate and compare with the previous unit's exam by the same group of students.

Assimilate, Reevaluate, or Dismiss: Based on the criteria for determining success, it seems that students need more exposure and opportunities for working with graphic organizers. Therefore, I will continue to use graphic organizers for the remainder of the semester and make my final decision based on the end-of-semester feedback.

Figure A.2 A Blank GARP Form

Area of Concern:

Information Needed:

Sources That Can Help:

Action Plan:
  Questions:

Instructional Procedures:

Determining Success:

Assimilate, Reevaluate, or Dismiss:

References

Alexander, J. E., & Cobb, J. (1992). Assessing attitudes in middle and secondary schools and community colleges. *Journal of Reading, 36*(2), 146–149.

Alexander, J. E., & Heathington, B. S. (1988). *Assessing and correcting classroom reading problems.* Glenview, IL: Scott, Foresman/Little Brown.

Alley, G., & Deshler D. (1979). *Teaching the learning disabled adolescent: Strategies and methods.* Denver: Love.

Alvermann, D. (1991). The discussion web: A graphic aid for learning across the curriculum. *The Reading Teacher, 45*(2), 92–99.

Alvermann, D. E., Dillon, D. R., & O'Brien, D. G. (1987). *Using discussions to promote reading comprehension.* Newark, DE: International Reading Association.

Alvermann, D., & Phelps, (1994). *Content reading and literacy: Succeeding in today's diverse classrooms.* Needham Heights, MA: Allyn & Bacon.

Alvermann, D. E., & Swafford, J. (1989). Do content area strategies have a research base? *Journal of Reading, 32,* 388–394.

Anders, P. L., & Bos, C. S. (1986). Semantic feature analysis: An interactive strategy for vocabulary development. *Journal of Reading, 29,* 610–616.

Anders, P., Bos, C., & Filip, D. (1984). The effects of semantic feature analysis on the reading comprehension of learning disabled students. In J. A. Niles & L. A. Harris (Eds.), *Changing perspectives on research in reading language processing and instruction.* Rochester, NY: National Reading Conference.

Anders, P. L., Bos, C. S., & Wilde, S. (1986). *The effects of vocabulary strategies on the reading comprehension and vocabulary learning of junior high students.* Paper presented at the Thirty-Sixth National Reading Conference, Austin, TX.

Anderson, J. (1987) *1787.* Orlando, FL: Harcourt Brace Jovanovich.

Anderson, R. C., Heibert, E., Scott, J., & Wilkinson, I. (1985). *Becoming a nation of readers: The report of the commission on reading.* Washington, DC: National Institute of Education.

Anderson, T. H., & Armbruster, B. B. (1984). Content area textbooks. In R. Anderson, J. Osborn, & R. Tierney (Eds.), *Learning to read in American schools: Basal readers and content texts.* Hillsdale, NJ: Lawrence Erlbaum.

Anderson, T. H., & Armbruster, B. B. (1986). Readable textbooks, or, selecting a textbook is not like buying a pair of shoes. In J. Orasanu (Ed.), *Reading comprehension: From research to practice.* Hillsdale, NJ: Lawrence Erlbaum.

Anderson, T. H., & Armbruster, B. B. (1991). The value of taking notes during lectures. In R. F. Flippo & D. C. Caverly (Eds.), *Teaching reading and study strategies at the college level* (pp. 166–194). Newark, DE: International Reading Association.

Angell, A. V. (1991). Democratic climates in elementary classrooms: A review of theory and research. *Theory and Research in Social Education, 19,* 241–266.

Armbruster, B. B. (1991). Framing: A technique for improving learning from science texts. In C. M. Santa & D. E. Alvermann (Eds.), *Science learning: Processes and applications* (pp. 104–113). Newark, DE: International Reading Association.

Armbruster, B., & Anderson, T. (1981). *Content area textbooks* (Reading Education Report No. 23). Urbana-Champaign, IL: University of Illinois, Center for the Study of Reading.

Armbruster, B. B., & Anderson, T. H. (1984). Content area textbooks. In R. C. Anderson, J. Osborn, & R. Tierney (Eds.), *Learning to read in American schools: Basal readers and content texts* (pp. 193–226). Hillsdale, NJ: Erlbaum.

Armbruster, B. B., & Brown, A. L. (1984). Learning from reading: The role of metacognition. In R. C. Anderson, J. Osborn, & R. J. Tierney (Eds.), *Learning to read in American schools: Basal readers and content texts.* Hillsdale, NJ: Lawrence Erlbaum.

Armstrong, D. P., Patberg, J. P., & Dewitz, P. (1989). Reading guides: Helping students understand. *Journal of Reading, 31,* 532–541.

Ashton-Warner, S. (1963). *Teacher.* New York: Touchstone.

Atwell, N. (1987). *In the middle: Writing, reading, and learning with adolescents.* Portsmouth, NH: Heinemann.

Aukerman, R. C. (1972). *Reading in the secondary school.* New York: McGraw-Hill.

Baker, L. (1985). Differences in the standards used by college students to evaluate their comprehension of expository prose. *Reading Research Quarterly, 20,* 297–313.

Baker, L. (1991). Metacognition, reading, and science education. In C. M. Santa & D. E. Alvermann (Eds.), *Science learning: Processes and applications.* Newark, DE: International Reading Association.

Baker, L., & Brown, A. L. (1984). Cognitive monitoring in reading. In J. Flood (Ed.), *Understanding reading comprehension.* Newark, DE: International Reading Association.

Bandura, A. (1987). Self-regulation of motivation and action through goal systems. In V. Hamilton, G. H. Bower, & Freijda (Eds.), *Cognition, motivation, and affect: A cognitive science view.* Dordrecht, the Netherlands: Martinus Nijhoff.

Bandura, A., & Walters, R. (1963). *Social learning and personality development.* New York: Holt, Rinehart & Winston.

Banks, J. A., & Banks, C. A. M. (Eds.). (1989). *Multicultural education: Issues and perspectives.* Boston: Allyn & Bacon.

Barrett, T. C. (1972). *Taxonomy of reading comprehension.* In Reading 360 Monograph. Lexington, MA: Ginn.

Barron, R. F. (1969). The use of vocabulary as an advance organizer. In H. L. Herber & P. L. Sanders (Eds.), *Research on reading in the content areas: First year report* (pp. 29–39). Syracuse, NY: Syracuse University Press.

Bartlett, F. (1932). *Remembering.* Cambridge, UK: Cambridge University Press.

Bean, T. W., & Steenwyk, F. L. (1984). The effect of three forms of summarization instruction on sixth graders' summary writing and comprehension. *Journal of Reading Behavior, 16,* 297–306.

Berlak, H. (1992). The need for a new science of assessment. In H. Berlak et al. (Eds.), *Toward a new science of educational testing and assessment.* New York: State University of New York Press.

Berthoff, A. (1981). *The making of meaning.* Upper Montclair, NJ: Boynton/Cook.

Bloom, B. (1956). *Taxonomy of educational objectives: Handbook I, cognitive domain.* New York: Longman, Green.

Brown, A. L. (1980). Metacognition development in reading. In R. J. Spiro, B. C. Bruce, & W. F. Brewer (Eds.), *Theoretical issues in reading comprehension.* Hillsdale, NJ: Lawrence Erlbaum.

Brown, A. L., Campione, J. C., & Day, J. D. (1981). Learning to learn from texts. *Educational Researcher, 10,* 14–21.

Brown, L. (1991). Metacognition, reading, and science education. In C. M. Santa & D. E. Alvermann (Eds.), *Science learning: Processes and applications.* Newark, DE: International Reading Association.

Brown, M. H. (1981). *Laying Waste: The poisoning of America by toxic chemicals.* New York: Pantheon.

Brown, R. (1991). Testing and thoughtfulness. *Educational Leadership, 46,* 31–33.

Brozo, W. G., & Simpson, M. L. (1991). *Readers, teachers, learners: Expanding literacy in secondary schools.* Englewood Cliffs, NJ: Merrill/Prentice Hall.

Brozo, W. G., & Simpson, M. L. (1995). *Readers, teachers, learners: Expanding literacy in secondary schools.* Englewood Cliffs, NJ: Merrill/Prentice Hall.

Brussell, E. E. (1970). *Dictionary of quotable definitions.* Englewood Cliffs, NJ: Prentice Hall.

Buckley, W. F., Jr. (1993). A discussion with William F. Buckley, Jr., concerning the book *Happy days were here again* [television program]. Washington, DC: C-Span.

Bunting, E. (1990). *The wall.* New York: Clarion.

Burns, M. (1992). *About teaching mathematics: A K-8 resource.* White Plains, NY: Math Solutions Publications.

Burns, P. C. (1980). *Assessment and correction of language arts difficulties.* Englewood Cliffs, NJ: Merrill/Prentice Hall.

Butzow, C. M., & Butzow, J. W. (1989). *Science through children's literature: The integrated approach.* New York: Libraries Unlimited.

Calder, N. (1979). *Einstein's universe.* New York: Greenwich House.

Calkins, L. (1986). *The art of teaching writing.* Portsmouth, NH: Heinemann.

Calkins, L. M. (1994). *The art of teaching writing (new edition).* Portsmouth, NH: Heinemann.

Calkins, L., & Harwayne, S. (1987). *The writing workshop: A world of difference* [Video]. Portsmouth, NH: Heinemann.

Carter, P. (1990). *Borderlands.* New York: Farrar, Straus & Giroux.

Catterson, J. (1979). Comprehension: The argument for a discourse analysis model. In C. Pennock (Ed.), *Reading comprehension at four linguistic levels.* Newark, DE: International Reading Association.

Caverly, D. C., & Orlando, V. P. (1991). Textbook strategies. In R. F. Flippo & D. C. Caverly (Eds.), *Teaching reading and study strategies at the college level* (pp. 86–165). Newark, DE: International Reading Association.

Center for the Study of Social Policy (1991). *Kids count data book: State profiles of child well-being.* Washington, DC: Author.

Chatton, B. (1989). Using literature across the curriculum. In J. Hickman & B. Cullinan, (Eds.), *Children's literature in the classroom: Weaving charlotte's web.* Needham, MA: Christopher Gordon Publishers.

Clay, M. M. (1985). *The early detection of reading difficulties* (3rd ed.). Portsmouth, NH: Heinemann.

Collins, M. (Ed.). (1990). *The last rain forest: A world conservation atlas.* Oxford, UK: Oxford University Press.

Cooter, R. B. (Ed.). (1990). *The teacher's guide to reading tests.* Scottsdale, AZ: Gorsuch Scarisbrick.

Cooter, R. B., & Alexander, J. E. (1984). Interest and attitude: Affective connections for gifted and talented readers. *Reading World, 24,* 97–102.

Cooter, R. B., & Chillcoat, G. (1990). Content-focused melodrama: Dramatic renderings of historical text. *Journal of Reading, 34*(4), 274–277.

Cooter, R. B., & Griffith, R. (1989). Thematic units for middle school: An honorable seduction. *Journal of Reading, 32*(8),676–681.

Cordell, A. S., & Cannon, T. L. (1985). Gifted kids can't always spell. *Academic Therapy, 21,* 143–152.

Count the ways technology works for schools. (1990, September). *Electronic School,* pp. A25–A35.

Cowan, E., & Cowan, G. (1980). *Writing.* New York: John Wiley & Sons.

Crichton, M. (1987). *Sphere.* New York: Ballantine Books.

Crichton, M. (1990). *Jurassic park.* New York: Ballantine Books.

Crichton, M. (1972). *The Andromeda strain.* New York: Ballantine Books.

Cronin, H., Meadows, D., & Sinatra, R. (1990, September,). Integrating computers, reading, and writing across the curriculum. *Educational Leadership,* pp. 57–62.

Crook, P. R., & Lehman, B. A. (1991). Themes for two voices: Children's fiction and nonfiction as "whole literature." *Language Arts, 68,* 34–41.

Cunningham, D., & Shablak, S. L. (1975). Selective reading guide-o-rama: The content teacher's best friend. *Journal of Reading, 18,* 380–382.

Cunningham, J. W., Cunningham, P. M., & Arthur, S. V. (1981). *Middle and secondary school reading.* New York: Longman.

Cunningham, P., Crawley, S. G., & Mountain, L. (1983). Vocabulary scavenger hunts: A scheme for schema development. *Reading Horizons, 24,* 45–50.

Cunningham, P. M., & Cunningham, J. W. (1976). Improving listening in content area subjects. *NASSP Bulletin,* pp. 26–31.

Cutler, C., & Stone, E. (1988). A whole language approach: Teaching reading and writing to behaviorally disordered children. In Zabel, M. (Ed.), *Behaviorally disordered youth* (vol. 4). Reston, VA: Council for Children With Behavioral Disorders. (ERIC Document Reproduction Service No. ED 305 785)

Dewey, J. (1909). *The school and society.* Chicago: University of Chicago Press.

Dewey, J. (1916/1966). *Democracy and education.* New York: The Free Press.

Dinnel, D., & Glover, J. H. (1986). Advance organizers: Encoding manipulations. *Journal of Educational Psychology, 77,* 514–521.

Dizenzo, P. (1977). *Why me? The story of Jenny.* New York: Avon.

Dreikurs, R., Grunwald, B. B., & Pepper, F. C. (1971). *Maintaining sanity in the classroom: Illustrated teaching techniques.* New York: Harper & Row.

Durham, P., & Jones, E. L. (1969). *The adventures of the Negro cowboys.* New York: Bantam.

Durkin, D. (1978–1979). What classroom observations reveal about comprehension instruction. *Reading Research Quarterly, 14,* 481–533.

Duthie, J. (1986). The web: A powerful tool for the teaching and evaluation of the expository essay. *The History and Social Science Teacher, 21,* 232–236.

Earle, R. A. (1969). Developing and using study guides. In H. L. Herber & P. L. Sanders (Eds.), *Research in reading in the content areas: First year report* (pp. 78–87), Lawrence, KS: Kansas Department of Human Development.

Edwards, P. R. 1992). Using dialectical journals to teach thinking skills. *Journal of Reading, 35*(4), 312–316.

Eeds, M., & Wells, D. (1989). Grand conversations: An exploration of meaning construction in literature study groups. *Research in the Teaching of English, 23,* 4–29.

Egan, K. (1992). *Imagination in teaching and learning: The middle school years.* Chicago: University of Chicago Press.

Eldredge, J. L., & Quinn, D. W. (1988). Increasing reading performance of low-achieving second graders with dyad reading groups. *Journal of Educational Research, 82,* 40–46.

Ellis, A. K., & Fouts, J. T. (1993). *Research on educational innovations.* Princeton Junction, NJ: Eye on Education.

Fader, D. N. (1976). *The new booked on books.* New York: Berkley.

Farr, R. (1991). *Portfolios: Assessment in the language arts.* (ERIC Document Reproduction Service No. ED 334 603)

Farr, R., & Tone, B. (1994). *Portfolio and performance assessment.* Fort Worth, TX: Harcourt Brace College Publishers..

Farr, R., Tulley, M. A., & Pritchard, R. (1989). Assessment instruments and techniques used by the content area teacher. In D. Lapp, J. Flood, & N. Farnan (Eds.), *Content area reading and learning* (pp. 346–356). Englewood Cliffs, NJ: Prentice Hall.

Fielding, L. G., & Pearson, P. D. (1994, February). Reading comprehension: What works. *Educational Leadership,* pp. 62–68.

Fisher, L. E. (1990). *The Oregon trail.* New York: Holiday House.

Flavell, J. H. (1981). Cognitive monitoring. In W. P. Dickson (Ed.), *Children's oral communication skills.* New York: Academic Press.

Fleming, L. E., & Leet, J. (1989). *Becoming a successful student.* Glenview, IL: Scott, Foresman.

Flesch, R. (1955). *Why Johnny can't read.* New York: Harper & Row.

Flesch, R. (1981). *Why Johnny still can't read.* New York: Harper & Row.

Flood, J., & Lapp, D. (1990). Reading comprehension instruction for at-risk students: Research-based practices that can make a difference. *Journal of Reading, 33,* 490–496.

Flood, J., Lapp, D., & Farnan, N. (1986). A reading-writing procedure that teaches expository paragraph structure. *The Reading Teacher, 39,* 556–562.

Flynt, E. S., & Cooter, R. B. (1993). *The Flynt/Cooter reading inventory for the classroom.* Scottsdale, AZ: Gorsuch Scarisbrick.

Flynt, E. S., & Cooter, R. B. (1995). *The Flynt/Cooter reading inventory for the classroom* (2nd ed.). Scottsdale, AZ: Gorsuch Scarisbrick.

Forgan, H., & Mangrum, C. (1989). *Teaching content area reading skills* (4th ed.). Englewood Cliffs, NJ: Merrill/Prentice Hall.

Fraser, B. J. (1986). *Classroom environment.* London: Croom Helm.

Frayer, D. A., Frederick, W. C., & Klausmeir, H. J. (1969). *A schema for testing the level of concept mastery* (Working Paper No. 16). Madison: University of Wisconsin, Wisconsin Research and Development Center for Cognitive Learning.

Fry, E. (1977). Fry's readability graph: Clarifications, validity, and extensions to level 17. *Journal of Reading, 21,* 242–252.

Fulks, D. G. (1985). Invigorating interior design makes schools more conducive to learning. *American School Board Journal, 172*(8), 31.

Fulwiler, T. (1985). Writing and learning, grade 3. *Language Arts, 62,* 55–59.

Gall, M. D., Gall, J. P., Jacobsen, D. R., & Bullock, T. L. (1990). *Tools for learning: A guide to teaching study skills.* Alexandria, VA: Association for Supervision and Curriculum Development.

Gamberg, R., Kwak, W., Hutchings, M., & Altheim, J. (1988). *Learning and loving it: Theme stories in the classroom.* Portsmouth, NH: Heinemann.

Gambrell, L. B. (1985). Dialogue journals: Reading–writing interaction. *The Reading Teacher, 38,* 512–515.

Gard, W. (1969). *The Chisholm trail.* Norman, OK: University of Oklahoma Press.

Garner, R., & Reis, R. (1981). Monitoring and resolving comprehension obstacles: An investigation of spontaneous text lookbacks among upper-grade good and poor comprehenders. *Reading Research Quarterly, 18,* 439–447.

Garner, R., Wagoner, S., & Smith, T. (1983). Externalizing question-answering strategies of good and poor comprehenders. *Reading Research Quarterly, 18,* 439–447.

Gee, T. C., & Rakow, S. J. (1987). Content reading specialists evaluate teaching practices. *Journal of Reading, 31,* 234–237.

Gilles, C., Bixby, M., Crowley, P., Crenshaw, S., Henrich, M., Reynolds, R., & Pyle, D. (1988). *Whole language strategies for secondary students.* New York: Richard C. Owen.

Glasser, R. J. (1979). *The body is the hero.* New York: Bantam.

Glazer, S. M., & Brown, C. S. (1993). *Portfolios and beyond: Collaborative assessment in reading and writing.* Norwood, MA: Christopher-Gordon Publishers.

Good, T., & Brophy, J. (1991). *Looking in classrooms* (5th ed). New York: HarperCollins

Goodlad, J. I. (1994). *Educational renewal: Better teachers, better schools.* San Francisco: Jossey-Bass.

Goodman, K. (1986). *What's whole in whole language.* Ontario, Canada: Scholastic.

Goodman, K. S. (1992). Why whole language is today's agenda in education. *Language Arts, 69,* 354–363.

Gove, M. K., & Kennedy-Calloway, C. (1992). Action research: Empowering teachers to work with at-risk students. *Journal of Reading, 37*(7), 526–533.

Graham, S., MacArthur, C., Schwartz, S., & Page-Voth, V. (1992, February). Improving the compositions of students with learning disabilities using a strategy involving product and process goal setting. *Exceptional Children,* pp. 322–344.

Graves, D. (1983). *Writing: teachers and children at work.* Portsmouth, NH: Heinemann Educational Books.

Groom, W. (1986). *Forrest Gump.* New York: Pocket Books

Gunn, R. M. (1963). *Tumblin' Creek Tales and other poems by "Pek" Gunn.* Nashville, TN: Tumblin' Creek Enterprises.

Guthrie, A. B. (1979). *The way west.* New York: Bantam.

Guthrie, J. T., Seifert, M., Burnham, N. A., & Caplan, R. J. (1974). The maze technique to assess and monitor reading comprehension. *The Reading Teacher, 28*(2), 161–168.

Haggard, H. L. (1982). The vocabulary self-collection strategy: An active approach to word learning. *Journal of Reading, 26,* 203–207.

Halliday, M. A. K. (1977). *Learning how to mean: Explorations in the development of language.* New York: Elsevier.

Hammond, D. (1979). *Anticipation activity.* Paper presented at the Great Lakes Regional Reading Conference, Detroit, MI.

Hannah, G. G. (1984). Jazzing up your classroom. *Learning, 13,* 68–71.

Harwood, A. M. (1991). *The difference between "democracy sucks" and "I may become a politician": Views from three high school civics classes.* Paper presented at the annual meeting of the American Educational Research Association, Chicago.

Hawking, S. W. (1988). *A brief history of time: From the Big Bang to black holes.* New York: Bantam Books.

Heathington, B., & Alexander, A. J. (1984). Do classroom teachers emphasize attitudes toward reading? *The Reading Teacher, 37,* 484–488.

Helfeldt, J. P., & Henk, W. A. (1990). Reciprocal question–answer relationships: An instructional technique for at-risk readers. *Journal of Reading, 33,* 509–514.

Hennings, D. G. (1993). On knowing and reading history. *Journal of Reading, 36*(5), 362–370.

Herber, H. L. (1978). *Teaching reading in content areas* (2nd ed.). Englewood Cliffs, NJ: Prentice Hall.

Herber, H. L., & Herber, J. N. (1993). *Teaching in content areas with reading, writing, and reasoning.* Boston: Allyn & Bacon.

Hersey, J. (1975). *Hiroshima.* New York: Bantam.

Hidi, S., & Anderson, V. (1986). Producing written summaries: Task demands, cognitive operations, and implications for instruction. *Review of Educational Research, 56,* 473–493.

Hiebert, E. H. (1991). *Literacy for a diverse society: Perspectives, practices, and policies.* New York: Teachers College Press.

Hinchman, K. 1987). The textbook and three content-area teachers. *Reading Research and Instruction, 26,* 247–263.

Hokanson, R. A., Agasie, K. M., & Beebe, K. (1993). *Information delivery: Education.* Chicago: Kemper Securities, Inc.

Holliday, W. G. (1991). Helping students learn effectively from science text. In C. M. Santa & D. E. Alvermann (Eds.), *Science learning: Processes and applications* (pp. 38–47). Newark, DE: International Reading Association.

Holmes, E. E. (1991). Democracy in elementary school classes. *Social Education, 55,* 176–178.

Honig, B. (1988). The California reading initiative. *The New Advocate, 1,* 235–240.

Huck, C. S., Hepler, S., & Hickman, J. (1993). *Children's literature in the elementary school* (5th ed). Orlando, FL: Harcourt Brace Jovanovich.

Hurd, P. D. (1983) Middle school/junior high science: Changing perspectives. In M. J. Padilla (Ed.), *Science and the early adolescent* (pp. 1–4). Washington DC: National Science Teachers Association.

Jenkins, C., & Lawler, D. (1990). Questioning strategies in content area reading: One teacher's example. *Reading Improvement, 27,* 133–138.

Johns, J. L., & Lunn, M. K. (1983). The Informal Reading Inventory: 1910–1980. *Reading World, 23*(1), 8–18.

Johnson, D. D., & Pearson, P. D. (1984). *Teaching reading vocabulary.* New York: Holt, Rinehart & Winston.

Johnson, D. W., Johnson, R. T., Holubec, E., & Roy, P. (1984). *Circles of learning: Cooperation in the classroom.* Alexandria, VA: Association for Supervision and Curriculum Development.

Johnson, N. M., & Ebert, M. J. (1992). Time travel is possible: Historical fiction and biography—passport to the past. *The Reading Teacher, 45,* 488–495.

Kelly, B. W., & Holmes, J. (1979). The guided lecture procedure. *Journal of Reading, 22,* 602–604.

Kershner, V. (1993, June 21). Why immigration laws are so hard to change. *San Francisco Chronicle,* p. A7.

Kohlberg, L., et al. (1975). The Just Community School: The theory and the Cambridge Cluster School experiment. In *Collected papers from the Center for Moral Education* (pp. 1–77). (ERIC Document Reproduction Service No. ED 223 511)

Kohlberg, R., & Gilligan, C. (1972). The adolescent as a philosopher: The discovery of the self in a post-conventional world. In J. Kangan & R. Coles (Eds.), *Twelve to sixteen, early adolescence* (pp. 144–179). New York: W. W. Norton.

Langer, J. (1981). From theory to practice: A prereading plan. *Journal of Reading, 25,* 152–156.

Langer, J. A., Applebee, A. N., Mullis, I. V. S., & Foertsch, M. A. (1990). *Learning to read in our nation's schools.* Washington, DC: Office of Educational Research and Improvement.

Lapp, D., Flood, J., & Farnan, N. (1989). *Content area reading and learning: Instructional strategies.* Englewood Cliffs, NJ: Prentice Hall.

Lasky, K. (1986). *Beyond the divide.* New York: Dell.

Lathlaen, P. (1993). A meeting of minds: Teaching using biographies. *The Reading Teacher, 46*(6), 529–531.

Lawson, D. (1988). *The United States in the Indian wars.* Boston: HarperCollins.

Lazarus, B. D. (1988). Using guided notes to aid learning disabled students in secondary mainstream settings. *The Pointer, 33,* 32–36.

Levin, J. R., & Pressley, M. (1981). Improving children's prose comprehension: Selected strategies that seem to work. In C. M. Santa & B. L. Hayes (Eds.), *Children's prose comprehension: Research and practice.* Newark, DE: International Reading Association.

Lewin, K. (1935). *A dynamic theory of personality.* New York: McGraw.

Lewin, K. (1936). *Principles of topological psychology.* New York: McGraw.

Loup, K., et al. (1991). *The system for teaching and learning assessment review (STAR): A holistic classroom observation alternative to measures of student perceptions for research on classroom learning environments.* Paper presented at the annual meeting of the American Educational Research Association, Chicago, IL. (ERIC Document Reproduction Service No. ED 335 756)

Lyman, F. (1988). Think-pair-share, wait time two, and on. . . . *Mid Atlantic Association for Cooperation in Education Cooperative News, 2,* 1.

Macaulay, D. (1978). *Great moments in architecture.* Boston: Houghton Mifflin.

MacAulay, D. J. (1990). Classroom environment: A literature review. *Educational Psychology, 10,* 239–253.

MacGinitie, W. H., & MacGinitie, R. K. (1986). Teaching students not to read. In S. De Castell, A. Luke, & K. Egan (Eds.), *Literacy, society, and schooling.* Cambridge, UK: Cambridge University Press.

Macrorie, K. (1980). *Searching writing.* Rochelle Park, NJ: Hayden.

Macrorie, K. (1988). *The I-Search Paper.* Portsmouth, NH: Heinemann.

Manzo, A. V. (1969). The ReQuest procedure. *Journal of Reading, 2,* 123-126.

Manzo, A. V. (1975). The guided reading procedure. *Journal of Reading, 18,* 287–291.

Manzo, A., & Manzo, U. (1990). *Content area reading: A heuristic approach.* Englewood Cliffs, NJ: Merrill/Prentice Hall.

Manzo, A., & Manzo, U. (1993). *Literacy disorders: Holistic diagnosis and remediation.* New York: Harcourt Brace Jovanovich.

Martinez, M. (1993). Motivating dramatic story reenactments. *The Reading Teacher, 46*(8), 682–688.

Mason, J. M., & Au, K. H. (1990). *Reading instruction for today* (2nd ed.). Glenview, IL: Scott, Foresman/Little, Brown.

Mathewson, G. C. (1985). Toward a comprehensive model of affect in the reading process. In H. Singer & R. B. Ruddell (Eds.), *Theoretical models and processes in reading* (3rd ed.). Newark, DE: International Reading Association.

May, F. (1994). *Reading as communication* (4th ed.). Englewood Cliffs, NJ: Merrill/Prentice Hall.

McGee, L. M., & Richgels, D. J. (1985). Teaching expository text structure to elementary students. *The Reading Teacher, 38,* 739–748.

McKenzie, G. R. (1979). Data charts: A crutch for helping students organize reports. *Language Arts, 56,* 784–788.

McWhirter, A. M. (1990). Whole language in the middle school. *The Reading Teacher, 43*(8), 562–565.

Meadows, N. (1994). *Classroom management and organization for inclusion settings.* Unpublished manuscript, Texas Christian University, Fort Worth, TX.

Meese, R. L. (1992). Adapting textbooks for children with learning disabilities in mainstreamed classrooms. *Teaching Exceptional Children, 24,* 49–51.

Menlo, A., Maraichj, M., Collet, L., Evers, T., Fernandez, R., & Ferris, L. W. (1990). *Secondary school teachers' perceptions of their work in the United States.* Paper presented at the annual meeting of the American Educational Research Association, Boston.

Mercer, C. (1992). *Students with learning disabilities* (4th ed.). Englewood Cliffs, NJ: Merrill/Prentice Hall.

Mercer, C. D., & Mercer, A. R. (1993). *Teaching students with learning problems* (4th ed.). Englewood Cliffs, NJ: Merrill/Prentice Hall.

Meyer, B. J. F. (1979). Organizational patterns in prose and their use in reading. In M. L. Kamil & A. J. Moe (Eds.), *Reading research: Studies and applications.* Clemson, SC: National Reading Conference.

Meyer, B. J. F., & Freedle, R. O. (1984). Effects of discourse type on recall. *American Educational Research Journal, 21*(1), 121–143.

Meyer, B. J. F., & Rice, G. E. (1984). The structure of text. In P. D. Pearson (Ed.), *Handbook of reading research.* New York: Longman.

Mills, J. F. (1973). *Treasure keepers.* New York: Doubleday.

Moffit, M., & Wartella, E. (1992). Youth and reading: A survey of leisure reading pursuits of female and male adolescents. *Reading Research and Instruction, 31,* 1–17.

Moore, D. W., & Arthur, S. (1981). Possible sentences. In E. K. Dishner, T. W. Bean, & J. E. Readence (Eds.), *Reading in the content areas: Improving classroom instruction* (pp. 138–143). Dubuque, IA: Kendall/Hunt.

Moore, D. W., Moore, S. A., Cunningham, P., & Cunningham, J. (1986). *Developing readers and writers in the content areas.* White Plains, NY: Longman.

Moore, T. (1992). *Care of the soul.* New York: HarperCollins.

Morgan, R. F., Meeks, J., Schollaert, A., & Paul, J. (1986). *Critical reading/thinking skills for the college student.* Dubuque, IA: Kendall/Hunt.

Moyers, B. (1993). *Healing and the mind.* New York: Doubleday.

Mullis, I. V. S., Campbell, J. R., & Farstrup, A. E. (1993). *NAEP 1992 Reading Report Card for the nation and the states* (Report No. 23-ST06). Washington, DC: National Center for Education Statistics, U.S. Department of Education.

Mullis, I. V. S., Dossey, J. A., Foertsch, M. A., Jones, L. R., & Gentile, C. A. (1991). *Trends in academic progress* (Report No: 21-T-01). Washington, DC: National Center for Educational Statistics, U.S. Department of Education.

Murray, D. H. (1985). *A writer teaches writing* (2nd ed.). Boston: Houghton Mifflin.

Muth, K. D. (1987). Teachers' connection questions: Prompting students to organize text ideas. *Journal of Reading, 28,* 254–259.

Myers, D. (1988). *Fallen angels.* New York: Scholastic.

Nabokov, P. L. (Ed.). (1972). *Native American testimony: An anthology of Indian and white relations, first encounter to dispossession.* Boston: HarperCollins.

Nagy, W. E. (1988). *Teaching vocabulary to improve comprehension.* Newark, DE: International Reading Association.

Nagy, W. E., & Anderson, R. C. (1984). How many words are there in printed school English? *Reading Research Quarterly, 21,* 304–330.

Nagy, W. E., & Herman, P. A. (1984) *Limitations of vocabulary instruction* (Technical Report No. 326). Urbana, IL: University of Illinois. Center for the

Study of Reading. (ERIC Document Reproduction Service No. ED 248 988)

National Academy of Science. (1984). *High schools and the changing workplace: The employers' view.* Washington, DC: Author.

National Center for Education Statistics. (1992). *Targeted forecast.* Washington, DC: U.S. Department of Education, Office of Educational Research and Improvement.

National Council of Teachers of Mathematics. (1989). *Curriculum and evaluation standards for school mathematics.* Reston, VA: Author.

Nelson-Herber, J., & Johnston, C. S. (1989). Questions and concerns about teaching narrative and expository text. In K. D. Muth (Ed.), *Children's comprehension of text.* (pp. 263–279). Newark, DE: International Reading Association.

Newkirk, T. (1990). Research currents: One teacher, one classroom. *Language Arts, 67,* 58–69.

Niles, O. (1965). Organization perceived. In H. L. Herber (Ed.), *Developing study skills in secondary schools.* Newark, DE: International Reading Association.

Nolan, E. A., & Berry, M. (1993). Learning to listen. *The Reading Teacher, 46*(7), 606–608.

Norton, D. E. (1993). *The effective teaching of language arts* (4th ed.). Englewood Cliffs, NJ: Merrill/Prentice Hall.

Norton, D. E. (1995). *Through the eyes of a child* (4th ed.). Englewood Cliffs, NJ: Merrill/Prentice Hall.

Novelli, J. (1990). Design a classroom that works. *Instructor, 100,* 24–27.

O'Neal, Z. (1986). *In summer light.* New York: Bantam.

Ogle, D. (1986). KWL: A teaching model that develops active reading of expository text. *The Reading Teacher, 39,* 564–570.

Olson, L. (1995, April 12). *Education Week,* p. 15.

Orlando, V. P. (1986). Training students to use a modified version of SQ3R: An instructional strategy. *Reading World, 20,* 65–70.

Palincsar, A. S., & Brown, A. L. (1984). Reciprocal teaching of comprehension-fostering and comprehension-monitoring activities. *Cognition and Instruction, 2,* 117–175.

Palincsar, A. S., & Brown, A. L. (1986). Interactive teaching to promote independent learning from text. *The Reading Teacher, 39,* 771–777.

Palincsar, A. S., & Brown, A. L. (1988). Teaching and practicing thinking skills to promote comprehension in the context of group problem solving. *Remedial and Special Education, 9,* 53–59.

Palmatier, R. A. (1973). A notetaking system for learning. *Journal of Reading, 17,* 36–39.

Panati, L. (1994). *1001 things everyone should know about science.* New York: Bantaam.

Pappas, C. C., Kiefer, B. Z., & Levstik, L. S. (1990). *An integrated language perspective in the elementary school.* New York: Longman.

Paradis, E. E. (1984). *Comprehension: Thematic units* [video tape]. Laramie: University of Wyoming.

Pardo, L. S., & Raphael, T. E. (1991). Classroom organization for instruction in content areas. *Journal of Reading, 44*(8), 556–565.

Paris, S. G., & Myer, M. (1981). Comprehension monitoring, memory, and study strategies of good and poor readers. *Journal of Reading Behavior, 13,* 5–22.

Pauk, W. (1974). *How to study in college.* Boston: Houghton Mifflin.

Pauk, W. (1988). *How to study in college.* Boston: Houghton Mifflin.

Paulsen, G. (1991). *The monument.* New York: Delacorte.

Pearson, P. D. (1985). Changing the face of reading instruction. *Journal of Reading, 29,* 724–737.

Pearson, P. D., & Gallagher, M. C. (1983). The instruction of reading comprehension. *Contemporary Educational Psychology, 8*(3), 317–344.

Pearson, P. D., & Johnson, D. D. (1978). *Teaching reading comprehension.* New York: Holt, Rinehart & Winston.

Peterson, R., & Eeds, M. (1990). *Grand conversations: Literature groups in action.* Toronto, Ontario: Scholastic-TAB.

Piaget, J. (1955). *The language and thought of the child.* New York: World.

Pine, G. J., & Hilliard, A. G. (1990). Rx for racism: Imperatives for America's schools. *Phi Delta Kappan, 71,* 593–600.

Preston, M. (1994). *The hot zone.* New York: Random House.

Provensen, A., & Provensen, M. (1987). *Shaker lane.* New York: Viking.

Puckett, M. B., & Black, J. K. (1994). *Authentic assessment of the young child.* Englewood Cliffs, NJ: Merrill/Prentice Hall.

Ramirez, A. G. (1985). *Bilingualism through schooling: Cross-cultural education for minority and major-*

ity students. Albany, NY: State University of New York Press.

Raphael, T. (1984). Teaching learners about sources of information for answering comprehension questions. *Journal of Reading, 27,* 303–311.

Raphael, T. (1986). Teaching question/answer relationships, revisited. *The Reading Teacher, 39,* 516–522.

Raven, J. (1992). A model of competence, motivation, and behavior, and a paradigm for assessment. In H. Berlak et al. (Eds.), *Toward a new science of educational testing and assessment.* New York: State University of New York Press.

Raygor, A. L. (1977). The Raygor readability estimate: A quick and easy way to determine difficulty. In P. D. Pearson (Ed.), *Reading: Theory, research, and practice* (pp. 259–263). Clemson, SC: National Reading Conference.

Readence, J. E., Bean, T. W., & Baldwin, R. S. (1992). *Content area reading: An integrated approach* (4th ed.). Dubuque, IA: Kendall/Hunt.

Reed, A. J. S. (1994). *Reaching adolescents: The young adult book and the school.* Englewood Cliffs, NJ: Merrill/Prentice Hall.

Reutzel, D. R., & Cooter, R. B. (1992). *Teaching children to read: From basals to books.* Englewood Cliffs, NJ: Merrill/Prentice Hall.

Reutzel, D. R., & Cooter, R. B. (1996). *Teaching children to read: From basals to books* (2nd ed.). Englewood Cliffs, NJ: Merrill/Prentice Hall.

Rieck, B. J. (1977). How content teachers telegraph messages against reading. *Journal of Reading, 20,* 646–648.

Risko, V. J., Alvarez, M. C., & Fairbanks, M. M. (1991). External factors that influence study. In R. F. Flippo & D. C. Caverly (Eds.), *Teaching reading and study strategies at the college level* (pp. 195–236). Newark, DE: International Reading Association.

Robinson, F. P. (1946). *Effective study.* New York: Harper Brothers.

Roe, B. D., Stoodt, B. D., & Burns P. C. (1987). *Secondary school reading instruction: The content areas.* Boston: Houghton Mifflin.

Rogus, J., & Wildenhaus, C. (1991). Programming for at-risk learners: A preventive approach (The principal's challenge). *NASSP Bulletin, 75,* 1–7.

Rosenfield, P., Lambert, N. M., & Black, A. (1985). Desk arrangement effects on pupil classroom behavior. *Journal of Educational Psychology, 77,* 101–108.

Routman, R. (1991). *Invitations: Changing as teachers and learners K–12.* Portsmouth, NH: Heinemann.

Ruddell, M. (1993). *Teaching content reading and writing.* Boston: Allyn & Bacon.

Ryder, R. J. (1994). Using frames to promote critical writing. *Journal of Reading, 38*(3), 210–218.

Santa, C. M., & Haven, L. T. (1991). Learning through writing. In C. M. Santa & D. E. Alvermann (Eds.), *Science learning: Processes and applications* (pp. 122–133). Newark, De: International Reading Association.

Savage, J. F. (1994). *Teaching reading using literature.* Madison, WI: Brown & Benchmark Publishers.

Schack, G. D. (1993). Involving students in authentic research. *Educational Leadership, 50*(7), 29–31.

Schatz, E. K., & Baldwin, R. S. (1986). Context clues are unreliable predictors of word meaning. *Reading Research Quarterly, 21,* 439–453.

Schmid, R. (1980). *Final report: The national secondary school survey.* Unpublished manuscript, University of Florida, Gainesville.

Schnitzer, S. (1993). Designing an authentic assessment. *Educational Leadership, 50*(7), 32–35.

Schommer, M., & Surber, J. R. (1986). Comprehension-monitoring failures in skilled adult readers. *Journal of Educational Psychology, 78,* 353–357.

Schumaker, J. B., & Deshler (1984). Setting demand variables: A major factor in program planning for the LD adolescent. *Topics in Language Disorders, 5,* 22–40.

Schumaker, J. B., Deshler, D. D., Alley, G. R., & Warner, M. M. (1983). Toward the development of an intervention model for learning disabled adolescents: The University of Kansas Institute. *Exceptional Education Quarterly, 4,* 45–74.

Schwartz, R. M., & Raphael, T. E. (1985). Concept of definition: A key to improving students' vocabulary. *The Reading Teacher, 39,* 198–205.

Shenkle, A. M. (1988). Shaping the classroom landscape. *Learning, 17*(2), 61–64.

Simpson, M. L. (1986). PORPE: A writing strategy for studying and learning in the content areas. *Journal of Reading, 30,* 45–50.

Simpson, M. L, & Dwyer, E. J. (1991). Vocabulary acquisition and the college student. In R. F. Flippo & D. C. Caverly (Eds.), *Teaching reading and study strategies at the college level.* Newark, DE: International Reading Association.

Simpson, M. L., Hayes, C. G., Stahl, N., Connor, R. T., & Weaver, D. (1988). An initial validation of a study strategy system. *Journal of Reading Behavior, 20,* 149–180.

Simpson, M. L., Nist, S. L., & Kirby, K. (1987). Ideas in practice: Vocabulary strategies designed for college students. *Journal of Developmental Education, 11*(2), 20–24.

Sizer, T. R. (1992). *Horace's school: Redesigning the American high school.* Boston: Houghton Mifflin.

Slater, W. H., & Graves, M. F. (1989). Research on expository text: Implications for teachers. In K. D. Muth (Ed.), *Children's comprehension of text.* Newark, DE: International Reading Association.

Slavin, R. E. (1983). *Cooperative learning.* London: Longman.

Smith, C., & Bean, T. W. (1980). The guided writing procedure: Integrating content reading and writing improvement. *Reading World, 19,* 290–298.

Smith, F. (1977). The uses of language. *Language Arts, 54*(6), 638–644.

Smith, F. (1988). *Understanding reading* (4th ed.). Hillsdale, NJ: Lawrence Erlbaum.

Spady, W. (1988). Organizing for results: The basis of authentic restructuring and reform. *Educational Leadership, 46*(2), 4–8.

Spady, W., & Marshall, K. J. (1991). Beyond traditional outcome-based education. *Educational Leadership, 48,* 67–72.

Spiegel, D. (1987). Using adolescent literature in social studies and science. *Educational Horizons, 65,* 162–164.

Speigel, D. L., & Fitzgerald, K. (1986). Improving reading comprehension through instruction about story parts. *The Reading Teacher, 39,* 676–682.

Stahl, S. A. (1983). Differential word knowledge and reading comprehension. *Journal of Reading Behavior, 15,* 33–50.

Stahl, S. A. (1985). To teach a word well: A framework for vocabulary instruction. *Reading World, 24,* 16–27.

Stahl, S. A., & Fairbanks, M. M. (1986). The effects of vocabulary instruction: A model-based meta-analysis. *Review of Educational Research, 56,* 72–110.

Stahl, N. A., & Henk, W. A. (1986). Tracing the roots of textbook study systems: an extended historical perspective. In J. A. Niles & R. V. Lalik (Eds.), *Solving problems in literacy: Learners, teachers, and researchers. Thirty-fifth yearbook of the National Reading conference* (pp. 336–374). Rochester, NY: National Reading Conference.

Stark, N. (1979). *The formula book.* New York: Avon.

Stauffer, R. (1969). *Directing reading maturity as a cognitive process.* New York: Harper & Row.

Stepien, W., & Gallagher, S. (1993). Problem-based learning: As authentic as it gets. *Educational Leadership, 50*(7), 25–28.

Stieglitz, E. L., & Stieglitz, V. S. (1981). SAVOR the word to reinforce vocabulary in the content areas. *Journal of Reading, 25,* 46–51.

Taba, H. (1967). *Teacher's handbook for elementary social studies.* Reading, MA: Addison Wesley.

Tarver, S. (1986). Cognitive behavior modification, direct instruction and holistic approaches to the education of students with learning disabilities. *Journal of Learning Disabilities, 19,* 368–375.

Taylor, B. M. (1986). A summarizing strategy to improve middle grade students' reading and writing skills. In E. Dishner, T. Bean, J. Readence, & D. Moore (Eds.). *Reading in the content areas: Improving classroom instruction* (pp. 274–278). Dubuque, IA: Kendall/Hunt.

Temple, C., Nathan, R., Temple, F., & Burris, N. A. (1993). *The beginnings of writing.* Boston: Allyn & Bacon.

Thomas, L. (1978). *The lives of a cell: Notes of a biology watcher.* New York: Penguin.

Tierney, R. J. (1992). Setting a new agenda for assessment. *Learning, 21*(2), 61–64.

Tierney, R., Carter, M. A., & Desai, L. E. (1991). *Portfolio assessment in the reading-writing classroom.* Norwood, MA: Christopher-Gordon.

Tierney, R. J., Readence, J. E., & Dishner, E. K. (1995). *Reading strategies and practices: A compendium.* Boston: Allyn & Bacon.

Tompkins, G. E. (1994). *Teaching writing: Balancing process and product* (2nd ed.). Englewood Cliffs, NJ: Merrill/Prentice Hall.

Tompkins, G. E., & McGee, L. M. (1989). Teaching repetition as a story structure. In K. D. Muth (Ed.), *Children's comprehension of narrative and expository text: Research into practice* (pp. 59–78). Newark, DE: International Reading Association.

Toms-Bronowski, S. (1983). An investigation of the effectiveness of selected vocabulary teaching strategies with intermediate grade level students. *Dissertation Abstracts International, 44,* 1405A. (University Microfilms No. 83-16, 238)

Torgesen, J. K., & Kail, R. J. (1985). Memory processes in exceptional children. In B. K. Keogh (Ed.), *Advances in special education: Basic constructs and theoretical orientations.* Greenwich, CT: JAI Press.

Tutolo, D. (1977). The study guide: Types, purpose and value. *Journal of Reading, 20,* 503–507.

United States Department of Education. (1990). *National Education Longitudinal Study (NELS). of 1988: A profile of American eighth graders.* Washington, DC: Author

Vacca, R. T., & Vacca, J. L. (1989). *Content area reading* (3rd ed.). Glenview, IL: Scott, Foresman.

Vacca, R. T., & Vacca, J. L. (1993). *Content area reading* (4th ed.). Glenview, IL: Scott, Foresman.

Valencia, S. (1990). A portfolio approach to classroom reading assessment: The whys, whats, and hows. *The Reading Teacher, 43*(4), 338–340.

Valencia, S., McGinley, W., & Pearson, P. D. (1990). *Assessing reading and writing: Building a more complete picture for middle school assessment* (Technical Report No. 500). Urbana, IL: Center for the Study of Reading. (ERIC Document Reproduction Service No. ED 320 121)

Valencia, S., & Pearson, P. D. (1987). Reading assessment: Time for a change. *The Reading Teacher, 40*(8), 726–733.

Vallecorsa, A. L. (1990, September). Story composition skills of middle-grade students with learning disabilities. *Exceptional Children,* pp. 48–54.

Vaughan, J. L., & Estes, T. H. (1986). *Reading and reasoning beyond the primary grades.* Boston: Allyn & Bacon.

Vygotsky, L. S. (1978). *Mind in society.* Cambridge, MA: Harvard University Press.

Wark, D. M., & Flippo, R. F. (1991). Preparing for and taking tests. In R. F. Flippo & D. C. Caverly (Eds.), *Teaching reading and study strategies at the college level* (pp. 294–338). Newark, DE: International Reading Association.

Weaver, C. (1991). *Alternatives in understanding and educating attention-deficit students: A systems-based whole language perspective.* Urbana, IL: National Council of Teachers of English. (ERIC Document Reproduction Service No. ED 337 755)

Wepner, S. B., & Feeley, J. T. (1993). *Moving forward with literature: Basals, books, and beyond.* Englewood Cliffs, NJ: Merrill/Prentice Hall.

Werner, P. H. (1991). *Purposes of writing assessment: A process view.* Unpublished manuscript, Southwest Texas State University, San Marcos, TX.

Wong, B. (1978). The effects of directive cues on the organization of memory and recall in good and poor readers. *Journal of Educational Research, 72,* 32–38.

Wood, K. (1987). Fostering cooperative learning in middle and secondary level classrooms. *Journal of Reading, 31,* 10–18.

Wood, K. D. (1992). Fostering collaborative reading and writing experiences in mathematics. *Journal of Reading, 36*(2), 96–103.

Zigmond, N., Sansone, J., Miller, S. E., Donahoe, K. A., & Kohnke, R. (1986). Teaching learning disabled students at the secondary school level: What research says to teachers. *Learning Disabilities, 1,* 108–115.

Zigmond, N., Sansone, J., Miller, S. E., Donahoe, K. A., & Kohnke, R. (1991). Instructional style meets classroom design. *Instructor, 101,* 26–30.

Name Index

Subject Index